# ELLY PETERSON

Elly Peterson in 1969

# ELLY PETERSON
## "Mother" of the Moderates

*Sara Fitzgerald*

*With a Foreword by Haynes Johnson*

The University of Michigan Press * Ann Arbor

Copyright © by the University of Michigan 2011

Published in the United States of America by
The University of Michigan Press
Manufactured in the United States of America
♾ Printed on acid-free paper

2014   2013   2012   2011      4   3   2   1

A CIP catalog record for this book is available from the British Library.

Library of Congress Cataloging-in-Publication Data

Fitzgerald, Sara, 1951–
    Elly Peterson : "mother" of the moderates / Sara Fitzgerald.
       p.      cm.
    Includes index.
    ISBN 978-0-472-11787-1 (cloth : alk. paper) — ISBN 978-0-472-
02762-0 (e-book)
    1. Peterson, Elly Maude, 1914–2008.   2. Women politicians—
Michigan—Biography.   3. Politicians—Michigan—Biography.   4. Republican
Party (Mich.)—History—20th century.   5. Republican Party
(Mich.)—Biography.   6. Republican Party (U.S. : 1854– )—
History—20th century.   7. Republican Party (U.S. : 1854– )—Biography.
8. Women's rights—United States—History—20th century.
9. Conservatism—United States—History—20th century.
10. Michigan—Politics and government—1951–   11. United States—Politics
and government—1945–1989.   I. Title.
F570.25.P47F47      2011
324.2092—dc22
    [B]                                                        2011003380

Frontispiece: Photo by Capitol and Glogau Photographers, Washington, DC,
courtesy of the Bentley Historical Library, University of Michigan, Michigan
Republican State Central Committee Papers.

*For my mother,*
*and the women of the Greatest Generation*

# Foreword

Haynes Johnson

At the Republican Party's contentious convention in the summer of 1964, a woman from Michigan left an impression on more than one teenage girl in her audience when she deftly fielded questions from network television correspondents and became the first woman to address her party's convention in prime time. It was Elly Peterson, then the GOP's assistant national chairman and a candidate for a seat in the U.S. Senate.

Decades later, after a distinguished career at the *Washington Post* and other publications, one of those teenage girls, Sara Fitzgerald, tells Peterson's story in this superb and timely biography. It carries a message that deserves the widest audience as the nation struggles to find needed consensus on critical issues amid poisonous political partisanship that has made it increasingly difficult for public officials to bridge their differences. I hope that every American reads it.

Judged solely as a political biographer, Fitzgerald has done an outstanding job. Her writing is clear, her research scrupulous, her analysis incisive. Perhaps more noteworthy, her narrative is free of the ideology that mars so many attempts to examine the role of gender politics in American life. Not that Fitzgerald avoids the problems inherent in sexism; the continuing struggle of women against discrimination is central to her account of Elly Peterson's life and career. "It is easy for those of us who followed to forget what the women of Elly Peterson's generation had to endure to achieve the successes that they did," she writes. "It has been a privilege to try to recapture at least some of that here."

Recapture it she does, memorably and eloquently. The result, on one level, is a classic American story of how one person triumphs over adversity to become an inspiration for so many others. The account of how "Elly," a girl from a small town on the Illinois prairie, became leader of moderates in the Republican Party—the "mother," as they admiringly came to call her—is especially relevant now in our divisive political environment. What makes this story more compelling is that Peterson did not begin as an ideological firebrand, nor, in fact, was she ever one. She was in many respects typical of women of her time and place: born Ella Maude McMillan in the isolated, comfortable pre–World War I years in New Berlin, Illinois, she never harbored political ambitions then. It was not for six years after her birth in 1914 that women even won the right to vote.

For women then, politics was not an option, or even an idea as a career. It was a man's world. Women were destined to become housewives. If they had jobs, they invariably worked as secretaries, as did Peterson. For them, feminism and the women's movement were far into the future. Their involvement in politics was more social than cause. As Peterson herself recalled, "In Illinois, socially-minded girls around 21 usually joined a political party, and at that time, Republicans were so much more fun than Democrats. They had by far the nicest parties and we were never bothered with having to learn what was going on."

For her, as for all Americans of her generation, the defining, life-altering event was World War II. She was married, and working as a secretary, when Pearl Harbor shattered the nation and changed the world. Her husband went into the Army, and fought his way with Gen. George C. Patton across Europe. Elly joined the American Red Cross in 1943 and was assigned to an Army field station hospital as "secretary and go-fer." Her life was never the same afterward. Her experiences forever expanded her horizons: sailing on the *Queen Mary* with fifteen thousand service men and women; following the forces from England to France after D-Day; proceeding across the continent into Germany two years later to set up a Red Cross operation there. Those wartime experiences, Fitzgerald writes, exposed Peterson "to the real diversity of America—and the rest of the world. Far from home, and cut off, sometimes for weeks, from the lifeblood of her family's letters, she fashioned a new family from the motley mix of soldiers and sailors, nurses, doctors, and dentists that she met along the way. She was not yet the 'Mother' that dozens of her political colleagues would come to love. But she was already an outgoing leader with a wise-cracking enthusiasm for life."

Then for her, and the rest of that "greatest generation," it was home and the forging of new lives. Elly drifted into politics, first as a volunteer, then working at the state Republican headquarters as "receptionist, secretary, typist, mail clerk, janitor, cook, helper to all, and mimeograph operator." She quickly became indispensable, even more so as she began crisscrossing the state as the party's chief organizer. She also encountered disgraceful sex discrimination. Republican finance officials denied her promotion as organizational director, for instance; no women were active in high places in Michigan's automobile industry, the men proclaimed. She also found herself battling the growing conservatism of Michigan's Republican women's clubs, a fight between the old ways of wealthy, socially prominent women versus the new kind of woman, represented by Peterson, who believed women should play a more important, professional role in campaigns.

Those ideological tensions intensified in the early sixties as the Republican Party was riven with conflict between the right-wing elements of Senator Barry Goldwater's rising forces and the more moderate GOP brand of Peterson and Governor George W. Romney, whom Elly served loyally, even if Romney annoyed her by his oft-quoted characterization: "She thinks like a man, looks like a woman, and works like a dog."

By then, Peterson was the most prominent woman in Michigan's internal Republican ranks. She became assistant chairman of the Republican National Committee in Washington, then a U.S. Senate candidate in 1964. That was a cynical move by Romney, who knew she would lose but who hoped her candidacy might garner enough women votes for his own gubernatorial race. She did lose, by a crushing margin of 2-to-1, but won enough women voters to help assure Romney's election, bolstering his slim presidential prospects. At that point, only two women served in the U.S. Senate—Margaret Chase Smith of Maine and Maurine Neuberger of Oregon—and both entered Congress after assuming seats held by their late husbands.

Elly never ran for office again, but she went on to become the first woman to chair a Republican state party organization and later to do another, ultimately frustrating, stint at the RNC as the Nixon White House moved the party rightward. Still, she remained active in political causes, increasingly those for women's rights for which she became an acclaimed national leader. She became a champion of the Equal Rights Amendment, joining forces with Liz Carpenter, the liberal Democrat from Texas who was close to Lyndon Johnson, to lead ERAmerica, a coalition of the pro-amendment groups. That effort, too, failed, but it was an example of how far Elly had traveled in seeking to put aside party labels in a joint bipartisan national effort to achieve important social goals, and especially to advance the cause of women.

During all those years, as her reputation soared, she continued to experience repeated acts of sexism—so many, and so degrading, that I found myself cringing in reading Fitzgerald's descriptions of them. Example: When Elly was invited to address a men's club, with no other women present but her sister, the male emcee introduced her to the audience by saying: "And now, Mrs. Peterson, we hope you will not give us your bra speech as that only covers two points but instead launch into your girdle speech as that covers everything!" Elly never let those insults deter her; if anything, they strengthened her resolve to combat them.

It was against all that personal background that Elly made a dramatic break with her party in the cause of true moderation. The year was 1982, and the Michigan GOP had chosen Richard Headlee as its candidate for governor, a man who loudly opposed virtually every issue that was important to moderate Republican women. Elly led a group of them in endorsing his Democratic opponent, four-term Congressman James Blanchard, orchestrating the endorsement in a way that was designed to capture the maximum media attention.

In words that foreshadow the nation's political climate nearly thirty years later, she said one of the reasons for so dramatically breaking ranks with her party was the "polarization of Michigan." She was denounced furiously by party regulars, most of them men. Replying to critics, she said she had endorsed the Democrat, "To wake up the Republican Party, wake up the male leadership and make them understand that women are here, they're here to stay and they're a potent force." Blanchard won the race, and Elly's courageous leadership became a model for all moderates.

When asked about her political affiliation late in life, Elly described herself as an independent. Although she still believed in fiscal conservatism, she said, "I don't believe that I would work in the Republican Party today." But, in the message that Sara Fitzgerald's wonderful book makes clear, if Elly Peterson were still involved in politics, surely she would continue seeking to forge moderate forces, from all sides of the political spectrum, in the interests not only of women but of all Americans.

* * *

*Haynes Johnson won the Pulitzer Prize for his coverage of the civil rights crisis in Selma, Alabama. Six of his books have become national best-sellers.*

# Author's Note

As a young teenager growing up in a Republican family from Michigan in the 1960s, I remember being astounded when a network television correspondent interviewed a middle-aged woman at the 1964 Republican National Convention. She was the party's assistant chairman, a candidate for the U.S. Senate, and, even to my youthful ears, clearly a woman who knew what she was talking about. It was Elly Peterson. I believe the moment made an impression on me because I was struck by the novelty of seeing a female politician on the national stage—and proud that she came from my home state.

By 1973, I was graduating from the University of Michigan with a major in history and a special interest in the new field of women's studies. During the years when I was preparing to write a senior thesis, Elly Peterson was beginning to capture her own story, even if it was only for the benefit of her close family and friends.

Fast-forward two decades and I finally got the chance to meet Peterson when she moved to a retirement community in North Carolina and became close friends with my parents. My mother underscored my sense that she had many interesting stories to tell.

In 2005, when she was ninety-one and I was going through another life transition, I approached her about writing her biography. Out came the memoir on which she had worked for many years, *Elly! Confessions of a Woman Who Walked the Streets,* which became the foundation of this book. Over the next years, Peterson was generous in sharing herself and her memories through interviews and letters.

This book might never have been finished without the support of several other people. Peterson's friends and protégées Margaret Cooke and JoAnn Hawkins provided ongoing encouragement, as well as key documents and photographs from their files. The enthusiasm and advice of Jim Reische, formerly of the University of Michigan Press, helped to keep me moving forward during periods of discouragement. Peterson's relatives—Holly Shrader, Mary Ann Richmond, Ann Murrah, and Denise Bolman—were always responsive to questions and concerns. I am also grateful for the hospitality that Holly and Buck Shrader extended when I visited Peterson in Colorado and the home that my friend Susie Thompson provided during research trips to Ann Arbor. To friends and relatives who continued to ask, "How's the book going?" my thanks—never underestimate how much that means to an author. Finally, I want to thank my husband, Walt Wurfel, for providing thoughtful second opinions on everything from politics to grammar and for patiently tolerating my research trips and other distractions over the course of half a decade.

It is easy for those of us who followed to forget what the women of Elly Peterson's generation had to endure to achieve the successes that they did. It has been a privilege to try to recapture at least some of that here.

# Bibliographical Notes

Elly Peterson was a prodigious writer, and the onetime secretary also kept well-organized files of the letters she wrote and received. During her lifetime, the bulk of her personal papers were donated to the Bentley Historical Library at the University of Michigan, a collection that was augmented by her heirs after her death in 2008. Citations from these papers are identified as "EMP Papers." Peterson also gave the author a copy of *Elly! Confessions of a Woman Who Walked the Streets,* a memoir that Peterson published for a small group of family and friends in 1997. Citations from this work are identified as "EMP, *Elly!*" Since her death, a copy of the memoir has been provided to the Bentley Library. Peterson wrote a shorter—and slightly different—memoir entitled *Elly! Memoirs of a Republican Lady!,* which is now also part of the Bentley collection. Quotations from this volume are identified as "EMP, *Republican Lady.*" The precise location of some documents in Peterson's papers changed slightly after materials were added to the collection following her death, but the author has tried as best she could to reflect the new locations of cited documents.

The author is grateful to the many friends, family members, and former colleagues of Peterson who shared memories, either through correspondence or interviews, as well as photographs and other materials. The author is particularly grateful to Margaret Cooke, who shared the work she did for the biography she had hoped to write of her friend and mentor. The author is also grateful to JoAnn DiBella Hawkins for sharing her copy of the memoir Peterson began writing in 1971, which Hawkins helped edit. The author is also grateful to have been able to draw from Bill McLaughlin's self-published memoir of his years in politics.

Among the many useful materials that Cooke provided were transcripts of lengthy interviews of Peterson that Karen Farnham Madden conducted in 1996 and 2000 for her 2002 doctoral dissertation at Michigan State University, "Ready to Work: Women in Vermont and Michigan from Suffrage to Republican Party Politics." In 1995, William S. Ballenger, editor and publisher of *Inside Michigan Politics,* conducted an interview with Peterson that is now part of the Michigan Political History Society's Governor James J. Blanchard Living Library of Oral Histories. (The author reviewed videotapes of several of Peterson's contemporaries that are found in this collection.) In 2003, Peterson was also interviewed by Kathy Banfield Shaw for a videotape she produced for the Michigan Women's Hall of Fame under the auspices of the Michigan Women's Studies Association. Shaw made the author's job easier by sharing the photographs that she had compiled for that project. Finally, Steve Lilienthal volunteered the fruits of an interview he conducted of Peterson in 1979.

The author augmented these recollections with her own interviews of Peterson over three days in February 2006 and regular correspondence until Peterson's death in mid-2008. Peterson reviewed those portions of the author's manuscript that were completed before her death and corrected a few factual errors. She was supportive of the project but sought no preapproval of the text.

The author appreciates the help that Karen Jania and the friendly staff of the Bentley Library gave her during visits over several years. In addition to Peterson's papers, the author accessed files of the Michigan Republican Party and the Walter DeVries and Virginia Allan papers there. The author also visited the Gerald R. Ford Presidential Library at the University of Michigan to review additional materials related to Peterson's work with the President Ford Committee and Ford administration.

Former secretary of commerce Barbara H. Franklin, an alumna of Pennsylvania State University, was instrumental in the compilation of oral histories conducted between 1998 and 2000 of several persons, primarily women, who tried to advance women in government between 1969 and 1974. The author appreciates the help of librarians at Penn State's Special Collections Library in accessing transcripts from this collection, entitled "A Few Good Women." Meanwhile, in 1983–84, women affiliated with Smith College's Sophia Smith Collection conducted oral histories of twenty-nine women involved in the drive to ratify the Equal Rights Amendment as part of a project called The Fight for ERA: Leaders, Strategies, and Directions. The author appreciates the assistance she received from librarians in accessing several of these. Records of ERAmerica have been organized by the Manuscript Division of the Library of Congress, where the author received additional help from the library's Women's History Roundtable.

The author visited the Miller Center of Public Affairs at the University of Virginia to review a 2004 oral history provided by James A. Baker III as part of its Presidential Oral History project and made use of transcripts of histories provided to the center by Stuart Spencer and Lyn Nofziger.

Certain national television broadcasts involving Peterson were reviewed through the Vanderbilt University Television News Archive and The Paley Center for Media in New York City, formerly the Museum of Television and Radio. Eddy Palanzo of the *Washington Post* and Faye Haskins of the DC Public Library helped the author review photographs of Peterson in those collections. The Eaton County Museum at Courthouse Square in Charlotte, Michigan, is the repository of additional photographs and Peterson memorabilia.

Through the newspaper and periodical collections of the Library of Congress, the author accessed coverage of Peterson in the *Detroit Free Press, Detroit News, State Journal* (Lansing), and *Grand Rapids Press* (Booth Newspapers). The Web site www.newspaperarchive.com provided searchable access to stories, particularly wire stories, that appeared in several smaller Michigan newspapers. Scrapbooks in Peterson's personal papers were the source of dozens of other clippings from newspapers around the country.

Finally, the author wishes to acknowledge the use she made of "The Political Graveyard" (http://politicalgraveyard.com), a Web site created by Lawrence "Larry" Kestenbaum, Washtenaw County, Michigan, County Clerk and Register of Deeds, that bills itself as the Internet's "Most Comprehensive Source of U.S. Political Biography."

# Contents

Illustrations *following page 122*

# Prologue

THE WOMEN WERE NERVOUS as they drove down the dirt road to the farmhouse in Charlotte, Michigan, that summer day in 1982. Ten years of work for the Equal Rights Amendment had come up short of victory. And now the Republican Party had chosen a candidate for governor who loudly opposed them on every issue that was dear to their hearts.

"Mother" was waiting for them at Holiday Hill. It had been twelve years since Elly Peterson stepped down as the top woman at the Republican National Committee and three years since she had cochaired ERAmerica. Still, she was the leader to whom they turned.

As they turned onto Tirrell Road, some had memories of happier days, of rollicking parties and backyard barbecues at the farm. For some, the memories went back nearly two decades, to the time when they had backed "Elly" for the U.S. Senate.

But this time was different. The women convened quietly, discreetly, many of them fearful that their professional and political futures were at stake. The farmhouse offered privacy, a place where no reporter would stumble onto their bumper-stickered cars.

They were all moderate Republicans, elected officials and activists, women at different stages of their lives. More than twenty years later, one recalled that it felt like she was going to a meeting of the Symbionese Liberation Army because it was so "under cover." But at Elly's farmhouse, she remembered, "the women who came felt safe."

The question now before them: should they throw the equivalent of a Molotov cocktail into the heart of the Michigan Republican Party?

The week before, Richard Headlee, a conservative insurance executive, had won a surprise victory in the Republican gubernatorial primary. Headlee was a vociferous opponent of both abortion rights and the Equal Rights Amendment.

Each news cycle only seemed to add to the women's outrage. Told that female voters were concerned about economic issues such as day care, Headlee responded in all sincerity, "I understand that. And that's why my goal is to make every household a one-income household where the mother can stay home with her children."

The old friends weighed their options. And for one last time, Peterson was willing to be their general. Over the course of twenty-five years in politics, she had learned how to count votes and play the press. She knew how to deliver the kind of quote that made a reporter's story sparkle.

At times in her career, she had kept her mouth shut—and sometimes paid a price for doing so. But she was sixty-eight now. There were no more campaigns to run, no more fences to mend. And if *she* spoke, someone was still bound to listen.

But timing was everything in politics, and timing was important now. And so she advised the women that they needed to be patient. They needed to wait for just the right moment and then make the most of it.

"You can only do this," she reminded them, "if you are going to win."[1]

# CHAPTER ONE

## The Girl from New Berlin

IT WAS AN ACCIDENT OF GEOGRAPHY that Ella Maude McMillan became a Republican in the first place. But it didn't hurt that Republicans also seemed to have more fun.

She was born in the Land of Lincoln, in the same Illinois county where the most celebrated Republican president launched his own political career. It was a state, she once told a reporter, "where people enter politics like they enter church."[1]

"If the Lord had known what a holy terror you were going to be," an old woman once told the little girl, "He certainly would never have put you on His earth." But, Peterson observed, "the Lord evidently didn't know, so He put me here, starting me meekly and mildly in a small town in Central Illinois."[2]

With only six hundred residents, New Berlin was small enough that the telephone operator always knew if the town's doctor was "in" because he lived across the street. The doctor was John Charles McMillan, who had gone to Washington University, then returned home to start a practice.

His wife, Maude Ella Carpenter, was born on a nearby farm but joined the tide of women who ventured into the workplace at the turn of the twentieth century. In 1898, she left home at nineteen to teach at the Illinois School for the Deaf in Jacksonville. Though Maude never used the word, her daughter Elly thought she would have qualified as an early "feminist."[3]

In 1901, a year after the McMillans married, their first child arrived. John Charles Jr. was a serious young man who eventually became a doctor. Four years later a daughter, Mary Catherine, was born and two years later another son, Lee Gibson.

Then, on the morning of June 5, 1914, their mother's helper awakened Mary and said she had a surprise. Mary correctly guessed it was a new little sister. She and her brothers called her Baby.

Elly McMillan's childhood was, by all accounts, a happy, comfortable one in a civic-minded family. The McMillans' three-story home had thirteen rooms, with the doctor's office in the basement. Although they had household help, they did not consider themselves wealthy. Charles's patients sometimes paid him in chickens or farm produce, and his children thought they were poor because his patients always owed him money.

From an early age, Elly McMillan was an extrovert and a performer. Before she was old enough for school, "Doc Mac's girl" often accompanied her father on his rounds. Maude used to say that her daughter knew more people than her husband did and "the lower they were, the better she knew them." Told she could invite a few friends to her seventh birthday party, she invited forty-two. She sang at all the "entertainments," even though, she acknowledged, she couldn't carry a tune.

In 1920, at the age of forty-one, Maude McMillan finally earned the right to vote. Ever after, her daughter remembered, she made sure she exercised that right. Charles was a Democrat, but Maude voted Republican—because, her daughter believed, she wanted "to kill off" her husband's vote.

But the McMillans were not political activists. "It would make a much better story," Peterson acknowledged, "if I could say we discussed politics at the dinner table and father and mother inspired me to take part."

But, she was quick to add, "it would also be a big fat lie."[4]

\* \* \*

As a girl, Peterson's horizons were defined by the roads and railroads of the Illinois prairie. New Berlin's "library" was set up in a lawyer's office, and he would take Elly to Springfield occasionally and let her pick out books. The telephone operator would also let her tag along on her monthly trip to the state capital.

But the McMillans wanted their children to see the world beyond New Berlin, and insisted they attend college. Charles went to medical school, and Lee went to dental school. Mary started at Illinois College for Women, then transferred to the University of Illinois.

When Elly graduated in the early 1930s, only about one out of ten

Americans her age went on to college. Winding up as salutatorian of her fifteen-student class, she was the only girl who did.[5] But she didn't agonize over where to go. She chose William Woods College in Fulton, Missouri, then an all-girls school affiliated with the Christian Church (Disciples of Christ), simply because Lee's girlfriend went there.[6]

She made good grades, because it was expected, but found she did not enjoy the liberal arts and had no interest in math or science. "I had no real desire to go to college," she recalled, "because I had no idea what I wanted to do."[7]

On New Year's Eve 1932, during her sophomore year, she went to a party celebrating the inauguration of Missouri governor Guy Brasfield Park. Prohibition was nearing an end but still in place. "They served drinks, and we just took one," she recalled. "It wasn't that we were drunk, we only had one drink. . . . It was pretty stupid on my part. We were so naive."

When she was caught, the college expelled her. Her father, a strict Baptist, was "furious"; her mother, "heartbroken."[8]

Mary came to her sister's rescue. Though nine years apart, the sisters were already very close. Mary suggested that Elly should come and live with her and her husband in Chicago and attend business school. And so Peterson transferred to Suburban Business College in Oak Park to pursue secretarial studies.

Her youthful indiscretion, she said, "was never mentioned again. It was just wiped out. I don't think anyone even knew it in New Berlin." Nor did her new friends in Oak Park.[9] She glossed over the episode in the memoir she later wrote for her family; official biographies generally noted that she had "attended" William Woods.

In contrast to her first years in college, Peterson loved everything about business school—shorthand, typing, and accounting. And while many of her friends stayed home both before and after marriage, she found that she wanted to work and "be on my own."

For the next two years, she was a secretary to the president of Ross-Coles Company, a merchandiser with a Chicago showroom. She discovered that she liked "the contact with the people" and that she liked to sell. She also discovered that she loved to organize an office. She was a successful secretary, she said, because she "understood the organization, and that was really my basic skill." Later, she told a writer, "A good secretary can learn the business as no other position can."[10]

In 1934, Martha McMackin, her best friend from William Woods, invited her to a University of Illinois football game and set her up with a blind date. She sent her own date to the train station to meet her friend, and he corralled a half dozen of his Alpha Sigma Phi fraternity brothers to go along. One of them was "Pete" Peterson.

W. Merritt Peterson was born 3 1/2 years before Elly in Brownstown, Illinois, near Vandalia. His father, Roy, had farmed and then worked as an assistant sheriff. But as Pete approached adulthood, Roy decided he didn't want to work anymore. It fell to his wife, Caddie, to support the family—and her son's college plans.

At Pete's suggestion, they moved into a house near the University of Illinois campus and took in male boarders. Caddie worked "like a dog," her daughter-in-law recalled. Pete provided the financial smarts, exercising strict portion control so that they wouldn't lose money.

Pete was very much "a man's man" whose greatest passions were hunting, golf, and the military. But he was also, in the words of his wife, "quite a 'dude.'" Years later a friend recalled the first time she saw him, tooling around Charlotte at the age of fifty: "a red and black MG convertible occupied by a tanned, handsome man in a fine tweed jacket, a silk ascot, an English country hat, and smoking a cigarette in a long holder!"[11]

Over the course of trips between Chicago and Champaign, Elly and Pete's relationship flowered. And after about a year and a half, Pete proposed.

"We had just been going together and it just happened," Peterson recalled. "He began going home with me, and I went home with him and we just decided to get married. But there was nothing especially romantic about it."[12] In fact, Pete actually presented his engagement ring in the false bottom of a slop jar, the kind of prank family members enjoyed playing on each other.

They were married in her family's home on October 11, 1935, her parents' anniversary. Elly wore the same high-necked, floor-length taffeta wedding dress that her mother and grandmother had worn. For their honeymoon, the couple spent a night at the Palmer House in Chicago, and then, on Monday, they went back to work.

They moved into an apartment in Oak Park near Mary and her husband, Park Richmond. The men hunted and played golf, and the couples played bridge and socialized together.

Elly fell in with the Young Republicans as "a social thing."[13] In one version of her life story, she wrote:

In Illinois, socially-minded girls around 21 usually joined a political party, and, at that time, Republicans were so much more fun than Democrats. They had by far the nicest parties and we were never bothered with having to learn what was going on. We wouldn't have known an issue if we met one face to face and we were never asked to meet the candidates, or hear what they had to say. We knew that if we did a simple chore now and then, we would end up in a neat bar in Franklin Park where beer and sandwiches with hot mustard were served![14]

Those years produced a story that Peterson loved to tell about her first real experience in politics. It was October 1936, and Kansas governor Alf Landon was challenging Franklin D. Roosevelt for the presidency. Peterson and several friends were recruited to go downtown and hand out Landon's trademark sunflowers. "Well, that [idea] was sort of fun," she recalled in one version. "We'd all [go] down and then we'd all go out to lunch. It was more of a party than anything."[15] Colonel Robert R. McCormick, publisher of the Chicago Tribune and a strong Landon supporter, promoted the event with banner headlines in his paper: "City Acclaims Landon Today: Great Parade to Escort Him Up Michigan Av."[16]

But when Saturday dawned, it was pouring rain. Nevertheless, Peterson said, McCormick "had planned to hand out sunflowers and—come hell or high water—they were going to be handed out. Down Michigan Avenue we went, we young ones walking, trying to get people to take the damned sunflowers that were dripping yellow paint down our arms, and onto our clothes, and all the time, Col. McCormick riding slowly down the avenue, in his big, black car, exhorting us ONWARD!"

It was, she concluded, "an amazing thing that I did not become a Democrat then and there."[17]

Peterson took away lessons from her first political experiences. Politics could be social, and politics could be fun. Years later Margaret Cooke, one of Peterson's many protégées, recalled how Peterson had urged her to join a Young Republican club when Cooke got out of college in the mid-1960s. Back then the Young Republican clubs in Detroit and its suburbs were boasting thousands of members. "It was acceptable," Cooke recalled, "it was legitimate. . . . You were going to a Republican meeting. It didn't have the tarnish of going to a bar."[18]

Back in Chicago, Pete Peterson was offered a sales job with Standard

Oil, and the couple moved 150 miles to Kalamazoo, Michigan. There, in 1941, in the middle of making plans for Christmas, they heard the shocking news on their radio. The Japanese had attacked a U.S. military outpost on what seemed like the other side of the world. And within a matter of months, the cozy little world they were building for themselves would be turned upside down.[19]

* * *

"Once upon a time," Peterson wrote, "the Great Powers gave a war and EVERYONE came! Not just soldiers and sailors and Red Cross and doctors and nurses—but civilians all pitched in with them."[20]

The Petersons were no exception. Still childless after six years of marriage, they set aside diagnosing their fertility problems when the war broke out. Almost immediately, Pete announced that he was enlisting in the army. Though not much of a mechanic, he was assigned to aircraft maintenance in California. "There goes the war!" Park Richmond joked when he heard the news.[21] Later Pete attended Officers' Training School, and was assigned to the Ninetieth Infantry Division of the Third Army under Gen. George C. Patton.

Meanwhile, Elly returned home. She worked briefly at a military installation in Springfield, then reconnected with Jane Allen, a friend who had just been divorced and was now living in Chicago. The two decided to rent an apartment on the near North Side, over a dress shop close to the Oak Street beach.[22]

Peterson's own memories of the dissolution of her marriage were fuzzy late in life. At ninety-six, Jane Allen Edelheit recalled that the Petersons' marriage had already broken up when the women moved in together, but Elly said it was the Petersons' wartime separation that led to their divorce. "I was in a city which had been captured by soldiers from all over," she recalled more than sixty years later, "and everyone catered to them and life was quite a party for the young (and I guess 'foolish')."[23] More than a third of all navy personnel passed through the Great Lakes Training Station in North Chicago during the war; another half a million men and women were processed into the army at nearby Fort Sheridan.[24]

In later years, Peterson still had second thoughts about her behavior. It demonstrated, she said, "a lack of maturity on my part." Everybody did it, "so I did it, too." She and Pete "just sort of drifted apart."[25]

She sought and obtained a divorce in 1943. It was difficult for the rest of her family because they were all very close to Pete.

In her memoir, Peterson devoted one sentence to the episode. The Petersons were, in fact, divorced for five years. Later in life, they continued to count their years of marriage from the time of their first wedding. JoAnn DiBella Hawkins, a longtime friend, recalled, "Pete took great delight in extolling the virtues of his first wife when they were with a group that didn't realize that Elly was wife number one *and* two."[26] Some good friends never knew that there had been a time when the Petersons had been apart.[27]

"Thinking it over," Peterson wrote later, "it was just as well we were divorced as we both stepped into a different life."[28]

But by the fall of 1943, she was "feeling at loose ends" and walked into the offices of the American Red Cross while on a weekend date in Washington. She walked out with a job overseas.

With the death of her father the previous year, her brother Charles had become the family patriarch. "He gave me quite a lecture on how stupid I had been . . . and now that I had done it, I had made my bed, I could never complain about ANYTHING that happened to me, etc., etc."[29]

Regardless of what happens, her brother added, "do not distress your mother!"[30] It was advice, she acknowledged later, that helped her get through some difficult times during the war.

Peterson was assigned to the U.S. Army's 280th Field Station Hospital. The standard Red Cross hospital team consisted of a field director, recreation director, and Peterson's job, "secretary and go-fer." From the start, her relationship with her team members was a frosty one. They had run a hospital unit stateside for more than a year, and "they made it very clear they needed a secretary like a hole in the head."[31]

It was during her years overseas that letter writing became a lifetime avocation for Peterson, the way she kept connected with friends and family. Forty years after the war, Peterson discovered that her sister had saved all the letters that she and other family members had written home. Her letters reveal a young woman learning to cope with the rigors of life near the front but still retaining her core of humor, common sense, and optimism.[32]

Peterson chose her words carefully, conscious of the wartime censors and concerned about distressing her mother. Nevertheless, it was clear that she did not get along with her Red Cross roommates. But, heeding her brother's admonition not to complain, it would be more than sixty years before she explained why the situation had been so awkward: she had to share accommodations with two lesbian partners.

Although she was the daughter of a physician, Peterson professed that as a young woman she had known virtually nothing about the human body. Thus she did not know what a lesbian was, only that her roommates always kissed each other before they went to bed at night.[33]

Christmas 1943 found Peterson headed for England on a troopship with fifteen thousand servicemen and women. Years later, she recalled:

> We boarded the ship at night, marching up the gangplank, gas masks and all. Someone whispered to me, "The Queen Mary," but I could see nothing but soldiers and nurses. It WAS the Queen Mary, and I felt so fortunate. I shipped over in Winston Churchill's suite, with its walls covered with silk and with only 16 of us in bunks three high in what had been his living room.[34]

The whisperer on the gangplank was Dr. Robert Allen. He was a dentist from Plano, Illinois, who was assigned to the 280th Field Station Hospital, and during their ocean crossing, she recalled, "we found we had quite a bit in common." Allen was "a big, strapping fellow," who had played football for the University of Alabama.[35] He was estranged from his spouse and had a young son. Before very long she was writing her sister, "The officers living here at present all have me earmarked 'Allen.'" In another letter, she observed, "He's a comfort to me as he's fun without being silly."[36]

In Peterson's first two weeks overseas, her letters bubbled over with the excitement of adapting to a strange, new world: "I spent all day yesterday in an accounting lesson as I have to keep the books in pounds sterling. . . . I can sleep through the alerts now and never seem to be awake for the All Clear. . . . We had roast GOSLING for dinner with the inevitable Brussels sprouts and boiled potatoes." Still, the main crisis was the disappearance of her foot locker, which did not show up for seven weeks.[37]

A month after her arrival, her unit began setting up a hospital on the cricket field of a seventeenth-century manor house in Saffron Walden, about sixty miles north of London. Their "landlady," she wrote, was a Mrs. Slater, "a sweet old lady" who occasionally invited them for dinner. Peterson had resumed using her maiden name, and Mrs. Slater, like several others, assumed that "Ella McMillan" was a "good Catholic" rather than the Baptist she still professed to be.[38]

Their unit was supposed to help figure out the best way to set up a tent hospital for the inevitable invasion of Europe. Two months after she arrived, Peterson wrote, "I principally run the office, keep books, cash checks, change money, run the library, keep up supplies for the patients, handle the correspondence which ranges from telling Mama all is well to trying to find a set of drums. In between I listen to a lot of bitching, how wonderful my wife is—or isn't—and look at 50 pictures a day of assorted women and children. I copy things for them (many are great on wanting copies of poems), mend every kind of rip or sew a button and SMILE."[39]

One of her first jobs was to make blackout curtains for all the tents. "Yes," she informed her mother, "I CAN sew—strange what you can do when you have to."[40]

In the months leading up to D-day, there was no shortage of men available for an attractive twenty-nine-year-old divorcée. In her first month in London, she took "Col. Hart, Major McGuire and Capt. Otis" on a tour of London and to see "Panama Hattie." A month later, she attended a dance in Hull and reported that she "had quite a swingeroo with a handsome English captain."[41]

Peterson was reunited with Bob Allen when their hospital was set up at Saffron Walden, and they continued to spend time together during their months overseas. "A date was to go over to the officers' club and have a drink or go to a movie—that's all there was to do—or take a walk."[42]

But two weeks before D-day, she had a surprise visitor. In a May 22, 1944, letter to her mother, she worked up to it slowly.

> The weekend turned out quite interesting after all. I didn't write Saturday as on Friday night I worked for the gals. . . . Saturday night we couldn't seem to get the urge to go anyplace. . . . Sunday morning I slept in . . . and then I got up and washed and ironed and was just heading for work [about] 10 when I got a phone call—Pete. I was about floored. He was in London until evening and could not make it out to camp so I told him I would come in there . . . whereupon I changed my clothes, got permission, got a jeep to catch the train— and it was an hour late—so I stood out in the cold for that hour and then stood on the train for two getting there. Rode next to a Captain . . . and he was quite interesting so it wasn't too bad.
>
> Not having seen Pete for nearly two years, I was wondering if I would know him and he has changed—he was fat as a pig for one thing—his face so filled out and he looks so different from most over

here as he still has the tan he acquired on the desert—then his hair is much much grayer—and of course I had never seen him in an officer's uniform. Incidentally, his promotion is up so he should soon be a First Lieut.

Pete said he had arrived in London "quite unexpectedly" the night before, and had obtained her phone number from her brother Charles. He had gone to church at Westminster Abbey that morning and then "decided that was all of London he wanted to see so we just spent the day visiting . . . and had a very nice one."

She went on to share Pete's news of his family and his assignment as executive officer in the headquarters division of the Military Police. Then she shifted gears to report that she had received her new field coat—"a wool lined gabardine water proofed thing with a hood—more practical to wear with slacks and much warmer than my dress coat, which I shall sluff off shortly."

She then returned to her ex-husband. "Pete thought the only change in me was I am fatter (which I am in reality not—but I think it is these darned suits) and my hair much grayer. He said I still wobbled as much as I used to!"

She concluded, "I had to come back on the early train, Sunday travel is so difficult, so left several hours before he did—had a dull ride back— Bob met me and we got some coffee and called it an evening. I was really tired as that is quite a trip to take all in one day.

"I won't be seeing him again—but anyway it was nice to get it over for the first time."[43]

In fact, five days later, Pete called her again, but this time she could not get a pass to see him.

Within a matter of weeks, Peterson turned thirty. "The gang" organized a party, and Bob took her out to dinner, but her letters reflected no particular introspection on passing that milestone.[44]

The day after her birthday, the Allies invaded Normandy. On June 8, she wrote her mother, "I can imagine you were glued to the radio most of the day and you probably know more than we do about what is going on. I do know the skies are filled with planes day and night."

Within two weeks, Pete wrote the Richmonds from the invasion force, "So this is France! Have been sorta busy and not much I can tell you." In fact, his transport ship, the *Susan B. Anthony* (an ironic twist for the husband of a future feminist), had exploded and sunk after hitting a mine during the landing. However, none of the twenty-five hundred soldiers and sailors onboard was lost.[45]

By late September, Elly was also moving on to France. A letter home showed how much her outlook had matured. "I am sitting in what is probably one of the dirtiest barracks in existence," she wrote, "just waiting. However, it looked mighty good to us when we arrived—in the rain—after carrying our 50 lb. blanket rolls, mussette bags, helmets and gas masks. There was some degree of heat—straw mattresses and blankets—the only thing: not enough and filthy. However, after 9 months dirt has no bother for me at all and we just slept 3 in a single bed and slept good."[46]

On October 11, 1944, she wrote, "If this isn't one helluva place—and, Ma, don't say 'Ella Maude!' THAT is a kind description of the place. We are in a cow pasture with all the glories therein." They slept on cots in a hut with a mud floor, and drew water from a well in the nearby village. They had "advanced from honeybuckets to straddle trenches." She added that she thought "I would never get the system but when you gotta go—you go—and thankfully!"[47]

Shortly after that, Peterson was assigned to the headquarters building in Paris, which, she reported, was "as cold as a barn. . . . I will remember when I used to complain about a temp of 65—this is steadily 40 or below." She missed her friends at the 280th Field Hospital: "I am hoping that something has developed and we are on the move—so I can get back. I have had enough of Paris at the moment . . ."[48]

The war was now being delivered to their doorstep. Each day, she said, the army was providing up to a thousand GIs with forty-eight-hour passes to Paris: "You should see them—they are really pitiful—one fellow had been in combat without rest for 56 days—he was really dead. . . . Everyone carries guns and they are the toughest hombres you ever saw—they don't care for nothin. . . . I guess I wouldn't either if I had been through what they have."[49]

By the end of the month, she was happy to be "getting home" to the 280th, particularly when forty letters were awaiting her. "My situation has eased considerably. I will have more responsibility—there is so much work. I will really have charge of the office, which I never had in England."[50] In addition, she was serving doughnuts—as many as two thousand a day—in the Recreation Hall. "Never want to see another donut," she concluded.[51]

In November 1944, the letters included a rare comment about politics. "I suppose people are excited about the election at home," she wrote her Republican mother. "I wrote for my ballot but it came just as we were moving and couldn't get things done so I didn't vote. We do not talk about it as it seems so far away but I wonder if anyone could beat Roosevelt."[52]

In a letter written later that month, she noted that it had been a year since she left home: "A lot has certainly happened since then but I can truthfully say I wouldn't have missed any of it (or do I care to go through it again). There are plenty of times when you doubt if you are doing any good at all, or times when you get so sick and tired of being uncomfortable, dressed in uniform, dirty, etc.—but mostly, you are satisfied to do what you can when you can—and your sense of values change[s] enough that you don't put the importance on the things you once did. . . ."[53]

At the end of the month, she wrestled with her unit's financial records, a task she never learned to enjoy. Then it was then back to wrapping Christmas presents for the patients: "At the present count I have 71 wrapped out of 1,000 to be done—how am I doing? It will probably turn me against Christmas for the rest of my life!" She also had to wrap fifty prizes of candy bars and gum for a bingo party. "I think I'll get a job in [Marshall] Field's basement when I get back," she quipped.[54]

The letters also began to reflect more about the progress of the troops.

Orders continue to come in and they say there might possibly be as much as a 50% turnover in personnel. I should hate it as I know everyone so well and after being together this long it is like your own family but they seem to be putting these fellows up to the front and pulling back some others for a rest which has merit behind the idea. I really get sick of radio announcements and newspapers which go on about our advancing, etc. every day, every day, like we were going to take Berlin at any minute and we were rolling along . . . believe you me, it is not that simple. . . .[55]

As Christmas approached, the mail stopped coming: "I have never seen morale at such a low pitch among the men," she wrote. "Christmas is bad enough but to go days without mail is just more than they can take. . . . I pray for a lot of mail for them for Christmas or things are going to be bad."[56]

But the holiday celebrations then took an even more tragic turn. On

Christmas Eve, a converted Belgian passenger ship, the *S.S. Leopoldville,* set off from Southampton with more than two thousand members of the U.S. Army's Sixty-sixth "Panther" Infantry Division, destined as reinforcements for the Battle of the Bulge. Just over five miles offshore of Cherbourg Harbor, the ship was sunk by a German submarine. In the ensuing chaos, some eight hundred American servicemen lost their lives.

For years afterward, the U.S., British, and Belgian governments withheld details of the tragedy from family members. In a letter the next day, Peterson wrote:

> I am going through a Christmas which I shall long remember—but not for its gaiety. . . . We . . . were just in the midst of opening our presents when an "incident" occurred which canceled all parties, celebration and thoughts of Christmas. Things happened fast—and we got little sleep. We have been busy all day trying to make up a little Christmas cheer. . . . The only thing good about last nite was it took the enlisted men's mind off their homesickness.[57]

Years later she added, "Our hospital, of course, ceased everything and every able person was put to work from hauling in people pulled out of the water to vital statistics—That's what I did all night. It was gruesome and it was hateful."[58]

A week into the new year, the mail started to flow again, including a letter from her ex-husband. "Finally heard from Pete," she wrote to her mother, "and he seemed to enjoy the box I sent him, although he complained about the shorts being too big. He seems to be fairly comfortable and not in the danger zone I thought he might be in."[59]

But there were still plenty of other male companions around—and some early signs of the "Mother" she was destined to become.

> A bunch of the enlisted men left yesterday for the infantry and they all came to tell me goodbye. My office, being about 4 × 4, was packed—and I really felt bad to see them go up front. They stammered and stuttered around and finally they got almost out of the door—one turned around and said, "We just come to tell you, Mac, we wanted you to know we'll miss you more than anything in the 280th . . . —I felt like sitting down and bawling—because one of them may [n]ever come back again . . . well, so it goes. First I think

I'm hardened to anything—then something happens like that and I feel like a first class sissy![60]

As the weeks and months rolled on, she began to display a more mature political awareness. "Those V-2's are something that should rankle long in English minds when peace is made. They have absolutely no military value and in almost every sense have demolished something that is entirely civilian—homes, stores, hospitals, schools—and killed thousands of helpless civilians. . . . Just the fact of them [has] made me hate the Germans more and more."[61]

She had decided not to request a thirty-day furlough home, even if she qualified for one. "When I come home I want it to be for good and not for [a] visit and I keep hoping that suddenly something will turn for the better and we can start thinking about home."[62]

As spring came, the end of the war was finally in sight. On April 30, she wrote, "The war news looks grand—just came over that Hitler is dead but we're all wondering if it's another rumor like peace. In Paris, they woke people up in the clubs, started dancing and carrying on at great rate—only to find it another rumor so I guess we won't celebrate this until we really hear."[63]

Pete, meanwhile, was continuing to move across Europe with Patton. On May 4, Elly wrote her sister that her ex-husband had been promoted to captain: "Guess that comes of combat and being with the General—but what ever it is it must be okay. He said it was pretty rough. I suppose he'll get to come home—at least for a brief spell before the E.B.I."[64]

Within a week, V-E Day arrived. "I, for one, am glad the celebrating is over as the Post Office has been closed for three days now—and I'm ready for mail," Peterson wrote home. "Probably today they'll be so tired from their celebrating we won't get any again."[65]

In June, her mother received a letter from "Cherbourg, France," from "Gus," a young man Peterson had previously described as "my Greek boyfriend who is always bringing something."[66] Gus wrote:

If Elly is a representation of the McMillans, well, I'll have to cope with a swell bunch of people. I have a snapshot of her which she gave me and autographed it. I shall always keep it with me. I gave her one of me to always remember her pal who is so noisy yet so very sincere. Everytime I get candy from home I try and pick out what she likes

and bring it to her. You should see her scold me for bringing it. She
always tells me to give it to my French girlfriends. I want her to enjoy
it instead of them that is why I bring it to her in the first place. . . .

Please tell the rest of the McMillans that their pride and joy Elly
is still our sweetheart and pal and always will be.

He then added in a postscript: "Where does she get all that personality?"[67] It was a question legions of admirers would continue to ask for the
rest of her life.

After seventeen months overseas, Peterson could finally write an un-
censored letter. On May 15, 1945, she wrote her sister, "I have often wondered just how I would feel like writing when we finally were permitted to
tell of our trip over. Now I think back it is a confused memory. . . . But
from it all, I have quite a picture of my first taste of the Army."

She remembered "cockroaches all over" the Red Cross building where
they were quartered in Louisiana and her "complete surprise and 'what do
I do now' when I received my first salute." She recalled the long, long train
trip north. ("By the end," she said, the women "looked like '90 days of
Bataan.'")

On the trip across the Atlantic, she had played bridge in the cabin of
the troopship commander and become seasick: "So they fixed the table so
I could play, get up quickly to go throw up and then a few minutes later return to the game! Never say die McMillan, I was called."[68]

A few months later, she moved on to Marburg, Germany, to set up the
Red Cross operation there. This time she was in charge, as her two
coworkers had been sent home.

"It was a grim time in Germany," she recalled. Marburg was filled with
German soldiers and sailors who were missing body parts "so the sights
around the town are horrible." Also, "with no fighting left to do the white
and black soldiers kept mixing it up so all nurses and Red Cross were
confined to post unless accompanied by the military. This certainly did
not add to anyone's comfort."[69]

She arrived back home on October 22, 1945, this time aboard a large
troop transport—"no Queen Mary"—that landed in Boston. She took a
train to Washington, "where we checked out as fast as possible."[70]

In an interview more than fifty years later, Peterson could not point to
any specific political skills she acquired during her days overseas.
"Frankly," she said, "the only politicians I encountered during the war

were real pains"—congressmen whose visits forced the hospital staff to work overtime in preparation.[71]

But the experience undoubtedly shaped her in subtle ways. She would have observed firsthand how officers could lead troops into battle and keep them fighting when they were weary and discouraged. Not surprisingly, in later years she often referred to her campaign workers as "the troops." And if you had slogged your way through the mud of wartime France, it was no big deal to crisscross Michigan's Upper Peninsula in the dead of winter. A protégée later recalled with admiration, "She carried her own bags, didn't worry about her appearance . . . she just wasn't high maintenance."[72]

Peterson's wartime experiences also exposed her to the real diversity of America—and the rest of the world. Far from home and cut off, sometimes for weeks, from the lifeblood of her family's letters, she fashioned a new family from the motley mix of soldiers and sailors, nurses, doctors, and dentists that she met along the way. She was not yet the "Mother" that dozens of her political colleagues would come to love. But she was already an outgoing leader with a wise-cracking enthusiasm for life.

The journey led to a lifetime love affair with foreign travel.[73] More important, she met persons from ethnic and cultural backgrounds that she might never have met in the small midwestern towns where she had spent most of her life. Years later she recalled that Bob Allen's roommate was the first Jewish person she had known.

There were, of course, stereotypes to overcome, and not all of her experiences were positive. "Rode with 2 GIs," she recounted soon after arriving in England, "one an Italian from South Chicago and I could get nothing from his 'dis, dese, and dem'. . . [and] the other was a Spaniard. I changed trains and drew a good Joe from Mass. . . . Then I changed again and drew some potato merchants playing whist and a Polish flyer who could not speak English but grinned at me for 3 hours."[74]

Early on, she wrote her mother:

I meant to tell you that so many of the English girls go out with negroes here just like they were white—not in London as you don't see many in the city—but out in the provinces where they are located and one of the Clubmobile girls was telling me you see white girls wheeling negro babies, etc., and the black lads really think they are in. That is one trouble Red Cross girls have working in those sections as the fellows think they should be free just like the English girls and, on top of that—can you imagine how some of these southern girls are—woo. . . . I surely can't understand it.[75]

But on another occasion, she wrote with admiration, "Guess I'll go watch the Negroes stand retreat. They make such a great show of it."[76]

Peterson did acknowledge one character trait that grew out of her wartime experiences: her patriotism.[77] She recalled how her commanding officer would ask the Red Cross staff members to join him on the reviewing stand. The patients, she wrote home at the time, "were wheeled out to the flag pole and the entire complement stood to attention. How beautiful and how thrilling to see the American flag lowered against the English sky with everyone at attention and every eye on the flag."[78]

"It was a great thing to be an American in those days," she remembered years later. "You were proud of it then and proud of the way men were doing. . . . Some of [the men] seemed so young and of course there were lots of tragedies. But there were a lot of wonderful moments, too. When you saw people rise above. And when you were over there that long you weren't homesick anymore."[79]

In October 1945, she finally returned to "home sweet home," still a single woman. In her memoir, she did not dwell on those particular memories, writing only, "I had been away nearly two years, and it was good to be back, with another life to build for myself."[80]

# CHAPTER TWO

---

# Hooked on Politics

---

HER LIFE RETURNED TO "NORMAL," but Peterson still felt at loose ends. The years after the war ended, she recalled, were an empty time when she just "couldn't seem to get settled."

She continued to date Bob Allen, and he eventually proposed. But Peterson turned him down. "Bob was an awfully nice fellow," she recalled, "but I knew I didn't want to live in Plano." She was also concerned about becoming the stepmother of a twelve-year-old boy.

The couple broke up, and Allen reconciled with his wife. Peterson continued to follow his life closely enough to know that he died within the decade.[1]

Meanwhile, Pete stayed in Europe, eventually serving as provost marshal of the Second Constabulary Brigade in Munich. There he helped set up the school that trained American military police for the occupation of Bavaria. Those two years, his wife believed, "were the best of his life." He "lived high" and had German girlfriends. She still wrote to him, as did her family members. Pete, she believed, "continued to feel closer" to them than he did to his own family.[2]

She took a stab at a new career: journalism. Before the war, Peterson had taken some night courses at Northwestern University. And in July 1946, in a foreshadowing of her future feminism, a new column, "To the Ladies," appeared under the byline "Elly McMillan" in the monthly *National Bowlers Journal and Billiard Revue.*

> Shades of Amanda Bloomer! The women have gone and done it again! Broken into the sacred precincts of the almost entirely mascu-

line *Bowlers Journal* to come up with their own page—devoted to women, for women, and by women. With progress like this you can't tell what they'll do—might even get the vote. Let's see what we can make of it—let us know what you're doing—and why.

In February 1947, she reported on a "quick trip" to Cuba:

[A]ll you bowling lasses had better be mighty happy Pappy has never taken you to Cuba to live, or you'd be missing all your fun. In talking to some of the gentlemen in Havana, they were positive in their opinion that women's place is in the home—and couldn't see them in any sport, much less bowling. . . . . they were aghast at the idea of mama taking off in the middle of the morning for a bowling league meeting.[3]

But in the end, Peterson felt she lacked the "self-discipline" to pursue a writing career.

When Pete was discharged from the army, he looked up his old friends Park and Mary Richmond. Elly was in San Francisco, but he phoned her long distance, and "when he called," she said, "I realized I was still in love." They remarried, this time in Oak Park, on February 5, 1948.

By then, Peterson was nearly thirty-four, too old, she said years later, to start trying again to have a family.[4]

Keith Molin, one of Peterson's "political children," said they sometimes talked about the fact that she had none of her own: "That subject would come up, and she would blow by [it]. 'Kids. They're all my kids.' She would do it in a way that said, 'You don't have to pursue it.'"[5]

Margie Cooke, another Peterson "kid," said Peterson told her their childlessness "was not an issue" for them. "They both had active lives and didn't care one way or the other. . . . She and Pete were jealous of the time they could carve out for each other. I really got the sense that children were not something she wanted or missed having."[6] Peterson doted instead on her nieces and nephews, godchildren and political protégées.

Late in life, Peterson acknowledged that if she had had children, she would not have been able to travel the way she did, for politics or for pleasure. Instead, she said, she would have ended up as "a housewife and volunteer."[7]

She also wrote, "Many people could not . . . and probably don't now . . . understand my submitting to the name of 'Mother' from people of all ages, races, creeds and colors. I always felt it was used in affection, and, in truth, I felt as close to many of them as their own mothers. . . . Most of them remained very special to me and will be so always."[8] Nearly fifty years after she gave up trying to have children, she told an interviewer that fifteen to twenty people began their letters to her "Dear Mother."[9]

* * *

In 1948, the Petersons moved back to Michigan, this time to Charlotte, a small county seat twenty miles west of Lansing, where Pete resumed working as a salesman for Standard Oil.

"Anyone driving through Charlotte, Michigan would find it a pleasant place: clean, tree-lined streets, a magnificent old red brick court house, well-kept brick and white houses," Peterson wrote later in life.[10] Joyce Braithwaite-Brickley, one of Peterson's closest friends, recalled the place as "typical small town America, a bit backward, unsophisticated, a farm town."[11]

The Petersons moved into a big stone house at 733 N. Cochran Street, the town's main street, which had an upstairs apartment for Pete's mother. But after she decided to move back to Illinois, the couple looked for a farm to satisfy Pete's hankering for some land. They found one, with sixty-four acres and close to the courthouse. It came with a white frame farmhouse, a barn, and a supply of pigs, sheep, cows, and chickens that Pete proceeded to name after people they knew. They invited old Chicago friends for a weekend housewarming party. One, in jest, said the place should be called "Holiday Hill." The name stuck and was installed on their mailbox.

Peterson gravitated to volunteer work with her friends. She took a particular interest in the American Red Cross, working to establish a local blood bank and organizing a new group of volunteer Gray Ladies at a nearby hospital. She volunteered with the American Cancer Society and joined the American Legion Auxiliary. The Petersons also joined the First Congregational Church in Charlotte. (When they first moved to town, they tried the Baptist church, she recalled, but they "did not make friends nor did we feel especially welcome." Most of their new friends turned out to be Congregationalists and kept after them until they joined.)[12]

Peterson drifted back into politics in much the same way. Most of her friends were Republicans, and party work was a natural outgrowth of other volunteer projects.[13] But her situation was different from that of her friends. Pete was offered a commission in the Michigan National Guard, and began traveling around the state. And Elly found herself home alone, with time on her hands and energy to burn. "I just naturally kept spending more and more time" on politics, she recalled.[14]

In fact, the Republican Party *was* attracting more women voters. In the 1952 election, women were 5 percent more likely than men to vote for Dwight Eisenhower—the first discernible gender gap since Herbert Hoover's 1928 race. Some pollsters concluded that women blamed the Democrats for the Korean War, inflation, and corruption in Washington. Other observers contended that women were more inclined to prefer fatherlike figures such as Ike. But journalist Marion K. Sanders wrote that "well-trained Republican women" were making the difference: "The telephone . . . was used on a scale never before attempted."[15]

Peterson attended her first Republican National Convention in 1952, working as a "gofer" for Rice Fowler, her local party chairman. "From then on," she recalled, "I was sort of hooked."[16] But she was frustrated by the casualness of the Republican campaigns, particularly compared with those of the union-backed Democrats. "The order of the day" was that "Republicans don't do things like that," she noted. "And the campaigns of 1950 and 1952 were sad indeed."[17]

In 1952, the Republican candidate for governor was Fred Alger, a wealthy Grosse Pointer who had served as Michigan's secretary of state. Peterson recalled, "Fred would cruise across the state with no rhyme or reason to his travel, appearing in one town in the morning; later on he would frequently have the 'happy hour' stop. He would then appear late and sometimes a little worse for wear. Still no one took the time to ride herd on him and, as a result his campaign was sloppy and disorganized."[18]

She was drafted as a traveling companion for Alger's wife, Suzy. Mrs. Alger was "a dynamic, bright attractive woman; every inch a socialite." She was willing to support her husband's political ambitions, "but she would not give an inch on her personal schedule." Women weren't expected to campaign. "Wives were wives and that was that; nothing very substantive.[19]

In the end, Alger lost by fewer than ten thousand votes to incumbent Democrat G. Mennen Williams in what was otherwise a landslide for the Republicans. But from Peterson's perspective, it marked the start of a downward spiral. The state party was still controlled by Arthur E. Summerfield of Flint, even after he became President Eisenhower's postmaster general. "He ran the state party with a tight little group of thirty-four men who decided on the candidates, raised the necessary money and, I believe, then prayed a lot for they did little constructive building," Peterson wrote.[20] By 1956, Williams was able to post a plurality that was bigger than even Eisenhower's.

But at the 1957 state Republican convention, it was time for change. A younger group succeeded in electing Larry Lindemer, a thirty-five-year-old attorney and former state legislator from Stockbridge, as the new party chairman.[21]

Peterson did not attend the state convention that year, but when she returned from a Virgin Islands vacation, she got a full report from her close friend, Gert Powers. Powers had already met with Lindemer and told him, "There's a gal you ought to get in here. . . . Her name is Elly Peterson and she's a crackerjack."[22]

Gert Powers was Peterson's earliest female political mentor. The wife of a longtime Eaton County commissioner, she had "a better political sense than a lot of men I ever met," Peterson recalled. Gert was in charge of all of her husband's get-out-the-vote efforts, including promoting the use of absentee ballots. In those days, Peterson recalled, women could "see the value of the small things, of putting together a person, a person, a person. Men didn't want to be bothered by that kind of thing."[23]

But Powers had some baggage that Peterson did not: she "had to clear everything through her husband," Peterson recalled. On one occasion, Powers declined to be recognized for her work on behalf of the local party unless her husband shared in the recognition.[24]

Initially, Peterson balked at going to talk with Lindemer. At forty-three, she was happy with the "little job" she had and didn't want to commute twenty miles to Lansing. But Powers kept nagging her until she set up an interview.[25]

From Peterson's perspective, Lindemer "could sell almost anything to anybody." To Lindemer, Peterson was "very intelligent and full of energy . . . and we hit it off well, right from the get-go." The same afternoon, she agreed to take the job. Arnold Levin, the party's press person, recalled his new boss running down the stairs to announce, "Arny, I've found a secretary!"[26]

The state party headquarters was in an old red-brick building on Capitol Avenue, dubbed "Lincoln House" after the large, decrepit gold statue that stood in the front hall. Peterson's first impressions were characteristically feminine.

> It was indescribably filthy. . . . Beside [the statue] was the reception-
> ist's desk with about 10 boxes of envelopes and the biggest mess I
> ever saw. . . . Filing had accumulated for months on top of files,
> desks, tables, the floor and everything was covered with dust and
> mixed up with old newspapers and other junk. When Larry said he
> needed me, he wasn't kidding. He needed me and fourteen other po-
> tential charwomen, to clean the place and get it in some kind of
> working order.[27]

So Peterson pitched in to straighten up the office, with help from her visiting nephew and Lindemer's wife, Becky. Overnight, she became "receptionist, secretary, typist, mail clerk, janitor, cook, helper to all, and mimeograph operator."[28]

"She kept going and going and going," Levin recalled. "After one problem was solved, she kept solving problems. We finally found someone who agreed to clean up the files. It was not easy, but we went at it. It turned into quite a chore, but it led to everything Elly accomplished."[29]

Some men might have resented a woman who moved in and immediately began straightening things up. But Levin said that was never an issue: "We had so many papers, from one spot to another, we didn't know what to do with them. . . .We thought it was wonderful to have someone there to take charge immediately." Lindemer took to calling Peterson "Mother," mimicking the teenager on *The Aldrich Family* radio comedy show, who responded to his mother's nagging with, "Coming, Mother." The rest of the staff followed suit and the name stuck.[30]

The next year, 1958, Peterson actually made her first try for elective office, running for city alderman in Charlotte's Third Ward. In a letter to voters, she touted these qualifications.

> 20 years of active interest in government
>
> 22 months overseas, World War II, with an Army hospital.
>
> 10 years in Charlotte of continuous participation in civic affairs: I
> helped originate the idea of the free blood program and have
> worked continually for it; have served in various capacities with the

American Red Cross, American Cancer Society, American Legion
Auxiliary and in Congregational Church work.

Have always been a city taxpayer and never missed voting in an
election.

She asserted, "I know you want sensible, progressive, efficient govern-
ment," and concluded, "THERE IS A PLACE TODAY FOR A WOMAN'S
VIEWPOINT ON THE CITY COUNCIL. YOUR ELECTED OFFICIALS
SHOULD BE THOSE WHO WANTED TO RUN, WERE INTERESTED
IN RUNNING AND HAVE A PROGRAM TO BENEFIT THE COMMU-
NITY. I'm sure you don't want officials who were drafted to round out a
ticket and who have never previously indicated any interest in civic af-
fairs."

A full-page newspaper ad pictured an attractive woman wearing
pearls, a standout among the six males on her slate. She was described as a
"joint property owner with her husband" and a "graduate of William
Woods."[31]

Peterson made no mention of the City Council race in her memoir
and rarely alluded to it in later speeches. Perhaps it was because the race
marked a rare defeat for her and took place in a small town. When asked
years later, she recalled that "Charlotte was deeply divided between Republicans and Democrats and the local elections were important. We
campaigned door to door. That year, a popular Democratic businessman
won the mayor's seat and swept Democrats into office."[32] However, the
campaign materials in her personal papers actually included no party
affiliation.

Despite her loss, she was still filled with entrepreneurial zeal for her
political job. Because the party could not afford a full-time salary for its
chairman, Lindemer had to stay close to home to tend to his law practice.
Peterson, on the other hand, was free to crisscross the state. By the end of
her first year, she was on the road nearly full time as the party's chief organizer. "In those days," she recalled, "people organized every precinct and
I found that more fascinating than anything I had ever done in my life."
Among those Peterson later cited as her "best precinct workers" was six-
teen-year-old Dennis Dutko of Macomb County, a future Democratic
member of the state House of Representatives.[33]

Lindemer recognized from the start that Peterson was destined to be more than just a secretary. Because she spoke up at brainstorming sessions and was well organized, he did not hesitate to send her to make speeches. No one ever complained. In fact, he said, "I may have had guys who said, 'Thank God you sent Elly instead of yourself because we had a good meeting!'"

Later, when they reflected on their years working together, he teased Peterson that he should have gotten out of her way and let her run the party because she came up with so many good ideas. One was the party's annual summer conference on Mackinac Island. Lindemer remembered that he was "a little bit leery. But she said, 'Let's put together a conference to get the Republicans together up there and try to stir up some spirit,' so we did, and it worked."[34] The conference has continued on a biennial basis ever since.

Lindemer and Peterson could see that the Democrats—with labor's Committee on Political Education—were working hard to teach their foot soldiers how to run successful campaigns. "That is what we tried to do—identify Republicans," she said. "Then that really became my whole life."[35]

Voter canvassing became a key tool for both parties in the second half of the twentieth century. As Peterson recalled:

> It was a matter of securing the voter's name and address, and then, through various methods, identifying their politics. This could be done door-to-door or over the telephone. In some cases, the direct question could be asked and in some cases it would be approached by questions about their interest in Republican candidates, taking a Republican paper, or attending Republican meetings.
>
> A common card was designed to keep things uniform. . . . We found out that to demonstrate the card and to get the story across, without any deviation, we had to hold at least FIVE meetings. What seemed so simple to us was not simple. . . . One method we found effective was to gather our group after a couple of informational meetings and go out on a blitz, working in teams with specified areas to cover. Then when we returned to our starting point, we could compare the cards, see where the weakness was, and have a sandwich and a beer before calling it quits.[36]

During this time, Peterson had her first brush with sex discrimination. Lindemer wanted to promote her to organizational director, but, she said, "the finance men wouldn't let him because they said no women were active in the automobile business in high places." But she brushed it aside and often said that if women *had* been involved with the auto industry, "they wouldn't build a backseat that was so hard to get into with a girdle on."[37]

Late in life, Lindemer said he could not recall ever receiving pushback on Peterson's role. But, he acknowledged, "I could understand that from Elly's point of view, there might have been subtle things that I missed completely."[38]

Lindemer himself, Peterson recalled, was "very broadminded. He didn't see any reason for my not doing these things as long as I worked well with the people in the counties. They got used to me and so, it wasn't much of a problem."[39]

By then, Peterson was so deeply involved that "title or not, I wanted to do the work anyway and proceeded to give up most of my social life to travel the state."[40] She visited many small towns and counties, trying to get Republicans to fill out their voter cards. "We never sat around and talked about what was being voted on in the legislature."[41]

The woman who had dreaded the prospect of a twenty-mile commute now had no qualms about driving across the state. Lindemer recalled that he had been concerned about Peterson driving at night, but "Elly disabused me of that rather forcefully early on."[42]

On one occasion, she decided to make a three-hour trip home after a late-night meeting. A lone driver began playing passing games before pulling off, apparently expecting her to join him. Peterson managed to elude him, but afterward kept a tire iron on the floor of her car.[43]

In April 1958, Peterson's personal papers suggest that she was beginning to ruffle some feathers among the leaders of some clubs in the Republican Women's Federation of Michigan. All across the country, the relationship between the party and the clubs—and the clubs' growing conservatism—was a growing source of tension.[44]

Peterson wrote two prominent women that when she had begun organizing the party's office "it was with the idea that I could take as much detail as possible off the shoulders of any of the officers, coordinate efforts of ALL groups, and keep a record for future use." But she said an officer in one of the local clubs had accused her of "spying" on her organization. Peterson provided details of the dispute but concluded that "there is no point of arguing this. We just don't agree on it. . . . There is too much to do to spend time in quibbling about who said what."

To avoid future problems, she said she would resign as vice chairman of her local club and work directly with the county and city committees "and therefore will not interfere with the other conception of the duties of a woman's club." She concluded by saying, "Since most of this seems to simmer down to being 'me,'" she would withdraw from all federation activities "as I believe there is plenty to do elsewhere."[45]

Although Peterson apparently backed off from this particular skirmish, it would not be the last time she butted heads with more conservative club leaders.

In November 1958, the Republican Party made progress behind its gubernatorial candidate, Paul Bagwell, and did even better in 1960 when Williams did not seek reelection. That year Bagwell lost to the Democratic nominee, Lt. Gov. John Swainson, by only about forty-one thousand votes. Peterson recalled Bagwell's defeat as the most painful of her career because "if we had only reached a few more voters, we could have won."[46] In her memoir, she observed, "It was obvious to all involved that there just weren't enough Republicans to win an election. We had to reach out to and gain the support of Democrats and Independents if we were to win elections in this state."[47]

After four years as chairman, Lindemer was ready to step down as 1960 drew to a close. But Peterson was "not ready to give up the fight." With encouragement from her political mentors, she decided to run for state vice chairman, the traditional woman's post, now that Ella Koeze was moving on to become national committeewoman from Michigan.

"My program is simple," Peterson wrote in announcing her candidacy. She intended

> to emphasize the educational and organizational work which has been under way the past couple of years. Organization is the key to eventual political victory and a determined effort will put the Republican Party ahead.
>
> I would like to see an acceptance of women and young people in responsible posts at both county and state levels—and as candidates on our ticket. I believe this can only be accomplished by a program which trains them for their responsibility in party work.[48]

Despite her pledge not to get involved with the women's clubs, Peterson wrote in her memoir that she had wanted to recruit a strong candidate for president of the Republican Women's Federation of Michigan to help build up the clubs and leave her free to focus on the overall organization.

Her choice was Lois Nair, who had served as chairman of the Wayne County committee and run unsuccessfully for Congress. But Nair and Helen Dean, a wealthy Grosse Pointe dowager and "the Mrs. Republican of the state," had another plan. They called on Peterson and came right to the point: Nair wanted to be vice chairman. "She felt her long years of service, her work in many capacities in district and club organization, and the fact that I had been a paid organizer and secretary fitted her for the post much better than my qualifications fitted me," Peterson recalled.[49]

Recounting the battle, Peterson reflected the professional she had quickly become: "I told them, as honestly as I knew how, that Lois did not have a chance. I had my commitments and knew that even if she could break some of them away I would have enough of the nearly 1,500 votes to win. I added that at this stage of the game I was not backing down."[50]

Although no one characterized it that way, the battle amounted to a fight between the "old ways," when "the Republicans were the well-to-do people in town so it was sort of chic to belong to the Republican Club," as Peterson put it, versus a vision that women could actually play a more important, professional role in campaigns.[51] At the time, it was expected that the vice chairman would be a woman because parity was required and the chairman was always a man. Thus it followed—for some—that the vice chairman should focus on women's activities.

When Nair made her own pitch for support, she wrote:

> Consequently, the vice chairman of State Central must have enormous experience working with women. This I have been doing for many years, and the number of organizations of women I have worked with and for is indeed great. It ranges from women's Republican clubs, through civic and patriotic organizations to Chairman of the Wayne County Republican Committee.[52]

Peterson checked with her supporters and found that with Nair in the race she would lose a few votes in Wayne County, as well as in the Tenth Congressional District around Midland, where Nair was grooming the wife of a Dow Chemical executive to take over her spot on the State Finance Committee.[53] Nevertheless, Peterson still believed she had the votes to win.

Always concerned about ethics, Peterson stopped drawing a paycheck from the State Central Committee, but continued to do her party work. Nair had to recruit drivers to visit outlying districts while Peterson drove herself. It made a difference, Peterson felt, particularly with the men. Nair also made much of Peterson's "newness in politics," even though most of the people "had seen me in their counties countless times while she was virtually unknown outstate."[54]

Gert Powers stepped in to help, and their team fashioned large cardboard circles that read "Elly" for supporters to wear at the state convention. It was the beginning of what contemporary political consultants would probably call the Peterson "brand."

When party leaders gathered in Detroit the first weekend in February 1961, Peterson received word that "an especially malicious" friend of Nair's had been circulating the story that Peterson and Lindemer were having an affair. Lindemer's response was to laugh. ("Now I grant you," Peterson recalled, "it might have been funny, but just because I was 10 years older and 20 pounds heavier, did he really have to LAUGH?") She advised her supporters to remain calm.

Part of the story was that her husband, then attending the Army War College in Carlisle, Pennsylvania, "was not around and did not want me to be in politics." But Pete "ruined that story" by driving through on Friday night to arrive in time for the vote on Saturday.[55] Despite their many separations and his disinterest in politics, Pete tried to be present for the big moments in his wife's career.

Peterson recalled the episode as her first brush with "gutter politics." But it would not be the last.[56]

In the end, she won by a substantial margin, 1,057 to 462. "The thrill of surviving a roll-call vote," she acknowledged, "simply can't be understood unless you are the one with your head on the block."[57]

The detail with which Peterson recounted the battle in her memoir may have been out of proportion to its significance in her long career. Still, it *was* a victory, a victory that represented the payoff for the long hours she had spent in the backwaters of Michigan. For a woman who had started out as a secretary and charwoman, it was a resounding vote of approval from her constituents.

A decade later, a Michigan newspaper editor recalled "the torrid convention battle in which Elly battled and defeated" Nair. In her own memoir, Peterson did not cast the episode as a battle between moderates and conservatives. But the editor said it was "really a portent of things to come, because Mrs. Nair was the candidate of the right-wing elements in the party at that time, and Mrs. Peterson never felt comfortable with them."[58]

The vote came on Saturday, and by Monday she was back at her desk, facing a month full of Lincoln Day speeches. Former House Speaker George M. Van Peursem was the new party chairman, and observers contended that he needed to move quickly to assure some party leaders that his election was not a step backward.[59] One way he did it was by promoting Peterson to manager of field services.

Van Peursem, she recalled, "was a brilliant speaker." But he had no interest in "talk[ing] to six people about organizing a precinct. Whereas if I got six people together, I thought it was a great night."[60]

One newspaper described Peterson's field services role as "a fresh, new approach to a particular aspect of politics." According to the "best records available," she was believed to be the first woman to have ever served either state party in that role.[61]

* * *

As 1961 began, three events occurred that had a major impact on the course of Peterson's career. She was elected to a more visible and demanding job. She met the man who would become her next political mentor. And she gained a new source of strong support in her personal life.

A sea change was occurring in Michigan. In April 1961, voters approved a call for a convention to revise the state's constitution for the first time in more than fifty years. The vote marked the culmination of years of work by the League of Women Voters, the Junior Chamber of Commerce, and a brand new nonpartisan group, Citizens for Michigan, which George W. Romney, the president of American Motors, had created. Over the next months, Republicans captured 99 of convention's 144 delegate seats, and Romney was elected one of its three vice presidents.[62]

It was during the Constitutional Convention (known as Con-Con) that Peterson first met Romney. Describing his charisma, she said, "The first place he was extremely charming. The second place he was a very successful businessman, turning his attention now . . . to the public good. I think those two things grabbed people."[63]

But Romney was also "the most ill-fitting Republican since Fiorello

La Guardia," concluded political writers Stephen Hess and David S. Broder. A Romney acquaintance once said, "When he meets with party professionals, it's like a Salvation Army girl in a burlesque house."[64] Another contemporary observed that Romney displayed "the bouncy optimism of a teen-age boy" and "the patient strength of a man who believes that sincere honest work will win over all adversity."[65]

Romney was no stranger to government or the Republican Party. But he had become skeptical about what political parties could accomplish. Even when he stood at the top of his party's statewide ticket, he would say, "I'm a citizen who is a Republican not a Republican who is incidentally a citizen."[66]

The party was not unified in its support of a new constitution. Under one proposal, the state would be reapportioned in ways that would reduce the power of the traditionally Republican rural legislative districts. But the earnest Republican delegates who supported reform were to become, in the words of one journalist, "the first wave of Romney's assault and a permanent addition to party activists"—and the group with which Peterson would be closely aligned in the coming years.[67]

As she was settling into her new job, Peterson was jolted by a death in her close-knit family.

On New Year's Eve 1960, Park Richmond died in Chicago at the age of fifty-four. Park's health had never been strong, and as a result, he had been exempted from military service during the war. He left behind Mary and a twenty-six-year-old son.[68]

The Petersons urged Mary to move to Charlotte and live with them, and after a time she agreed. She moved into one of the upstairs bedrooms and took charge of tending the garden. Eventually, she found a job as a housemother in a women's dormitory at Michigan State University in nearby East Lansing. For most of the next 40 years, she and Elly would live or travel together for a good part, if not all of, the year.

The sisters were devoted to each other, despite their differences in age, personality, and interests. Mary, Elly would write later, "helped me through every trouble and was the confidante of my deepest secrets."[69] Pete was also very close to his sister-in-law; she, after all, had helped to keep him tied to the McMillan family following his divorce.

And so the household worked as a troika of equals that would be rare in contemporary society—and was rarer still in the early 1960s. Mary helped run the Petersons' household when Elly was traveling. And as Pete enjoyed the company of male friends on the golf course or in the duck blind, Elly had her own regular female companion.

"Elly and Mary were closer than any two sisters I've ever known," said Joyce Braithwaite-Brickley. "Mary was quieter, and, I thought, somewhat in awe of the life that Elly led. She was enormously talented herself, but she hadn't Elly's dynamism. But she quietly held her own. She and Elly shopped together all over the world, traveled, and it was enormously inspiring. Their bond was very clear."[70]

Mary "was very different from Elly," recalled Mary Ann Richmond of her mother-in-law. In contrast to Elly, Mary "was not an easy person to get close to. Where Elly [was] warm, loving and outgoing, Mary was reserved, proper and introspective, even with her son and granddaughters. She loved them, but in her own way."[71]

"Mary was a staunch supporter," said Larry Lindemer. "I think she was very important to Elly." Of the family's living arrangement, he added, "That was a great credit to all three of them, because those things are sometimes not easy."[72]

"Elly and Mary and Pete all had their own space, their own lives," acknowledged Keith Molin. "They complemented each other, they didn't get in each other's way." They displayed "small-town values, but modern philosophies."[73]

As the newly elected party vice chairman, Peterson wasted no time in carving out an expanded role. Part of that involved supporting the constitutional revisions. Peterson and Romney's wife, Lenore, each made more than 160 speeches in support of the reforms, sometimes in homes before only a half dozen people.

Peterson recalled her Con-Con work as probably her introduction "to the way of Democrats." Somewhat to her surprise, she discovered that they were "much like Republicans!" After energetically debating state Democratic vice chairman Harriet Phillips over the Con-Con proposals, the women would share a cup of coffee. The experience, Peterson recalled, taught her "to enjoy the give and take with [the] opposition."[74]

As Con-Con was meeting, Peterson developed a six-part program called "A Better Citizen" to help Michigan voters learn more about their political system. The project was designed to keep party members engaged during off years in the election cycle and to help get Republican materials

into schools and libraries where they might be read by independents. She
began by organizing a Women's Advisory Council (whose members she
called the WACs), with women from every county, because "in a state 750
miles long" she could not manage the task on her own.[75]

She was already impatient with the pettiness she had encountered in
dealing with some political women. In a later memo, she said she began by
contacting fifty women she knew.

> I chose them for their political know-how—and their demonstrated
> ability to be flexible in their thinking, tolerant in their opinions.
> They included some elected party officials. . . , a number who had
> served in these capacities but no longer had any function in the party
> (this was good as it gave them a home instead of turning them out to
> pasture), and some of them were new people I felt could be trained.
> I asked NO ONE to this original meeting that I did not personally
> know to be this type of woman . . . and I asked NO ONE for the sake
> of including them. I also carefully avoided women who were contro-
> versial, who had intolerant narrow opinions or who were ineffective
> in their own counties.

She stressed an important lesson.

> Choose only proven, qualified women. Don't take someone to "rep-
> resent the Federation—the Young Republicans—the ethnic
> groups"—just for that reason. . . . If you have one ineffective woman
> in the group "just because"—you will lose your total effectiveness.

There was also a foreshadowing of the painful divisions that she would
soon encounter:

> Clear the air definitely on attitudes. If they feel they can live only
> with Goldwater—or Rockefeller—or Joe Blow—they are not for
> you. In fact, you should not have asked them in the first place. Flexi-
> bility and tolerance are two of the highest qualifications.

She conceded that she had once made the mistake of taking "someone
else's advice about a woman I didn't know really well. In my instance, the
woman turned out to be a devoted [John] Birch [Society] member. I sim-

ply had to sit down and talk with her and tell her why we could not include her. She had by then decided we were lost souls anyway—and hardly
worthy of her attention."[76]

It was on one of Peterson's swings through the Upper Peninsula that
Molin, then head of the Young Republicans at Northern Michigan University, fell under her spell. They got together to discuss bringing in a
speaker to help build the Republican Party in Marquette, an enclave for
organized labor.

Afterward, Peterson wrote to say that she had lined up Fred C. Scrib-
ner Jr., a former undersecretary of the treasury and legal counsel to the
Republican National Committee. Molin wrote back to the effect that "if
we're not worth somebody" like a presidential candidate, "then we probably don't need to do this at all."[77]

Molin recalled that Peterson responded with "a very nice stern,
'Mother-like' letter, saying, 'No, Keith, that's not the way it works. This is
the way it works.'" And then she helped the Young Republicans line up a
group of young, up-and-coming, Republican state legislators that included future governor William Milliken.

The experience, he said, "was one of my first lessons in terms of how
to follow leadership, but secondly, from her, how to exercise leadership:
'Don't get yourself drawn into an unnecessary battle or fight. Work your
way through this.' It was a learning experience for me and a teaching moment for her."

Molin freely attributes what success he had in life to Peterson, who, he
said, "gave me more second chances than most people would give to anybody. . . . To this very day, when you sit at the desk with one of those 'how
do I solve this problem?' the question you ask yourself is, 'What would Elly
do?'"

Within a short period of time, Molin gained a Con-Con internship
and then was assigned to Romney's subcommittee—"all of which had
been orchestrated by Elly Peterson in the background." And before long,
he had a full-time job in politics.

The thing that was so amazing about her is that . . . there were never
any fingerprints. But that's the way she operated. . . . You would *never*
hear Elly say, "Well, I made a call . . . or I've suggested to somebody.
. . ." You'd go to her and say, "Elly, I need to ask you a question. I got
a call from so-and-so and they asked me to think about this, and

what are your thoughts?" And she'd say, "Well, I think that's something you ought to consider," and she'd give you all the reasons why.
And years later you would understand that the reason you got the
call was that she suggested they make that call. Which was another
one of her great strengths. She *never* put the spotlight on herself.[78]

When the spotlight *was* on Peterson, it still frequently focused on
feminine pursuits. In September 1961, the society editor of the *State Journal* in Lansing described a fashion show fund-raiser at which Peterson, a
guest of honor, wore "a royal knit jacket dress with contrasting headband
hat of russet pheasant feathers."[79] Two months later, the same reporter
covered a luncheon honoring six Republican women delegates to Con-
Con, where Peterson announced that a Republican women's group had
produced a new cookbook, with "pretty red covers" that "added to their
charm for holiday gift giving."[80]

But in January 1962, the *Detroit News* ran a more substantive profile of
Peterson and Phillips, her Democratic counterpart. "The coffee klatch and
the tea party are competing with the smoke-filled room in shaping the
destiny of politics today," it read. "From precinct level to top party posts,
the ladies are having their way—and what's more, the men are listening."

The article attributed the increased interest to Peterson and Phillips,
who, "although poles apart in their political philosophy, . . . share the view
that the feminine upsurge is a natural trend of the times."

Still, reporter Corinne Smith noted, "Although both women thrive on
politicking, each admits to daydreams about more time for home and
family, and each makes the most of precious time at home." Peterson was
said to spend one day a week at her desk, and the rest of the time on the
road. By then, she had visited sixty-eight counties and planned to have organizations built in all eighty-three by August.[81]

The fruits of Peterson's outreach and her blunt humor were evident in
a twenty-two-page confidential report found among her papers. Presumably written by Peterson, it described each county's organization.

This "good Republican county" has slipped constantly since a high of
71.6%. It is still safe but losing around 300 Republican votes every
two years and apparently attracting no new ones. The Chairman
Hague is an able person but apparently totally disinterested; holds
no meetings, attends none and does nothing. . . . I have not found

anything Tom McAllister approves of except himself in every possible role from national delegate, ConCon to Co. Chairman. He has discouraged group after group which we have activated from doing anything for organization or fund raising. . . .The whole trouble with this county, organization and financewise can be summed up in one man: Carlton Morris. He has bucked completely all forms of education and organization (even told George he didn't want the people educated for then they would discuss candidates and he didn't want that).

Of Gratiot County, she wrote, "This is an outstanding county—and a woman did it all." For Oakland County, she wrote simply, "Be my guest."

The reports are also sprinkled with helpful "people" details: "His wife owns Joyce of Leland, smart dress shop. . . . A ball of fire in Shelby named Ruth Harrison good on finance and other matters. . . .Doc Kelsey is a character but has the county committee moving with the help of Ollie Britten who is in the Sheriffs office and Ruth Willis of St. Helen who is a real fireball . . . . Lowell Geneback, former Finance Chr. A fine person but on the outs with Agnes Lord."[82]

Meanwhile, as the state's political insiders were buzzing about Romney's political ambitions, he summoned Peterson to a Lansing meeting where he told his closest advisers he had decided to run for governor. It was the first time she felt included in a meeting of the power brokers.[83]

Romney made his formal announcement on February 9, 1962, midway through Con-Con. Because Peterson had been working hard to build up the party, "it was not with a great deal of joy" that she learned her campaign job would be to shepherd Lenore Romney around the state. She had willingly accompanied Suzy Alger a decade before, but now thought her experience "rated more than another hand-holding position." But she put aside those feelings for the good of the cause. "Remember," she noted in her memoir, "women did not account for much in those days, and I think the men thought they were getting rid of 'two birds' at once—Lenore and me!"

Peterson had time to craft a plan before the campaign moved into high gear later in the summer. She was concerned because Mrs. Romney "seemed. . . to be very fragile." She decided to begin with a June 5 luncheon at the Lansing Civic Center, and then accompany her to a luncheon every other week in other cities and towns.

Mrs. Romney, an aspiring actress in her youth, asked Peterson if there would be a press conference in connection with the Lansing event. In her memoir, Peterson described her reaction: "A press conference for a woman—and 'only a wife' at that???? Perish forbid! No woman EVER had a press conference, and no newsman would have come if she did."

But Mrs. Romney was so serious that Peterson badgered the political press corps to attend. She "cajoled and wheedled and pled and used every other way I could think of to get their bodies out of the Capitol and over to the Civic Center." In the end, she said with evident pride, "they came— and they were conquered."[84]

"If the reaction of some 700 Republican women is any indication, [Mrs. Romney] is on her way to becoming a one-woman political task force," wrote Ray Courage of the *Detroit Free Press*. He dutifully described what she was wearing, then added, "But when she talked, it was clear she hadn't come to model clothes." Mrs. Romney, he noted, spoke "without a text or notes" and "covered the political spectrum with ease and humor and impressed the women with her sincerity."[85]

Meanwhile, Glenn Engle of the *Detroit News* wrote: "A petite and vivacious grandmother, Mrs. Romney left her women listeners cooing over the success of her political debut. The few men at the luncheon, mostly Republican officials, were outspokenly thankful that she was on their side. . . . With her knowledge of state affairs and her articulation of Michigan problems, she belied the appearance of a fashion model in a fresh green and white print."[86]

Afterward, Peterson "raced back to the office—to change the entire format of her campaign." She resolved to take Mrs. Romney to places her husband would never have time to get to—and to do it with "women power." If, in fact, the new strategy was not put in place until *after* Mrs. Romney's speech, Peterson must have moved extremely quickly: in his story, Engle noted that Mrs. Romney had scheduled appearances in fifteen cities over the next two weeks, and planned to visit every county before a potential August 7 primary.

Peterson said she consulted her Women's Advisory Council on how to organize Mrs. Romney's campaign. Could they raise enough money to cover the cost of her travel, even if it meant adding twenty-five cents to the cost of a luncheon ticket? (The men, Peterson noted, "would faint dead away if I suggested much of a budget.") The women felt the plan was doable and suggested recruiting other prominent local leaders to introduce Mrs. Romney to help position her as an independent.

Mary Richmond agreed to help with the driving, freeing her sister to focus on "the political chores." On some trips, the women were also accompanied by the Romneys' fifteen-year-old son Mitt, who went on, forty years later, to serve as governor of Massachusetts and then to run for president. On one trip near Traverse City, Peterson recalled how the religious convictions of his father could be a source of amusement for the rest of the family.

> We consulted the maps which showed a road that looked like it went over the water. In talking about it, Mitt kept returning to the fact that the road had to be okay because the map showed it.
>
> Finally, his mother, in exasperation, said, "Oh, Mitt, you know good and well a road will not go over water unless there is a bridge."
>
> "Oh, that's right," Mitt comes back, "Dad isn't here!"

Local women handled the details of Mrs. Romney's trips, including selling "everything that was saleable." Mitt Romney, Peterson noted, "was in seventh heaven doing the selling."[87]

In the end, the purchases added up, Peterson recalled, with $14,000 to spare, money that was put toward purchasing more television time at the close of the campaign. The gubernatorial campaign itself cost more than $450,000, then a record for the state.[88] ("Nowadays," Peterson acknowledged, "they'd laugh you off the block if you gave them $14,000. Today you couldn't even make one commercial.")[89]

Republicans, Clark Mollenhoff wrote at the time, discovered Mrs. Romney could be as good a campaigner as her husband—"some even said she was more effective." He credited Peterson for quickly recognizing her talent.[90]

By the close of the campaign, Mollenhoff noted, "George Romney needed Lenore's two hundred speeches and every other bit of help he could to fight the leadership of the United Automobile Workers and the AFL-CIO."[91] Peterson's plan enabled the candidate to focus on the nineteen most populous counties with the greatest potential for the ticket splitting his strategists hoped would carry him into office; his wife's tour helped to keep "the 64 outstate rural counties from feeling left out."[92]

In the end, Romney won by a margin of 78,500 votes. It marked the end of fourteen years of Democratic rule in the governor's mansion.

But that wasn't all. Republican leaders also trumpeted that they had captured a seat on the state Supreme Court, defeated two Democratic incumbents in the State Legislature, and attracted "the biggest off-year Republican vote in the history of the state." In addition, they had recruited "a record-number 25,000 precinct workers who proceeded to canvass some 500,000 homes, four times the number reached in the 1960 election." Peterson's field staff was credited with traveling 200,000 miles, holding 800 training meetings, and making more than 8,500 personal calls on local leaders.[93]

"It was a high campaign," Peterson recalled, "filled with peak excitement. No matter what you had done, you wanted to work another hour or so on another chore." Many nights she would check into a Detroit hotel at 10:30, then go over to headquarters and type a few more letters until the early morning hours. "Winning," she said, "was almost a let-down as the campaign had been so exciting."[94]

Six months later, Michigan voters approved the new Constitution. All the months of coffee klatches and speeches paid off when the revisions squeaked through by fewer than ten thousand votes. It was a major victory for Romney and ensured that, come 1964, Michigan governors would serve four-year terms instead of just two.

At Romney's first press conference after he was sworn in, Peterson began calling him "Governor." Romney noted the change and said, "You've always called me George." She replied, "It was no effort to call you George, but it required a lot to be able to call you 'Governor.'"[95]

She had the miles to prove it.

# CHAPTER THREE

## A Chapeau in the Ring

As she savored her first big statewide victories, Peterson was already reflecting on the progress that women had—or had not—made in Michigan. Writing for the state Chamber of Commerce's magazine, she noted that women had outpolled men in Detroit for the first time in its history. Women, she said, were "invading" the fields of theology, engineering, electronics, and banking.

"Yet," she wrote, "it is the field of politics in Michigan that still remains out of reach of women." Only one woman, Martha Griffiths, was in the congressional delegation, only four women sat in the State Legislature, there were few women mayors, and "the State Administrative Board and other top positions completely missed any powderpuff influence."

> Because women never have held status jobs to any great extent in politics, they haven't worried about being advisors or serving at the executive level. They have been willing to do the chores of political labor. . . . And they take great pride in knowing their precincts and their people, quoting their precinct voting records as easily as the newest recipe for lemon pie. . . .
>
> Today's housewife, homemaker and career gal recognizes the political opportunity facing her. She knows her qualifications are as valid as the men's. She has accepted—and proven—the authority given her to *assist* in running her party.
>
> Why then, she asks, hasn't she been given the authority to help guide and direct the party organization, help with decisions on a policy-making level? With the same, proven qualifications, why isn't

she equally as acceptable? Why, the women ask, should we arbitrarily be denied these goals and responsibilities just because we wear bouffant skirts and feathered cloches?

It has been said that women do not, and will not, have an opportunity to prove their capabilities in the field of politics in Michigan for one reason—women never have been recognized in the automotive industry as potential executives. Politically-minded women don't believe this.

These women have long since passed the stage of being complimented when a male politician intones "God bless the women" or "she thinks just like a man."

Women don't think like men. And they don't want to. They think like women and they want to keep it that way.

Peterson concluded by writing, "It wouldn't be surprising if the gals would grow weary of the political merry-go-round if they don't get the brass ring soon. They are in a position to take it. But they appeal to the men: 'Don't arbitrarily deny us the opportunity to catch the brass ring when we're qualified—just because we are women.'"[1]

Years later Peterson acknowledged that it had disturbed her when George Romney first introduced her at a dinner by saying, "She thinks like a man," a quotation that was often repeated. Romney, she recalled, "thought he was being kind." But, she said, "for years, it was like waving a red flag in my face, and I always answered as politely as I could: 'I think like men think they think.'"[2]

Pundits were beginning to speculate about the next Republican presidential candidate, and Romney was increasingly positioned as a potential rival to Barry Goldwater—particularly after Nelson Rockefeller decided to divorce his wife and marry a woman eighteen years his junior. Romney and Goldwater were "two strong-willed men," Peterson observed, and as time went on, they seemed to find more and more ways to antagonize each other.[3] Five days after Romney announced he was running for governor, Goldwater spoke to a sellout crowd of five thousand in Detroit. Without mentioning Romney by name, he declared, "This myth that business dominates the Republican party of Michigan should be exposed for the fraud it is." He then evoked nervous laughter by joking that the candidate had finally "decided to join the Republican party."[4]

In September 1963, Peterson was making a speech in Macomb County when Clare Williams, assistant chairman of the Republican National Committee (RNC), reached her by phone. Williams was planning to marry Carl Shank and move to Florida in a few months. Would Peterson be interested in taking over her job?

Peterson said that the phone call "bowled me over" because she "had never even dreamed of going to Washington."[5] But Pete told her "it was too much of a challenge to turn down, and surely a great way to wind up my political career."[6] Her husband, she said years later, "could stand me being gone and being in the public eye because he was absolutely confident of his own ability."[7]

It was the first of several instances in which Peterson "answered the call," moving up the political ladder in the process. At the age of forty-nine, she had no grand plan for building a career; rather campaign organizations began recruiting her when they needed her skills.

Years later Shank told Peterson that she had presented the party's top male leaders with a list of national committeewomen and state vice chairmen for consideration "and they agreed that it should be *you.*" Some of the national committeewomen "wanted it for themselves." But, Shank concluded, "I kept the gentle pressure" on U.S. Rep. William Miller, the party chairman, "'thinking only of him, etc.'"[8]

Press coverage of Peterson's appointment focused on the expertise she was expected to bring to the job. The *Detroit News* reported, "The darling of Michigan's Republican Party organization, Mrs. Elly Peterson, of Charlotte, was tapped Saturday to apply her political talents on the national level. . . . Word of her impending loss to the state organization shook party leaders."

The reporter said that as field services director, Peterson "had been the state party's guiding hand in dealings with local precinct organizations" and "unofficially" she had "also directed women's activities." It was noted that at the request of Romney and Arthur G. Elliott Jr., the new state party chairman, Peterson would retain her elected post as state vice chairman.[9]

Two days later the *Washington Post* reported that Peterson had received one of three "major appointments" that Williams was announcing in preparation for the 1964 campaign. Williams cited Peterson's "mobilization of the women of Michigan in the Romney campaign, and the maintenance of the organization to work for the adoption of the new state constitution."[10]

Meanwhile, the *New York Times Magazine* soon noted that "some 45,000 Republican women—twice as many as had worked in any previous gubernatorial campaign—rang doorbells, telephoned and raised funds" for the Romney campaign. Peterson was identified as "the lady in charge."[11]

In a profile later that fall, the Washington reporter for Booth Newspapers described Peterson as "a charmer, a lovely person with a great flair for the political soft sell." Her "most sparkling talent is winning persons to her without even trying. To put it another way, it's doubtful whether anyone has ever found it possible to dislike her."[12]

Ruth Hobbs, a party activist from Ann Arbor, wrote, "As of now I am still in a state of shock after reading of your new appointment! Naturally, I am thrilled for you but I cannot help feeling that is the worst calamity that ever happened to Michigan."[13]

Williams had proposed a transition period in which Peterson would serve for a few months as executive director of the Women's Division—a post that had not been filled since 1953. Over the ensuing years, the division had been reshuffled in the RNC's organizational chart, and tensions between the party apparatus and the National Federation of Republican Women had persisted.

In 1962, Williams had written, "There are some details of our inter-relationships as Republican women leaders . . . which need immediate and serious consideration for improvement." In a review of the composition of state party executive committees, Williams had found that only one-third of the state federation presidents, one-half of the national committee-women, and not all of the state vice chairmen were members. "One hundred percent inclusion of all our women leaders in all these Executive Committees should be an immediate goal to further women's influence and effectiveness," she asserted.[14]

Despite those concerns, it was generally accepted that the Republican Party treated its women better than the Democrats did—a point Peterson often made in her speeches. Until 1970, political scientist Jo Freeman found, Republicans were more supportive "of women party workers, more successful in organizing and educating women about politics and more likely to promote the feminist position on issues when there was one."[15]

Peterson moved to Washington on October 1, describing herself as "excited and fearless." She would be the first woman to serve as assistant chairman who had not previously served as a national committeewoman; fortunately, Williams took steps to help smooth her way, particularly with the women who had wanted the job themselves.[16]

Within a month, Pete also received a promotion. On September 19, the Michigan National Guard officer in charge of tracking more than one hundred million dollars' worth of Guard property died unexpectedly. As commander in chief of the Guard, Governor Romney appointed Pete to replace him.

Colonel Peterson served as U.S. property and fiscal officer for the next seven years. He was responsible for property ranging from combat boots and mess kits to eighty tanks and fifty-five jet aircraft located in the state.[17] The promotion also made it possible for Pete to travel to Washington a few times a month on legitimate government business. The couple took an apartment at 2500 Q Street NW, near Dupont Circle, and began a commuter marriage. "We may have to meet in air terminals," Elly said at the time, "but we'll meet."[18]

Williams was Peterson's first, and only, female boss in politics. Williams, she recalled, "was an experienced, practical perfectionist" who kept records of the clothes and jewelry she had worn—and the jokes she had told—so she wouldn't repeat them. Peterson acknowledged that, by comparison, she was "a slob at heart," who "just couldn't do things" Williams's way. Still, Peterson appreciated Williams's efforts to show her the ropes, and by the end of 1963 the two women had traveled together to four regional meetings and ten states. Peterson quickly assembled a staff, which included Nebraska senator Roman Hruska's daughter Jana, speechwriter Aileen O'Callaghan, and Pam Curtis, a recent college graduate who would work for Peterson for more than a decade.

Yet, Peterson noted, "Few men considered the job of Assistant Chairman as amounting to much more than a sop for women." She was never expected to report on her activities, and she never attended a staff meeting. "I could have spent several months in Hawaii or Puerto Rico," she recalled, "and I suspect no one would have worried or cared."[19]

The small-town girl experienced some wide-eyed excitement as she stepped onto the national stage for the first time. The "biggest thrill of all" was taking a limousine trip with Williams to visit Dwight Eisenhower at his retirement home in Gettysburg, Pennsylvania. She had met Ike after he spoke in Detroit the year before and described how she and Gert Powers had been "speechless with excitement." This time Peterson and Williams met with the former president for an hour as he showed them his paintings and Steuben glass collection.

Peterson recalled another outing with Williams to a dinner where Eisenhower was the featured speaker. She was wearing a lace dress she had purchased in Hong Kong. Suddenly, she recalled in her memoir, the seams split. The always-prepared Williams saved the day, pulling tiny safety pins out of her purse to patch the dress back together, enabling Peterson to produce a shy smile when she finally shook hands with the former president.

On another occasion, Williams took her to New York City for tea with Nelson Rockefeller's new wife, Happy. Rockefeller's divorce and remarriage had provided a feast for gossip columnists; thus, Peterson was surprised to discover that Mrs. Rockefeller "was far from the 'femme fatale'" she had expected and that she "could not believe this shy, attractive, but simply-dressed lady could be the one about which so much had been written...."[20]

During her first nine months, Peterson made visits to thirty states, some of which were more memorable than others. The southern regional meeting, held in South Carolina, provided "a lesson in politics." It was "something of a shock to see the Confederate flag flying and hear them sing 'Dixie' instead of the national anthem." But, she said, she "learned to live through that meeting, repeating to myself constantly that I should not be provincial."[21]

In Vermont, she was reminded that, in many respects, she was ahead of her time. She met the state vice chairman for breakfast, and after ordering, asked her to describe her projects. "Oh," the woman replied, "I don't do anything. I can't. I have a job and three children at home."

The exchange, Peterson recalled, "was such a letdown for me." But, she realized, that was the attitude of many vice chairmen. "They had to have the opposite sex, and there were no women chairmen, so it had to be a woman.... They named a nice woman who wasn't going to complain or cause trouble." Many of the national committeewomen "did absolutely nothing. They were wealthy women. They could write a check."[22]

Still, she was determined to make a difference. One of her innovations was "Dear Mabel Cards," postcards that Republican women could send to their friends or distribute door-to-door. "Those of us traveling the country have been both shocked and dismayed at the seeming total misunderstanding (or acceptance, which is worse) of what's going on in Washington," Peterson wrote in a cover letter. "Since it is impossible for our relatively few in number Republican leaders to personally cover all areas, it becomes the duty of Republican women everywhere to get this story told to the public. Then, if people really don't CARE, we can feel that at least they chose their path based on KNOWING."

Preprinted on one side of each card was a short handwritten note beginning "Dear Mabel"; the flip side featured short talking points. In one, a statement by President Lyndon Johnson—"We are going to take all the money that we think is unnecessarily being spent and take from the 'haves' and give to the 'have nots' that need it so much"—was compared to the words of Karl Marx.[23]

Within a week Peterson received an enthusiastic response from Mrs. John W. Lewis of Crothersville, Indiana: "We surely don't know what has happened lately at National Headquarters, but we sure like what we've been seeing lately." She cited the cards and other initiatives, and concluded, "Whoever has been dreaming these up should have an extra star in their crown. If there were as much initiative and inspiration shown by party leadership on the *local* level, victory this fall would be a foregone conclusion."[24]

On January 29, 1964, Peterson got her "first break on national television" when the Republicans scheduled fund-raising dinners in twenty-one cities, connecting twenty-five thousand guests by closed-circuit television. The "Go-Day" events were designed to liquidate the party's debt and begin building a war chest for the fall elections.

Peterson had hoped to attend the "Dinner with Ike" in Detroit, but Bill Miller assigned her to Cleveland, where she would share the platform with Rep. Bob Wilson of California and himself, and from which the broadcast would originate.[25]

Peterson's job was to introduce Romney in Washington, who would then introduce Eisenhower in Detroit. At the Cleveland dinner, she found herself sitting between Ohio governor James Rhodes and Vernon Stouffer, president of Stouffer Corporation.

> Gov. Rhodes was not all enthusiastic about being at the dinner, or sitting next to me—in fact, I gathered he wouldn't have been interested in sitting next to ANYONE!
>
> I tried to talk to him, and our conversation went something like this: I introduce[d] myself and mentioned I had started my political career with George Romney. He grunted, "Damn fool. I'm going to take a task force to Michigan and take all of his industry." Silence. An

aide came up and whispered to him to ask if he would speak to a Young Republican meeting the next week. "Hell, no," he growled, "they don't do a damn thing. If it's women, I'll speak. If not, to hell with it." Silence.

I ventured a question about his wife. "She never comes to these things and that's the way it ought to be." Silence.

He ate his salad, threw his fork on the table, and sat waiting for the ordeal to end. I thought, "And to hell with you, too" and turned to Mr. Stauffer [*sic*]. He said, in his quiet, very refined way, "Don't let him upset you, Mrs. Peterson. He is sometimes very abrupt!"

So I ate my meal, visited with Mr. Stauffer, and got my introduction out loud and clear.[26]

In a short amount of time in her new job, Peterson made an impact. At the end of February, she was invited to join a panel discussion with Allen L. Otten of the *Wall Street Journal*, David S. Broder of the *Evening Star*, and Democratic U.S. Rep. Neil Staebler of Michigan at a meeting of the Washington chapter of Sigma Delta Chi, the then all-male professional journalists' society. It was, she wrote her sister, "quite an experience." She arrived early with her speechwriter, and "the help wanted to know if 'we were supposed to be there.'" As club members drifted in, "they gave us side-ways looks—and several asked about us—NOBODY SPOKE." Finally, the officers arrived and straightened things out. One man told her that the only other woman who had ever addressed the club was Marguerite Higgins, a Korean War correspondent who had won a Pulitzer Prize.[27]

Looking back, Peterson reflected, "I was naive, to be sure, when I arrived, and like any new person in Washington, I had to learn the ropes." It was not long, she said, before she learned that "everyone on the committee was working openly for Barry Goldwater." "At first, I wondered why they had brought me in: was it to try to get Romney to knuckle under; was it to have a 'liberal state' on the [rolls] of the committee; or was I just the 'in house liberal?'" She enjoyed her work, her travels, and meeting scores of other Republican women. "But I could tell that I was really outside the family circle, coming as I did from Michigan."[28]

The Republican National Committee may have been a "family circle," but throughout the party's extended family, civil war was about to break out.

\* \* \*

In late February 1964, Romney summoned Peterson to his East Lansing home for a strategy meeting. The business on the table was the upcoming U.S. Senate race. Although Goldwater had not yet clinched the Republican presidential nomination, Romney expected that the Arizona senator would lead the ticket in the fall. The prospect, one aide recalled, had his team "just tearing out their hair."[29]

The group who gathered that day included longtime advisers Dick Van Dusen and Bill Stirton; Jack Dempsey, the TV newsman who had headed up Volunteers for Romney in 1962; Walter DeVries, a PhD from Michigan State University who had become Romney's chief pollster and government liaison; and Max Fisher, the oil magnate who served as the candidate's chief "moneyman." Besides Peterson, two other women were included: the governor's wife and national committeewoman Ella Koeze.

Romney's polls showed that Johnson would beat Goldwater in a landslide in Michigan but that Romney could win if he captured enough ticket splitters. Now they needed to find a Senate candidate who would improve the governor's chances.

Two Republicans had already entered the race against Phil Hart, the popular Democratic incumbent. James O'Neil was a Ford Motor Company executive and a member of the State Board of Education from Livonia, who had been running for a year without much progress. Edward Meany was from Grand Haven, a sales manager for a leather goods company. He had been campaigning longer than O'Neil but with even less to show for it. Both were considered to be from the party's conservative wing. "They were running their own campaigns pretty much independent" of the governor, DeVries recalled. "They were not part of the 'Romney team,' whatever that meant."[30]

The governor liked to take an idea and put it on the table for discussion. Some of his aides had already suggested approaching Peterson. But they also wondered, "How do we know she can do this, because it's never been done before?"

At the meeting, other potential candidates were discussed first: John Hannah, president of Michigan State University; Henry Ford II, president of the auto company; Joseph L. Hudson Jr., the Detroit department store executive; and Rep. Gerald R. Ford, the new U.S. House minority leader. Each had been approached about running, and each had said no.

Someone suggested that a "gimmick" candidate should be considered, someone who would be different, yet credible. Suddenly the governor turned to Peterson. "Elly, you have to do it. You have to run."

"I think we knew what we wanted," DeVries recalled of the meeting. "Just having her there and talking about it may have jelled it." Romney, he noted, was always willing to take risks.

But Peterson was flabbergasted: "If I had been hit in the head with a board or if he had suddenly come across the room and slapped me across the mouth, I would not have been more stunned." In her memoir, she contended that she was never sure whether the draft had occurred spontaneously or whether the advisers were following a script. But she wrote her sister, "The men all said 'Great'—'fine.' You could tell it had been discussed AND settled."

Peterson reeled off the reasons why she would not make a good candidate: "Nobody knows me outside of the party. I don't have any personal financial resources or the contacts to raise money. I don't know how to be a candidate, I only know how to tell someone else how to be one. Pete might not like to me to run. I had always worked for other people and that's the way I like it." When no one challenged her, she fell silent.[31]

As the meeting was about to end, Romney took her into his den for a private conversation. "I need you to do this," he said. "I want you to go home and talk to Pete. You are the only one who can hold this party together." By then, she recalled, she believed that Romney "was the star who had brought all our hours of work to fruition." If he wanted her to run, then she should.[32]

Fisher then took her aside and pledged that he would take care of the fund-raising. Man after man pledged his support, and then she drove home to Pete in a daze.

Expecting her husband to be surprised or upset, she was shocked when he laughed, shook his head, and said, "Go to it if you want to."[33] She confided to her sister that "Pete was stunned but not silent." After Lenore Romney called him, "he felt better—he had the feeling maybe I was a patsy, and that I would get my feelings hurt. Of course, I don't need to be told I am an underdog." On top of everything else, she knew that Hart would be able to draw on the financial resources of his wife, Jane, the daughter of Walter Briggs, the millionaire owner of the Detroit Tigers.[34]

Two days later Peterson's possible candidacy made the front pages. In the *Detroit Free Press,* Romney was described as "highly receptive to the idea."[35] The *Detroit News*, meanwhile, said Peterson's name "had been given casual mention for a couple of weeks by Republican leaders desperately searching for a formidable candidate." Peterson was described as "attractive" and "articulate." The paper noted that "her fans credit her with the working effectiveness of a man while maintaining her feminine charm."[36]

From the nation's capital, the *Washington Post*'s Maxine Cheshire cited Peterson for streamlining "heretofore soft and flabby Republican women's groups into svelte and peppy organizations wooed by politicos intent on victory." Romney's draft of Peterson, she wrote, was "his only hope of taking the women's vote away from Hart."[37]

Meanwhile, Jerald Ter Horst of the *Detroit News* said that Peterson's draft signaled a potential battle with Hart over "the housewives' vote" in the wake of the senator's support for truth-in-packaging legislation. Ter Horst acknowledged the "key role" Peterson had played in Romney's 1962 victory and saw her candidacy as part of an effort to solidify the governor's national reputation by winning more down-ticket races.[38]

Peterson continued to speak frankly with the media—suggesting that she was still adjusting to the new role of candidate. She acknowledged being "flattered and flabbergasted" and conceded that she was not widely known outside of party circles. "I'm still not at all sure whether voters are ready for a woman senator from this state," she told the *Detroit News*. "Women haven't gone as far politically in Michigan as they have in many other states, particularly in the East." Between 1944 and 1950, the article noted, women had been unsuccessful candidates for lieutenant governor, state treasurer, and auditor general in Michigan.[39]

Peterson's papers indicate that early on she phoned Meany (and probably O'Neil as well). "Elly," Meany wrote in return, "I have too much respect and admiration for you to consider any schism in our friendship as a result of your getting into the Senate race." He signed off, "Best, Ed, and with love, too."[40] Three days later, she responded, "I didn't want the occasion to pass for you to know that I very much respect you and am fond of you, and surely if it develops that I enter this race, the only regret would be the necessity of running against you and Jim O'Neill [*sic*] of whom I am so fond."[41]

Peterson put off announcing a final decision for nearly a month. On the one hand, she had been in her new job for only a few months. And, since her early race in Charlotte, she had never been interested in seeking elective office. But she had always been willing to do what was necessary for "the good of the cause." And she recognized that seven years' worth of party building in Michigan could be jeopardized by the coming campaign.

But she set three conditions before making the race: she wanted feedback from her statewide network, particularly the WACs. She wanted to know how the newspapers would respond to her candidacy. And she wanted to investigate "how the money sounded."[42]

Arny Levin was among those who received a phone call. He asked if she knew what she was getting herself into. She replied that no one else was willing to take on the race—or at least to take it on for Romney.[43]

Of the press response, Peterson wrote her sister, "The newspaper men from Michigan all tell me I'd help the ticket—I'd get miles of publicity and Hart would have trouble putting a hand on me. They also realize . . . the problem of his incumbency—money—the importance of Michigan etc. but the *good* part is they aren't wiping me out before I get under way even."

But money remained a major concern. She told her sister that her friends were asking, "Will I be given enuff money for a proper campaign or will it be like others where the candidate has gone in and then *not* received the proper financial backing." She figured she would need a minimum of fifty thousand dollars for the primary "so when [the financial men] hear this they may lose their enthusiasm."[44]

By March 9, Gert Powers and Nelle Taylor, a State Central Committee member from Grand Ledge, had formally launched a "Committee of 1000" in support of Peterson. "We hope it will help her make up her mind," Powers said. "We feel that a thousand women are as good as a million dollars." She then added that they were also seeking the signatures of a thousand male supporters.[45]

Expressions of support began to flow in. Audrey Seay, from Trenton, wrote that she had read about Peterson's possible candidacy in the morning paper. "I nearly leapt for joy. . . . The brightest individual on the political scene this year. It was the best that could almost happen."[46]

Katharine Willis, vice chairman of the Van Buren County Republican Committee, wrote, "I contacted every office holder, and political leader in my county, and I received the same favorable impression from all of them. Many comments were 'Well, there is a darn good chance she can do it, and I sure would vote for her.' And Elly, my county has had the *Pleasure* of getting to know you. In my humble opinion, you have everything to gain. . . . It surely goes without my saying I will do everything in my power to help you."[47]

Lillian Wright, vice chairman of the Genesee County Republican Committee, wrote:

> I don't think there is anyone more qualified for the office, nor who could run as good a campaign, as you, my dear. Boy, you'd really set this old State on its heels, from top to bottom, and, I believe, as soon as you got more exposure to the general public and the Independents saw what a terrific gal we have here, they'd flock to your side in this thing. Of course, the unknown factor is whether or not the women, bless their little pin-heads, would turn their back on any woman candidate. I, for one, think it deserves the old college try.

But Wright was concerned that Peterson would have to leave the RNC: "I am not sure that I feel the organization, nationally, can afford to let you make the try. They may have had organization people before, but they have never had anyone with your ability."[48]

Shirley McFee, who later was elected mayor of Battle Creek and a University of Michigan regent, wrote of her "mixed emotions." She had watched Peterson go to Washington

> with great pleasure . . . for we are well aware of your tremendous ability in the field of organizational politics. Surely your opportunity on the national level is not one to be brushed lightly aside. Yet we also are cognizant of the fact that you are one of the few individuals in Michigan who could give Phil Hart a run for his money. Obviously, the men of consequence have written off this engagement and will wait for more vulnerable opponents. A woman might just be unique enough to turn the trick. However, the senatorial bit is a gamble at best and you are sorely needed where you are.[49]

But Peterson was not swayed simply by the enthusiasm of her associates. On March 2, she wrote Dempsey, "One of the things . . . that I would have to be sure of is that the decision to run would not be simply 'the name on the ticket,' because I think you know me well enough to realize that if I went into it, it would be not only with the idea of winning, but with the idea of if I didn't I would make [Hart] know he had been in a race.

"Frankly, Jack, this takes some money, and I would have to see it or be pretty positive it was going to be there before I got involved."[50]

She scheduled a March 26 press conference to announce "whether I go or don't go." She wanted a meeting that week with Van Dusen and Fisher to discuss the financial arrangements; if necessary, she was prepared to schedule it as late as March 25.[51]

On March 24, she made appearances in Oakland County and Detroit. "I have not made up my mind," she told her audience in Bloomfield Hills. "I have one foot in the bathtub, but don't know which way I'll slip." She said she planned to talk to Pete on Wednesday night and would decide on Thursday.

But she was already playing party peacemaker. "I have had women tell me they would quit the party if the wrong man got the presidential nomination," she said in one speech. "If this is your position, I say to you, 'Go home right now. We've got to have card-carrying, all-the-way Republicans.'"[52]

Finally, she squeezed in a meeting with the finance men and then wrote her sister that the "big boys gave me a guarantee of a *base budget* so anything over that will be clover (and helpful). To date we have in around $200 and we plan to issue membership cards, sell jewelry, etc.—so much for money."[53]

Although she kept her options open, Peterson left nothing to chance when it came to planning her announcement. She scheduled a morning press conference in Lansing—complete with coffee and rolls for the reporters—early enough to meet the *State Journal*'s deadline. A meeting of the WACs was scheduled immediately afterward. Koeze wrote them that "Elly . . . will be at the meeting to shed some light on her plans and programs for this coming year" and urged members to make "a special effort" to show their support.[54]

By March 26, Peterson was ready to go. "No woman has ever been nominated for the Senate from Michigan," she said. "But precedents were made to be broken, and women, in the past, have established a fine record of breaking them."[55] She pointed to the two thousand signatures her supporters had collected in less than a month as a factor in her decision, and promised a "Peterson-to-People" campaign in which she would seek, in the words of one reporter, "the votes of factory workers at plant gates" and "women's groups at teas and coffee hours."[56]

Asked whether she considered herself "a particular type of Republican—that is a conservative, liberal, Goldwater, Eisenhower, Rockefeller or some other type," she replied, "I've never understood these labels people take. If you label yourself you don't judge the issues as they stand and I think you should judge each issue individually."[57]

From the vantage point of nearly a half century, press coverage of Peterson's announcement produced some cringe-inducing headlines as journalists tried to convey the novelty of her candidacy: "Elly's Chapeau in Senate Race," the State Journal trumpeted. "Millinery in State's Ring," read the headline on a Detroit Free Press editorial. It went on to say that if Peterson's primary opponents "expect dainty behavior, they're in for a surprise. Mrs. Peterson is a straight-from-the-shoulder political pro who will be as hard to deal with as a wife who wants a new dress."[58]

The Detroit News, meanwhile, resurrected a variation on the Romney quote she disliked: "She looks like a girl, thinks like a man and works like a dog."[59]

The Christian Science Monitor, however, played it straight, writing that Peterson had "taken some of her own advice" and after urging "other women to seek political office," was taking the plunge herself. "Recent polls," reporter James S. Brooks noted, "have indicated Senator Hart could win reelection in a walk against either Mr. Meany or Mr. O'Neil. But against Mrs. Peterson, political observers believe, the contest would be tougher."[60] Similarly, the Battle Creek Enquirer and News editorialized that "Hart may be in for real trouble" because if Peterson won the GOP primary, he "can figure on quite a loss in female support."[61]

Peterson's primary opponents took issue with any suggestion that she had polls showing she was the favorite. O'Neil noted that in his 1963 race for the State Board of Education, he had drawn more votes than any Republican candidate running statewide. Meany, meanwhile, said, "Elly is attractive, articulate and knowledgeable. But she is not too well known outside the party."

For his part, Hart said, "A candidate shouldn't be judged on the basis of sex, color or religion." For that, the Associated Press reporter described him as being "a little less gallant" than the two Republican men.

In conclusion, the article said that both Meany and O'Neil "admitted the chic Mrs. Peterson was the prettiest candidate. 'All I can do is get my suits pressed,' Meany said."[62]

By all accounts, Elly Peterson had the stamina of the Energizer Bunny and an uncanny ability to keep several balls in the air at the same time. Before opening her campaign headquarters in mid-April, she returned to Washington to direct the Twelfth Annual Republican Women's Conference, several days of events held during the Cherry Blossom Festival. The conference had involved three months' worth of work, and, she told a reporter, "it's no small matter. Twenty-five hundred women, and all their housing and meals to plan, not to mention the programming of the conference itself."

The article described Peterson as "a gray haired, breezy mannered, yet obviously efficient and capable woman." Her secretarial training, the reporter added, "is still something of an embarrassment to the staff at Republican headquarters" because, a colleague said, "she can type faster and take dictation faster than anyone in the office."[63]

The women's conference was programmed back-to-back with a meeting of eighty leaders of the National Federation of Republican Women, whom Peterson addressed, now as a candidate for the U.S. Senate. Ter Horst of the *Detroit News* had observed in mid-March that "since coming to Washington, Mrs. Peterson has distinguished herself by articulating counter-attacks on the Democratic administration."[64] President Johnson, she told the federation, "is speaking softly and carrying a feather, and this approach has never yet caused anyone to back down, certainly not the Communists." She characterized the War on Poverty as "a grab bag of merchandise assembled from the shelves of old warehouses marked 'New Deal' and 'Fair Deal' and even the 'New Frontier.'" She called the president a "huckster" and a "snake bite remedy salesman" who tries to be "all things to all people." Then she urged the women to unite behind whichever candidate was nominated that summer. "We will need every pair of available hands, every pair of willing feet, every loyal Republican heart, if we are to have tea in the White House" next spring.[65]

Three presidential candidates—Goldwater, Rockefeller, and Sen. Margaret Chase Smith of Maine—addressed the women's conference, along with Lenore Romney. At the conference's close, Peterson urged the delegates "to preserve the unity of purpose you have shown here because without this our cause would be lost."[66]

The conference represented another organizational challenge on which Peterson knew she would be judged. She recalled that she and her staff "worked frantically to make sure all the arrangements were perfect." But shortly before a morning program was to start, a wall in the auditorium at the Sheraton-Park Hotel collapsed. There were no injuries, and when the meeting reconvened, Peterson responded with a quip: "There's no truth to the rumor that the wall was put together with Johnson's wax and was therefore a little slippery."[67]

Peterson stepped down as state vice chairman when she became a Senate candidate but agreed to stay on as assistant chairman of the national party until that summer's convention. Although party chairman Miller and other RNC staff members supported her candidacy, "not all," she recalled, "was rosy." Clare Williams Shank "was most offended that I would give up the job for which she felt she trained me to run for almost certain defeat."[68] The day she announced her candidacy, Peterson wrote Shank, saying she was "sorry that you don't agree with my decision. . . . I have given this a great deal of thought, and there are a number of factors about it that I cannot explain to you in a letter but cannot be overlooked, not the least of which was the consideration of the National Committee."[69]

Back in Michigan, the same party leaders who had urged her to run now said they could not take sides until after the primary. Romney publicly declined to endorse a candidate. His decision, Peterson recalled, "hurt me at first," but she understood it "deep down."[70] Meanwhile, Chairman Elliott ordered his staff to stay out of Peterson's campaign. "I realize the deep fondness we have for her," he wrote to them. "Still we cannot allow State Central employees to become involved in any primary activity."[71]

The political and media environment was still not a welcoming one for women. Only two women—Smith and Maurine Neuberger—served in the U.S. Senate, and both had entered Congress by taking over the seat of their late husbands. Further, there were few, if any, women reporters assigned to cover campaigns; when stories appeared under female bylines, they were generally relegated to the society pages. It would be another seven years before membership in Washington's National Press Club was opened to women—and women were permitted to come down from the balcony when they covered news-maker luncheons there.[72]

One of Peterson's campaign aides recalled a visit with U.S. Rep. Catherine May, a Republican from Washington state who had won a seat in her own right six years earlier. She advised him, "One thing you've got to avoid is having your woman candidate look like she's a lot smarter than the other guy. Men voters aren't ready for this. . . . When I ran against the guy, the guy was a dope, and I had to really bend over backwards to keep from making him look like a total dope for fear it would backlash on me." The aide, John McClaughry, felt it was "a very shrewd observation."[73]

In an April interview, Peterson said she expected her Senate campaign would be easier than the one Smith would face for president: "The presidency is so tied in with military matters that many people just can't see a woman in the job. It isn't that way with the Senate—and besides, the way has been broken for women senators."[74]

In another story, James Robinson, of the *Detroit Free Press*, reported that Peterson had already figured out how to get elected.

All she has to do between now and November is become the "most-talked-about" woman in Michigan.

The way Elly has it figured, you call in your friends, especially the women, organize them into talking committees and tell them to "talk about Elly" every chance they get.

"Give them something to talk about, something a little new and different, and they will do the job," Elly explained, in outlining what promises to be one of the liveliest political campaigns Michigan voters have ever seen.[75]

But Peterson herself reflected her times when she contributed one of "Two Open Letters to Teen-Age Girls" that *Seventeen* magazine solicited from the parties' top women that year. Although she noted that "more and more women are running for office at every level," she did not specifically encourage her youthful readers to do that.

Rather, she wrote that "more and more men candidates are counting on their wives for helpful, knowledgeable assistance in their campaigns. A husband and wife team can cover twice as much ground, but disaster can strike the most promising candidate if his wife is unprepared to carry her end." She then raised the prospect that the teens might marry someone like Gov. Mark Hatfield of Oregon or state Rep. Russ Strange of Michigan, both of whom were first elected to office at a young age.

Although Peterson highlighted young women who were serving as key political and legislative advisers, and "the unbeatable combination of having fun while doing something worthwhile" that comes with campaign work, she did not mention her own candidacy.[76]

After the women's conference, Peterson returned to Charlotte for the grand opening of her headquarters. The *Detroit News* reported that "it was like old home week for neighbors who haven't seen much of Mrs. Peterson since she went to Washington. . . . Her organizational skill was demonstrated again yesterday. Friends who dropped in . . . just to say hello left as directors of countywide GOPeterson drives."[77]

Before the event, Peterson hosted a luncheon for the press. Virginia Redfern, the *State Journal*'s society editor, responded with a glowing report: "Elly Peterson lives in just exactly the kind of house that anyone who knows her would expect. That is that Elly . . . is practical, down-to-earth, warm, hospitable and known for good taste in the things she says and does. Her country home . . . has all these qualities."

She went on to describe Peterson's furnishings, which included "charming little framed prints" from countries she had visited and "lovely accessories brought from the Orient. . . . Other touches that make the Petersons' home unique and reflect facets of its mistress are the placement of antiques here and there, most of them with family connotations. . . . But all her talents are not in decorating. Elly's luncheon buffet, prepared with the help of a neighbor and friend, was delicious."[78]

The creative "branding" of "Elly" was already under way, thanks to Gert Powers. Peterson wrote her sister that "the pins, strips, etc., will all be ELLY. Instead of a bumper strip, we're having 4 1/2-inch *circles* for car *windows* with ELLY! and pins elly."[79]

Redfern noted that "a basket of logs (each labeled with an 'Elly' sticker)" had been placed by the fireplace and that the candidate and her staff wore "gold pins, spelling out 'Elly' in large letters." Another reporter quoted Peterson anticipating "department stores and novelty shops" that would soon be selling "'Elly towels' to help clean things up." Still another focused on "GOPeterson stationery, a money tree on which supporters placed dollar bills," and "for the ladies, there were white whimsies (veil-like hats) adorned with red and blue elephants."[80] ("I never was known as 'Mrs. Peterson,'" she observed years later. "I went from 'Elly' to 'Mother.'" In her memory, only the *Kalamazoo Gazette* "remained formal," referring to her as "Mrs. Peterson" in headlines.)[81]

Most observers believed Peterson would face an uphill battle. In April, the *Wall Street Journal* reported that the Republicans were having trouble enlisting "top-flight candidates." Party leaders, Allen L. Otten reported, "are lining up behind Mrs. Elly Peterson," the RNC's "dynamic" assistant

chairman. "She will wage a vigorous campaign, but few GOP leaders outside Michigan expect her to beat Sen. Hart."[82]

In June, DeVries conducted a poll that showed Hart was well ahead of
all of his potential opponents. But DeVries found that a Hart-O'Neil race
would be the closest—63.7 percent to 14.4 percent. Against Peterson, Hart
would win by 67.5 percent of respondents to 14.0 percent for Peterson because there were fewer undecided voters.

DeVries concluded that Peterson was drawing less support from the
ticket splitters who had put Romney into office. But, he noted, "Elly holds
up well with the straight Republican voters and those preferring Romney."
Against all the Republican candidates, most voters preferred Hart because
of his experience and party. "In this year when Hart is seen as a Democrat
and as an experienced, familiar figure, partyness is about all O'Neil has going for him," DeVries wrote in a memo. "Elly doesn't even have that."

If Peterson won the primary, he added, "she will have to be made
known to the public as quickly and widely as possible. Since the committed
voters think so highly of Hart's experience, she will have to counter with
her own experience, state and national party service. The fact of her being
a woman does not now appear to be either her downfall or her salvation."

The memo was labeled "confidential," and Peterson did not recall ever
having seen it more than forty years later. It's possible that the governor
did not want to appear to be taking sides; it's also possible that his team
did not want to discourage her by sharing the pessimistic findings.[83]

A month later the *Detroit News* published the results of a Market
Opinion Research poll that showed O'Neil leading in the primary
matchup with 30 percent of the vote, while Peterson trailed with 24 percent and Meany had 11 percent. O'Neil was leading among every category
of voter, including women, where his margin actually widened to fourteen
percentage points. (When the survey was expanded to include voters of
both parties, O'Neil was found to be favored by a margin of two to one.)
But, the paper reported, because 35 percent of Republicans remained undecided, "this contest is still wide open." And, it noted presciently, "presumably, the three-way contest will be decided by Republican voters. And
a Republican primary vote is susceptible to party organization."[84]

In her final days with the RNC, Peterson got a groundbreaking opportunity—the chance to address the Republican National Convention
during prime time. She was the first woman to be given that honor and
the only one to do so that year.

The San Francisco convention is remembered now for its divisive bitterness. As the delegates gathered at the Cow Palace, CBS correspondent Eric Sevareid observed, "This is a showdown fight for what many have called the soul of this party. The 1,300 delegates do not represent a family reunion. This is a gathering of eagles. Their talons are sharpened and their eyes are hard. I think we can expect little humor and little fun from them."[85]

A record number of women—230—were seated as delegates. Women also served in equal numbers to men on all major convention committees, the first time full parity had been achieved since the party adopted that goal in 1940. Women also chose the convention theme, "For the People," and served as treasurer, secretary, and parliamentarian.[86] Observed the *Oakland Tribune,* "For the women, it's the best Republican National Convention in history."[87]

Based on experience, Peterson was not sure how much of her speech would actually be televised. Helen Thomas of United Press International (UPI) reported that Peterson hoped the networks didn't "start selling ice boxes" when "her big moment" came. Thomas reported that women who had been lobbying the networks for more exposure "have been bluntly told that women speakers are 'poison' and the viewers don't like to hear them." But she said Peterson's speeches have a "hard-hitting, rip-the-rafters quality that just may prove the experts wrong."[88]

Under a headline that characterized Peterson as a "squaw" among the "big heap chiefs," Marie Smith reported for the *Washington Post*'s "For and about Women" section, "The scarcity of women speakers on the convention platform is not intended as discrimination against the fairer sex but rather to give television viewers of the convention what they want, a Committee spokesman said. Studies, the spokesman continued, show that viewers don't like to hear women give speeches."

Assigned to cover "distaff" events, Smith observed that "if women were forgotten in the program planning, they were certainly very much in mind in the planning of social events for convention-goers." Peterson hosted a fashion show luncheon for national committeewomen and the spouses of national committeemen, as well as a brunch for incoming national committeewomen and a brunch for fifteen hundred women.[89]

In another article, Smith said Peterson had become "a star in the game" through her work on Romney's behalf. She added:

For her major address Monday night, which she said will express the feelings she and other women have about the Republican Party, she will wear a Baron Peters café au lait suit with a pearl necklace and tiny pearl earrings.

She is leaving her party office with mixed emotions. "It has been a stimulating experience and we have made progress, but I feel you can't accomplish all the things you want to in such a short time. I would like to have worked on education programs with non-partisan groups," she said.

If she does not win election to the Senate, that may be her next venture in politics.[90]

Smith said Peterson was "not a feminist," and quoted her as saying, "People ask me if I encounter any special problems as a woman candidate. I just can't tell—I can't get any feeling on it as I talk to voters. . . . I have never consciously fought the battles of women. I just went ahead and did my job—maybe I had to work a little harder because I was a woman, but I didn't think of it that way." Still, the reporter said, Peterson felt that "women have a long way to go in politics before they get to the top. . . . As a candidate, I'm doing all the things I've preached," and "as a woman candidate you are a gimmick and you might as well put on a gimmick campaign."[91]

Ranny Riecker, who later worked closely with Peterson in the state party, recalled that at that time Peterson would become irked when Koeze complained loudly about her treatment at the hands of Republican national committeeman John Martin. "If she wouldn't tell everybody about it, nobody would know," Riecker recalled Peterson saying during the 1964 convention. "And," Riecker noted, "I think that was very much of a learning lesson for all of us as women. If you didn't complain, and you put on the right face, maybe people didn't know" the extent to which women were "second-class citizens."[92]

Peterson was allotted ten minutes on the first night of the convention, a warm-up to keynoter Mark Hatfield. Recalling that night, she wrote, "It was a moving moment for me as I rose to address that convention and looked down to see Gov. Romney, ex-Gov. [Wilber M.] Brucker, Jerry Ford and the entire Michigan delegation on their feet to lead the applause. I got through it with one difficult moment when I thought my throat was closing, and I would be unable to speak."

"Tonight," she started out:

I speak to the American mother whose son is even now crawling through the jungle muck of Vietnam, risking his life to stem the tide of communism in Southeast Asia. Tonight, I speak to all the American parents who fear for the safety of their children—be they black or white—as racial disturbances across our land lead to bitterness, anguish and violence. Tonight, I speak to American working men and women, alarmed at the gigantic bite the federal government takes from their pay checks. Tonight, I speak to every American, beset with the hopes and fears of everyday life in this complicated, confusing bewildering world we live in. And my message is this. . . .What has happened to the America we knew?[93]

The *Washington Post* said Peterson was "passionate" as she "overlooked the breach within her own party" and "lashed out at the Democrats." The speech, it said, was written the day before, after Peterson had "scrapped another address drafted earlier."[94] Peterson credited staffer O'Callaghan, former president of the Texas Federation of Republican Women, with helping to write it.[95]

In its coverage, UPI reported that Peterson "took off her kid gloves" and blasted the Democrats, saying, "I hold no brief for power-hungry politicians who would nibble away our freedoms. Even more distressing is the fact that a seemingly indifferent America is willing to permit them to do so." She questioned Johnson's call for a "Great Society," asking, "What is the matter with the free society?"[96]

Frances Lewine, of the Associated Press, reported that Peterson had "stirred the convention to drum-beating and applause" when she "used a house-keeping metaphor," telling the convention, "We cannot accept the present-day fashion of sweeping the scandals under the rug and whitewashing the walls as a substitute for a real spring cleaning. If there is something we should know about the Bobby Baker case, why aren't we told about it? "[97]

The speech, as it turned out, was broadcast in its entirety.

A tantalizing question is what role it may have played in shoring up Peterson's support among those who would be voting in the primary six weeks later. The day after the speech, the *State Journal* reported that Peterson "frankly admitted to newsmen she welcomed the opportunity to be seen and heard, and hoped it might help her primary campaign."[98] Her campaign had urged local supporters to push their newspapers and broadcast outlets to cover the speech and also purchased newspaper ads promoting it.[99]

A number of young women took note of the speech. Teenager Christine Todd Whitman, the future governor of New Jersey, attended the convention as a page to that state's delegation. A supporter of the party's moderate wing, Whitman recalled that Peterson's speech "was one of those that you remembered for someone being brave enough to stand up and say something. . . . Hers was a voice of reason, I remember."[100]

Meanwhile, Anita Stauffer, president of the Ogle County Teen Age Republicans in Mount Morris, Illinois, wrote Peterson that the speech was "outstanding" and it was "heartening to see a woman in politics who can really speak." She asked for a copy and information about how Peterson had gotten started in politics. Deborah Paul of Alexandria, Virginia, also praised the "excellent" speech and asked for a copy.[101]

The rest of the convention, however, was not a happy memory. Peterson recalled, "[W]hen I finished my speech, I was told not to sit on the platform again during the convention and [that I] would not be included in the planning meetings."[102] She was, however, given a reserved box, from which she watched the proceedings with relatives and friends from Charlotte.

In the end, Goldwater secured a first-ballot victory with 883 votes, followed by Pennsylvania governor William Scranton with 214 and Rockefeller with 114. Michigan delegates cast their 41 votes for their favorite son, George Romney.

Of the convention, Peterson wrote, "It would be difficult for me to repeat my feelings at the rudeness shown Gov. Rockefeller, as the right wing booed and hissed his speech." Then there was "the Eisenhower speech on the press, when he seemed to be as nutty as the nuttiest winger and finally Goldwater's acceptance speech, which spelled out the beliefs of the wingers. For those of us wearing Romney buttons, the convention became a nightmare for we were insulted and in some cases, even spit upon, by ultra-conservatives. The young men were especially rude, making loud and unbelievably crude remarks in elevators and restaurants and over-running convention seats and boxes, using counterfeit tickets."[103]

The morning after Goldwater accepted the nomination, Peterson received "a handwritten note (make that SUMMONS!)" to meet with the state party chairmen, Goldwater, and his new running mate, her old boss Bill Miller, for a briefing on the campaign ahead. She recalled running into eight moderate state chairmen, "who were being treated as if they had the plague." The conservatives were jubilant. As each person entered the room, she recalled, Talbot Peterson, the Wisconsin party chairman, yelled out, "Say, do you think there were 837 extremists at the convention last night?" drawing "a big laugh."

"At no time," she added, "did Goldwater speak to me or any of these eight leaders, and at no time did I ever receive an acknowledgement from him or his people that I was (to all intent[s] and purpose[s]) still National Assistant Chairman. They just took over the National committee and, like old soldiers, the moderates faded away."[104]

# CHAPTER FOUR

## The Reluctant Candidate

Peterson returned home to some bad news for a candidate still trying to build her name recognition: the unions at Detroit's two major newspapers had gone out on strike the opening night of the convention, so there had been no coverage of her speech in the state's two biggest papers. They would not resume publication until after Election Day.

But now, at least, she was finally free to campaign full time rather than just on weekends.

Gert Powers had become campaign chairman. Nelle Taylor and her husband, Bruce, took charge of finances. Pam Curtis moved to Michigan from the RNC staff. She drove from Washington with twenty-seven-year-old John McClaughry, who had been working for a struggling magazine published by Rockefeller Republicans. He showed up in blue jeans, carrying a guitar and an onion bag stuffed with his clothes. Peterson hired him as press secretary and speechwriter. Steve Royer, a law student who had met Peterson as a Teen Age Republican, signed on as bus driver, assistant press secretary, and gofer.

Mary Richmond, who had moved to Hawaii to take a job at the prestigious Kamehameha Schools, now returned to Charlotte to travel with Elly and manage her household. Other old friends from Charlotte pitched in, everyone from the women's circle at the First Congregational Church to members of the local Brownie troop, who helped with mailings and tacking up signs.

"Grass roots," Peterson observed, "don't get any grassier than that!"[1]

Among the Charlotte volunteers was Joyce Braithwaite, who took on the job of campaign scheduler and, over the years, became one of Peterson's closest friends and a political force of her own. From the start, Braithwaite-Brickley recalled, Peterson "struck me as a powerful person. She was larger of stature than most, walked with a very pronounced step. . . . And her voice was about an octave louder than most."

At the time, Braithwaite was the mother of two small boys and having marital problems. Peterson reached out to her, "and at the time," she recalled, "I needed that from someone." Peterson was, Braithwaite concluded, "a mesmerizing person to me."[2]

One supporter who stayed above the fray was Pete, whose job barred him from partisan politics. A feature story in the suburban *Observer* newspapers described Pete as "Michigan's undisputed political widower of 1964." The profile continued:

> "I always love to see her again," says Pete, "even if it's only on television."
>
> Pete claims he always misses Elly when she's gone, but says it gets especially acute about dinner time. Friends of the Petersons report, however, that Pete is no slouch as a cook. He is still famous around Charlotte for a concoction he labeled simply "soup." . . . Pete delights in suffering through his desertion on the golf links at Charlotte and Grand Ledge. . . .
>
> When Elly made a brief trip home last week, Pete claims she walked in, shook his hand and asked him to vote for her in the September 1 primary. "I did the average voter one better," he says. "I not only promised to vote for her, I kissed her. At least I hope that's one better."

This profile, like other contemporary news stories, dated the Petersons' marriage from the time of their first wedding.[3]

In the last weeks before the September 1 primary, Peterson made the most of the statewide volunteer organization she had built. On primary day, the weather was good and turnout was strong, in part because legislative and congressional districts had just been redrawn, pitting incumbents against one another in some races.[4] And when the votes were counted, Peterson had come from behind to defeat her two male rivals.

She garnered more than 210,000 votes, about 39 percent of the total, against the reputed favorite O'Neil, who captured 34 percent. Ed Meany was third with about 27 percent.[5] In vote-heavy Wayne County, O'Neil's home territory, Peterson trailed by about 11,000 votes. But she made up the difference across the rest of the state where she was well known among party regulars.

She ran her primary campaign on less than $25,000. Her brothers each contributed $1,000, as did GOP activist Jack Stiles of Grand Rapids and G. Frank Langford, a family friend. Romney and J. Willard Marriott contributed $200 each, Larry Lindemer, $110.[6]

Peterson credited her volunteers for her victory; the Associated Press cited her organizational work in building the State Central Committee "from the precinct level up" and "seven-days-a-week campaigning."[7] The latter, of course, was only possible in the final weeks before the primary.

In hindsight, at least one reporter concluded that Peterson won only because her two opponents had split the conservative vote.[8] O'Neil later pointed to the newspaper strike as the turning point in his loss.[9]

On primary night, Peterson was already playing party peacemaker. "I don't necessarily agree with Mr. Goldwater, just as I don't see eye-to-eye on all issues with Gov. Romney," she told the Associated Press. "But this is a big enough party to weather differences of opinion. Our basic philosophy is the same."

Romney, for his part, declared that his new ticketmate was "an exceptional woman who has demonstrated exceptionable [sic] ability."[10] The *Detroit Daily Press*, the slimmed-down strike newspaper, said Peterson's victory "promises a new kind of political campaign in Michigan. . . . Wags grabbed this contest early with the quip that 'Hart is too much of gentleman to wallop a lady even politically.'"[11]

The two-month general election campaign was on.

In her memoir, Peterson recalled of her team, "We used feminine guile, male power, and everything else we could find." Gert and Joyce set the schedule, and "Steve, Mary and I took off every morning about five to keep it going. Sunday was our day off for laundry, letters, recuperation—unless, of course, there was an important meeting to attend."

> Since there was virtually no money, we operated on basic necessities. Our women volunteers used every ingenuity they possessed to get every possible cent. They raised small sums of money in every possible way (except the world's oldest profession!) and they did it with enthusiasm. They put out home made signs in their yards and in the yards of any neighbor willing to cooperate. They went door to door

when we blitzed an area, a favorite way of campaigning. . . .We put out millions of pieces of literature. . . . While I covered a small town newspaper or radio station, the troops would go fast as they could covering the town, especially the business district.[12]

Peterson's campaign literature described her as "a working member of the Republican team" and "a woman of action," as well as a "Red Cross worker overseas, civic leader, blood program director, housewife, Republican organizer, top National Republican official." She would "represent all the people, show interest in Michigan and its problems." Next to a photo shot in front of her farmhouse, the text read, in a bit of a stretch, "Elly Peterson has been 'down on the farm' enough to understand the problems of Michigan's farmers—and the hopes and aspirations farm women, like mothers everywhere, have for their children."

The brochure included photographs of Peterson with Eisenhower, Richard M. Nixon, Romney, and Scranton. "As the number two Republican in the national party," it said, "Elly Peterson has had ample opportunity to meet governing officials of other states, investigate national problems and, by being Elly, 'learning by listening.' " She was also shown with Pete and their dog Jake, though the brochure asserted that she "seldom has time for relaxed moments like this one . . . in her vigorous campaign to find out what all the people of Michigan think, what they want in their national government."

Peterson, it said, "believes 'it's a man's world—and a woman's world,' and there should be equal opportunities for both, equal chances for present and future generations to be educated, to exercise talent, without prejudice because of sex, race, creed or color." And, it asserted that "the halls of the Senate and the legislative process will be as familiar to Elly Peterson as the Michigan highways and byways she so constantly has traveled."[13]

Without the Detroit papers' free media coverage, Peterson needed more money if she was going to build her name recognition beyond party regulars. But the financial support she had expected from "the money men" never materialized. Further, she regretted that Powers had to endure the "degradation" of having to "beg for every cent" she got from Max Fisher.[14]

As campaign chairman, Powers tried to shield her friend from the campaign's financial woes. When Peterson found out, she was "just sick" that Powers had had to go begging. Finally, Peterson went to Romney and reminded him that he had been present when Fisher had promised his support. She understood that Fisher had calculated that she couldn't win, so there was no point in providing more financial resources. "But," she maintained, "he shouldn't have told me in the first place that he was going to give me money."[15]

A close observer of the campaign recalled, "A lot of money was coming [into the party] from the right wing," and "they were particularly cool to her by the end" of the campaign. Fisher, he observed, "concluded he would get her enough money to make a respectable race, but would not lean on people too hard."[16]

"There was always tension because Max Fisher would promise you the world and then you wouldn't get it," recalled DeVries. "Or he'd be very tight in handing out funds. And of course in '64, the key thing was to get Romney reelected. Everything else was subservient to that."[17]

The lack of media attention also was frustrating. Although she worked with McClaughry on speeches and policy positions, Peterson concluded that most of their work was for naught. "Press," she recalled, "was almost impossible to get." Hart did not have to campaign very hard because he was sitting on a big lead, and most reporters were focused on the presidential and gubernatorial races and the growing divide between Romney and Goldwater.

McClaughry recalled, "Nobody was much interested in Elly's campaign. . . . The big question was, 'Can freshman governor Romney overcome the tide that is ebbing rapidly because of Goldwater and stay in office?' . . . So this was one of the least demanding chores a campaign press secretary ever had."[18]

In the end, Peterson concluded, the best coverage she got was when her bus became stuck in the mud and she had to hitchhike to her next appearance. On the day her headquarters opened, a friend hung a sign on the Petersons' doghouse that read, "If you can't vote, bark it up." The photo, she said, "went all over Michigan." Sadly, she concluded, "Gimmicks were much more apt to make the news than issue discussions, and I got more press out of the battery falling out of my campaign van than I ever did on important speeches."[19]

What coverage there was often ended up on the society pages or was laden with feminine images, some of which Peterson underscored in her speeches. "The lady daintily slipped off her gloves" and let Hart have it, one report said. "The rustle of political petticoats will set the scene. . . ." A strong endorsement from former president Eisenhower was "tucked firmly in her handbag."[20]

In a story on plans for a joint appearance of women candidates and candidates' wives, the reporter noted, "The new strategy in campaigning may create a few problems—like what is the proper way to greet a lady politician, GOP officials mused today. No problem, they say. 'Just shake her hand and don't worry about squeezing too hard—the gals are developing a pretty good grip.'"[21]

Late in life, Peterson said she had not been troubled by the way her campaign was covered. But later on, the sexism rankled. "It came to me as I worked more and more for the Equal Rights Amendment," she recalled. "I could see where we were constantly put down. Now all this didn't bother a lot of people. It didn't bother me at the time. There are just so many things you can do, you couldn't do anything about that."[22]

As the election approached, the Booth newspaper chain assigned a reporter to cover the Peterson campaign on a full-time basis. Jon Lowell was a twenty-two year old with a degree in playwriting, who had been hired by the *Muskegon Chronicle* even though he admitted he couldn't type.[23]

Peterson's campaign, he noted, was "not a campaign a lot of people were fighting to cover." He remembered the struggle it faced in small towns "to get the press to listen to [Peterson] on substantive issues, and get beyond the fact that she was a woman running for high political office."

In her memoir, Peterson took pity on Lowell. "We could tell he suffered, literally suffered, being hooked up to the campaign of a woman. And, on top of that, a woman who didn't have a chance!"[24]

But Lowell had a different perspective. He was thrilled to cover a statewide campaign so early in his career. And Peterson, he said, "was just terrific and understanding" about his inexperience. It was, he concluded, "a great way to start."

On one campaign swing, Peterson introduced him to Nixon, then doing time on the chicken dinner circuit after his loss in the 1962 California gubernatorial race. Peterson explained to Nixon that the reporter knew "almost nothing" about politics; Nixon, in turn, provided Lowell with "his version of Politics 101."

Peterson recalled in her memoir:

We did our campaigning in a Cortz bus, and [Jon] became a permanent fixture in the seat next to Steve [Royer], where they would argue politics and world affairs as we drove along. In the mornings, Mary would have his coffee ready, and in the late afternoon, our little refrigerator would frequently have a beer or martini for him. We thought it was a great joke on his last campaign trip with us, when we knew he had to catch a plane back to Muskegon, to have a farewell dinner in his honor, and present him with a case of beer he had to carry on board.[25]

Lowell agreed that they all had fun together. "It was remarkable," he reflected, "given the [lack of] resources and relatively unconventional nature of running a woman for Senate." Peterson, he recalled, was "unfailingly good spirited" and "absolutely tireless." She genuinely "liked reporters." You saw, he said, "none of the venom that you see in politics today."

Lowell contrasted Peterson with "Soapy" Williams, whom he covered later in his career. Williams, he said, "had a campaign image of being outgoing, a wonderfully accessible 'man of the people.'" But in fact, "he was a very oddly private, reclusive man. Very often in politics, what you see is not what you get in private. Elly was the same mold—the public persona was the same as the private."

A longtime political consultant who worked with Peterson early in his career described it another way: she had what he calls "inside charisma," when "people inside an organization love being with her," as opposed to the "outside charisma" that most candidates have. "You always wanted to be with her. . . . She was just incredibly gracious and funny."[26]

Lowell's career later took him to Washington. Reflecting on his first campaign, he said, "You really had to resist developing a vested interest in seeing them do better. . . . It was very hard not to like all of them. And that was certainly not true of campaigns I covered subsequently."[27]

A *Chicago Tribune* reporter observed that Peterson had "the gift of humor under pressure."[28] On a bitterly cold evening in October, Peterson recalled in her memoir, she was the twenty-second of twenty-four candidates scheduled to speak in an unheated barn at a rural fairgrounds.

You had to hand it to those Sanilac County Republicans who were bundled to the forehead. They sat through it all (or is it just possible they were frozen to the seats and couldn't move?) Finally, it was my turn and the Master of Ceremonies got up to introduce me. He was fulsome in praises. I had been his long-time friend, he had been mine. We had been [in] each other's house, we had worked together in party affairs and in civic affairs. He was proud to introduce, "The next Senator from Michigan, Mrs. Ella Koeze!" . . . . I could see right then how well I would do in the election . . . and that is about how well I did!

On another occasion, she ran into twenty-six-year-old Stewart R. Mott, the philanthropist and political activist, at a coffee hour in his hometown of Flint. "I mentioned I had been downtown handing out literature," she recalled. "He said he had been there, too—handing out condoms!"[29]

The *Tribune* reporter captured the campaign's frenetic pace.

"I need prayer, luck and help," [Peterson] told a supporter at 10:30 p.m. of the day she started at 5:45 a.m. She already had toured two huge manufacturing plants, ducking around machinery and hustling along assembly lines, to shake employees' hands.

She visited a business men's luncheon, toured a retirement home, visited the city hall of Pontiac north of Detroit, rushed to an interview at a local newspaper, dashed thru the rain to a coffee meeting at local Republican headquarters, then sped thru a vast shopping center for more meeting and greeting.

It was 5 p.m. then and, with no time to change the clothes she'd been wearing since 5:45 a.m., she went to a dinner, then to a rally, then to a home where 100 Republicans had gathered to hear her speak.

At 10:30 p.m., she had one more stop—a Young Republican rally. She was tired, her voice was getting ragged, but it had been "a good day," she said.

The story noted that Peterson planned to travel fourteen hundred miles in five days that week and expected that she would rack up fifty-five thousand miles by the end of the campaign.[30] Peterson recalled that she missed only two days on the campaign trail and only because she broke her toe while trying to put on a girdle. She estimated that she shook at least two thousand hands a day—about the same pace as her World War II doughnut distribution.

By October 20, Lowell reported, "Elly's Army" expected to have a hundred thousand volunteers across the state "as an integral part of one of the most unorthodox campaigns in Michigan history." Shelley Spann, the Birmingham homemaker who headed the effort, said most of them worked only for Peterson because they were such fervent admirers. "It's almost adulation," Spann said. "I've never seen anything like it, it's an Elly cult." The campaign had sent out fifteen thousand letters to groups such as the League of Women Voters and United Church Women, asking members to volunteer. Recruits would be asked to send a projected two million "personal endorsement" cards to names on their Christmas card lists and to make phone calls over the last three days of the campaign.

"We're not feminists," Spann said. "I don't think we should rally behind a woman just because she is a woman." But Spann herself resigned from the board of her local League of Women Voters chapter so that she could volunteer.[31] Years later Peterson recalled that women would come up to her after the campaign and say, "But I thought you'd win!"—something she said she never herself believed.[32]

Nevertheless, Peterson tried her best to run a tough campaign against Hart. She challenged his "effectiveness," declaring he was a "puppet" and "rubber stamp" for Johnson. Hart, she noted, had voted five times "to sweep the Bobby Baker case under the rug."[33] He was "a doormat and pushover for the Democrats in Washington."[34]

At a speech in Ann Arbor, she unveiled a plan for ending the draft.[35] In Birmingham, she called for a government-supported program to put more social workers into the fight against juvenile crime.[36]

Peterson said she and McClaughry "worked long and hard on issues, and he was a good teacher."[37] McClaughry observed that Peterson "was not an issues-oriented person at all. She was an organizer, which I am not." He said he would tell her what he thought she should say about a particular issue, but acknowledged he was nervous because his own experience was so limited. As it turned out, he said, "I don't think I got her into any trouble."[38]

Arny Levin agreed with McClaughry's assessment. Peterson "had knowledge of the issues, but no real touch with them."[39]

One hot issue was section 14(b) of the Taft-Hartley Act, which permitted states to outlaw the "union shop." McClaughry recalled that even though he tried to explain it to Peterson, "14(b) seemed to get tangled up in her brain somewhere. And every time somebody said '14(b)' she sort of went 'deer in the headlights,' like 'What the hell is that thing again? I cannot remember.'"

They gained more traction over legislation Hart had sponsored to acquire additional land to establish the Sleeping Bear Dunes National Lakeshore. A number of Detroit residents with cabins on Lake Michigan "were ripping mad about it," McClaughry recalled. "And Elly went up there and denounced the whole crazy scheme and won a roaring ovation." It was, he said, "the best reception she got in the whole campaign."[40]

Still Peterson and McClaughry knew she was barely laying a glove on the incumbent. Years later she observed that Hart was "a good man, good senator, good husband, good everything." She was, she said, "very fond of him."[41]

And the feeling was mutual. Hart's biographer said that, sitting on a thirty-six-point lead, Hart joked privately to a reporter, "Gee whiz. God, Jerry! Elly Peterson is one heck of a nice woman. I don't want to go out there and run against her. Why don't they give me somebody I can get my teeth into?"[42]

Hart scheduled his campaign's official kickoff only a month before Election Day. "Bad staff work" at the end of September led him to miss three important events where Peterson showed up. A Peterson aide said, "We may be the underdogs in this thing but if that nice senator just keeps on missing these dates he'll give us the election." The Hart camp reported that "Phil got pretty upset about it because, as anyone who knows him is aware, he doesn't want to slight people."[43]

The first week of October, the two opponents happened to run into each other in Muskegon. But, the UPI reporter noted, the meeting "was not the debate Mrs. Peterson had hoped for." Nevertheless, the paper reported that "Hart told Mrs. Peterson he had come to have high regard for Michigan's Republican women since bumping into the GOP candidates' wives blitz team in Port Huron" that week.[44]

In the end, all Hart really had to do was draw attention to Goldwater, who remained far behind in the polls, and coast to victory. But Romney had drafted Peterson not because she could win but to help assure his own reelection. After the GOP convention, Romney had announced he would "accept" Goldwater but not "endorse" him. His position did not change, even after Goldwater made a one-day visit to Michigan in late September.

The tensions meant Peterson often had to navigate through a political minefield. "People were bitter about Goldwater," she recalled, "and, time after time, would throw our literature back in our faces when we said, 'Yes, I am supporting the choice of the Republican Convention.' Some of the conservatives were just as unhappy when the answer was, 'Yes, I'm supporting Gov. Romney for Governor,' but the die had been cast, and we were not about to change it."

It was, she concluded, "almost impossible to split the campaigns away from each other."

> If I would say I was campaigning just for Peterson, that I knew my own road was rough and rocky and I would do my thing and let Goldwater and Romney do theirs, I satisfied no one. As the national election picked up, more and more hate was generated. I grew so discouraged at times. I had been a working Republican too long to leave the party in such a hassle as that election grew to be. I was a Republican and I wanted to remain a Republican. I believe the Romneys felt the same way. I perceived my job of the moment not being elected but keeping the party together coming out of the election with a Republican Governor and the troops to rebuild.[45]

Looking back, Lowell observed that "Peterson was a big believer in serious party unity, and 'thou shall not speak ill of Republicans.' As a result, she was much more inclusive than a guy like Romney, who viewed himself as being on God's side, and anyone who wasn't on his side, wasn't listening to the Almighty. She had to do more than a little bit of patching up on behalf of Romney, a role for which I'm sure he never gave her any credit."[46]

McClaughry recalled:

> She was fiercely loyal to Romney, even though she said early on she would support the presidential nominee of the party. Her job as I saw her do it was to try and heal over the divisions among Republicans around the state to the point where her Senate candidacy was sort of an afterthought. It was sort of a ticket to go out to the rural counties and meet with the party leaders and say, "Look, you know, the big thing here is getting George reelected, and if you want to beat the drums for Goldwater, that's fine, but you know Barry is not going to carry this state, so let's try and mute our differences and win what we can win." . . .

She's a very practical politician. She was a huge talent in her ability to bring people together and talk sense to them. A lot of women are reluctant to enter a confrontational situation. Women have different styles. Elly could easily adopt a male style. Sort of no-nonsense, "let's lay it out on the table, and look right in the eye and agree on how we are going to do this." Which certainly endeared her to me as a male.

You didn't have to decipher Elly. She gave you . . . the real deal.[47]

Peterson's campaign made it back onto the front pages in early October through an episode that foreshadowed what more than one major female candidate would experience over the next half century.

She was attending a tea in Jackson on October 8, when she was called to the phone to speak with a reporter. Romney had just fired the adjutant general and two other top officers of the state National Guard after the state auditor had turned up irregularities in sales of state-owned lots near Camp Grayling, the Guard's encampment in northern Michigan. Pete was among those who had purchased lots.

Peterson was "floored," then remembered that Pete *had* bought something a few years before. The reporter asked about the size of the lot; she said she didn't know. The campaign cut the tea short and headed back to Charlotte. Pete, it turned out, had bought less than half an acre of land with no road access. "The incredible part," Peterson recalled, "was not his buying it for profit but that he bought it at all!"[48]

The next day the *State Journal* reported that the Petersons had purchased twenty-three lots at $17.40 each. The average price of the sold lots was $29.00, with some near the Petersons' going for as much as $35.00.

Romney had directed state attorney general Frank J. Kelley, a Democrat, to recommend what legal steps should be taken to protect the rights of "innocent purchasers, if any," and to recommend how the state could recover any losses.[49]

Democratic state party chairman Zolton Ferency added fuel to the fire by immediately calling for a special investigation to determine whether the Petersons had benefited personally. Romney promptly came to their defense, declaring that Ferency's "innuendos are made out of whole cloth. Not only is he guilty of dirty politics in trying to frame an attack on Mrs. Peterson through her husband, but he is also guilty of questionable political judgment."

In the same UPI story, Peterson said, "To attack my husband's integrity is to attack me where I am extremely vulnerable—any woman can understand that."[50]

McClaughry remembered meeting at the Petersons' home over the weekend to deal with the crisis. He recalled that it was one of those " 'you bought a what?' moments in a marriage." Elly, he recalled, was "mightily embarrassed by the episode." And while everyone agreed the transaction was newsworthy only because she was a candidate, the campaign was "certainly in panic mode that Sunday morning."[51]

Peterson called a press conference to declare that her husband "was an innocent purchaser in no way involved in any of the illegalities or irregularities." Five years earlier, Pete had submitted a sealed bid of four hundred dollars for the lots, "totaling 1.26 acres of rather marshy" land. "No one solicited his bid. No one suggested how much he should offer. No one gave him any information about any property or procedures unknown to other officers and enlisted men of the Guard or to many residents of the Grayling area."

She added, "Obviously the Democratic leaders, speaking through their state chairman, singled out my husband from hundreds of others for only one reason—gutter politics. Their techniques have even included news commentaries reporting that my husband was one of the three officers dismissed by Gov. Romney. . . .What my husband did was honest, fair and in the open—which is more than I can say for my opponents in this affair."

When she undertook her race, she said, "I did not count on seeing rotten politicians attempt to ruin my husband's career. That is a price I will not pay. My husband is an honest man who can stand proudly on his long and honorable record as a soldier and who can weather all the lies and slime you can sling at him. And as for me, I am going to continue to hammer at my opponent's record in office."[52]

For his part, Hart forcefully declined to make an issue of the land sale. After Peterson's press conference, he went before reporters to declare, "I have said nothing about it because—except for what I have read in the papers—I know nothing about it. Politically, Mrs. Peterson and I are in sharp disagreement. . . . But at no time in this campaign have I questioned her integrity and I don't intend to."[53] Another story noted that Hart and Peterson had recently crossed paths in Detroit, but "the lot purchase was not brought up." In fact, Hart's press conference, the story said, marked the first time he had mentioned Peterson by name at a campaign appearance.[54]

The press conferences seemed to have the desired effect. The *Jackson Citizen Patriot*, for one, editorialized that Ferency's attack "stands out as a particularly disgusting bit of mud-slinging."[55]

As the land-sale story broke, UPI observed that it "came at a crucial time for Mrs. Peterson in a state where Republicans are split into two camps." Peterson, it noted, "was naturally considered an underdog" against Hart, "but her vigorous campaign gave signs she had been making headway in the battle. A row now involving the Peterson name, however innocently, could be a telling blow."[56] But the *Citizen Patriot* editorial asserted, "In the final analysis, we doubt that Mrs. Peterson's cause will be hurt. Although they like hard-hitting politics, most voters are repelled by unwarranted smears."[57]

In her memoir, Peterson wrote, "The story never really was cleared up properly and for weeks afterwards people would sidle up to me and ask, 'Say how much DID Pete make on that property?' "[58]

The imbroglio ultimately didn't change the outcome of the race, but its precise impact is unclear. Within a week, Lowell reported that the Peterson campaign was "apparently convinced that the furor . . . is dying down as fast as it started," mostly because of Romney's continued support and Hart's refusal to make it an issue.

The same story reported on a two-day swing to the Upper Peninsula, Peterson's first in the campaign. Her aides noted that "in her work within the Republican ranks she spent more time north of the Lower Peninsula than any GOP official in years" and that "the friendships she has developed created a hardy core of backers that give her a running start in the area."[59]

As the campaigns slogged to their conclusion, Romney came under direct fire from Republicans who complained that he was distancing himself from the rest of his ticket. The complaints broke into the headlines after an October 17 tour of St. Clair County by the "GOP team"—twenty or so candidates, including Peterson. At parades in seven communities, Romney marched alone at the front of the parade, and at four of the stops he was the only candidate to speak. In her memoir, Peterson wrote that "Romney, for some reason, did not acknowledge even one Republican in the crowd. The Secretary of State candidate was furious, but so were the press men traveling with me that day as they knew how hard I had been working."[60]

The UPI reporter covering the event said that "after questions had been raised," Romney agreed to share the rostrum with Peterson and U.S. Rep. James Harvey. As Romney tried to introduce another local candidate, an argument broke out over his access to the microphone.[61] The next day, Romney took issue with the story, contending there was not enough time for all candidates to speak.[62]

After that, the Peterson campaign decided to take what little money it had for television and get Romney to tape an ad. Peterson recalled:

> We went to the studio, and he was in a hurry, tired and out of humor. He kept telling everyone to hurry it along. He did not like to repeat the lines, and he didn't want to be kept waiting while they rehearsed me. A fly appeared and came buzzing around, creating more trouble for the camera crew and that did it. He turned to me and said, "I don't care where that fly goes. Ignore it and let's get it over." Intimidated, I started on my speech, with the cameras rolling, and the fly crawled across my forehead. I did not twitch, I did not falter. I gave those lines perfectly with that fly crawling near my nose. I was THAT afraid of George Romney. He had spoken! I was only grateful the damned fly didn't crawl into my mouth!! Well, it broke up the crew, and I must confess it broke up George Romney, too, when he saw the re-run.

Eventually, she completed a good take.[63]

There was another, more sinister concern. Over time, the Peterson campaign had been receiving postcards that were, in Peterson's words, "mean, vituperative, anti-women." Powers intercepted them before her friend could see them. But by the end of the campaign, the messages became threatening enough that they decided to notify the police. It turned out they were sent by a four-hundred-pound man from a small town in central Michigan who lived over a store and retrieved his food and mail by dropping a basket out his window. When the police asked him why he hated Peterson so much, he replied that the postcards simply gave him something to do.[64]

Election Day dawned with "a continued run of beautiful autumn weather," the *State Journal* noted, but "even the Republicans didn't make too many claims about the chances of Elly Peterson."[65]

Peterson voted in Charlotte, then Harold and Ruth Frank, friends from Detroit, hosted the campaign staff for dinner before they headed to the Statler-Hilton to await the returns. The campaign maintained its sense of humor up to the end: posted on the Franks' front door was an oversized photo of Peterson with the fly on her nose.

When the votes were tallied, Peterson lost by a margin of nearly two to one. But with a campaign budget of only seventy-five thousand dollars, she still managed to attract nearly 1.1 million votes. And she had two "great consolations": Romney defeated his opponent, Neil Staebler, by more than 380,000 votes, and she garnered more votes than Goldwater did. Considering the money that the presidential campaign had poured into the state, not to mention staffing a headquarters in every county, "we felt that was an accomplishment."[66]

One Romney biographer wrote of the governor's victory:

> That kind of showing in the middle of a Republican catastrophe is not easy to explain in terms of campaign techniques, though he improved them, or a two-year record, through he had a solid one. Something else was going on. A clue may be found in some of the dull projects that bored capitol reporters but made news in the neighborhood papers and on 40 Michigan radio stations. He had worked, as he promised on the '62 campaign trail, at the clumsy business of giving many more people a say-so in government.[67]

And, arguably, the WACs and programs like Peterson's "A Better Citizen" initiative had been important, if not fully appreciated, contributors to that.

Coverage of the results noted that Peterson "was well known among the party professionals as something of an organizational genius" but "a major blow to [her] hopes of gaining public recognition was the prolonged [newspaper] strike.... This, she admitted, hurt her campaign to an incalculable degree by virtually cutting off the most effective means of getting her views on the issues presented to the state's most heavily-populated area."[68]

Peterson conceded defeat about 11:30 p.m. In her speech, she blamed the Johnson landslide.[69]

Looking back, Lowell recalled, "She went a long ways toward legitimizing a serious role for women in politics generally in Michigan. It could have been a throwaway, stupid campaign, but it wasn't. A lot of serious political professionals, both Democrats and Republicans, were not expecting much, but came away impressed." Lowell said he talked to Democrats who had thought the campaign would be "a joke," but "they felt very differently by the end."[70]

"She couldn't overcome the head of the ticket," Molin noted. "But she could keep attention focused on herself and her role. She was a sacrificial lamb, and everybody knew that." Molin said Peterson's closest friends didn't want her to run "because nobody should have to go through that." But she did, he concluded, because she felt a strong "call to service."[71]

Added DeVries, offering the perspective of the Romney staff, "Elly did the job she was supposed to and ran a positive, issue-oriented campaign. ... She did so much better than people thought, not in terms of the result, but in terms of the way the campaign was conducted. ... She didn't want to do it ... but in many ways it sort of set her up for life in the Republican Party, in Michigan as well as nationally, in terms of the kind of campaign she ran."[72]

Romney's victory gave the Peterson team something to celebrate that night. But, she recalled, "The sad part was the devastation of the rest of the elective offices. We lost five Congressmen in our Michigan delegation, as well as control of both houses of the State legislature, all the educational posts, Supreme Court seats and many county races. It was a holocaust, leaving the party about a quarter of a million dollars in debt."[73]

She had succeeded in getting Romney reelected, but she vowed she would never again be a candidate. "It was grim, it was difficult, and it was heart breaking. Worse, it was degrading. You knew from the beginning you could not win but you could never let your troops know that."[74]

Years later, she recalled, "I could ask anybody to vote for you, and if they turned me down, it didn't bother me. But it was very embarrassing for me to have to go into a restaurant and interrupt people when they were eating, ride the train and shake hands with people who were trying to read their morning paper, half of whom didn't know what the heck I was talking about." She also hated having to grovel for financial support that she felt had been promised.[75]

Molin noted, "You have to have more ego than Elly Peterson has, or a different kind of ego than Elly Peterson has, if you're going to be a candidate."

Nevertheless, he said, "she loved to campaign for people. When you listen[ed] to her campaign for George Romney, or Bill Milliken, or Nelson Rockefeller or whomever it [might] happen to be . . . there was a kind of an excitement and an enthusiasm that was almost contagious. When you heard her campaigning for herself, it was quite obligatory, always quite proper, again she was always the lady."[76]

In McClaughry's assessment, "She was not a natural candidate. Her natural role was a leader and organizer. There are some people who are 'face people,' . . . who go to campaigning like a fish to water. And Elly was really the organizer, an extremely valuable commodity, by the way."[77]

"I have no regrets now at having been in that campaign," Peterson wrote in her memoir. "However, its bitterness left many scars. As for me, I presumed I had wound up my political career."[78]

On Election Night, she told a reporter, "I guess I'll go back to work with the troops—in the precincts where they need me." Asked if she would run for state party vice chairman again, she replied that she would not. "I'm a firm believer in the policy that the old ought to move out and make room for the new. That's what has been wrong with this party at times."[79]

## CHAPTER FIVE

# The Click Moment

THE MORNING AFTER ELECTION NIGHT, Peterson woke up without a race to run or a job to do for the first time in seven years. It had been more than a year since she had lived anything close to a normal life in Charlotte. But she was fifty now and didn't want to return to her old organizational work. She had made up her mind that in her political career "what came, came."[1]

But what she needed first was a break. So she hit the road with her sister, traveling to New Jersey for the wedding of Mary's son and then to the Virgin Islands before meeting up with Pete in Florida for Christmas. They decided to buy an apartment in Sarasota, which she thought she might finally have time to enjoy.[2]

Back in Michigan, however, Republicans were already pointing fingers. Within a week of the November debacle, state chairman Art Elliott called a meeting of local chairmen. Romney asked them to speak up about their complaints. Knowing that Romney and Elliott were close friends, they didn't offer any. Romney left the meeting, telling reporters, "Art Elliott has done an outstanding job under very difficult circumstances."[3]

The Petersons returned after the holidays. The State Central Committee meeting was scheduled for mid-January at the Jack Tar Hotel in Lansing, and Elly and Joyce Braithwaite decided they "ought to go for laughs, attend the cocktail party and see what was going on."[4]

The day committee members were gathering, Romney announced that Peterson would become his special assistant. Peterson did not mention the job in her memoir, but news accounts described it as a part-time post, off the state payroll, handling Romney's "national correspondence and related matters" now that his reputation was growing beyond Michigan.[5]

Peterson and Braithwaite attended the cocktail party as planned and then stopped by the ladies' room. When they came out, they encountered two reporters, James Brooks of UPI and Robert Longstaff of Booth Newspapers. "They asked if I had heard that the state chairman would be dumped and that I would be the new state chairman," Peterson recalled in her memoir. "Again, I came up with my stock phrase in moments of stress—'You are out of your mind!'"[6]

But, in fact, the reporters were serious. Emil Lockwood, the Republican Senate leader, had told them that unless Romney gave Elliott a "clear-cut endorsement" he would push to elect Peterson instead. "I have nothing against Art Elliott," Lockwood told the reporters. "But I think Elly would be a tremendous asset. The Republican Party needs to get certain groups behind it, and if we had a woman chairman, we'd get the women behind us—and they outnumber the men in Michigan now."[7]

Peterson dismissed the idea. She had a nightcap with friends, then retired to her hotel room. But unbeknownst to her, "a steady trek of party leaders" had called on Lieutenant Governor William Milliken the previous afternoon, seeking a new chairman. After Milliken had heard from enough of them, he called Romney. They then began phoning Republicans around the state, phone calls that continued into the night.

As Braithwaite-Brickley recalled it, Peterson "went to bed about 10 (as was her wont) while I stayed up until about 3 (as was mine). I found it all incredibly interesting, and after midnight I began to hear 'gossip' about the idea of dumping" Elliott for Peterson. "This idea and the talk surrounding it kept increasing as the night wore on. I went to our room after midnight, woke her, and told her of it. She was astounded, told me that it had to be just talk, that it seemed like nonsense to her."

Braithwaite-Brickley observed, "There are those who say that Elly had some advance notice of Romney's intention to promote her for chairman. I don't believe that to be true."[8]

Peterson recalled telling Braithwaite, "George Romney is not going to have a woman state chairman" because the party's finance men would block it. Not a single state party had a woman chairman, and RNC chairman Ray Bliss did not even let women attend his state chairmen's meetings as proxies. Peterson protested, "I can't raise money, I was never any good at raising money."[9] But early in the morning, her phone rang. It was Romney, calling from his office across the street, asking her to come over.

Pete used to tease his wife that he could always tell when the governor was on the phone because her casual voice would be transformed into a clip of "Yes, sirs" and "No, sirs." "If George said, 'jump,'" he used to tell her, "you would ask, 'how far?'"[10]

"I don't know how I got dressed," Peterson recalled, "or how I got my lipstick on, but all of a sudden, I knew the whole story was true. I knew he was going to ask me to be State Chairman and I panicked."[11]

Romney, she believed, "was a little more than irked" that party leaders had not spoken their minds two months earlier. "I think this meeting was all too typical of many held with those who worked for and with him. They were too afraid to speak their minds for fear they would be in opposition to him and incur his wrath. . . . So they waited and took their story to Lt. Gov. Milliken and, like many things in politics, it just grew."[12]

The episode was, in the words of biographer D. Duane Angel, one of Romney's "more serious political transgressions," an episode made all the more awkward because he had just appointed Peterson to another job.[13]

In an early story, Peterson told the *State Journal*, "I won't say I wouldn't consider this—but I would assume I won't run for state chairman." It would be, she added, "a tremendous undertaking for a woman to run for that. It's a very difficult job—and is it a job for a woman?"[14]

But when Romney offered the job, she did not hesitate to accept.

From then on, she recalled, "things happened fast." Elliott agreed to resign. At a hastily called press conference, he said he was stepping down out of concern for "my family, my business and my future." And Romney announced he would endorse Peterson at the state convention in February. He said he had made his decision Friday night, unaware of Lockwood's own "draft Peterson" movement.[15]

By afternoon, she and Braithwaite were headed back to Charlotte, with Pete still in the dark about her new job. Braithwaite, she recalled, "made some comment en route home about how strange it all was, . . . that 24 hours ago we had not even dreamed of this and now I was going to be state chairman. My comment to her was, 'Yes, and remember this, Joyce, we may be on top now but two years from now, you and I may be driving down this road and we will be the ones who have been shafted!'"[16]

Peterson was clearly humbled by the prospect of being the first woman to serve as a state party chair. She had no role models to follow. Later political scientists noted that Mary Norton, a Democratic congresswoman from New Jersey, had served as her state's party chair in the 1930s and 1940s, but Peterson was the first Republican and commentators viewed her as a groundbreaking pioneer.[17] An "exclusive interview" with the local Associated Press reporter was carried by newspapers as far away as California, Florida and South Carolina.[18]

One reporter wrote, "Many Republican leaders from Gov. Romney on down hope State Chairman–apparent Elly Peterson can present a better party image to the public and its workers than has outgoing chairman Arthur Elliott. . . . A prominent Democrat said Mrs. Peterson. . . 'ought to give the organization some fire.'"[19]

Reporters made clear that Peterson was already a well-regarded political professional, even as they still described her physical appearance and personal charms. One said she was "a silver haired, blue eyed, let's get-down-to-business type who is matronly enough to appeal to women and quick-witted enough to keep men's attention."[20]

Another article said she was "an attractive, sharp-witted party veteran with a reputation as an organizational expert and tireless worker." She was "a woman with determination," who was "astute, politically knowledgeable and has a delightful knack of getting along with people—both men and women. They admire her and they respect her. And more importantly, they like her. She's an adept strategist. She's an idea gal. And when she gets an idea she acts. She makes decisions and then sees to it that the project gets done."[21]

A profile in the Toledo *Blade Sunday Magazine* that spring described her as "an extremely feminine, yet businesslike woman. . . . A friendly, down-to-earth woman, a devoted wife, relaxed hostess, and capable executive."[22] Another story described her as "a no-nonsense political veteran who looks deceptively like a Hoskinson lady," a reference to an archetypical *New Yorker* cartoon matron.[23]

Among those quoted was Democratic Chairman Ferency, who only three months before had been the subject of a blistering attack by candidate Peterson. A reporter wrote:

Ferency probably got his relationship with . . . Peterson . . . off on exactly the wrong foot when he described her as "an old political warhorse covered with a lot of battle scars from political infighting. She'll be able to take care of herself in this job."

Asked if he wasn't being a little indelicate in his description of the attractive Mrs. Peterson, Ferency said, "Oh, no! She's not asking for any quarter. She's getting into a man's game."

"I have a high regard for Elly. She is well qualified for her job."[24]

DeVries recalled of Peterson's rise, "Prior to that time, [women] served coffee, they took notes, they cleaned up the office, they did the phone banks and all that kind of stuff. But they were never really an integral part of any sort of . . . campaign strategy apparatus. She was the first, and because she was so good, I think it made it possible for others to do it. . . . She just blazed a whole new trail."[25]

Arny Levin was one person who remembered Peterson from her days as the secretary, when she "learned how to con the electric people into believing that the check had been in the mail for three months."[26]

"She just set out to do what she wanted to do," he said. "I don't think she had in her mind that one day she was going to be Republican chairman. There were just a series of steps that let her step into the breach. And she had an awful lot of friends. A lot of people admired her. All of it put together made a compelling modus vivendi."[27]

Peterson continued working part time for Romney until the state convention. The gathering should have been the high point of her career—at least up until then. Instead, it produced what she recalled as her "click moment," that episode in a woman's life that first awakens her feminist consciousness.[28]

"Over and over again, it was emphasized to me that I was the only person who could 'lead the party out of the wilderness,'" Peterson wrote in her memoir. "'This is the time when your organizational skills and your knowledge of Michigan Republicans can be of utmost value.'"[29]

But as she was about to go onstage to accept the chairmanship, she was stunned when Max Fisher "came up to congratulate me—then added: 'But of course, we can't pay you what we paid Art—you are a woman.'"[30] He told her she would be paid only fifteen thousand dollars; Elliott had earned six thousand more.

Peterson did not dwell on the episode in her memoir, but it continued to rankle for the rest of her life. "How dare they think I'm supposed to save the party!" she said in a later interview, "they lost everything in 1964. They are the ones who thought I could do it, but I'm not worth the money because I'm a woman. And I think that really was the first time I began to observe things of that kind, it bugged me and it bugs me to this day when they put women down like that."[31]

She also wrote, "Then and there I realized women needed more help than the Republican Party! I thought it very strange that men all felt I was vital to the cause—but not worth any more money—and my thoughts more and more went to encouraging women to be active in all roles. I was, I guess, a 'born again feminist.'"[32]

Margie Cooke, then running to become the first female vice chair of the Michigan Federation of College Republicans, had been drafted to introduce Peterson. Cooke has vivid memories of the night because her mother had come to hear her speak. Cooke recalled that "after Elly won the nomination, there was a bit of a pause and some bustling around, on stage and off. I was sitting on stage but was given no signal to move to the podium. In fact, I was told a couple of times to wait as Elly wasn't ready. Then after several minutes, Elly walked on stage without introduction or fanfare. Everyone stood up and cheered and she gave her speech." No one, Cooke realized, thought anything was amiss, except for her mother, who wondered what had happened to her daughter's introduction.[33]

Backstage, Peterson was forced to think fast. She acknowledged that she "thought about crying" but in the end came up a clever twist of her own.[34] She went out on the stage, and brought the delegates to their feet with what press accounts described as an "emotional plea for party unity." "Let's grow up and become completely realistic," she said. "We're going to need complete teamwork for a complete victory in 1966—and we have to remember that our only goal is to win."[35]

Then she noted that after their recent losses, the party was $250,000 in debt. So she said she would contribute $6,000 of her salary, "and I expect you folks to do the same."

Of course, she wasn't contributing real money. "I never would have gotten" that salary, she later said. "I thought it was sort of outsmarting the old guy that told me that."[36] She recalled that she would have liked to have her women "pass the hat," but knowing how strapped many of them were, she instead asked everyone to contribute at least ten dollars. Romney "started the ball rolling by giving me $100."[37]

The press fell for her story, as did Bill McLaughlin, who was elected vice chair. In his memoir, he said, "Elly returned $6,000 to emphasize our tough financial position."[38]

Ever the good trooper, Peterson did not go public with her anger. Other political contemporaries never knew the backstage story; nor did she name Fisher until late in life.[39] Braithwaite-Brickley recalled that Peterson shared her emotions with her, "but not to Max. She smiled to Max, accepted gracefully and set about to do her job. It was a disgusting thing that he did, a power play, [a] child's play and it was very small."[40]

Within a few days, Peterson announced that Fisher and Don Ahrens, who had chaired the Republican State Finance Committee since the 1950s, would become "honorary chairmen" and Harold McClure Jr. and Wendell Anderson Jr. would replace them.[41]

As she took charge, the party's right wing was still rumbling, and the concerns of African Americans were moving to center stage. In her first major interview as party chairman, she was asked whether "right-wing extremists are a problem for the Republicans." She replied:

> I cannot state the extent to which this class of people is willing to go. Many of them are sincere people who have a great concern for their country, and this is their way of expressing it. I hope we can somehow reach through to them that this is not the broadest sense of the Republican Party, and that we simply cannot be permitted to have a party of exclusion.
>
> If they are willing to come in and be with us, a party of inclusion, then they are welcome. But they must be willing to subscribe to our general principles.

There was still some expectation that Michigan Republicans could attract a significant share of the African American vote. When asked how her party would "communicate with the Negro," Peterson replied:

> When we speak integration, we must mean it in the fullest sense. That means going into the block clubs and the neighborhoods. We have never been as good as the Democrats at this. We haven't developed fully the people to do this.
>
> We Republicans have traditionally run the good part of our affairs through the area of clubs which were more or less exclusive. I think we have taken great steps and strides to change that within the past six years, but I don't think we have gone far enough.

Finally, asked about the challenges she would face as a woman, she replied:

> The unique problem is that there are male meetings, for example, the state chairmen's national meeting. But there aren't many problems that can't be solved. Women should be active in politics and seek the status elective posts. To me, there's nothing more exciting in life than a campaign. I can't understand why more women aren't doing the same thing.[42]

The first hurdle Peterson faced was the party's "money men." She recalled, "Before I became State Chairman, women had not been included in the top finance meetings, but here I was, the State Chairman, and I had to make the report and tell the story so the door had to be opened." Max Fisher told her the Finance Committee was going to have lunch at the Detroit Athletic Club, which was then closed to women, and that she "could go down and have lunch in the basement with his secretary." She recalled, "I quietly replied that I would walk out and go home if I wasn't to be a full and equal participant."[43]

McClure stepped in, made arrangements so that women could enter the club, and invited several other women to attend the historic occasion. Peterson recalled that he ended his remarks by encouraging the women to "take your shoes off, relax, and sit back knowing you are welcome."

Peterson responded: "Obviously it is good that women are finally here." Then she couldn't resist adding: "But apparently Harold does not know it is not our shoes we take off when we want to relax! . . ."[44]

DeVries recalled, "She had to compete with all those men to start with, the smoke-filled rooms, and for most of the people in there, dealing with a woman at that level was new." Although he noted that the male Con-Con delegates had worked with women as political peers, "It's hard to remember how backward we were even back then."[45]

As historian Sara M. Evans observed:

> It is startling to realize that in the early 1960s married women could not borrow money in their own names, professional and graduate schools regularly imposed quotas of 5–10 percent or even less on the numbers of women they would admit, union contracts frequently had separate seniority lists for women and men, and sexual

harassment did not exist as a legal concept. It was perfectly legal to pay women and men differently for exactly the same job and to advertise jobs separately: "Help Wanted—Men" and "Help Wanted—Women."[46]

The next barrier Peterson faced was the Republican State Chairmen's Association. At the first meeting, Peterson recalled that every time RNC chairman Ray Bliss swore, he would say "Excuse me." Finally, she said, "Ray, let's knock it off. My husband's in the Army. I know probably more words than you know." She made sure to stay "in the background" at her first meeting.[47]

But she quickly forged good relationships with several of her male peers, particularly midwesterners like Robert Ray of Iowa and John Andrews, the new Ohio party chair. "Just forget the color of my dress and my earrings and I'm like any other party chairman in the country," she told one reporter. It would be a full two years before another woman, Lorraine Orr of Nebraska, joined the group.[48]

Meanwhile, back in Michigan, she began building her own team. Within a few weeks, she decided she wanted to hire Braithwaite, who was then working as a secretary to Bill Bishop, manager of the State Accident Fund. Braithwaite was separated from her husband, and "with two small boys, it was a very frightening time for me. I was unsure. I was in no position to gamble with my work."

Peterson met privately with Bishop to talk about Braithwaite's future. Afterward he told Braithwaite that if she wanted to try it he would hold her job open in case she changed her mind. "Wow," Braithwaite-Brickley recalled, "I was gone in a flash."

On her very first day as Peterson's administrative assistant, she said, "I learned that things were going to be different from anything I'd done before. . . . The very first hour with Elly, I was in her office and she began to dictate things to me which needed to be done, and she didn't stop for about 8 HOURS. I'd never seen so much work in my life."[49]

Braithwaite began traveling with Peterson, particularly on weekends when her sons were visiting their father. "How wonderful it was to go," she recalled. "I began to meet her friends around the state, to see ways in which I might be helpful to her. She hated driving. I loved driving. So I drove most of the miles we traveled, all over the state, from one end to the other, her giving her grand and inspiring speeches, me soaking it all up."[50]

Braithwaite soon told a reporter that working with Peterson was "like working in the eye of a hurricane. It's lots of excitement, fun and gives you a worthwhile feeling."[51]

Braithwaite-Brickley believes that politics cannot be taught, that "you're either blessed with an understanding and affinity for it or not." As it turned out, she had the knack, and went on to serve as appointments director and chief political liaison for Governor Milliken. But she recalled her time with Peterson as "the best experience of my life . . . the best and most productive time ever."[52]

In June, Peterson offered McLaughlin a full-time job as executive vice chairman at twelve thousand dollars a year. The salary, McLaughlin noted, was substantially more than he had earned as director of publicity and advertising for the Cinerama Theater in Detroit and was "extremely generous," particularly in light of Peterson's salary cut.

His new boss, he learned, "knew everyone and had the special gift of being able to remember faces and names. . . . She was a terrific public speaker with a deep, booming voice that always was upbeat, hopeful and cheery."

McLaughlin began driving nearly 180 miles round trip from St. Clair Shores to Lansing every day, working "seven days a week and usually five nights." Never, he said, "have I seen a team so motivated." He gave speeches—"it seems like I gave a speech a day"—sometimes to four hundred people, sometimes to "two, three or four." But, he added, "I stayed pumped. No matter how large or how small the crowd, each speech was a performance, each performance part of the crusade."[53]

Jerry Roe was hired as director of organization and Molin as an organizer in the Upper Peninsula. "You always knew when Elly was upset, but that was not necessarily a death sentence," Molin recalled. "She'd put her 'Mother' voice on—firm, articulate. No twinkle, no laugh. Instructive, not abusive."

Referring to Peterson's staff "kids," he noted, "the one thing we were determined not to let happen was to disappoint her. . . . She let her 'kids' have a good time. But she never let her 'kids' lose sight of the mission."[54]

Margie Cooke first worked for Peterson as a summer intern, doing research on state legislative races: "She didn't suffer fools gladly. . . . She just seemed to find good people, and she seemed to always have room for what you wanted to do. If you were interested in working hard, then she was interested in working for you. The people who wanted glory without putting in the work didn't last long."[55]

In her first weeks as chairman, Peterson attended twenty-seven Lincoln Day dinners. She and Braithwaite drove sixty thousand miles across the state in the first year, and Peterson flew thousands more to meetings and speeches around the country. (Racing once to a speech a few hours away, she and Braithwaite managed to take a car from a parking lot attendant and drive it twenty miles before realizing it wasn't theirs.)[56]

"There was much unhappiness left over from the Goldwater-Romney campaigns," she wrote, "and we first had to raise some money to pay off the debts. I had to be tough to the workers around the state, and I made [it] clear (to paraphrase Winston Churchill) that I had not become Chairman to preside over the liquidation of the Republican party. I figured they either got the picture and helped or there was little we could do."[57]

Recalled DeVries from the vantage point of the governor's office, "It was always, 'If you can't get anyone else to do it, Elly will do it.' . . . And not just clerical stuff. It was telling the county chairman or somebody else that what they were doing was wrong and 'you have to change it.' Or telling a contributor, or tough stuff like that that typically men did and women wouldn't do. She would do it and she would get it done and usually done in the right way."[58]

One of the first major things the staff organized was ten dinners across the state on the same night, featuring prominent Republicans. Conceptually, it was similar to the nationwide dinners that Peterson had been a part of at the RNC. Ten top Republicans, including Rockefeller, accepted invitations to speak. But, Peterson recalled, one did not. Ronald Reagan was then making speeches as a warm-up to running for governor of California. "He would come only if he got a big percentage of the take or $20,000 flat," Peterson recalled. "He didn't come. We didn't want him. Overnight we paid off a big sum."[59]

During these years, Peterson had ample opportunity to hone her speaking skills and provide whatever the occasion required—be it inspiration, humor, or simply to stand up and sit down quickly. Having listened to "too many awful speakers" herself, she recognized the importance of training potential candidates in the art.

George and Lenore Romney were "skilled speakers," Peterson recalled, "but sometimes they didn't know when to quit." "Even a simple introduction should require some time and thought," she wrote in her memoir, "and not just the dull reading of biographical data, as if it were an obituary."[60]

Braithwaite-Brickley recalled Peterson's "searing eloquence. She dealt in reality but had a way of making an audience laugh along the way. But in the end, she really came back on point and slammed an audience. . . . She wasn't the delicate type. I think this made her lightness, followed by powerful instructions, all the more powerful."[61]

Over the course of her speech making, Peterson developed favorite themes and metaphors. "I find it easy to understand why our party is having so much trouble attracting independent and disillusioned Democrats," she told the Berrien County GOP committee in January 1966. "It's because we're so cotton-picking busy tearing down our house from the inside that we haven't time [to see] who might be at the front door wanting to come in."[62]

She was introduced so many times that by the end of her career she had developed a set speech built largely on anecdotes of her introductions. In her memoir, she recalled giving a speech at a men's club when she and her sister were the only women present. The emcee turned to her and said, "And now, Mrs. Peterson, we hope you will not give us your bra speech as that only covers two points but instead launch into your girdle speech as that covers everything!"

At a women's club luncheon, the president turned to her and asked, "Elly, do you want to speak now or let them enjoy their luncheon a little longer?" At a meeting of a Young Republicans club, the membership chairman preceded her remarks with a rousing sales pitch that concluded, "And if we get more members, we can get better speakers!"

In Kansas, an emcee wound up by saying, "And I give you the BIGGEST woman in the Republican Party, Elly Peterson." At a Rotary Club function, a district chairman summed up by saying, "Why, there isn't a man in this audience who isn't familiar with her!"

A favorite introduction was provided by her good friend Wendell Hobbs, party chairman in the Second Congressional District around Ann Arbor, who said, "There goes one of the finest women that ever walked the streets!" The audience laughed, and Hobbs apologized, but Peterson was quick to reply that "It's the nicest thing said about me lately." She incorporated the quote into the title of her lengthiest memoir.

Peterson was not one to quote poetry, but she liked to use a particular poem at women's gatherings, where, she said, "it never failed to get a laugh," particularly among party vice chairmen.

I'm not allowed to run the train
Or see how fast twill go.
I ain't allowed to let off steam
Or make the whistle blow.
I cannot exercise control
Or even ring the bell
But let the damned thing jump the track
And see who catches hell![63]

Molin recalled that no matter where she traveled Peterson tried to connect with the county chairman, always a man in those days. He recalled traveling through Schoolcraft County with Peterson when she decided she wanted to say hello to its party chairman, Charles Varnum. "If she would ask somebody, 'You know where I would find Mr. Varnum?' she'd never say, 'Well, I'm the Republican state chair.' She'd just say, 'Well, I'm a friend of his from Lansing and I was passing through town and I just thought that maybe I would try and say hello to him.' "[64]

By the time Cooke graduated from Michigan State, a College Republican chapter had been organized on every major campus. Peterson, she said, "treated us like we were important. We didn't always deserve it." If Peterson had a few extra tickets for a hundred-dollar-a-plate dinner, she would pass them along to the students. If the students needed a ream of paper for their annual convention, they knew Peterson would look the other way if they raided the supply at party headquarters.[65]

In her first six months as party chair, Peterson engaged in a behind-the-scenes battle to keep the leadership of the 8,500-member Republican Women's Federation of Michigan in the hands of moderates who supported party unity. At stake was the role the federation would play in the next presidential election; the battle amounted to an early test of a broader national strategy that moderates like Peterson were pursuing against conservative activist Phyllis Schlafly. And as a newspaper observed afterward, the Michigan women "proved that moderates can win this kind of intra-party fight."[66]

"Angry charges and denials of ballot rigging, illegal procedures and stacking the convention are flying between member clubs," the *Detroit Free Press's* political reporter observed as the federation convention approached in September. "The dispute was touched off by women who feel federation leadership is ingrown, unrepresentative, and harmful to the party cause. In large measure, it is part of a continuing feud between conservatives and moderates."

Seven years earlier, as a more junior party employee, Peterson had been more circumspect about meddling in federation activities. But now the stakes were higher. Realtor Ruth Hobbs, the Republican state chairman of women's activities, had agreed to oppose Bernice Zilly for the federation's presidency. Zilly, a former president of the Grosse Pointe Republican Women's Club, was a longtime friend and supporter of Richard Durant, the ultraconservative chair of the Fourteenth Congressional District.

Zilly was actually the choice of the federation's Nominating Committee, but Peterson and Hobbs did not want her in charge of an organization that would be called on to support Romney's 1966 reelection campaign. "Peterson, who might be expected to wave a neutral flag under ordinary circumstances, makes no bones about her support" for Hobbs, the *Free Press* observed.[67]

Peterson did not mention the battle in her memoir, but in a memo to moderate allies across the country, she described what happened. She acknowledged strategic advice she had received from California leaders, then went on:

> The battle was vicious with the opposition slate standing in the lobby of the hotel with two cries—"All liberal Republicans are Communists so all on the Hobbs slate are Communists" and "This is your opportunity to beat George Romney!". . .
>
> That they attacked me was an obvious ploy. Their theme that I was taking over the Federation and that State Central wanted to run it was naturally expected.
>
> I think the part that struck terror in my heart was the obvious hatred on the faces of about twenty women. Since they controlled the machinery of the Convention, they ran roughshod over many people and things—it was only by the sheer weight of numbers that we could keep the thing in control. The parliamentarian ruled for us on many occasions, and the President refused to take a vote. This had the effect of cementing our own forces and bringing some others into the fold. However, during the middle of the night on Tuesday,

the President met with a few women and decided they would abandon the Convention rules and let anyone vote. . . . By 10 a.m. on Wednesday morning, we had 16 counts of fraud or irregularities completely documented. The choice we had to make was whether to try to win with our gals or declare the election illegal. We decided to go for broke.

The ensuing balloting was, Peterson wrote, "the longest three hours of my life." In the end, her forces won by a vote of 150 to 99.

Among the tense moments was a challenge to the candidacy of Dovie Pickett, a "quiet, retiring" African American from Detroit, because she was a member of the paid staff of the Wayne County GOP district office. "The candidate," Peterson wrote, "walked to the front and spoke quietly but magnificently about the fact that she had been a Republican all of her life and if she chose to give every moment of her free time to the party also, she didn't think it should be condemned." Pickett received a standing ovation, and was elected recording secretary. (Peterson noted that although there were about "850,000 Negroes" in the state, there were only about 10 in federation clubs.)[68]

In her luncheon address, Peterson played peacemaker:

I hope that if there is any unhappiness among you about the last two days that you will blame me and not the Federation which has done a wonderful job.

What we are accomplishing here will affect the future of our families and our way of life. We must be united (not that we all should think just exactly alike) in working together as Republicans against the Democrats.

Being a state chairman is not all beer and skittles. . . . It requires the patience of Job, the strength of Atlas and the wisdom of Socrates. I think I have the first two qualities, but the wisdom must come from all of you. And I never make any move before I consult with county chairmen.

I am tough-minded where my party is concerned and I intend to be.[69]

Afterward, Peterson wrote her moderate friends, "We swept the whole slate and since that time have had an influx of letters and phone calls of congratulations (even money) and a new spirit throughout the entire state. I am convinced that we were right, and we are beginning to gradually pick up the pieces of those who are saveable."[70]

Peterson apparently took some steps to wipe away any fingerprints that might have been left behind. She wrote Koeze that she had removed certain items from Koeze's "expense account for the Womens' Federation inasmuch as I have given my word that we were not charging anything to State Central in connection with this battle." After Koeze returned from a trip, she said, the two women could "figure out how to handle this."[71]

In the aftermath of the meeting, Peterson received several appreciative notes. One attendee said she would "always remember the way you conducted yourself. . . . You were planning such perfect strategy, making the right move at the right time, pre-counting the votes so accurately—all done in your lady like style."[72]

Art Elliott sent a telegram, congratulating her on "an important victory" and declaring, "I am proud of you."[73] Jim Hayes, secretary of the Michigan Bakers Association, called her "a courageous lady and an impressive leader." The entire effort, he wrote, "showed excellent pre-planning and astute on-the-scene generalship. . . . You put your career in jeopardy to wage the fight. Very few people (including me) would have the fortitude to do it. . . . In my association with Republican Party work, I've had the opportunity to watch three state chairmen at work. In my judgement, your victory over the 'bigots' is the most outstanding achievement recorded by any party leader that I have known."[74]

More personally, Ruth Hobbs wrote, "Talk about courage! It was strictly a team effort with you as the leader and probably would never have been attained if you weren't our state chairman. . . . You'll never know how very much I appreciate all you do for me."[75]

As the months passed, party leaders turned to identifying and recruiting strong candidates to run in 1966. Five Republican members of Congress had gone down to defeat in 1964, and the party had lost control of both chambers of the State Legislature. There was nowhere to go but up.

McLaughlin recalled:

I don't think there is a book on candidate recruitment—at least there wasn't one in 1965. . . . We first studied election statistics for all State House, State Senate, and Congressional races. This wasn't easy because the 1964 results were so non-typical because of the Goldwater rout. The precincts and the districts had changed since 1962. We studied and studied and eventually got a good handle on millions of figures.

Then we started looking for candidates. We pushed the local committees to find them. When we found them, we had to make a determination if they were good enough to win. Where there was more than one candidate, sometimes we decided who had the best chance to win. Then we did what we could to get that candidate the nomination. This was not always appreciated. Elly had the guts to say, "Do it." She wanted to win.

In the end, they targeted twenty districts in the state House (they needed a net gain of nineteen seats to take control). In the state Senate, they targeted five districts, needing all of them to gain the majority. For the U.S. Congress, they identified four districts where they believed incumbent Democrats could be defeated and four Republicans who they felt could do it—Marvin Esch, Philip Ruppe, Garry Brown, and Jack H. McDonald.

In a fifth district, the Seventh District, surrounding Flint, the twenty-eight-year-old son of the former mayor wanted to enter the race. Donald Riegle Jr., then a Republican, was fresh out of Harvard Business School but was so "very attractive and very persuasive," in McLaughlin's words, that his race was added to the priority list.

Congressman Robert Griffin emerged as the party's choice to run for the Senate. In April 1966, his campaign got a break when the Democratic incumbent, Patrick McNamara, died in office. Within two weeks, Romney appointed Griffin to fill the vacant seat, enabling him to run as an incumbent, albeit a short timer. He would have his work cut out for him, facing former Democratic governor G. Mennen "Soapy" Williams.

When the August 2 primary arrived, all the fresh young Republican recruits won their congressional primaries. "This wasn't easy," Peterson recalled. "We had to knock a few heads together . . . but we did what had to be done."[76]

Peterson had proposed that the party run a "United Republican Campaign," a concept that was foreign to Romney. Her reasoning was both practical ("to save on expenses" by operating out of a single campaign headquarters) and strategic ("to assist in pulling in some candidates" with

Romney and "to lay to rest once and for all the conversation 'he is a loner'").[77] Romney bought the plan, and the campaign's advertisements touted the "Action Team for the Action State," linking Romney, Milliken, running for re-election as lieutenant governor, and Griffin at the top of the ticket.

The day after the convention, party leaders were ready with a training session for all of the candidates. Field staff members were deployed to support the key congressional campaigns. Each Tuesday night top staff members met to coordinate campaign stops and advertising buys—and to help support the down-ticket candidates. The targeted races also received funding from both the state committee and the RNC—no more than ten to twenty thousand dollars from each, but still, McLaughlin recalled, "amounts unheard of at that time."[78]

College Republicans were put to work, particularly those who had learned how to do precinct work and raise money at a "campaign school" Peterson had organized the previous year.

Attention was also paid to ethnic groups. One-fifth of Michigan's population—more than 1.8 million persons—were thought to have strong immigrant ties, mostly to Europe, including 255,000 Poles and more than 100,000 Ukrainians.[79]

In 1962, Ilmar Heinaru, a young Holocaust survivor from Estonia, had volunteered to do whatever he could to help Romney win. "Until Ilmar came along," Peterson recalled, "the Republicans had never made such headway with ethnic groups." They had support in the Dutch communities in western Michigan "as they tended to be Republicans," but among the Poles and Italians around Detroit, they had "failed miserably." That began to change in 1962, when Heinaru quickly created twenty-seven ethnic groups in support of Romney and organized them into a Nationalities Council.

In 1966, Peterson launched "Operation Accent" with Heinaru's help. Each week about three hundred newly naturalized citizens received a personalized congratulatory message from the governor. In addition to learning that the state flower was the apple blossom and the state bird the robin, recipients were told, "The Republican Party was organized more than a century ago in a spontaneous revolt against the spread of slavery. Today, it remains the party of human freedom and equal justice." Political writers David Broder and Stephen Hess pointed to the initiative as a sign that "State Chairman Peterson knows her business."[80]

For Romney, there was even more at stake in the 1966 election. As Hess and Broder observed, "A candidate seeking the presidential nomination is not unlike Hercules performing his twelve labors. In 1966, Romney had two labors to perform." First, he had to "win big." Second, he had to hang onto Griffin's U.S. Senate seat and recapture at least some of the lost congressional districts.[81]

This time, Romney was willing to do what he had to. As Angel described it, Romney cast off "all independent garments" and "kissed every Republican in sight. He ignored his Democratic opponent and put his image on the line in behalf of almost every person on the GOP ticket, giving special attention to Robert Griffin. For the first time, Republicans spent more money than the Governor, who spent roughly $200,000." The Romney Girls became GOP Girls, and the campaign was run by a tight group of professionals instead of an army of volunteers.[82] Romney even put on elephant neckties.[83]

On the final weekend, Peterson, McLaughlin, and Braithwaite made a swing through all the campaign headquarters in Wayne County. The schedule for Saturday alone started at 9:00 a.m. and ended at 8:45, seventeen offices later. "It was a fabulous two days," McLaughlin recalled. "Every headquarters was as busy as a beehive. Spirits were high and Elly, so popular, was a magic tonic to the volunteers."[84]

On Election Day, the results were, in Romney's words, "sensational" and better than his "most optimistic expectations."[85] He won by a margin of more than 527,000 votes, the second-largest plurality in state history. Griffin won by nearly 300,000 votes to become the state's first elected Republican senator in fourteen years. The party captured all five of the targeted congressional seats, regained control of the state Senate, and achieved parity in the House. Among the notable successful Republican candidates that year was N. Lorraine Beebe of Dearborn, who had been recruited to run for the state Senate and, by a 908-vote margin, became only the third woman elected to that body. The Republicans also elected a state Supreme Court justice and captured all eight seats on the state Board of Education and the boards of the public universities.[86]

The morning after, a tired Peterson told a reporter, "I've been in election after election where we didn't win. This is the culmination of 10 years of my life. . . . I feel like Christmas came early this year."[87]

Braithwaite-Brickley remembered that Peterson was "the one who set the stage for . . . the sensational Republican blow-out" that year. "She'd envisioned it, and she made it happen. And I've never heard her take a moment of credit."[88]

United Press International credited Romney as "the engineer of a mammoth Republican landslide which catapulted him to the forefront of the GOP presidential picture." The reporter pointed in particular to the victory of Griffin, "a largely colorless Romney appointee who campaigned in Romney's bigger than Michigan shadow," over Williams, who was "as traditional to Michigan Democrats as cars are to Detroit."

Contrasting the campaign to the rout of 1964, the reporter wrote, "With the team victory behind him this time, the win left Romney at center stage in the presidential speculation drama."[89]

The *New York Times* agreed. Walter Rugaber wrote that Romney "had moved deeply into contention" for the 1968 GOP presidential nomination. The governor, he said, had to be able to carry along at least two or three other candidates. "In this," the reporter concluded, "he far exceeded everyone's expectations, including his own."[90]

# CHAPTER SIX

# Minding the Middle

WITH A SUCCESSFUL CAMPAIGN BEHIND HER, it was time for Peterson to turn her attention to another longtime goal: broadening the base of the Republican Party, especially in urban Detroit.

At mid-decade, that was not necessarily an impossible dream. A "Big City Committee" led by Bliss had called on the party to turn its attention to the cities. Between 1962 and 1966, Romney's support among black voters had, in fact, increased from 10 to 34 percent; in the most recent election, the governor had also captured nearly 50 percent of the union vote.[1]

Since the early 1960s, Michigan Republicans had been putting more money and staff into their Detroit field office, but Peterson concluded that they weren't making progress fast enough. "Inner-city people," she decided, "were not going to get involved easily with organizations of women or youth or new groups."[2]

Her answer was the "action center." She had gotten the idea from Charles H. Percy, a former Bell and Howell executive who had just lost a race for governor of Illinois. Percy was rechanneling his energies into a "Call for Action" program similar to the one Ellen Sulzberger Straus had already pioneered at WMCA, her New York City radio station. Public service ads encouraged listeners with problems to phone volunteers who tried to help solve them.

"The need was apparent," Peterson recalled in 1971. "We had to crack the inner-city vote to win big. We had to change our fat-cat image because basically our party was one of volunteers, but also one of poor public relations. We had to find a way to involve minorities as no party could be strong if mired in the WASP image. . . . We felt the Democrats simply packaged people as 'union,' 'poor,' 'black,' and catered to them as groups, not as individuals. That was the key: individuals."

As her chief lieutenant, she hired John Marttila, a Wayne State University law student. Marttila, she recalled, "was inclined to look down at Republicans with their stuffed-shirt image," but he was "open to ideas" and "grew as excited about this as I did."

" 'How,' we asked ourselves, 'can we expect people who are troubled with rats attacking their children, drunks lying across their front doors, their gas turned off, [to] be interested in lowering the tolls on the Mackinac Bridge?' Real help had to start at the level of their immediate concerns." Inner-city residents, she said, often didn't know that there were programs that could help them, if only they knew about them.[3]

Marttila noted years later, "It was just amazing that we had the stupidity or the guts to do what we did."[4]

It was not an easy sell. "Money is always scarce in politics," Peterson observed, "new ideas are suspect, and old-line leadership was not about to encourage new people who might take over their jobs." Most of the political establishment, she added, "thought community involvement was a nutty idea. To many of them, John was a wide-eyed liberal, and I was a WOMAN . . . what could you expect from them? And from a combination of the two?"[5]

But Peterson and Marttila persevered. On April 6, 1967, the Metropolitan Action Center opened for business in a separate room of the party's Thirteenth District headquarters at 3533 Woodward Avenue near Grand Boulevard. They made more than three hundred contacts with leaders of neighborhood organizations, service clubs and churches. Milliken served as chairman and joined Marttila in calling on Detroit mayor Jerome Cavanagh; Romney also lent his support. They won the backing of Clyde Cleveland, head of the Congress on Racial Equality in Detroit, and Roy Williams, who was developing youth programs for the local branch of the Urban League. And once they got prominent Democrats like Cleveland involved, WJLB, an inner-city radio station, agreed to air their public service announcements.

"The hardest thing to sell to our politicians," Peterson recalled, "was the idea that (1) it would have to be an ongoing program for perhaps eight to 10 years before we picked up much benefit in the way of votes and (2) it required a deep, personal commitment to the idea of brotherhood and equality. Strangely and sadly," she concluded, "the latter was harder to sell than the former."

For the project to succeed, she knew it could not be positioned as a partisan effort or "political gimmick." Marttila, she recalled, "being aware of the image we had in the inner-city, was questioning whether we would ever be able to come out as Republicans."

But in just four months, she said, "we found out people in trouble don't care what your politics are." As a result, they renamed the office the Republican Action Center. It cost them their public service ads—"our greatest chance of building"—but, she concluded, "it was a gamble we had to take."[6]

From the day black and white volunteers began answering calls, as many as fifty persons a day phoned 832-0800 seeking help. While organizers were not sure the volunteers would be able to address every problem, it helped to have a sympathetic governor, supportive members of Congress, and good business connections.

In a report to Romney, Peterson summed up the mix of calls that were fielded.

A twenty-one-year-old mother had twins. One died and lay in the mortuary for eleven days because there wasn't money to bury it. The Aid to [Families with] Dependent Children people were boxed in by their rules. We found the child's father, who paid for the burial. . . . A couple 67 years old had worked past their Social Security retirement, and when they needed the money, they couldn't get it. They were starving. A call to Senator Griffin got them the check in five days. We've handled a number of Social Security complaints. . . . We found one old couple with two feet of sewage in the basement. We went after the landlord. . . . We've got a group making a price study to see why the poor are being overcharged, and how to get credit from somebody other than the loan sharks.[7]

In a November 1967 report to Peterson, Marttila acknowledged, "We have been greeted with much more enthusiasm and acceptance than I ever anticipated."[8]

Peterson had observed that in many communities, it was the Republicans who were running the blood banks, leading the churches, and coordinating fund-raising drives for charities. Now, under the banner of "Mission Involvement," local party volunteers were encouraged to "look around them, see something that needed to be done to improve the quality of life and fix it in the name of the Republican Party."[9]

In Eaton County, Republican women organized an art exhibit to spotlight local artists and raised enough money to support an art scholarship at Olivet College. In the Upper Peninsula, Republicans opened a teen center, provided staff, and covered the operating budget. In Livingston County, twenty-three disabled persons were employed at a dilapidated workshop; the Republicans opened up a better building, which provided space for forty-eight. In Wayne and Oakland counties, Young Republicans tutored underprivileged children and organized cultural tours for them.[10]

By the end of 1967, 154 projects had been started in forty-five counties.[11] Once again, Peterson observed, it gave party members something meaningful to do between elections.

Peterson wanted to "establish a bridge between outstate people who simply were unable to relate to the problems of those living in the inner-city and those accepting our help."[12] In the summer of 1967, the Detroit riot, tragically, finally provided the opportunity for that connection.

"For those of us who lived outstate," Peterson recalled in her memoir, the riot "began as something happening in the big city far removed from us. We watched on television, read about it in the papers, oohed and ahed, regretted, and were glad we didn't live there. Suburban people were frightened, bought guns and locked their homes. Stories flew—all of them dramatic—and most of them distorted." The National Guard, including Col. Pete Peterson, was dispatched to Detroit to help restore order.[13]

Within thirty-six hours, Peterson received a call from John Marttila, who had gone to their headquarters, from which he could hear gunfire. The residents, he said, desperately needed food because the big stores had closed and the small family groceries had been burned.

Within a matter of hours, Marttila contacted all the Republican Party offices in the metropolitan area and Peterson reached the offices in fourteen more counties. Donation centers were set up at party offices and radio stations notified to help spread the word. By the end of the day, four truckloads of food arrived in the riot zone; over the next three days, thirteen more arrived from outstate counties. Republicans worked alongside union members and Interfaith Emergency Assistance, a ministers' group; together they eventually distributed eighty tons of supplies. Peterson recalled, "We helped to unite families, clothe some who had lost all of their belongings in fires, and never before had 'out state' and 'inner-city' cooperated in this way. It was one of our finest hours."[14]

Inevitably, though, she was disappointed that the Republicans did not get more positive publicity. The papers, she noted, reported on the churches' food distribution efforts, but "no one wrote about how it got there or where it came from!" Nevertheless, she recognized that the volunteer initiative "would fall on its face if it was blown up, and looked like 'Lady and Lord Bountiful.'"[15]

The Detroit action center initiative was successful enough that Mary Brooks, the RNC's assistant chairman, asked Peterson to speak about it at regional RNC meetings. Plans for action centers in Dallas and Hartford were soon launched.

* * *

In mid-1967, what the *New York Times* called "one of the bitterest political fights now under way in the nation" broke into the headlines—the struggle between Phyllis Schlafly and Gladys O'Donnell for the presidency of the 500,000-member National Federation of Republican Women (NFRW).

In 1964, when she had written *A Choice Not an Echo* to promote Goldwater's candidacy, Schlafly had been elected first vice president of the federation and thus was in line to become its next president. At the time, the RNC provided "nearly two-thirds to three-fourths" of the money that the federation used to operate.[16] And, as the *Times* put it, "Some Republican leaders believed [Schlafly's] outspoken right-wing views would be a divisive force in the party during a presidential election year."[17] O'Donnell, a relatively conservative older Californian and "garden-variety Republican," emerged as an alternative who would promote party unity in 1968—and could still win a federation vote.

"Depending on whose perspective one takes," historian Catherine E. Rymph observed years later, "the battle over the Federation presidency was either an attempt to purge conservatives from the Federation and squelch women's independent voices or an attempt to return the Federation to its traditional role as a noncontroversial auxiliary that would help the party rather than be a divisive force. Complicating this conflict was the fact that it was simultaneously one between moderates and conservatives *and* one between party regulars and party outsiders. In either case party regulars clearly did not want Schlafly to become leader of the Women's Federation."[18]

Peterson does not mention the national federation battle in her memoir other than to cite Schlafly's campaign as an example of the right wing's single-minded determination to win.[19] Nor did she draw attention to her own role in the battle when the topic came up in later interviews. But her personal papers make clear that she was a general, if not *the* general, for "the party regulars" who wanted to block Schlafly's ascension.

In every war, there are inevitably two sides—and two points of view over exactly what transpired and whether the ends justified the means. A rereading of the history of the battle suggests that Peterson could quietly and capably play hardball if she believed the circumstances warranted it.

On the surface, Peterson had many things in common with Schlafly, who was ten years her junior. Both were midwesterners. Both were effective public speakers and communicators and born political organizers. They had shared the experience of running unsuccessfully for Congress, and both were becoming increasingly concerned about the limited role that women were permitted to play in their party.

Nevertheless, over more than a decade, the two women became increasingly bitter antagonists. Peterson's notion of her party's "big tent" never extended far enough to the right to include Schlafly. And she abhorred what she viewed as Schlafly's personal aggrandizement and self-promotion, even as she was willing to acknowledge that "the women who adored her, adored her."[20]

Peterson always remained suspicious of where Schlafly was getting her financial support and believed some was coming from the John Birch Society. But years later she told Schlafly's biographer that reporters who had investigated Schlafly's funding sources were "not finding a thing and, as much as I hate to admit it, neither am I."[21]

Schlafly, never one to be muzzled, published a short book, detailing her side of the story. In a chapter entitled "The Purge," she wrote about herself in the third person and adopted a perspective that, from the vantage point of more than forty years, seems surprisingly feminist.

> The behind-the-scenes forces which directed the campaign against Phyllis were not only the liberals. They were joined by all those who feel it is to their own interests to keep Republican women neutral-

ized. The Republican Party is carried on the shoulders of the women who do the work in the precincts, ringing doorbells, distributing literature, and doing all the tiresome, repetitious campaign tasks. Many men in the Party frankly want to keep the women doing the menial work, while the selection of candidates and the policy decisions are taken care of by the men in the smoke-filled rooms. All those building their own political machine want only machine-people who can be controlled. In Phyllis, they recognized one who could not be neutralized or silenced, and who would fight for women to express their ideals in matters of policies and candidates commensurate with the work the women do for the Party.[22]

The anti-Schlafly forces pursued several strategies to deny her the presidency. In August 1965, O'Donnell advised Peterson that the federation's board would propose a bylaw change to delay the meeting by a year. "Time is a great insulator and the ideal cure for many problems," she wrote. "It would also give us time—which I feel is on our side." Peterson responded that she supported the change and also expressed her wish that "there were a way [the convention] could be held in the middle of the nation instead of [in Los Angeles]. It would be most helpful to those on the east coast."[23] The next month, the board voted to delay the convention until 1967, asserting that it made more sense to hold the meeting the year before a presidential election.

Typically, the federation alternated its convention between East and West Coasts. But in May 1966, the federation's Executive Committee followed up on Peterson's recommendation and voted to move the convention to Washington, DC, farther away from Schlafly's base of support in Southern California and closer to the moderates' strength in the Northeast and Midwest.

That year, Republican National Committeewoman Katherine K. Neuberger of New Jersey wrote Peterson that she "was delighted that you are taking the leadership in the National Federation struggle. It is something that has got to be done and if we just drift on and hope it will all go away we will wake up some morning and find out that the Federation has been taken over by the extreme right wing which will be a catastrophe for the entire party."[24] Another western state leader contacted Peterson after being advised that Peterson was "the 'key' to the whole thing."[25]

The correspondence is sprinkled with references to "007," "agents," and "counter-intelligence." As an RNC meeting approached in mid-1966, Peterson advised another member, "I am sure I don't have to tell you that if they start talking about Phyllis Schlafly I would be very careful. I would prefer that you don't mention anything any of us are doing or thinking of doing."[26] Later in the year, Peterson wrote another Republican national committeewoman, "I think it is time the men realized the seriousness and helped us and so I will move in that field to discuss with some of the leaders on the National Committee, State Chairmen, etc., so they are with us."[27]

Finally, in March 1967, the federation's Nominating Committee formally proposed O'Donnell when it prepared its slate of nominees; Ruth Hobbs was nominated for treasurer. But instead of retreating quietly back home to Alton, Illinois, Schlafly moved to challenge O'Donnell.

Peterson recognized that she and her allies faced a tough fight to get their candidate elected; "the nut fringe is beautifully organized," she observed to one friend.[28] They kept close tabs on the composition and leadership of each state delegation, a process Peterson had begun in Michigan in 1965. In December 1966, Peterson described what she viewed as an effort to stack the Michigan federation with conservative clubs: "We just voted them down on the basis they had not cooperated with any projects we had for the past two years and why should they join now for the purpose of sending delegates to a convention? I stopped their clocks then— but I am sure just temporarily."[29]

As the convention approached, Peterson stepped up her efforts to recruit friendly delegates. When she learned that Hawaii would send only one of the eleven delegates to which it was entitled, and that she was a Schlafly supporter, Peterson wrote Sen. Hiram Fong, asking if his wife could attend, along with any staff members who were registered to vote in the state: "Republican women throughout the nation would take a giant stride backward if a woman of Phyllis Schlafly's coloration were to become national president. . . . We feel we can win this, but we want to have every possible delegate we can muster."[30]

She had wanted to make the request over the phone but resorted to a letter when she could not reach Fong. She wrote Bobbie Mills, president of the Hawaii federation, "This is not the way it should have been handled." She added, "For your ears alone, I think our fight looks pretty good. Our problem is concentrated on getting our delegates to Washington." She hoped to take "about 145 bodies from Michigan for the O'Donnell slate."[31]

The final battle unfolded in the first week of May 1967. It was marked by days and nights of credentials challenges and charges and counter-charges over everything from voting fraud to the creation of phantom federation clubs to the busing in of delegates.

In a later speech, Peterson recalled, "It was a test of parliamentary skill. How well I remember our little lady delegates from Michigan, not understanding what was going on really—told to sit in their seats, never leave them and BE PREPARED TO VOTE. They sat as though pole axed."[32]

Patricia Reilly Hitt, comanager of O'Donnell's campaign, recalled the time as a "harrowing, harrowing experience," even as she acknowledged that she and Patricia Hutar, cochairman of the National Young Republican Federation, had worked out a seating arrangement to put all of the Schlafly delegates in the back of the hall to try to "keep it calmed down and low-key."[33] Schlafly later complained that the delegations from Michigan, New York, and Pennsylvania were given the best spots.[34]

By the end of the meeting, O'Donnell had prevailed by a vote of 1,910 to 1,494.

In her postconvention book, Schlafly cast the moderate women as tools of the RNC's male leaders, especially Bliss, though Peterson's correspondence suggested otherwise. But Schlafly also specifically named Peterson as one of those who had conspired against her, pointing to a story that was published in the *Grand Rapids Press* on May 1, 1967. Schlafly referred to Peterson as "Governor George Romney's State Chairman," and wrote:

> Mrs. Peterson talked too much and revealed more than she intended. After publicly attacking Phyllis, she predicted that the next NFRW Convention would be held in Washington in May 1967. Why Washington? Why in May? By tradition, the convention alternates east and west of the Mississippi; and it was time to go west. September was *always* the NFRW convention month. Mrs. Peterson was not a member of the NFRW Board and had no proper way to be privy to confidential advance information.
>
> It turned out that Governor Romney's employee knew more about the site of the Convention than the Executive Committee which subsequently picked the site.[35]

Afterward Peterson wrote Mills that the convention "frankly, was exhausting emotionally and it was just terrible."[36] But in a long report to federation members in Michigan, she tried to be conciliatory. She noted, in an understatement, that the Nominating Committee's choice of O'Donnell "was not acceptable to Mrs. Phyllis Schlafly." On a slightly defensive note, she acknowledged her friendship with O'Donnell and outgoing President Dorothy Elston, another pro-unity strategist. But Peterson professed her innocence by asserting that she did "not have an extensive National Federation background or have I attended their Board meetings."

Always at issue was who was really providing the financial support for the women's activities since neither the women—nor their clubs—had substantial resources of their own. Years later, Peterson still recoiled at the memory of Schlafly supporters who had called moderate delegates "Rockefeller whores." But at the time she wrote the Michigan women:

> There were other charges. "Nelson Rockefeller paid for many delegates"—I don't know, perhaps he did. He surely didn't help any of our women, and I found no evidence that he helped any in states other than his own. Our Michigan delegates (1) paid their own way or (2) had help from their own clubs or (3) sold candy, etc., to raise funds—such as our Negro delegates from Detroit, led by Dovie Pickett, which was the largest Negro delegation from any state. Mrs. Schlafly did not answer press on the question of where she obtained her funds for a $3,500 reception, gifts of perfume and tape measures to over 4,000 delegates, brochures, printed material, hair ribbons, etc. . . . So let us assume both forces raised their money from friends rather than from Nelson Rockefeller, the John Birch Society and the Liberty Lobby.[37]

Schlafly's forces, she noted, had charged that "'O'Donnell's age would preclude her from getting youth'—I'm not too far removed from her age, and I don't quite feel ready to be through on that account. I feel I can help youth, too!" But she also challenged some on her side: "Some O'Donnell supporters felt Mrs. Schlafly should not take a job which would take her away from her six children. I think that is Mrs. Schlafly's business. Every mother, as far as I am concerned, has the right to decide who she wants to raise her family and how much time she wishes to spend with them."

Near the end of the report, she wrote, "I do regret these things: that

Mrs. Schlafly did not prove to be the gracious lady Bernice Zilly was two years ago." (After she lost, Zilly had made a motion to approve Hobbs's election unanimously.)[38] Peterson wrote that she was "proud" of the Michigan delegation, which, even though it included Schlafly supporters, did not have "the overtones of hate" she had observed in some delegations.

"Presumably the road ahead will be rocky for the National Board," she concluded, "but they are dedicated, sincere women, and they will do their best to pick up the pieces." Only two members of the sixty-member board, she noted, "supported the Schlafly story of [a] 'crooked election.'" She added, "Whether all will join or whether, as we see here in Michigan, there will be those who will prefer to be dissidents and who find their pleasure in dissension—well, that remains to be seen."

When Schlafly left the federation convention, she vowed to form "a grass-roots organization made up of just plain American women and mothers who believe in the cause of constitutional government and freedom."[39] Three months later she launched *The Phyllis Schlafly Report*, mailing the first issue of the monthly newsletter to the 3,000 supporters within the federation. Eight years later, she incorporated the Eagle Forum. Both were to serve as a base for her opposition to the Equal Rights Amendment in the 1970s. By 1980, the federation's membership would drop by nearly half, to 280,000 members.[40]

Schlafly biographer Carol Felsenthal noted that "one of the more intriguing ironies of the Federation battle was that if there was a feminist on the front—a strong-willed woman who was not going to tolerate any dictation from the boys in the bureaucracy—that was Phyllis Schlafly."[41]

Peterson had been quietly raising similar questions about women's role in the party. But their political goals were very different. Schlafly wrote books when she lost; Peterson kept mum about her victories. And while Peterson raised money by selling jewelry featuring her name and sent out chatty memos to party leaders from "Elly," she never would have dreamed of using those devices to finance her own political movement. Reflecting on Schlafly's approach, she wrote in her memoir, "While she can't get elected to an office, she can keep the waters stirred, can cause a lot of trouble for issues like ERA and tends to get the publicity and the notoriety she seems to crave."[42]

In 1967, the moderates won their battle, but they would eventually lose the war.[43]

* * *

Among the men who ventured into the NFRW convention that year was George Romney, thought to be "the closest thing to a presidential candidate" among the party leaders who spoke at the event.[44]

Peterson asserted that she "was not involved in any of the decisions that began Romney's campaign," mostly because she was busy implementing the Action program and traveling around the state. In her memoir, she wrote:

> The Romney for President campaign was such a can of worms that it is hard to describe it from my viewpoint. . . .
>
>   In hindsight, it would have been much more productive if he had remained in Michigan most of the time instead of moving early into the campaign. However, he had an eager staff and, My Lord, they were advising right and left! It is not possible . . . and surely not necessary . . . to name all of them who were taking part in decisions. But it created a big problem: No one was top dog and everyone had his own axe to grind so it became a battle of wits, or "Who's on top?"

She was quick to qualify her observations by saying, "[R]emember, this opinion comes from the vantage point of an outsider, who attended a meeting now and then, or spoke for the Governor at some rally. I was sort of on the outside looking in and not really able to follow what their principal program was all about. . . . If I went to a meeting, then I skipped two, in disgust."[45]

The leaders of Romney's campaign team were all males. The Washington-based headquarters operation was led by Leonard W. Hall, a former RNC chairman. Advisers included old Michigan hands such as DeVries, Lindemer, Fisher, and Dick Van Dusen, as well as J. Willard Marriott, an old friend of the governor's, and Travis Cross, an associate of Mark Hatfield.

Although there is no indication that Peterson sought a campaign job, there is also no indication that anyone tried to recruit her.[46] Despite her own good national party connections and the role she had played in the Romney victory, it would still be another nine years before a woman—Peterson—was hired for a high-visibility post in a presidential campaign organization.[47]

There was good reason for early optimism among the Romney team. A Louis Harris poll taken just after the 1966 election showed the governor would defeat Johnson by a margin of 54 to 46 percent, the best showing of any of the potential Republican candidates. Even the Detroit riot did little to tarnish his reputation.[48]

But all of that changed on August 31, 1967, when Romney sat for an interview with Lou Gordon, the host of *Hot Seat* on UHF station WKBD-TV in Detroit. Gordon asked about apparent inconsistencies in the governor's positions on the Vietnam War. Romney replied, "Well, you know, when I came back from Vietnam, I had just had the greatest brainwashing that anybody can get. When you—"

*Gordon:* "By the generals?"
*Romney:* "Not only by the generals but also by the diplomatic corps over there. They do a very thorough job."[49]

Peterson recalled in her memoir, "No one with Romney that night caught the significance of the remark. . . . It didn't strike until about the middle of the week when the press picked it up and leaped on Romney with both feet."

When the story broke nationwide, Romney was out of town campaigning and Peterson was in Washington for an RNC meeting. Hall dispatched her to meet Romney at National Airport, keep him away from the press, and "spirit him" to a downtown hotel. When they arrived, she recalled:

Len immediately spoke to him about the seriousness of his remark. Romney became so furious I thought he would explode; he did not believe he had said the wrong thing, and simply did not believe there would be any consequences. Len told him quietly, but firmly and honestly, that it was an error of the greatest magnitude. All this time I was scrunched up against the headboard of the bed, wishing I was anyplace in the world but in this bedroom, as the two thrashed out this issue!

When other aides supported Hall's damage assessment, Peterson recalled, "the governor, red in the face, completely and utterly routed, stalked out of the room. When he returned an hour later, he was quiet and self-contained."[50]

Romney said he would work on a statement, and labored on it all night. When he delivered it, Peterson thought he did a "superb" job and that many RNC members agreed. But the governors who had been on his Vietnam trip—even the Republican ones—disputed his version of their briefings.

The episode quickly took on a life of its own, fueled by editorial cartoonists, stand-up comics, Democrats, and competing Republican campaigns. Within two weeks of the first headlines, Richard Nixon's lead among Republican voters had widened to 26 percentage points. Still, in early October Peterson wrote a woman party leader in Wisconsin, "The brainwash thing was bad—let us not kid ourselves—but the press blew it out of proportion. . . . It seems to be calming down now."[51]

Romney forged on, formally declaring his candidacy on November 18, 1967—with the help of the public relations apparatus of the Republican State Central Committee.[52] Nevertheless, by early 1968, when, Peterson noted, "things should have been all set and ready to go, they were not."

In retrospect, Peterson was among those who felt the campaign might have fared better if it had concentrated more resources in Wisconsin rather than "first-in-the-nation" New Hampshire. "Wisconsin citizens were our kind of people," she wrote. "George was known there from his days with American Motors, there are many Mormons in Wisconsin, and they wanted to help. Crowds turned out, the press was better, and generally speaking, things looked encouraging."[53]

But the die had been cast in New Hampshire. Early in the year, Peterson said she received a "panic call" from the campaign, asking her to come help out in New Hampshire and Wisconsin because "Lenore's schedule was not going so well." She took a leave of absence from the state committee and flew to Concord, where she quickly realized that "Lenore was just not going to be able to come through as she had in Michigan" because all of the local Republicans were "lock, stock and barrel" for Nixon. The state just wasn't large enough for two Romneys, and press coverage, by both national and Massachusetts-based media, was still hard to come by.

Instead, someone hit on the idea of identifying "home headquarters," where local families could host a gathering to promote Romney. But when Peterson was given a list of potential hosts for follow-up, "I soon found out that about 50 percent of those I called had never agreed to be a home headquarters, did not want to be and were really irked to be called."[54]

On another campaign trip, this time to Dallas, the women met with "a group of money people at a very elegant private club." Peterson recalled:

> The waiters were black and as they bent over the table, giving perfect service, one of the wealthy hosts said, "One thing you can't do, Mrs. Romney, is work with the niggers. They ain't to be trusted"—and on and on and on. She and I did not look at each other and we surely did not look at the black waiter![55]

In the weeks leading up to the New Hampshire primary, the campaign's own polls indicated that Romney would lose to Nixon by a margin of 70 to 10 percent.[56] On February 28, less than two weeks before primary day, Romney announced that he was withdrawing.

Peterson recalled:

> In a hotel room in New Hampshire, the men working closely with Romney decided he would not make it and should throw in the sponge. Max Fisher was in Israel at the time, and they could not reach him. He did not like the fact that the decision had been made without him, but money was not coming in, and large sums of money were desperately needed for the primary contests. People were discouraged, the brainwash statement hurt, and the press, forgetting all that George had done for Michigan, portrayed him as a dum-dum. It was a tragic time for the Romneys and a bitter pill for a proud man like George to swallow.[57]

Romney decided to make his announcement just before the Republican governors gathered for a meeting in Washington. Lenore Romney got only a few hours' notice, as did Peterson, who was back at her desk in Lansing.

In "The Story of Wednesday, February 28, 1968," Braithwaite and Peterson captured their memories of the day. Braithwaite wrote that when the phone call came she could tell by the look on Peterson's face that the governor had decided to withdraw.

Peterson added:

> I was so stunned I couldn't answer so he continued by saying that he was not getting through to the people and inasmuch as he had promised the governors at White Sulphur Springs that he would

carry on until he felt he couldn't—so since their meeting is today he had to do this now so they could discuss things. Otherwise they wouldn't meet until June. . . .

He was just great—but at the end he said, "Well, Elly,—one good thing—I'll be in Mich. And I'll see more of you and *that's* good." So with [illegible] almost in tears, I said, "I love you" and he laughed and said, "Well, I love you, too."[58]

A *New York Times* story said Peterson "wept at the news" and quoted her as saying, "I was completely floored. George Romney is a great governor and would have made a great president. It takes a man of exceptional stature and courage to move as he has done toward getting the strongest possible candidate for the Republican Party."

Peterson demurred when asked whom she would support now. But she told the *Times*, "I will be strongly inclined to support anyone who receives the endorsement of the Republican governors."[59]

It was a depressing time for Michigan Republicans. When she heard the news, Peterson recalled, "I thought of the hours of sacrifice of the Romneys and the thousands of dollars and thousands of hours, and then the deep disappointment of having the race end almost before it began."[60]

But she was also becoming frustrated with the inability of the party's moderate wing to fight aggressively for its beliefs. The moderates, she concluded later, "reached their apex" in 1968. "They had so many outstanding governors, senators, congressmen, but after losing, this group seemed almost blurred in the party structure and many dropped out of sight."

"Moderates," she wrote just a few years later, "just don't care enough to fight constantly to win. They will pour out their life's blood for a month, or even three months, but when the battle is over, they want to go on to other things. It doesn't seem to matter that much to them. Life goes on.

"Not so the right wing. . . . They have tasted victory and they have tasted power . . . and they like it. They will make NO concessions to moderates, or liberals, but they expect to have concessions made to them."[61]

Rockefeller and Scranton both scrambled to take on Nixon, but by the time the party gathered in Miami Beach in August he had sewn up the nomination. He won on the first ballot, capturing 692 votes to 277 for Rockefeller and 182 for Reagan. Peterson seconded the nomination of "favorite son" Romney, who drew 50 votes, 44 from Michigan and 6 from Utah.

In the next roll call, Romney captured 186 votes for vice president, while Nixon's choice, Maryland governor Spiro Agnew, received the party's blessing with 1,128. Peterson and Romney were asked to join the escort party for Nixon and Agnew. Romney told reporters afterward that through the unsuccessful drive to nominate him for vice president, "the poison that was spreading was lanced and the party leaves Miami united." He said he had not sought the vice presidency and had asked the Michigan delegation not to take the lead in promoting him.[62]

Once the Democrats nominated Hubert H. Humphrey at their chaotic convention in Chicago, the battle was joined. "The day Richard Nixon was nominated," Peterson wrote, "he was my candidate, and in my simple mind, that was the way politics worked. You fought for your guy, but if he lost, you worked for the winner: In this case, Nixon."[63]

In early September, commenting on Nixon's prospects in Michigan, Peterson told the *New York Times,* "The only thing that concerns us Republicans is becoming too complacent." She predicted Nixon would win the state. "I would have told you three months ago that he couldn't win," but "the bandwagon is for us. The Democrats are still trying to pick up the pieces."[64]

But by late October, even Peterson's perpetual optimism had been dulled. A *Washington Post* report from the campaign trail recounted:

> En route to Battle Creek, the second stop, Michigan's Republican chairman, an able and tough-minded matron named Elly Peterson, says, "I've never been in such a tough campaign as this one, or at least one where it's been so hard to get our own people stirred up." There are no major state contests to attract voters' interest, and Nixon was the third choice of Michigan Republicans, behind George Romney and Nelson Rockefeller.[65]

McLaughlin remembered, "For the only election in my time, we did not rent a hotel for an election night party. Elly, I and a few of the staff got the returns at Party headquarters and kept the Governor and Milliken posted at their homes." Before 9:00 p.m., NBC called the state for Humphrey.[66]

In the end, Nixon drew 41.5 percent of the Michigan vote compared to Humphrey's 48.2 percent, with George C. Wallace capturing another 10 percent. But by the next morning, it was clear that Nixon had won nationwide.

Peterson wrote a Republican friend that they "were fortunate" to hang on to their congressional seats, a feat she considered "a miracle." But "the Nixon bomb cost us eight educational posts, one Supreme Court Justice and control of the Michigan House of Representatives."[67]

Still, a Republican was back in the White House—for the first time in eight years. There was a Cabinet to pick, an inauguration to plan. And as the party chairman in one of the eight largest states, Peterson was summoned to California for a meeting with the president-elect.

Each of the other state chairmen came on his own. But John Mitchell, Nixon's campaign chief and soon to be his attorney general, asked Emil Lockwood, chairman of Nixon's Michigan campaign, to accompany Peterson. "The poor man didn't know Michigan's organization or Michigan's finance picture, but his gender comforted them so we muddled through," Peterson recalled. But Mitchell's action, she said, spoke louder than words: "Never Trust a Woman."

It was an ominous way to begin a new administration. Later, she acknowledged ruefully, "I should have remembered the first meeting."[68]

The children of John Charles and
Maude McMillan: (*from left*) John
Charles Jr., Mary Catherine, Lee
Gibson, and Ella Maude, circa 1920.
(Photo courtesy of Holly Shrader.)

Elly McMillan in her Red Cross
uniform, Washington, DC, 1943.
(Photo courtesy of the Bentley
Historical Library, University of
Michigan, Elly M. Peterson Papers.)

Elly Peterson with (*from left*) Allie Marriott, Mitt Romney, J. Willard Marriott, and Lenore Romney, October 1963. (Photo courtesy of the Bentley Historical Library, University of Michigan, Elly M. Peterson Papers.)

Lenore and George Romney with Elly and Pete Peterson at a January 1964 dinner honoring Peterson following her appointment as assistant chairman of the Republican National Committee. (Photo by Lawrence Belland, courtesy of the Bentley Historical Library, University of Michigan, Elly M. Peterson Papers.)

Elly Peterson with young volunteers during her 1964 U.S. Senate campaign. (Photo by Douglas G. Ashley, Birmingham, Michigan, courtesy of Margaret Cooke.)

Elly Peterson at a campaign stop during her 1964 U.S. Senate campaign. (Photo courtesy of the Bentley Historical Library, University of Michigan, Elly M. Peterson Papers.)

Richard M. Nixon, George
Romney, and Elly Peterson
during the 1964 campaign.
(Photo courtesy of the
Bentley Historical Library,
University of Michigan, Elly
M. Peterson Papers.)

Michigan Republican Party
chairman Elly Peterson
with party public relations
director John Toepp outside
the state Capitol in Lansing.
(Photo by Tom O'Reilly,
*The Blade* [Toledo], April
18, 1965, reprinted with
permission. Courtesy of the
Bentley Historical Library,
University of Michigan,
Michigan Republican State
Central Committee Papers.)

Pete and Elly Peterson with their dog, Jake, at their home, "Holiday Hill," in Charlotte, Michigan, early 1965. (Photo by Tom O'Reilly, *The Blade* [Toledo], April 18, 1965, reprinted with permission. Courtesy of the Bentley Historical Library, University of Michigan, Michigan Republican State Central Committee Papers.)

Elly Peterson straightens Gov. George Romney's tie at a political dinner. (Photo courtesy of the Bentley Historical Library, University of Michigan, Elly M. Peterson Papers.)

Elly Peterson (*front row, far right*) at a meeting of the Republican State Chairmen's Advisory Committee, Washington, DC, January 16, 1969. (Photo by Capitol and Glogau Photographers, Washington, DC, courtesy of Margaret Cooke.)

Republican National Committee chairman Rogers Morton (*second from left*) and Republican National Committee assistant chairman Elly Peterson at an Oval Office meeting with President Richard M. Nixon, November 1969. (Photo courtesy of the Bentley Historical Library, University of Michigan, Elly M. Peterson Papers.)

Elly Peterson with members of her staff at the Republican National
Committee: (*from left*) Jackie Fernald, Nancy Risque Rohrbach,
Christine Todd Whitman, and Pam Curtis. (Photo courtesy of the
Bentley Historical Library, University of Michigan, Elly M. Peterson
Papers.)

Elly and Pete Peterson with the "Mother" ice sculpture created for
the party marking her retirement from the Republican National
Committee, December 15, 1970. (Photo courtesy of the Bentley
Historical Library, University of Michigan, Elly M. Peterson Papers.)

Elly Peterson and President Gerald R. Ford in the Oval Office, 1976. (Photo courtesy of the Bentley Historical Library, University of Michigan, Elly M. Peterson Papers.)

ERAmerica executive director Jane Wells and cochairs Elly Peterson and Liz Carpenter review map showing the states that had ratified the Equal Rights Amendment, February 1976. (Photo by Joe DiDio, National Education Association Communications Services, ERAmerica Records. Courtesy of the Library of Congress.)

Elly Peterson, former first lady Betty Ford, and Bella Abzug listen as first lady Rosalynn Carter addresses the ERAmerica rally at the International Women's Year Conference in Houston, November 1977. (Photo by Carolyn Salisbury, National Education Association, ERAmerica Records. Courtesy of the Library of Congress.)

Protestors, including Elly Peterson, march in Detroit in opposition to the 1980 Republican National Convention's failure to endorse the Equal Rights Amendment in its platform. (Photo courtesy of the Bentley Historical Library, University of Michigan, Elly M. Peterson Papers.)

Martha Griffiths, James Blanchard, and Elly Peterson at the luncheon where Peterson and other moderate Republican women endorsed Democrat Blanchard in his 1982 race for governor of Michigan. (Photo courtesy of Margaret Cooke.)

Elly and Pete Peterson and her sister, Mary Richmond, vacationing in Maui. (Photo courtesy of Mary Ann Richmond.)

## CHAPTER SEVEN

# Back to Washington

THE WEATHER FORECAST FOR Richard Nixon's first inauguration was "a fifty-fifty chance of rain," an apt prediction for Peterson's own future as she traveled to the event.

It was time, she had decided, to move on. She would continue as national committeewoman from Michigan but would step down as state party chair after the convention in February. And George Romney was moving on, too—this time to Washington as secretary of housing and urban development.

If Peterson was excited about the prospect of attending a Republican inauguration, it was not reflected in her memoir. But she was still optimistic about the new administration. She recalled, "I had complete confidence [Nixon] would be one of the great Presidents. I felt his background fitted him for the job as no candidate in history had been fitted. I had the utmost confidence he would cut the great costs of government, cut the fat, cure the nation's ills if they were curable . . . in short, I was a True Believer!"[1]

And "her guy"—the governor of Michigan—*had* been rewarded with a Cabinet post that, if not at the very top of the Washington pecking order, was at least well suited to his skills.

This provided Peterson, at age fifty-four, with some opportunities of her own. In late December 1968, Nixon's transition office solicited information about her qualifications and interest in an "appointment to high Federal office."[2] As she recalled, "President Nixon had asked every Cabinet member to have an outside project, and, remembering the volunteer program we had been operating in Michigan, assigned that to George." She and Romney made some preliminary plans, and two of his aides began working on it in Washington. She begged off lunch with one old friend, saying, "I have had to spend so much time in Washington working with the Governor on a volunteer program."[3]

She was no longer the same wide-eyed innocent who had moved to the capital five years before. Her self-confidence was demonstrated by some of the short letters she fired off in her final weeks as state party chair. She chided William H. G. Fitzgerald of the Nixon Inaugural Committee for sending three copies of the same telegram, urging her to sell inaugural gala tickets. ("Bill," she said, "I nearly died at the way national Republicans waste money—I was raised in the wrong state!")[4] To Rep. William Broomfield of Michigan, recently appointed to the House Republican Campaign Committee, she offered some advice for the 1970 campaign: "I think you will find that most State Chairmen agree with me that it is a decidedly wrong approach to announce to the press and say publicly that certain specific seats can be won and the states which can be won or lost. . . . [I]t is discouraging to the State Chairman who is told he cannot win anything no matter what!"[5]

As she prepared to step down, Republican members of Congress praised her in the *Congressional Record*. In his remarks, Griffin wrote:

It is easy to see why Elly has earned the respect and admiration of friends and political foes alike. A part of her success is due to the fact that she is, by nature, a problem solver. She speaks out on the issues and, like many women, she has her own opinions—and the courage to stand by them. Moreover, she combines a business-like attitude and penetrating wit with a gentleness unusual in the hectic world of politics.[6]

Rep. Garry Brown noted:

To again recite the tributes and plaudits expressed by my colleagues regarding her good sense, tireless effort, and political agility would be repugnant to Elly, for she has never sought nor expected the praise that has been due her. But, like a good warrior, she has derived her satisfaction from jobs well done and an examination of her record establishes that her entitlement to self-satisfaction is almost limitless.[7]

Two years later, David Broder provided his own assessment of Peterson's impact on the state party.

> [Mrs. Peterson] managed to convince Romney that governing was easier if he had party support than if he was attempting to function as a one-man band. And she managed to convince some awfully skeptical Republicans that Romney's personality and grass roots appeal could be made a vehicle for building a stronger party organization.
>
> The party conferences she ran in those years were about as close to town hall democracy as it is possible to get in a mass society, and the enthusiasm they generated had a practical payoff in the election of an additional senator and five more Republican congressmen.[8]

Not all of the state party's problems had been solved, of course. McLaughlin, who succeeded Peterson as chairman, recalled, "When Elly was elected, we were in debt. We were still in debt when she left and for the next decade." The source of the debt, he said, was bills from candidates' campaigns that got dumped on the state party. "In most cases, they were accepted by the State Finance Chairmen, who were most eager to impress the powers to be with promises to pay the bills. It was difficult for us in the political end to undo the agreements once they were agreed upon."[9]

Lindemer noted, "I think the only thing Elly would rather have someone else do is to make the pitch for money." Jerry Roe also pointed to fund-raising as Peterson's one weak point as state chair. "She never grasped raising money," he recalled in a later interview. Peterson, he said, often ended up going to Max Fisher for help in meeting her payroll. Nevertheless, at the end of 1968, the Finance Committee reported that the party had become the first in the state to raise more than two million dollars in a year, achieving nearly 80 percent of its goal.[10]

After the convention, the Petersons took a three-week vacation to Hawaii. When they returned, the first phone call Elly received was from Romney, summoning her to Washington.

News reports said they were to meet about "a possible federal appointment." Peterson coyly told a reporter "she had no idea what Romney had in mind," but a source in his office reported that "it would be in the area of the administration's huge proposed volunteer program."[11]

On her arrival at Romney's office, his secretary told Peterson that she had received a call from Rep. Rogers C. B. Morton of Maryland, the new RNC chair. Peterson called back and set up an appointment. Finally, she met with Romney. But it turned out there had been a change of plans. She recalled:

> I found out that Max Fisher had taken over the project in my absence and had drafted people from every agency to talk about it. He had scrapped our original plans, and then he went on to offer me the job of Executive Director at about the same kind of salary (and about as complimentary a way) as the one he offered me as State Chairman![12]

Later news stories reported that Peterson had been in line to set up a volunteer program within the Department of Housing and Urban Development (HUD), working as a deputy director of the agency.[13] But in the meantime, Nixon had decided to make voluntarism "a central theme" of his administration under the leadership of Romney and Robert Finch, the new secretary of health, education and welfare (HEW). A week after the inauguration, the initiative made page-one headlines in Washington as plans were unveiled for "a governmentwide and nationwide drive to pit millions of citizen volunteers against the country's social ills."[14]

"After Mrs. Peterson returned from Hawaii," the Grand Rapids Press reported, "more conversations [with Romney] ensued, and [her] job was upgraded to a point where Fisher, Detroit millionaire, became interested. He had been a personal friend of Romney's since the early 1960s; knew exactly what Romney's thinking was and is on volunteer cooperation among citizens, and set out to help his friend again."[15]

After Romney dropped out of the presidential race, Fisher had thrown his support to Nixon, ultimately raising nearly 10 percent of the 36.5 million dollars that Nixon spent in the campaign according to Fisher's authorized biography. Fisher declined an offer of an ambassadorship or a seat in the Cabinet, according to biographer Peter Golden, because he did not want to be indebted to Nixon. All he really wanted was access. He had helped to engage business leaders in rebuilding Detroit and now wanted to do the same at the national level. It was not long before he was spending three days a week in Washington as an unpaid special presidential consultant on voluntary participation, with offices in the Executive Office Building and at HUD.[16]

Peterson had received a quick lesson on what could happen when you failed to protect your turf in the sharp-elbowed opening months of a new presidential administration. But that was not her style; she had been more focused on wrapping up her work as state party chair and owed her husband his time on the golf courses of Oahu. And in a battle with Fisher or the Nixon White House, she was, of course, outmatched.

In her memoir, Peterson recalled her first meeting about the volunteer initiative.

> Around the table sat people from 10 or 12 agencies, plus about ten bright governmental aides. The first statement immediately put me off. A young intellectual rose to say he felt our first duty would be to define the word "volunteer." I thought: "This is not my bag, a pseudo-intellectual I am not, define 'volunteer' I won't do" and excused myself, saying I would be back later (I thought "much later") after they decided what a volunteer is! The truth: I was never cut out to be a bureaucrat![17]

As the architect of a successful volunteer program, Peterson concluded that the new committee "was going to be more talk than substance." But she was probably also perplexed about how she was expected to fit into the new organization.

So she went to meet with Morton. Because she had never worked with him before, she professed that she was surprised when he offered her a job.[18]

> He told me about his ideas for the Party, the need to broaden it, to include minorities, youth, ethnics, women, and then he offered me the job of Assistant Chairman at a salary that would have made Max Fisher wince!
>
> He said: "I want the Assistant Chairman to be more than a sinecure for women. I want you to share with me the direction of the Committee in all its programming and planning. I know you have had more experience in party organization than I have had and I know you know more of the workers around the nation. I recognize your abilities, and I want you to use them."[19]

Peterson then described the offer she had received from Romney and her interest in getting his volunteer program off the ground. But Morton persisted, saying, "Do this for the party, Elly."

It did not take long for Peterson to decide that "politics was really 'my thing' and that this position would make it possible for me to continue selling 'involvement' to the people around the nation."[20]

Thus, when the Cabinet-level Office of Voluntary Action was unveiled, with Fisher in charge and Romney as the Cabinet-level chairman, a reporter observed that Fisher "got the prestige," Peterson "got the job she wanted," and Romney "got the satisfaction of seeing a lifelong ambition fulfilled."[21] In a reflection of the times, Peterson's new job was described in another account as "the top post which can be achieved by a woman in a national political party."[22]

If Peterson harbored any resentment over how her HUD appointment had been handled, if she felt Romney should have fought harder on her behalf, she did not express that, other than to acknowledge in her memoir that she was happy not to have to work for Fisher. She put the most positive spin possible on the turn of events—and remained close to both Romneys.

In fact, Peterson probably *was* better suited to the familiar, fast-paced world of politics than the glacial pace of the federal bureaucracy. Still, if there was a place in the administration for a person with her organizational skills, it was not likely to be identified because no one was focused on recruiting women. That job would eventually fall to Peterson herself.

As news of her appointment made headlines, the *Washington Post* reported, "Although Mrs. Peterson didn't say so, some of her friends indicated they were disappointed that she was not offered a job in the Administration commensurate with the service she has rendered the party." The article added that some had expected her to take a job as "special assistant" to Romney, "but apparently Mrs. Peterson preferred to work in the area of politics."[23] Peterson, it was reported, again planned to take a Washington apartment and commute to Charlotte on weekends.[24]

The *Post's* "For and about Women" section had transformed itself into the "Style" section only two months before, but Peterson's appointment was still covered there, not in the national news section. Nevertheless, Peterson asserted that she was going to play a more important role than women had in the past. The *Washington Star* reported, "The GOP assistant chairman traditionally goes to a woman, for it's her job to coordinate the party's women's activities. But yesterday, Mrs. Peterson said it was broader than that. 'There's a little different concept today than just women's.'"[25]

A Michigan reporter wrote that Peterson had undertaken "the most wide ranging and responsible assignment ever given a woman in an American political organization."[26] A month later he said that, as a result of an RNC reorganization, "Peterson has been given more responsibility than has ever before been given a member of her sex in a national political organization."[27] Another reporter said that Peterson's job "holds the promise of making her one of the most important people in the Republican party structure," with "an upgrading of the job of assistant chairman, which traditionally has been a sop to the female wing of the party."[28] Five months later, a veteran Washington woman reporter wrote that Peterson "would not have accepted the position . . . if her role was to be so limited. After all, she had that job back in 1964 and knew the limitations."[29]

As spring flowers were beginning to bloom, Peterson captured her thoughts: "[Washington] *is* a beautiful city. I hope I like to live here better than I think I will!! At least I know I'll like my work." After a dinner party a few nights later, she observed, "What you *are* and what you *do* in Wash[ington] are separate—the women all seem to have their thing and much talk is over how hard everyone works."[30]

Before she left Michigan, her friends organized "An Evening with Elly" dinner at the Statler Hilton as a sendoff. Zolton Ferency stole the show when he arrived disguised as a Western Union messenger boy. But the audience really broke up when Milliken, now the governor, declared, "I am so proud to say I have had a part in making Elly Peterson."[31]

Back in Washington, Morton made good on his word that she would have more responsibility than her predecessors. Within a few months, she was serving "as liaison with the White House and government agencies on patronage, a brand new assignment for that position."[32] In that job, she was trying to help women get more administration appointments. And she anticipated she would "continue selling 'involvement' to the people around the nation."[33]

In Morton, Peterson found another boss who was her kind of guy—a "great bear of a man: handsome, charming, radiating warmth, in shirtsleeves and bright suspenders." Morton, she recalled, "never quibbled about my being a woman, or alluded to it in any way. He truly made me a part of the management team. . . ."[34]

Their admiration was mutual. A few months after she took office, a reporter wrote that Peterson was an easy choice for Morton because "most Republicans will tell you she is the best woman pro in politics."

As he said in introducing her at a recent [RNC] meeting, everyone he consulted recommended Mrs. Peterson as the most efficient, the most knowledgeable and the most likeable.

"Now that I have had the privilege of working with Elly, I find that even her most ardent booster underestimated her," he said. "She is great."[35]

From May to August, Peterson's speaking engagements included twenty-one events in nine states and Washington, DC—in addition to commuting back to Michigan on the weekends.[36] After six weeks, Morton admonished her:

I am concerned that you are traveling too much. The job is beginning to manage you instead of you managing the job.

You are exceedingly important to the planning and management of the overall Republican thrust. Your current schedule which I have seen scares me to death. . . .

Please don't kill yourself![37]

While in Washington, Peterson rented a small apartment close to Dupont Circle. She kept three sets of clothes, one in her bags, one in the closet, and one at the cleaners, and shopped at stores that knew her tastes. She eschewed nighttime social events to try to get a full eight hours of sleep.[38]

She told a reporter that the Washington cocktail circuit "is not my thing" and that if she had an evening off she preferred to curl up with a book.[39] "I can adjust to anything," she told another reporter. "As long as I'm with stimulating people, nothing bothers me."[40] When she did go out after work, it was often for a drink with her younger colleagues.

Peterson's memoir makes clear that she enjoyed her day-to-day work ("God was in my Heaven and all was right with the world"). The RNC staff quickly implemented plans to change "the shape, the sound and the look of Republicans with a new elephant, new publications and new programs. I can truthfully say that everyone of us was eager to get to work in the morning and never wanted to leave at night!"[41]

One of those publications was a forty-eight-page booklet titled *Women Power*, designed to help the party's women leaders perform their

jobs. In addition to providing information on the party's structure, parliamentary procedure, and public relations, it included three diagrams explaining the protocol for seating dignitaries at a head table.[42]

Christine Todd Whitman, the former Republican governor of New
Jersey and Environmental Protection Agency administrator, was among
those who worked at the RNC at that time. In her autobiography, she provided the perspective of a woman thirty years Peterson's junior. "Young
women in Washington," she wrote, "were only just beginning to occupy
jobs that didn't involve getting coffee for the men in the office. Many of
the men had no idea how to interact with us—especially when we were in
rooms that had long been the exclusive domain of men."

The daughter of a leader of the New Jersey Republican Party, Whitman recalled that in describing her new job, "an assistant to the first assistant," the state party's newsletter said, "She's papa bear's pretty bundle of
charm, wit and political savvy." More than thirty-five years later, Whitman
acknowledged, "The condescending tone of that tidbit retains its capacity
to rankle even now." But "fortunately," she wrote, "the attitude at the RNC
was quite a bit more evolved."[43]

In a later interview, Whitman said that, while she technically reported
to Morton, "I really worked *with*" Peterson. "She was just a great mentor.
She *was* 'Mother Peterson' in many respects because she went out of her
way to engage young people." Referring to the RNC's staff, she added, "Elly
was sort of the center of a lot of that young activity."[44]

JoAnn DiBella (now Hawkins) was another young RNC staff member
who developed a lifelong friendship with Peterson as she helped write her
speeches. "She *was* like a Mother to us, giving us advice, helping to shape
our careers, and it was so natural," Hawkins said.[45] When Peterson asked
for help with a speech, she recalled, "She'd say something like, 'I want it
short, pithy, with a message—something like the Bible.' "[46]

"It was a good team," Whitman concluded, referring to the leadership
of Morton, Peterson, and Jimmy Allison, the Texan who served as deputy
party chairman. "Everybody had a great deal of respect for one another
and worked well with one another.[47]

In her memoir, Peterson wrote that she looked forward to working
with Morton and his team "for four years," suggesting that she had not yet
determined what she would do when Pete retired at the end of 1970.[48]

Describing life at the RNC, Peterson recalled:

> We had every reason to believe the White House would give us 100%
> cooperation because, following his election, Richard Nixon had told
> the National Committee he planned to devote some of his time to
> building a powerful party. He told us we were the leaders within our
> states and we were going to have a lot to say and he would listen. Pa-
> tronage and items of [a] political nature were ours. He said there
> never would be a National Chairman with the mandate Rog Morton
> had, and he would back him 100% in every decision, at all times.

"At the beginning," she added, "we all thought we were part of the 'family.' "[49]

*  *  *

After eight years, there was no shortage of Republicans jostling for jobs in the new administration. It was a time when members of Congress still handpicked local postmasters and rural mail carriers, before there were well-funded presidential transition offices. Peterson stressed that Nixon had promised state party leaders they would control patronage.[50] Morton had been assured that the RNC would be involved to help build a stronger party, and Peterson had been told that she was in charge. But instead White House aides had asserted control—and were stepping on toes.

From the perspective of government reformers, of course, less parti-san involvement would probably be a plus. But Morton and Peterson also sought to bring more women and minorities into government. Further, Peterson grew increasingly frustrated when she could not do the job that she thought she had been hired to perform.

In truth, most of the openings probably involved more show than substance. The same month Peterson assumed her new job, the *Washington Post's* "Federal Diary" column observed that members of Congress "don't seem to realize that Mr. Nixon has only about 2,000 honest-to-goodness political and policy-making slots to call his own. And many of them have already been filled, although the White House still gets about 1,000 letters a day concerning employment."[51]

A few months later, Peterson acknowledged as much. Although one newspaper reported that "every proposed nominee for federal appoint-ment—from federal marshal to federal judge—is supposed to be referred to Mrs. Peterson," she noted that "most of the administration's glamour jobs were filled before she took her present position."[52] There were, however, another seven thousand, mostly honorary jobs on boards ranging from the Mental Retardation Board to the Commission for the Preservation of the White House.

In a May memo to Republican national committeewomen, Peterson urged them to "appoint an able group of women to work with you who can talk to business women and civic groups and get their ideas" on potential female appointees. "There is a commission for almost everything—every type of disease, education, industry, and so on," she wrote. She emphasized that the names should be accompanied by biographies with the nominee's "complete background AND THE PARTICULAR AREA OF COMPETENCE." She reminded them that "this is a very important assignment."[53]

Personnel matters at the White House were first handled by Nixon's political adviser, John Sears, with support from Harry Flemming, a special assistant to the president, and Peter Flanigan, a Wall Street financier and Nixon friend.

The operation was, by several reports, distrusted by party regulars. John Osborne, *The New Republic*'s White House correspondent, wrote:

> John Sears, with his clinically intelligent approach to politics and politicians, and two other Presidential assistants dealing with personnel matters, Harry Flemming and Peter Flanigan, simply did not strike orthodox Republicans as the proper types to be vetting candidates for high-level, high-pay appointments before they were approved and announced by the President. It was not so much that Nixon's talent hunters scorned Republican applicants—they didn't; far from it—but they looked first for good *Nixon* Republicans, second for good *party* men, and that they actually seemed to believe all that Nixon stuff about quality first and party next.[54]

Meanwhile, Rowland Evans and Robert Novak reported that Flanigan insisted on using "a cumbersome, unevaluated list of job applicants" that Flemming had compiled and computerized, but that was "a laughingstock among practicing politicians" and "filled with names solicited . . . from such unlikely sources as 'Who's Who.'"[55]

After years of crisscrossing the country and serving as a state party chair, Peterson had a Rolodex as big as anyone's. But she found herself caught in the middle between the White House and her state-party friends.

> [The state people] bitched and bitched about this. Roger, Jimmie and I bore the brunt of it every time we communicated with the troops across the country.... Suspicions ran high at 1600 Pennsylvania Avenue. As stupid as it is, they must have thought the National Committee and the leaders in the states were trying to cut in on THEIR personal power, instead of wanting to be helpful. Anyone who knows the no-win situation of handling political appointments knows there is no glory to it.[56]

"The problem of rewarding the party faithful," Evans and Novak wrote at the time, "has plagued President Nixon and . . . Morton out of all proportion to the potential party benefits involved."[57]

By mid-May, Harry Dent, the South Carolina party chairman, was brought in to replace Sears and smooth ruffled feathers. The move helped placate the southern chairmen, but the patronage battles continued. "The inability of the National Committee and the White House to coordinate their competing patronage systems," Evans and Novak observed, "led to bizarre results," including competing lists of appointees developed by Cabinet members and the national committee, and a presidential appointment for one of the biggest Democratic contributors in New Jersey without a head's up to that state's Republican leaders.[58]

On one occasion Peterson went through an intermediary to try to set up a meeting with Flanigan to discuss appointments for women. She recalled, "He sent back word, 'Elly is not my dish of tea.' I considered sending him a formal note announcing the fact I was not requesting a bedding down with him; I simply wanted to discuss business."[59] The committee staff, she said, laughed about it and then advised the state committees to contact Flanigan directly.

But she could not laugh it off forever.

> There were many people displeased with the appointments but we, at the National Committee, . . . tried to convince our state organization people that we could all work together.
>
> Then, I began to find out, bit by bit, that there was no "working together." Moderates were not only outside the circle, but also "sus-

pect." At one point, Harry Dent told some of his southerners, who rushed to repeat it to me: "We don't quite trust her at the White House."[60]

She added, "I found out about this time [that] I had changed from being a purely Republican political animal. It just didn't seem worth it to fight the small time bores like Harry Dent and the White House crowd .. [.] and in a very short time, being the 'in-house woman liberal' was a drag to me!"[61]

Another time she observed, "My principal task at the National Committee on some days seemed to be nursing back to happy life the various good Republicans [Charles] Colson and the Palace Guard stepped on during the course of the day."[62]

On another occasion, she wrote:

None of us realized the power of the Nixon inside staff: the Palace Guard. In their eyes, I (and some of the others) were rank outsiders ... anyone who had been with Romney, Rockefeller or Scranton ... HORRORS! And then to add to that—being a woman!!! They did not forget my earlier transgressions or the fact that at the Convention I cast my vote for Romney for Vice President. Looking back, I can see how their minds worked. Later, having many occasions to see their repugnance at working with women, their total lack of perception of any political worth of women, I can understand the situation better than I did at the time.[63]

In *Nixon's Civil Rights,* an overview of the contradictions of the Nixon administration's civil rights policies, Dean J. Kotlowski observed that the president's conservative advisers "expressed contempt for women's abilities and equal rights." White House chief of staff H. R. Haldeman, for instance, refused to hire women for advance positions in Nixon's 1972 campaign, saying it was "a stupid idea which will cause more trouble than it's worth." Kotlowski noted, "Sexist comments were far more common than racist slurs in Nixon's administration." Regarding women's rights, he added, "[T]he president and his aides were too steeped in traditional roles to offer anything beyond halfhearted leadership."[64] From her own vantage point, Peterson observed that Haldeman "was so anti-women, he wouldn't even have any on his staff. He used male secretaries, even."[65]

In the final weeks of the 1968 campaign, Nixon had asserted, "We cannot and will not miss bringing qualified women into positions of government they can fill." He noted that there had not been a female Cabinet secretary since Eisenhower named Oveta Culp Hobby to be secretary of health, education and welfare.[66]

At an early White House press conference, Vera Glaser, then Washington bureau chief of the North American Newspaper Alliance, decided to raise the issue again. She observed that women had received only three of the two hundred high-level appointments that Nixon had made. "Could you tell us, sir, whether we can expect a more equitable recognition of women's abilities, or are we going to remain a lost sex?"

Nixon replied, "Would you be interested in coming into the government?" a response that Glaser thought "was a little snide." But, she added, he must have realized, " 'I'm on television with 50 million people watching,' and he turned quite serious."

"Very seriously," the president responded, "I had not known that only three had gone to women, and I shall see that we correct the imbalance very promptly."[67]

But it didn't happen overnight. In late May, Peterson reported to Morton that out of 1,170 appointments, fewer than 20 had gone to women, and she complained with exasperation, "THE MEN SAID THEY SIMPLY HADN'T THOUGHT OF IT." The Cabinet, she said, should be pushed to hire more women.[68]

Peterson launched a survey to identify the extent to which women were, in fact, working in high-level federal government jobs. Her goal was likely two-fold: to try to develop a positive public relations message but also to uncover vacancies and identify competent women who could fill them.

She found two volunteers, Katherine "Kitty" Massenburg, the Republican national committeewoman from Maryland, and Robenia Smith, to work on the project. The task, she said, proved challenging because of the "buttoned-up operations of the White House staff. Some of the agencies felt you were up to something if you inquired, and some probably didn't even know."[69] Smith eventually came on full time.

Appointments were set up at federal agencies, and the women tried to update the numbers in "Women in Public Service," a 1959 study by the RNC women's staff. It was not an easy task. As Peterson recounted in her memoir:

Then there was the splendid gentleman from [the] Commerce [Department] who listened to the women's story, sat back in his chair with his paunch properly adjusted, and his feet on the desk, and came forth with, "Now, ladies, I do not presume to advise you."

"Oh," breathed Robenia, "please do. We could use any advice you care to give us."

"Then," said our gracious, friendly diplomat, "let me make this clear. We are all friendly here to the Administration. [By inference Kitty and Robenia weren't!] We believe it is unethical for you to come through the back door to try to get jobs for women." At this point, the "ladies" left—furious! Since Commerce failed to appoint any visible women during this era, I suppose this was his out![70]

At the Justice Department, Peterson recalled with tongue-in-cheek, "they found warmth and friendship! 'All you need,' said the man interviewed here, 'is to come up with some women with the proper qualifications.'" When they inquired what those were, he replied, "They should have graduated at the head of their class, been Phi Beta Kappa, should have had about 10 years of experience in civil or criminal courts and should be under 30, if at all possible!"

The survey extended to the statehouses. "One southern governor wrote us a charming letter, telling us he had nothing against women," Peterson recalled. "He had not appointed one, but if he ever came across one he felt could serve, he would surely be glad to appoint her!" Other inquiries went unanswered; when reports could be found, they usually confirmed that there were very few women in the top jobs.[71]

Peterson faced a difficult balancing act as she tried to put a positive spin on the Nixon administration's record on appointments while pushing internally to improve it.

In July, four "irate" Republican congresswomen—Florence P. Dwyer of New Jersey, Margaret Heckler of Massachusetts, Charlotte Reid of Illinois, and Catherine May of Washington—met with the president to complain about his lack of progress. In a memo to Nixon, Dwyer asserted that "none of us are feminists . . . we seek only equal opportunity." The administration "has done absolutely nothing of significance in the field of women's rights, responsibilities and opportunities."[72]

According to a subsequent news report, the congresswomen "professed surprise to learn how many women held top administration positions." The women arrived with a list with only twenty names, but left with one showing thirty-seven, presumably a tally that Peterson was keeping. Peterson, it was reported, "will have the continuing responsibility for working with the lady lawmakers on this problem" and she had "put together a list of several hundred competent women who are available for appointment."[73]

Still, the numbers her staff eventually produced were discouraging. With the exception of women serving as mayors of cities larger than twenty-eight thousand people, the number of women serving in Congress, state elective positions, and legislatures had actually declined since 1959. In a report to the Republican Women's Federation of Michigan, she noted that in his first nine months Nixon had appointed 135 women to "key posts in the Federal Government, in International Affairs and on important Committees and Commissions." Still, the list actually included women described as "confidential secretary," "special assistant," "executive assistant," or "personal secretary." Peterson herself faulted the White House for including "Agnew's mail clerk" on one list. The survey, she later advised the Michigan women, "offers little excitement in the advance[s] women have made. . . ."[74]

Before the end of the year, the administration hastily assembled a President's Task Force on Women's Rights and Responsibilities that included Glaser and Massenburg and was chaired by Virginia Allan, the past president of the National Federation of Business and Professional Women's Clubs. Within two months, they produced "A Matter of Simple Justice," with recommendations for addressing women's concerns. Among other things, they suggested that the president hire a special assistant for women's rights.

Allan recalled, thirty years later, that Peterson "was in there pushing all the time" as the task force rushed to complete its work in time for the president's State of the Union address.[75] But, as Kotlowski described it, "Unprepared for the task force's agenda, top Nixon aides buried it" and the release of the report "became a public relations nightmare."[76] Not one word was mentioned in the State of the Union address. And, as Peterson recalled, "Many of the people on the Commission were asked to speak about it. Many members of the press wanted to know about it. The White House staff handed out excuses. That made newspaper people all the more eager. Women's groups asked for copies for study. Excuse after excuse was given. Finally, someone leaked it to a Florida paper, and the re-

port was finally printed." A promised dinner at the White House, an opportunity to brief the White House staff, never materialized, according to
Peterson. Nor were any recommendations included when the next State of
the Union address was prepared in January 1971.

Peterson observed:

> At a time when women were becoming more and more disen-
> chanted with government, at a time when almost all of the well-
> known women's national organizations were beginning their fight
> for equality, there was a blindness in the resistance in the White
> House. I believe they felt the women would continue to do their vol-
> unteer work regardless. They felt women would continue to take or-
> ders and perform, but it ain't necessarily so!
>
> The Republican Party started their gender gap in these areas.
> The male politician will continue to intone "God bless the ladies"
> and some will listen but many will turn their heads and go into work
> other than politics. . . . And it was obvious from the beginning that to
> most of the men, women were second class citizens.[77]

* * *

Over the years, Peterson had learned how to multitask. If one project
wasn't going particularly well, she could always focus on another one. In
this case, it was taking the action centers nationwide.

In late June 1969, Morton announced that Peterson would direct a
new program called "Action Now." Tina Harrower, the national committeewoman from Connecticut, would head teams that would develop projects to address local problems such as "narcotics, conservation, pollution
and consumer protection," and John Marttila would work to establish new
action centers, based on the Detroit model. There was no apparent coordination with Fisher, who was reported to be seeking support from the
private sector and asking women's volunteer organizations about their
priorities.[78]

In an RNC brochure, Peterson described the initiative this way.

> The Community Action Program is a Republican answer—not alto-
> gether new but often unpracticed. It is a call for voluntary commu-
> nity involvement—a call to individuals to work together to bring
> about solutions to the problems of their cities and towns. . . .

We must mobilize this great volunteer working force and give it the direction it needs. By doing this, we can accomplish two things: Republicans everywhere can make a personal investment in their country, taking a little time for America; and, it is a way to gain for the Republican Party an acceptance among groups who have previously regarded Republicans as aliens.

Politically speaking, the key word is "acceptance," for we are not now looking for votes or party members. It is enough, initially, to establish an honest and effective working relationship with the people who most need our help—we can then understand, from first-hand experience, the real truth about the problems of America.

There are 162 million adults in our country. Fewer than a third of them are Republicans. Many are not interested in their communities. Nevertheless, it is our job to provide the stimulus that will make them want to help.[79]

Based on the missionary work Peterson had done when she was state chair, action centers had already been launched in Hartford, Dallas, and Wilmington, Delaware. By January 1, 1970, it was expected that additional centers would open in Baltimore, Oakland, Pittsburgh, Philadelphia, Washington, DC, and a small town in the Midwest.

"The action center," she said, "is the most meaningful thing the Republican Party can do with its headquarters operation. I deplore the kind of center opened in so many cities where you have a woman to answer a phone that doesn't ring and a pile of literature not relevant to their concerns. . . . We say look around you, determine what needs to be done, and move in and do it in the name of the Republican Party."

In Detroit, she said, the character of the GOP had changed "from stagnant leadership to a group of young black and white activists. We just didn't have these young people before." Recalled Marttila, "We won elections we shouldn't have won, we recruited young people we shouldn't have." The party, he added, "was stunned by who the face of that district became—young, sophisticated black professionals who otherwise could have been Democrats. . . ."[80]

Peterson anticipated that it would take six or seven years for the projects to make inroads into the Democrats' traditional urban strongholds. She acknowledged that the action program "resembles the function once performed by old-style political organizations." Still, David Broder observed at the time, the fate of the initiative "will be important to those in both parties who are intrigued by the possibility of using local political headquarters as social action centers."[81]

Meanwhile, Peterson also announced plans to scrap the annual Republican women's conference in Washington, which, for seventeen years had, in Glaser's words, "drawn thousands of little old ladies to view the cherry blossoms and soak up GOP gospel from party wheelhorses." Instead, Peterson planned to bring five hundred activist women, particularly from the African American, Jewish, and ethnic communities, to brainstorm with GOP national committeewomen and state vice chairmen (still overwhelmingly female) on how to broaden the party's base. Between July and September, she convened meetings of women from each targeted group to enlist their support. Peterson was, Glaser concluded, "shaking the GOP right down to its elephantine toenails."[82]

The progress that the Detroit action center had made in just two short years was cited as evidence that the idea could work in other parts of the country. In Detroit, Willie Lipscomb, a twenty-six-year-old psychology major from Wayne State University, had been recruited to run for party chairman in the district where the center was located. Lipscomb said he had been attracted through a mailing from the "Metropolitan Action Center." Now the center's communications messages would become much more overtly political.[83]

Broder noted that the center's Republican staff members and volunteers had, in at least one case, applied overt pressure on a landlord who was a major Republican contributor to get repairs made for a tenant. In another case, they got the state to shut down an insurance company whose sales practices were preying on inner-city residents.[84]

Peterson was heartened by the positive press coverage the initiative received. Paul Hope of the *Evening Star* wrote:

> Other women may get more glamorous assignments in the Nixon administration, but Elly Peterson is likely to have a more lasting effect on the Republican party than any of them.
>
> Mrs. Peterson, one-third of a triumvirate that built the Republican organization in Michigan a decade ago, has been given the job of building the party in the cities.
>
> Her office is not in a plush town house, and she won't be hostess at fancy parties for dignitaries. Her desk is in a partitioned section of

the Republican National Committee headquarters that presently is half white and half blue because workmen have finished only half of a repainting job. Many of the parties she gives are likely to be in the ghetto, attended by people who never thought they would see the inside of a Republican precinct headquarters.

She doesn't believe for a minute the many reports that the Nixon strategy for reelection is a Southern-oriented one that largely writes off the Negro vote and the industrial states of the Northeast.[85]

Peterson acknowledged that "we may not get results for years." But in the same article, there was the first hint of retirement. Hope said that when Pete retired in 1971, Peterson planned "to hang up her political running shoes." But he was skeptical, "for as Elly Peterson once said: 'I get more fun out of a precinct organization than six no trump, doubled.'"

The initiative was launched at a time when the Nixon administration was sending out mixed messages on its vision for the party. Kevin Phillips, then an aide to Attorney General Mitchell, had just published *The Emerging Republican Majority*, which called for writing off blacks, Jews, liberals, and northeasterners and focusing instead on voters from the South, West, and Midwest. The White House took steps to keep Phillips under wraps. Asked for a comment on what became known as the "southern strategy," Peterson replied tartly, "The idea came from a book by a young man I'd never even heard of. . . . I just don't buy the concept, and neither does Rogers Morton."[86]

Virginia Knauer, White House special assistant for consumer affairs and one of the top female appointees, reflected this tension in a speech she delivered the same month to the National Federation of Republican Women: "There are some critics who say that this administration doesn't care about the Negro vote—that it doesn't care about the industrial states of the Northeast. Elly's programs demonstrate that that philosophy is a lot of hogwash. The Republican Party, the party of the people, cares about people in the North, in the South, in the East and in the West."[87]

Nixon's public posture supported widening the party's base, while his aides were pursuing policies that sent the opposite message. After eight months on the job, Peterson was invited to the White House with Morton and two other RNC officials to discuss their plans with Nixon and Dent. She recalled:

If it had been hard to sell the programs to working politicians in the states, it was not difficult for this politician President to grasp their import. He was strongly in favor of both the action program and the involvement of women—my other "thing.". . .

When I told him of the women's advisory groups I had organized: Jewish women, the Council of Black Involvement, and the ethnic groups because these three groups seldom had a chance to get elected to party positions, and this was one way of involving them, he said, "Elly, continue to work with the black people. They should be made to understand what our party can do for them and will do for them. This is the group where we can make the greatest impact, and I hope you will continue this with all you have. Don't worry about the Jews. You won't get 'em anyway." I remembered this statement often when black groups attacked him, and I found that all too often I was considered by minorities to be an Administration woman and one of the few willing to work with black groups.

The president, she recalled:

was interested in every item of our programs, made comments and suggestions on each. When I told him how difficult it was to get male leadership to understand what the action program could mean to them, he would, he said, write them a letter giving it his blessing and encouraging them to participate. He did this, and while it helped some, the fact that we could secure no meaningful assistance from the White House staff took the strength away from his help. . . .

It was a friendly, interesting meeting which lasted 45 minutes, and the President sent us away feeling he was sincerely interested in helping us build a strong organization.

In fact, it was the last time she spoke with Richard Nixon.[88]

A photograph of Peterson and Nixon was featured on the front of the RNC's weekly "Monday" newsletter two months later, noting that "Elly" had "reported on her great ACTION NOW! Program—a model of GOP volunteer service in the nation's inner cities."[89]

But, as Kotlowski notes, Nixon's national political strategy "practiced the politics of exclusion or inclusion as circumstances dictated. By 1969, the president viewed African Americans as strong Democrats and expended little effort to gain their votes. The National Association for the Advancement of Colored People (NAACP), he complained, 'would say [my] rhetoric was poor [even] if I gave the Sermon on the Mount.' . . . On civil rights, he warned aides not to 'expect any credit for what you do, or any real PR gains, just do what is right and forget it.' "[90]

For a time, at least, the Action Now initiative did, in fact, provide the party with positive public relations, as Peterson urged Republicans, particularly women, to take on projects. "A week with Mrs. Peterson would be a strenuous one for a woman half her age," one reporter concluded, "as she travels to at least two and frequently three states to promote Action Now." In between trips, it was noted, she worked thirteen-hour days in Washington before returning to Charlotte to spend weekends with Pete. ("Her recipe for rest is to put everything that could cause tension or worry about her work out of her mind completely at night and on the weekend," the reporter added.)[91]

She told a regional conference in Albany that her voluntarism project was "more satisfying" than actual campaign work.[92] She told Wichita Republicans, "Call this an idealistic approach if you want to. I call it practical to clean up your own back yard."[93] She urged Tampa Bay Republicans to sell themselves as "the problem solver."[94]

In North Carolina in late 1969, Peterson acknowledged that problems were spreading to rural America, too. "I wouldn't have believed that possible, but in Charlotte, Michigan, a city of 10,000 population—a rural area—three of our finest high school students were picked up for drugs," she told the Buncombe County Republican Women's Club.[95]

Among those who were involved with the Action Now Committee was then representative George H. W. Bush, who chaired a Task Force on Earth Resources and Population Control. Two decades later, in his inaugural address, Bush spoke of a "thousand points of light" and called for "a new engagement in the lives of others, a new activism, hands-on and involved, that gets the job done." He then added, "The old ideas are new again because they're not old, they are timeless: duty, sacrifice, commitment, and a patriotism that finds its expression in taking part and pitching in."[96]

By the end of Morton's first year, the RNC could report that action centers were operating in Dallas, Milwaukee, Hartford, and New Haven, and a second center was open in Detroit. Meanwhile, Republicans were said to be conducting public information and education programs about national problems in twelve states, with the help of films and brochures about the problems.[97]

But there were still setbacks. An action center was initially planned for Miami to work with Cuban refugees. The Cubans, Peterson noted, "were desperately in need of help and we felt were candidates for Republicanism if we could help them." But, she recalled, the project faltered when a prominent Republican woman moved to strike the item from the party's budget, saying, "After all, you know, we don't really want to get involved with Negroes."[98]

"Sometimes the people were very receptive," Marttila recalled. "But at other times people would look like, 'Who is this lunatic?'"[99]

In October 1969, Peterson took a break from her RNC responsibilities to travel behind the Iron Curtain to the Soviet Union, Romania, and Yugoslavia as part of a Delegation of American Women for International Understanding. It was the first of several similar trips that Peterson would make over the next decade.

A few years later, she wrote:

> One thing that did stand out was the emphasis Russians have put on the ability of their women to be good propagandists. They use their Soviet Women's Committee as a strong propaganda arm, assigning them to other countries, encouraging them to bring in women from the Third World Countries.
>
> America could do more of this, it seems to me.

She went on to write, "It is because I feel so strongly about this country that I am interested in recognizing the potential of all women. We are part of America's vast natural resources and can contribute a great deal to the strength of our country. We must, for this burden is too heavy for men alone to carry."[100]

CHAPTER EIGHT

# A Crisis of Conscience

AS THE NEW YEAR BEGAN, Peterson was invited back to the White House. It was not to discuss political appointments for women, voluntarism in urban neighborhoods, or the upcoming congressional elections. Rather it was to attend church.

Dr. Norman Vincent Peale, of Marble Collegiate Church in New York, led the worship service, and the Vienna Boys' Choir sang. As she sat through the service, Peterson found herself pondering "the idea of the President inviting God to the White House, instead of going to church himself."[1]

In his sermon, Peale addressed two problems that were "upsetting people generally": dealing with stress and standing up to crises.[2] The message was well timed. Eight days later the president responded to the rejection of his first Supreme Court nominee from the South by naming U.S. Circuit Judge G. Harrold Carswell instead. Within days, newspapers revealed that twenty years before Carswell had supported segregation as "the only practical and correct way of life."

For Peterson, it was becoming increasingly difficult to be a Nixon cheerleader.

At the RNC, Whitman recalled, Peterson "was loyal on the surface," but the staff knew she was unhappy, particularly because of their after-hours conversations. "She wouldn't hesitate to confide in some of us who she knew were of the same persuasion," Whitman explained. It was "disappointment more than frustration," disappointment over "missed opportunities, disappointment in the message. . . . But she wasn't somebody who bitched and moaned and complained. She wasn't disloyal in that sense."

After Carswell was nominated, Whitman said the White House asked the RNC staff to make phone calls to state Republican chairmen to drum up support. Whitman didn't think Carswell was qualified and didn't want to make calls. Peterson's example, she said, "emboldened" her to refuse. Peterson's message was that "if you feel strongly about it, that's what you do, stand up for your principles."

There were no repercussions at the RNC. "The attitude," Whitman said, "was, 'Okay, if you don't want to do it, there will be somebody else here who does think he's qualified.' . . . I'm not sure the White House would have been happy had they known that . . . but the attitude at the committee was . . . 'We're all in this and we're not going to agree on everything all the time, but that doesn't mean we have to take it out on one another when we don't.'"[3]

She counts Peterson, along with her parents, as her role models. "You don't set out to be a role model, it's not something you consciously assume, but unconsciously she was an enormous role model for a lot of people. . . . She never compromised on her principles and that was a message that came through, without preaching, loud and clear to those of us who worked there at the time."[4]

The party's conservative wing, however, viewed things differently. The American Conservative Union's January 1970 newsletter noted with alarm that Peterson was listed as a member of the dinner committee marking the seventh anniversary of the liberal Ripon Society. A commentary observed, "Mrs. Peterson, thought to be a moderate Republican in her views, seems to have veered to the left. She apparently sees no clash between her official party post and lending her name to a GOP splinter group which constantly attacks the President."[5]

The Carswell nomination contributed to another decision of conscience that was personally painful for Peterson: the resignation of Marttila as coordinator of the action centers.

In a prominent story a few months later, the *Detroit Free Press* quoted Marttila as saying that he had resigned because he thought "the policies of the present administration are racist." The article noted that through their organizing techniques Marttila and his associates had captured 45 percent of the black vote the previous fall for an ultimately unsuccessful Republican candidate for mayor of New Haven, Connecticut. But, the article said, Marttila "had reached the point where he could no longer justify staying with the Republicans."

Marttila told reporter Clark Hoyt, "Here I was, under the guise of some social program, recruiting people to be involved in the Republican Party and the administration just wasn't responding to their problems. I'd go out and try to get minority persons involved, then I'd look at the front page the next day and see something like Carswell."

Marttila said that he was reluctant to talk publicly about his decision because "he did not want to jeopardize the Action Program or harm Mrs. Peterson," who had brought him to the RNC. Marttila added, "I don't want to become the public symbol of anything. I paid my dues. For 3 1/2 years I worked for internal reform in the Republican Party, and the seeds of what I left may be very positive. . . . But now it's time for me to work with the party that is speaking more forthrightly on the issues."[6] Marttila joined the first—and ultimately successful—Democratic congressional campaign of Father Robert Drinan of Massachusetts.

After the article appeared, Marttila sent Peterson a touching, eight-page, handwritten letter:

> I hope you realize that I had much more to say about you than "I didn't want to harm Mrs. Peterson." Unfortunately what has appeared I will have to live with. Although I wouldn't reuse the phrase "racist" again because it is far too emotional and prevents rational discussion, I believe Nixon is racist & destructive to this country.
>
> What genuinely disturbs me is that people may misinterpret how I felt about the past three years under you. As you know, I am far, far from ungrateful. My present job today is largely due to my past activity with the GOP. It makes an important difference to me that you know that I tried over & over in the interview to point this out—unfortunately, the news was that I was leaving for the Dems rather than I once worked for a *wonderful* human being named Elly Peterson. . . . You have taught me that decency & political participation are not incompatible. It is the way I plan to govern my political life. . . .
>
> More than any other human being, you have helped me become what I am, and I will never forget you for this. Although you may disagree with my decision, I know that I will not let you down—you and I are working for common principles.
>
> Knowing that I have undoubtedly caused you embarrassment & difficulty after all you graciously gave me will bother me for a long,

long time. I am deeply sorry for any trouble. Serving under you has been the greatest privilege of my life.[7]

In her memoir, Peterson recalled:

I took quite a beating over John's leaving, especially in his old district. As he had left to become a Democrat, the right wingers were convinced he had been a "Communist" from the start. They simply didn't understand John. He was, and is, a man of great compassion and conviction. As long as he felt he could have a part in the shaping of a new way for a political party to operate in human terms, he was willing to give it everything he had. He suffered the ostracism from the White House Staff, which was hitting many people, and he did not have the prior memories of Nixon or deep party loyalty to keep him going. It was, to my mind, a tragedy to lose him.[8]

More than forty years later, the episode still pained Marttila deeply. He had attempted to leave quietly, and said he had not nailed down the job with Drinan until after his departure. He was shocked by the prominence the story had received and "devastated for Elly." He recalled, "I was so embarrassed by it, I didn't call her. I'm sure she reached out to me, because I was stricken, honestly stricken" by the story. "She was loving and forgiving."

Looking back, Marttila rejected any suggestion that the idea behind the action centers was politically naive. Peterson, Milliken, and Romney, he said, "were people who were really committed to the concept of expanding the base of the Republican Party and in the right way, and on the right terms. . . . So therefore I think they deserve enormous credit for giving it a shot. . . . For a party that needed answers, some kind of experimentation was laudable."[9]

But without the attention of Peterson and Marttila, first in Detroit and later around the country, the action center initiative didn't survive—one of Peterson's "two regrets in my political career."[10] A few years later, a study by the Detroit–Ann Arbor chapter of the Ripon Society concluded, "Since the Detroit Center was the only one in the nation which was actually functioning at a meaningful level, its failure meant that the Republican party had a national program which existed on paper only."[11]

Some years later, Milliken ran into Marttila at the funeral of former Detroit mayor Coleman Young. He wrote Peterson about their conversation.

We recalled those early days when you were reaching out as chair of the party to a broader constituency; how you wanted the party to care about people, how you wanted compassion and concern to be a genuine part of the objectives of the Republican party. It was good to talk about those things again.

He told me about a meeting he had set up one time for you . . . with a group of young, very liberal, very suspicious—even hostile—Democrats. He said when you came into the room and started to talk, they were absolutely captivated. You were caring, you were funny, you were obviously totally honest and sincere. You mesmerized them, he said.

How far this party has come from those days![12]

* * *

In early 1970, another drama was unfolding that Peterson would remember as "surely one of the saddest experiences in my career in politics."[13]

Michigan Republicans had to find another credible challenger to Phil Hart. In January, Peterson was summoned to a meeting at Romney's HUD office, along with Ford, Griffin, and Milliken, now facing his first campaign for governor since succeeding Romney. "It was almost a repeat of 1964," Peterson recalled, "except this time I was not about to be asleep at the switch and thrust into another statewide campaign. Name after name was mentioned and discarded, and then out of the clear blue sky, George announced that Jerry wanted Lenore to run! There was a moment of silence, and I could well picture what was running through the minds of each man."

One concern was the prospect of a primary battle against conservative state senator Robert Huber of Troy, who had already announced his candidacy. No one wanted Milliken to have to run with Huber. Romney, she recalled, was not happy about the prospect of his wife running, but had decided "that if the party needed Lenore and if Milliken wanted her, then it would be okay with him."[14]

Peterson might have viewed Lenore Romney's candidacy as a wonderful opportunity to promote a capable woman for an important job. But instead she "began to think of the difficulty of the campaign, of how George and Lenore would have to be separated, how much he depended on her for help in his own difficult job, of the 'slings and arrows' I had taken in my own campaign, of being a woman, and, given the polls and the character of Michigan elections, how it would be almost impossible for her to win."[15]

After mulling it over for several days, Peterson decided to phone her friend and tell her just that. They talked for about an hour. "I was adamant," Peterson recalled. "I insisted she rethink her position, and we closed on a pleasant note. I wasn't sure in my assessment of the call whether she heard everything I said."

But later Peterson learned that while they were talking Milliken was meeting with George Romney in Chicago, reaching an agreement to put a Romney on the ticket. Peterson told her aide Pam Curtis, "There goes the ball game, and it shows how much my advice counted!" In hindsight, she concluded that she should have gone directly to the men since it was obvious that Lenore "was not in on the basic decisions!"

Peterson's recounting of Mrs. Romney's campaign reflects the challenges she faced as she tried to balance several roles. As a national party official and national committeewoman, she was expected to maintain an arm's length relationship—at least until the party had formally chosen its nominee. (Huber later said that if he won the primary, he would seek Peterson's resignation, contending she had unethically used an RNC postal meter to send out mailings encouraging volunteers to support Romney and insinuating that he was a member of the John Birch Society.)[16]

Peterson also said she wanted to give Milliken and her protégées McLaughlin, Braithwaite, and Molin some breathing space to pursue their own campaign strategy without second-guessing on her part. But at the same time, it was hard for her to stay on the sidelines; Lenore Romney was a close friend, and Peterson was still viewed as one of the state's preeminent political strategists.

For whatever reason, her memoir displays some sensitivity to suggestions that she was directly involved in what political reporter Tim Skubick described as "a comedy of errors and political pratfalls from the opening bell."[17] But at the same time, she was restrained in her criticism of old friends and political allies.

As reports of a Romney candidacy surfaced, the *Washington Post* said that "friends" of Mrs. Romney had been working to turn her personal popularity into votes at the upcoming consensus meeting to choose the party's candidate. The "most powerful support," the article reported, had come from Peterson and Republican national committeeman Harold McClure.[18]

But Peterson asserted in her memoir that she was "very cautious" and not that heavily involved until the day of the meeting that was designed to choose a consensus candidate. She denied making calls on Romney's behalf and said she was kept busy with her work in Washington and travels across the country.[19]

On February 21, several hundred Republicans gathered in Lansing to pick a candidate from among the two dozen people who had expressed interest. "It was every governor's nightmare," Skubick wrote. "You want to give the impression you are in charge and in control of your party but Milliken clearly was not."[20]

From the moment she arrived, Peterson recalled, "people were asking me what I thought, how I believed it would go, why wasn't the Governor indicating more of a preference, was it really true he wanted Lenore? It all smelled wrong to me. The attitudes were peculiar, and there was an aura of uncertainty in the air." But she decided that "the best thing to do was NOTHING" and referred questions to the governor's staff.

A late entrant into the race was U.S. Rep. Don Riegle. As the speakers rose in turn, his speech, she recalled, "was magnificent." He was "immaculate, intense, a hard charger all the way." Riegle spoke for ten minutes, and brought down the house.

Lenore Romney went next. "She was ill prepared," Peterson recalled, unaware that she faced a challenge. She did not know a campaign speech was expected rather than an acceptance speech.[21] "Lenore was dull and showed no fire," McLaughlin remembered. "The result was to contrast the young, hungry Riegle with the aging grandmother."[22]

The first vote was taken, with no one gaining the 75 percent required to qualify as the consensus nominee. Peterson had to leave early to make a speech in Marquette. "By this time," she recalled, "it was obvious" that two Milliken staff members were working the room in support of Riegle. "This, in itself, made me mad. What angered me is that those of us in the original meeting were not brought into this move. I delivered myself of some unladylike remarks to one of them as I left the room. I never forgave myself for letting them get to me, but I was boiling mad. My thoughts were all for Lenore, who had been put in a terrible situation through no fault of her own. (Because she was a woman????)"[23] (The extent of Peterson's fury on this occasion is underscored by the fact that she so rarely expressed anger in her memoir. In this instance, it was likely fueled by her own memories of how men had manipulated her at the start of *her* Senate campaign.)

Checking back after the speech, she learned that in a competition with "no consensus" her friend had managed to garner only 60 percent of the vote. She wrote her sister, "Suffice it to say *somebody* double crossed somebody. L.R. is out *I hope* and I am *most* relieved."[24]

But that was not to be the case.

On Monday, George Romney caught up with her in Oklahoma City. He had drafted a statement about his wife's candidacy and wanted to run it by Peterson. She was "horrified," and before she heard it she knew he shouldn't release it. But Romney was "adamant."[25]

In the meantime, Milliken called a press conference that Skubick recalled "was like covering a train wreck." One reporter asked Milliken if he had been run over by a Rambler driven by a little old lady, a reference to Romney's American Motors. "Would you turn around and let us see the tire marks?"[26]

"The evening press," Peterson recalled, "was brutal. George Romney was trying to take over Michigan! Bill Milliken wasn't running things at all, Lenore hadn't won, she had won, Don Riegle should have won, and so on."[27] "Romney's reassertion of power was quick and brutal," noted the *Detroit News*, "and the full force of it fell squarely on Milliken. It may well have irrevocably damaged the governor's ability to lead his party."[28]

"To a person the phone calls we received said it was the biggest mess Michigan Republicans had ever seen," Peterson observed.[29]

It was an uphill struggle for Lenore Romney after that. She managed to defeat Huber in the August primary but captured only 52 percent of the vote. Going forward, Peterson recalled, "the aura of George running the campaign from HUD in Washington always hung over the campaign, and Lenore never was able to establish herself as her own candidate." The Romney and Milliken campaigns went their separate ways, and "those who had promised to help Lenore Romney in the beginning suddenly were very busy elsewhere."[30]

* * *

It is not clear exactly when Peterson made up her mind to retire at the end of 1970. But as the months went by, she expressed her opinions more freely and leavened her personal disappointments by trying to have fun with her staff.

She told an audience of women journalists that it was a mistake for

Sen. Roman Hruska of Nebraska (the father of one of her early RNC aides) to defend the Carswell nomination by suggesting that "mediocrity" deserved representation on the Supreme Court. And she described the publication of then White House counselor Daniel Patrick Moynihan's recommendation of a period of "benign neglect" on race relations as "a tragedy," adding, "I happen to be a strong promoter of civil rights and I do not look forward to neglect of any kind."[31]

In April, the Republicans gathered in Washington for their national leadership conference, under the banner "Together We Can." This time Peterson was in charge of the retooled event, which replaced the women's gathering, as Peterson had vowed the year before. "Since I felt it would be my last hurrah, I wanted it to be good and loud," she recalled.

Among the twists she and her staff devised to spice up the program was a "reverse press panel" entitled "The Media Looks at the Republican Party," featuring five nationally known journalists, including Simeon Booker of *Ebony* and *Jet* magazines, columnist Marianne Means, and Dan Rather of CBS News. "For once," she said, "there were more people in the meetings than in the bars!"[32]

But the estrangement between the RNC and the White House was telegraphed by the fact that while the conference had been scheduled to accommodate Nixon's schedule, there was no guarantee that he would even show up for the final dinner with twelve hundred state leaders. Instead the president had planned his own "Evening with Johnny Cash" at the White House, where, Peterson recalled, all the Cabinet members were also expected. In the end, the president squeezed in a ten-minute speech at the RNC's gala.[33]

The story that Peterson recalled most vividly from the night involved Juanita Hunter, her young African American secretary, who had sought an RNC job after hearing about the Action Now initiative. At the last minute, Peterson and her staff realized they hadn't lined up anyone to sing the national anthem at the gala. Hunter said she could do it. Peterson recalled:

> We all looked at her, startled, not knowing if she could sing a note. But she insisted she could sing it and sing it well. Finally I told her, "Juanita, the hour is late. You sing, but if I find when you come on stage that you can't sing a note, I will personally chop you into bits." We all laughed, and the three staff members present kept worrying she would blow it.

That night my only regret was that her mother wasn't there to hear her. I introduced her by saying I hoped they would forgive a mother's pride, but this was one of my "kids." The Southern delegation, in front of the podium, stiffened as this stunning black girl walked on the stage. The top people in the Administration, in the cabinet, the Agnews, Mrs. [Martha] Mitchell—all were there. This child, looking exquisite in a long green evening gown, sang like an angel. Tears were in my eyes, I know, and when I looked down at the staff table, they were paralyzed in admiration.[34]

JoAnn Hawkins also volunteered the story, though in her version, Peterson went on stage after Hunter sang and boasted, "That's one of my children." Hawkins cited the story as an example of how Peterson "never sought glory for herself but went out of her way to highlight her staff."[35]

When the conference was over, Peterson gave her staff members bracelets with a charm that read "Together We Did." "That was the kind of attitude she brought to everything," Whitman said. "Together you can do anything." More than thirty-five years later, Hawkins also still cherished her bracelet.[36]

Peterson and her staff were also bonding around the concerns of the nascent women's movement. Theirs was a more moderate sort of feminism, still intent on working with men as team players.

The Leadership Conference marked the debut of "Mother Peterson's Political Players." For the "Where We Were" segment of the Republican Women's Leadership Council meeting, Hawkins wrote a skit, "Rights for Wronged Women or Little Nell at the Ballot Box," to celebrate the fiftieth anniversary of women's suffrage.[37] She interviewed eighty-five-year-old Alice Paul, founder of the National Women's Party, and other suffragists, and they loaned banners and vintage photographs for the staff members to use.

Said Hawkins, "We were trying to highlight the achievements of women and also emphasize the difficulty of the struggle and the bravery of the women involved. It was both a celebration of women's rights and a call to action for more equity. And, it was our attempt to indicate how women could achieve results without being particularly strident or offending men."[38]

The women were called on to repeat their program at a Romney campaign event in Michigan and at a conference marking the fiftieth anniversary of the Labor Department's Women's Bureau. At the latter, Peterson was once again frustrated that the president could not find time in his schedule to meet with participants. "Women came from all the states and left unhappy," she wrote. At the last minute, a tea with Pat Nixon was arranged.[39] Afterward, what the media described as "a small group of militant women" from the National Organization for Women (NOW) accused the president of abdicating his "responsibility as the leader of our country." They noted that the day before, he had found time to meet with a group of Boy Scouts.[40]

But Peterson, like many others of her generation and political persuasion, was still critical of the more militant feminists.

In a March 1970 speech to the American Newspaper Women's Club (ANWC), Peterson took "a dim view of the burgeoning 'women's liberation movement,' describing them as 'too few in number,'" according to Vera Glaser's summary. "In many cases, she said, they 'turn women off rather than turning them on.'"[41] A few months later an Ohio reporter quoted Peterson as saying that Martha Mitchell was a "welcome 'phenomenon' on the Washington scene" and that women's liberation leaders were "detrimental to their sex because 'they are so grim.'" The reporter added that Peterson was a "strong advocate of equal pay for equal work . . . but she doesn't think bra-burning and shrieking demonstrations are means to those ends."[42]

On August 26, NOW organized a "Women's Strike for Equality" to commemorate the fiftieth anniversary of women's suffrage. In the statement she released that day, Peterson focused more on the apathy of the suburban housewife.

> American women need to be shaken from their complacency, and women's lib, while offensive to some, is doing the job in their own way. . . .
>
> I urge the housewife who has no use for militancy and is satisfied at home, to look beyond her kitchen window at the other side of town. It's not enough to be happy yourself, you must also share that happiness with those who are not quite so fortunate. That's as much a part of women's lib as trying to get equal salaries. . . .
>
> An American woman belongs wherever she is needed—in the home, in the professions, in industry, in volunteerism. These doors have been opened by crusading men and women and it's up to the rest of us to give that final push and walk through.[43]

In general, Peterson preached a pragmatic, bipartisan approach to involving more women in politics. In her speech before the ANWC, she said, "There has never been a time in this nation's history when it needed excellence more. I'd like to see women give their full contribution to this country. If a woman can do that then I say go to it, and I'd be for her whether she's Democrat or a Republican."[44]

In May, she and Geri Joseph, then the vice chairman of the Democratic National Committee (DNC), announced that they were seeking foundation support for an in-depth poll on women's attitudes toward politics. The previous year, Peterson had surveyed state-level Republican women, but the results were discouraging. Wrote back one leader, "I hate to put into writing the attitude towards women candidates in this state . . . by the Governor, Senator and State Chairmen. The Executive Director at the headquarters made the statement that the women in the GOP should stay home in the kitchen."[45]

In a joint press release, Peterson and Joseph said that much of their concern "results from the fact that during the past ten years the number of women in public office has actually declined." The problem, they said, was bipartisan.[46]

After the lobbying of Peterson and others finally paid off in August 1970 when the army promoted its first two women generals, Anna Mae Hays and Elizabeth P. Hoisington. Peterson hosted a reception for them, "not as Republicans, but as women. We were so happy they had knocked down a barrier for women."[47] She underscored that point by inviting Harriet Cipriani, deputy vice chairman of the DNC, to help pour tea at the reception.[48]

Ironically, that same day the House approved, by a 350 to 15 vote, the Equal Rights Amendment, which Martha Griffiths had succeeded in getting discharged from the House Judiciary Committee two months before. In one of her regular, chatty memos from "Elly" to "Republican Women Leaders," Peterson commented, "You must all have been as excited—and surprised—as I was, when the Equal Rights Amendment passed by such a whopping margin. I guess that many of the members of Congress sensed that here too was a vast silent majority behind the militant organizations for equal status, and some just might have sincerely thought that it was time women emerged from the status of second class citizens."[49]

But for Republican audiences, she could retain her partisan edge. In another "Elly" memo a few weeks later, she noted that organized labor was still opposed to the amendment, and observed sarcastically, "[O]f course, it isn't because they wish to discriminate against women, you understand ... it is the PRINCIPLE OF THE THING."[50]

* * *

In May 1970, Peterson traveled to Portland, Maine, as the featured speaker for the Republican state convention. The night before, Nixon had announced on nationwide television that he was sending U.S. troops into Cambodia. Before the speeches began, the delegates adopted a resolution "of support for President Nixon, the job he has done to date, and 'the Cambodian Thing,'" in the words of a reporter who covered the event.[51]

"Elly was very much against the action," JoAnn Hawkins recalled, "but was put in an uncomfortable position and had to appear that she agreed with the group." At a press conference, Peterson said it was too early to predict what impact the Cambodian incursion would have on Nixon's reelection. "By 1972 many things can happen in Southeast Asia," she said. "We are all distressed, but we've got to think of it this way—what could the President have done? This will create an emotional problem that will affect America."[52]

In the prepared text of her speech, Peterson challenged Maine Republicans to think positively about their chances of defeating incumbent Democratic senator Edmund S. Muskie that fall. But she also practiced "tough love," adding, "Let me state clearly, I have not come here to win friends, but to gain workers and victory in the fall. I am simply not going to tell you that I think Republicans have done a good job and make simpering noises of congratulations."[53] The reporter observed, "If the opening day was dull, it certainly wasn't the fault of the orators." Peterson, he wrote, "is, in the opinion of many delegates, the best speaker which the national organization has sent trending into Maine for some time."[54]

Hawkins said she and Peterson were "particularly proud" of the speech Peterson delivered later that month when she received an honorary doctorate of laws at the hundredth annual commencement of William Woods College. The speech came a few weeks after four students were killed during an antiwar protest at Kent State University. She told the graduating students:

> Don't talk of the misery of the ghetto if you have never volunteered
> to work in one. Don't complain about the system if you have never

labored to change it from within. Don't speak of communication and reject your parents' advice and love. Don't demand academic freedom and close your college. Don't speak of peace and condone the burning of buildings. Don't advocate love if you are not willing to embrace all humanity—the poor and the unpoor, the white and the non-white, and young and the not-so-young.[55]

Undoubtedly mindful that she was a role model, she did not share the circumstances surrounding her departure from the college with either her audience or her youthful speechwriter. She graciously wrote the university president, "There just is no superlative to tell you how I feel at this honor. I can only say that in a lifetime of excitement, this is truly my 'finest hour.'"[56]

In July, Peterson ventured into what some Republicans would have considered enemy territory, addressing the convention of the National Association of Colored Women's Clubs. She said she was "not totally satisfied" with what the Nixon administration was doing to help blacks achieve their goals. Then she quickly added, "Before the reporters run out of the room to label me another critic of the Nixon administration, let me also say, I was even *less* satisfied with" the Johnson administration's record. Peterson's memories of the speech focus on the fact that the women were "totally surprised" as she detailed a list of advances minority groups had made under Nixon, because, she said, their papers and leadership "emphasized the LACK of Nixon interest."[57]

But the full text of the speech reveals this additional perspective.

Our job won't be over until there is no need for a White to reassure a Black that he cares. . . . until there is no longer a need for speeches like this. Our job is over when people judge each other by accomplishments and not by color or religion or occupation. . . .

I look for a day when we can dislike someone of a different color and not feel guilty about it. Sometimes, we are overprotective and cocktail party humanitarians will gush that all Blacks are their friends. That's ridiculous. I shouldn't expect to like all Blacks as I don't like all Whites. But civil rights is such a sensitive area that too many of us are afraid to be honest about our feelings. . . . I look for a day when Black and White neighborhood women can share koffee klatches and gossip indiscriminately about friends in either race without the cry of racist being hurled.

She pointed to the success of the action centers and then added:

> It's these unpublicized efforts that lead to harmony, not the scream-
> ing and bloody riots that foul our television screens and spill out
> abusive language and violence into our living rooms. Extremism and
> militancy, whether in the form of the clenched fist salute of a Black
> Panther or a hooded Klansman, [lead] only to anarchy. Violence
> leads only to destruction. . . . Both organizations are a dramatic way
> of expressing an opinion. Their fault is that membership in each is
> selective and discriminatory, their goal is superiority, and their
> means are destructive.[58]

The speech was later inserted in the *Congressional Record* and
reprinted in a special RNC brochure titled "A Coat of Many Colors."[59]

As the fall campaign season approached, Peterson gave up her Washington apartment because she would be spending so much time on the
road.[60] She focused on organizing several states and advising candidates'
wives on conducting parallel campaigns to support their husbands. Eight
years after she had managed Lenore Romney's travels, it was still a novel
concept. To help out, the RNC's Women's Division had prepared a pam-
phlet designed, in the words of a reporter, to teach wives "how to conduct
coffee hours, how to handle the press and how to make speeches. This participation by the wives of candidates enables them to recruit social friends,
church women and others who might like to work for the candidate personally but not full time for the Party."[61]

"Want to hear how this week's schedule is?" Peterson asked one
Florida reporter in early summer. "Yesterday I went to New York in the
morning and returned in late afternoon. Today I'm at my desk attempting
to catch up. Tomorrow, I'll be in Pittsburgh, Thursday means Minneapolis, Friday I'll spend in Duluth before heading back to Minneapolis Saturday morning. Saturday night it'll be Detroit." Each city included a speaking engagement.[62]

In September, Peterson and her staff decided to put their passion into
action and knock on doors for Louise Leonard, who was running for the
West Virginia state Senate. Leonard, a graduate of the George Washington
University School of Government, had worked with the Office of Strategic
Services and the State Department and, like Peterson, had bested two male
candidates in her Republican primary.

Hawkins recalled, "We had a great time on the trip—it was fun even though a lot of the people weren't particularly enthusiastic about Louise's campaign." Peterson, she said, "never asked you to do something she wouldn't do." Summing up the caravan, she added, "It wasn't easy going door-to-door, but she was right there with us."[63]

Peterson also took a leave from the national committee to do a swing through northern Michigan on behalf of Lenore Romney. (She later asserted to a reporter that she had made fifty-eight appearances in forty-three Michigan counties between June and November.)[64] But, she said, "the handwriting was on the wall."[65]

"There was no question Lenore had too much baggage working against her," she concluded, "not the least of which was being a woman. As one nicely dressed man in Clare told her: 'Up here, lady, we wouldn't vote for a woman or a nigger.'"[66]

A decade after he first met Peterson, Molin was now managing Milliken's campaign. He acknowledged that "a wide chasm" had opened between the Milliken and Romney campaigns. One day, Peterson walked into his office, closed the door, and said, "Keith-o, I'm here to say if there's anything I can do to help you down the stretch, you give me a call."

Peterson, he recalled, "never got in the way. [She] never said, 'This is what you need to do.' . . . She could have told me more than I would ever be able to learn in terms of what needed to be done, but she would let you learn on your own. But she knew the time had come that if we were going to win the gubernatorial campaign, we had to put this chasm between the two campaigns aside and get behind the one that had the opportunity to win. And that was another kind of leadership for which she was never really properly recognized. She had a great sense of timing."[67]

Although the press had speculated about Peterson's retirement for some time, she had not planned to formally announce it until November 1—two days before the election. But she was forced to announce it in mid-October, when Pete's retirement was announced in Michigan, prompting media inquiries about her own plans.

Peterson told Glaser, "I've always felt that the strength of any political party lies in new ideas and new people. . . . I never intended to hang on by my teeth forever. If I move on, it makes for more diversity and action."[68]

In an October 29 memo to the "Republican leadership," Peterson said she would spend most of December "in the office making up final reports on the various programs" she had managed. She added, "Of course I will be available to any of you who would like to consult with me about any of your future projects."

She concluded, "Politics has been an interesting and exciting career, but by far the nicest part about it is the warm friendships I've had with so many of you. I certainly hope that all of them will continue, and that we can keep in touch from time to time."[69]

In her November 1 resignation letter to Morton, she said her RNC job "has been the climax of a rewarding political career" and assured the chairman of her "appreciation and devotion."[70]

But others apparently received franker words. Her national party mentor, Clare Williams Shank, wrote back that Peterson's letter "brought back the flood of frustration and resentment and anger that I lived with most of the time I held the [assistant chairman] job. The rebuffs—the salary of about half what the men got who did less and ranked lower—the necessity to beg—to prod—to finally demand—it was always there to fight—and wearying endlessly. . . . I left too much of myself in the stresses of that job,—I never really regained all I had before that,—from pouring it out day and night, too intensely. So I do understand all your letter said, and didn't say. It never seems to get better there."[71]

While Pete's retirement made her own decision easier, at least one reporter observed, "Acquaintances who knew of her difficulties in pressing for a broader base for the party believe that she might have left before long anyhow." He added that "just about the last straw" for Peterson was "the purging" of liberal Republican senator Charles Goodell of New York. The administration had instead supported the election of Conservative James Buckley. Peterson, the reporter said, "attributes that strategy to a strain remaining in the Republican Party from the period when the Goldwater faction held control." But she avoided direct criticism of the White House, saying, "It's not my kind of politics to throw dirt at your opponent."[72]

In characteristic style, Peterson kept her real emotions in check until the election returns were in. She went back to Michigan for the final weekend of the campaign and joined McLaughlin in making a sentimental swing through twenty-five headquarters offices in Southeast Michigan. As he went trick-or-treating with his sons, McLaughlin recalled, "I tried to smile, but I was terribly depressed. I knew Lenore would be wiped out. I really didn't think Milliken could survive the Hart landslide. I wondered where I would find a job."[73]

Peterson returned to Washington for Election Night and sat up at the

RNC to watch the returns come in. One bright spot was Louise Leonard's defeat of the majority leader of the West Virginia Senate. But for the most part, the results were disappointing. As Hawkins recalled, "To me, it seemed like the end of an era and a defeat of everything that was important to us."[74]

"There were many fine men throughout the country who suffered defeat that year," Peterson recalled in her memoir. She counted among them Goodell; Rep. George H. W. Bush of Texas; Rep. Thomas S. Kleppe, who lost a bid for a Senate seat from North Dakota; and Sen. George Murphy from California, who lost his bid for reelection. Rep. Catherine May, one of the four congresswomen who had complained about the lack of female appointments, also lost her House seat.[75]

And in Michigan, Hart trounced Romney by a margin of 67 to 33 percent. (Six years earlier, Peterson had actually outperformed her better-known friend by a few percentage points.) State senator Lorraine Beebe also lost her race, a victim of her opposition to Parochiaid to Catholic schools, as well as her public acknowledgment that she had had an abortion.

Because of problems with new voting equipment in Detroit, it took until Thursday to confirm that Milliken had defeated his opponent, then state senator Sander Levin, by only 42,000 votes out of 2.6 million cast.

In his morning-after analysis, David Broder wrote that the Democrats had "repulsed President Nixon's bold mid-term election offensive" by retaining control of both houses of Congress and "totally erasing the Republicans' 2-to-1 majority in the nation's governorships." The prospect of retaking Congress, Broder noted, had impelled Nixon and Agnew to "lead the GOP forces in the most expensive and massive mid-term campaign the country has ever seen. Agnew's rhetoric, aimed at Democratic 'radical-liberals,' triggered disputes that made this the angriest mid-term election in a quarter century."[76]

A week later Peterson sent Morton a blunt, seven-page "Final Report." She started by arguing that 1968 had actually *not* been a great year for the Republicans, noting that they won the presidency with only 43 percent of the vote, lost strength in the state legislatures, and failed to pick up many congressional seats. "So where did the Republicans go in 1969? Did they recognize their own weaknesses? Did they weed out the inept, the disenchanted, the weary? Did they create an aura of broadening the base—of involvement of all citizens in a dramatic citizen volunteer oriented national movement? There can be only one answer—NO!"

She poured out her accumulated frustrations about the RNC's inter-actions with the White House, the "tokenism toward blacks, women and youth" and the failure to involve volunteers and minority groups in mean-ingful ways—"we blew this royally."

Noting that in 1968, women represented 51 percent of voters—the first time they were in the majority—she charged that "we studiously *blew* their interest" and listed eight specific points—including the lack of fe-male appointments and the caliber of the appointments that were made—to make her case.

She then went on:

> I am operating under the ground rules any woman who survives in Republican leadership has to operate under: i.e., looking at the prob-lems; hoping for a solution rather than glossing over them and deal-ing out the platitudes which brought us where we are today. I hope we can all sit back and look at the future without an over protection of our own programs or a sensitivity about their values. If we are to be merely an arm of the White House with funds and activities solely channeled there we should resolve a way to come out of that alive and breathing. I believe our time is short to face the facts and decide the road to 1972.

She called on the party to which she had devoted her professional life "to establish our national goals *honestly*."

> If our choice is to be a white, southern, boarder [*sic*] state oriented policy [*sic*], then let us quit kidding about it and move in a direct line to get the white so-called silent majority vote. Let us turn our publications, organizational efforts, money to rifle-shot where the ducks are and let us relieve ourselves of the expense and effort of tokenism. . . .
> If we are honestly interested in broadening the base, then let us move in *that* direction with something more than tokenism.

She outlined the specific accomplishments of her division and the steps that she thought should be taken next. But, she added, "If White House support is *not* there and if the current antipathy to women's active participation is the order of the day, then I would say be honest about it,—

cut the [Women's] Division to two or three and put the money, effort and action where the direction leads."[77]

Her frustrations also spilled out in a long Election Day interview with Richard Dudman of the *St. Louis Post-Dispatch.* She noted that her responsibilities for disenfranchised groups would be taken over by Richard Curry. "Men are my biggest stumbling block," she said. "I hope his presence will remove the stigma of having these things known as women's programs."

Dudman wrote that Peterson said "she has always thought that the best way to deal with discrimination against women was not to complain but to endure it and work around it. 'I never spoke about the doors that were closed to me,' she said. 'Too many women worry about not being at the head table. I always figured that if I was not invited to a strategy meeting it was their loss.'

"'But,' she continued, 'I'm not sure. I'm getting awfully weary of maintaining that attitude, I'm getting weary at the discrimination against women in all kinds of political life.' She noted her statistics on the decline in the number of female officeholders and added, 'I say, if men keep working at it, we'll be wiped out in 10 years.'"[78]

Then, as was often her custom, she left on a postelection vacation with her sister, this time to cruise the Rhine.

When Peterson returned, her mail included a poignant note from Lenore Romney, signed "love, love."

> Who would ever have thought as we talked of Hart's vulnerability little did I know how open and bare and wide my own vulnerability would be! You are so right: "Total Forget" is the only prescription to keep from total dissolvement. But my sub-consciousness isn't obedient. I still waken after a nightmare of seeing myself in print as distorted by our "friends." But this too will pass.
>
> How wonderful that you wrote—I needed *every* word. It was great to be talking to you that night and to have your elegant yellow roses adorning our suite. Your voice, so cheerfully accepting the inevitable.
>
> We've been through many things—but good grief—who ever could have dreamed up *this?*
>
> I'm aware of your labors—the trekking and organizing and stirring up the lazy ones—and hours after hours of all the nitty gritty.

It helps to know there are others who give their all because some things mean so terribly much. . . .

Yes, there are luminous "highs"—with the devoted sharing of many volunteers and the "believers" up there too.

But the body wounds are deep—I believe I've "had it"—but maybe someday I'll rise again to campaign for someone I believe in. . . . [H]e will have to be awfully good.[79]

Peterson then kept a date to address the Illinois Federation of Republican Women, the organization Schlafly had once headed. At the outset, she observed that "this is probably the only election when no one can really decide whether or not we won. It all depends on who you talk to." She said, "I personally believe we made some impressive gains for an off-year election," while noting that Illinois ended up in "the loss column."[80]

Peterson returned to the theme of how the party should permanently transform itself. "My answer to winning will never make a cover story. . . it will never be the subject of a political column. . . nor will it ever become professionalized, for it can't. For the way to win is to care—to care enough about this country and what it means to the entire world so that you care for *all* its citizens. . . . Unless we, as a party, include the non-traditional Republican we are going to grow old and obsolete. We will have outlived our time."

She also had a message for her female audience: "As women you should be interested in your own potential. Don't think of yourself in the context of the bra burning, radical Liberation, or 1001 ways to camouflage hamburger way, but in a loftier, more pragmatic sense. WOMEN YOU MUST TAKE THE LEAD IN BUILDING THIS PARTY IF IT IS TO SURVIVE."

But speaking to the press in Chicago, she assumed a tougher tone. She referred to the "devastating defeats" the party had suffered and warned that unless it abandoned its "exclusive club" image and worked to include the young, the old, and the poor, it would not survive. The reporter said Peterson "chastised the party for thinking that elections can be won by spending 'a bundle of money three months before the vote,' by ignoring the problems of big cities, or by assuming that people moving to the suburbs automatically think Republican."[81]

In a December 3 report to the party leadership, she made a final pitch for retaining the Action Now program. She observed that only 17 percent of Michigan voters still identified themselves as Republicans and that action centers provided a way of attracting and motivating new volunteers for the 1972 campaign. An action center, she wrote, "is simply a refinement of old ward politics. . . . Why is there such a block about having a headquarters open to solve people's problems?"[82]

By then it was known that most of her top RNC colleagues would also be leaving, including Morton, who was in line to be interior secretary. Staff members were described as "irked because they were shut out of high-level campaign decisions by White House aides, then blamed for bloopers" such as a controversial series of newspaper ads that sought to paint eight Democratic senators as "extremists." Peterson said the ads were the handiwork of White House special counsel Charles Colson. "Those ads were his baby," she said. "Everything we heard pointed to it. Then he tried to dump it on the committee."[83]

(Her comments were reported again in April 1973 as the 1972 Nixon campaign's political "dirty tricks" were beginning to be disclosed. The so-called Shipley ads were placed by the Committee for a Responsible Congress, headed by Carl L. Shipley, then the Republican national committeeman for the District of Columbia. Colson continued to deny that he had had any involvement with the ads, but others disagreed.)[84]

But Peterson had made enough good friends over the years that she could still leave on a high note. In an article likely written by one of her close colleagues, *The Republican* magazine said:

> Throughout her long and productive service to the Party, she has kept one objective in mind . . . expand the Party by offering all kinds of people work to do. Or, in her own words, "After twenty-five years, my one final point is the one I've tried to make all along: 'We cannot be an election year Party, based on the membership of a select few. In order to serve America, we must be representative of America. In order to understand her problems and solve them, we must confront them firsthand. In order to win the votes of her people, we must first win their confidence and affection. As Republicans, you must get out of your homes and into your communities.'"

Noting her plans to retire to Hawaii, the article closed, "But she'll never be retired in the minds of many Republicans. To her staff, her friends and her admirers, she'll always be 'Mother.'"[85]

December 15 was "the day to end days," Peterson recalled.[86] She opened that morning's *Washington Post* to find a column by David Broder headlined "Tribute to Elly Peterson." He wrote:

> In an age where the term is thought to be derogatory, Mrs. Peterson has always and unashamedly been a political pro. . . . It is, I think, accurate to say that her abilities would have earned her the national chairmanship, were it not for the unwritten sex barrier both parties have erected around that job. Certainly, her organizational talents made her views as respected and her advice as sought-after among her colleagues in the party as anyone in the past decade.

Broder continued:

> The role of a woman in politics is an inherently difficult one—especially if her forte is organization. Yet through the years there have been women in both parties who have overcome the obstacles and made an enormous contribution to the functioning of our political system. . . .
> One basic problem all talented women face is the tendency of the parties to shunt them off to some preserve of tea-party irrelevancies called "women's activities." Mrs. Peterson . . . fiercely resisted stereotyping and by sheer energy and capability won her right to operate at the full range of her talents.

"It was Mrs. Peterson's fate to serve on the National Committee staff in periods which were hardly conducive to her own brand of progressive Republicanism," Broder concluded. "But hard-headed as she is, Mrs. Peterson would say you should expect to be frustrated in many of your hopes if you get involved in politics."[87]

Broder later told Peterson that the column was "from the heart, and, if I were sentimental, would have said more."[88]

Her staff showered her with gifts at lunch; Curtis gave her a gold bracelet engraved with "Thanks for raising me—your dumb kid."[89] Then later that night, Morton and his wife, Ann, hosted a gala party at the Mayflower Hotel. Friends flew in from all over the country. Morton and Allison made speeches, praising Peterson's "dogged efforts to open her party and its philosophy to blacks, women and young people," wrote Saul

Friedman of Knight Newspapers. "But the biggest compliment, and the most incisive," was paid by Hart, "the only Democratic officeholder at the party." Standing at the back of the room, he said quietly, "My hope is that Elly's counsel will continue to go unheeded."

Friedman continued:

> The Republican Old Guard never did take much of a liking to Romney and his maverick messianic ways. And they condescendingly indulged Elly Peterson in her efforts to build "action centers" and a GOP base in the ghettos.
>
> It did not seem important to them, in their safe outstate districts, that organization, philosophy and political techniques put the Michigan GOP far head of most State Republican parties. . . .
>
> Mrs. Peterson is quitting partly because she has not been of the same mind as White House political operatives . . . who believe that dividing and conquering can bring us together. One would not think she would agree to run the Republican National Committee, as long as their counsel was accepted at the White House.
>
> Mrs. Peterson is a political pro who understands that politics is for governing, not merely winning. And she prizes good political form.[90]

Peterson asked that no one from the White House be invited, but friendly reporters like Helen Thomas made hay of the apparent snub when none showed. One supporter said Peterson had never been forgiven for supporting Rockefeller. Nixon did send her a book of his collected speeches as "a token of my appreciation for the important contributions you have made toward the cause of good government."[91]

Evans and Novak observed that if Nixon had come, "he might well have felt a kinship for Capt. Bligh on the bridge of the H.M.S. Bounty." Working the room, the columnists gathered eight off-the-record anecdotes that they said reflected "distrust, disillusion and alienation" among the Republicans present.[92]

Peterson was particularly touched by a telegram she received from twelve of Washington's top political reporters. It read:

> Since you say you are giving up politics, we feel we can give up nonpartisanship and express our admiration for you as a great pro and a

good friend. Your honesty, good humor, enthusiasm and realism throughout the years we have been covering you make it possible for us to answer the enemies of Women's Lib who ask: "Yeah, but would you want your son to marry a politician?"

It has been a pleasure, boss lady, and we wish you and Pete the very best in the years ahead.

It was signed by Broder; R. W. "Johnny" Apple of the *New York Times;* Jack Germond, then of Gannett; Jules Witcover of the *Los Angeles Times;* Paul Hope of the *Washington Star;* Loye Miller of Knight Newspapers; Walter Mears of the Associated Press; John Lindsay of *Newsweek;* Bruce Winters of the *Baltimore Sun;* Bruce Biossat, political columnist for the Newspaper Enterprise Association; William Theis of Hearst Newspapers; and Bill Kulsea of the Booth chain. They said they had wanted to attend her party but had to cover Agnew's speech to the Republican governors in Sun Valley "to record what should be a high point in the continuing saga of Republican unity."[93]

The telegram, Peterson wrote later, "made the evening perfect for me, along with my wonderful political friends, and the ice sculpture running the length of the table spelling out one word: MOTHER."[94]

About this time, Morton apparently sent her another heartfelt letter. It read: "At the moment my country seems far away. Where have gone the blood, the sweat, the tears which were shed to bind its greatness? They seem to have washed away. . . . Our association—yours with all of us at the committee—makes me more determined than ever to restore wherever I can a faith in America and its leadership. The alternative to success is too grim to contemplate."[95]

Of Peterson's Washington years, Joyce Braithwaite-Brickley observed later:

Elly never changed. She grew, of course, through experience and disappointment and triumph. She became stronger and stronger, and for a darned strong woman in the beginning, it was inevitable and wonderful to see. Her experience in Washington came from knowing what was right and trying to do it while so many of the people she worked with there were poseurs, fighting for a place in the light. I think she had never worked with such people and was stunned. It caused her to seem much less effective than in past positions. There were exceptions, of course, . . . people from whom she received positive vibes and enthusiasm. But for each of those, she found so many of the immature and positioning people, struggling to look important. They made her experience there difficult and dimmed her enthusiasm.[96]

As Peterson herself observed to Dick Dudman, "A lot of people will be glad to see the last of me."[97]

# CHAPTER NINE

---

# A Path out of Exile

---

In January 1971, Peterson finally *did* retire—this time for more than a month—as she and Pete took up a "self-imposed exile" on an island seven time zones from Michigan.[1] "I doubt if I'll ever be totally out of politics," she told a reporter, "because I've been tied up with it so long." Yet she confessed she would "enjoy being disorganized" for a change, traveling and doing volunteer work—"solely for pleasure."[2]

The couple purchased a two-bedroom condominium on Honolulu's Ala Wai Canal, and Mary settled in with them permanently. Elly professed to be "a nut on Hawaii" and loved wearing a muumuu whenever she could. The Petersons planned to return to Charlotte during the summer months.[3]

Many years later Peterson confided that she had always thought that when she and Pete retired they would live in England or France for half the year. "I'd always talked about it. It was my dream." But Pete flatly said, "No."

"He said he had given up a lot and now he planned to do nothing but golf and hunt," she recalled. It was the only time that her husband had expressed any resentment about the demands her work and travel had placed on their marriage. "So I woke up that he might have wished me to be home—but why didn't he say so?"[4] Elly continued to travel extensively, with Pete, Mary, and others, but now, more than before, their relationship was on Pete's terms.

From Hawaii, she watched as some of her old White House adversaries were sent packing. In mid-January, the White House proposed Anne Armstrong, the national committeewoman from Texas, and Delaware national committeeman Thomas B. Evans Jr. as "cochairmen" to serve under Sen. Robert Dole of Kansas, who was replacing Morton as chairman.

Armstrong's appointment, David Broder wrote, "was viewed as a bow to women members" of the RNC, "some of whom had been critical of Mr. Nixon for failing to elevate" Peterson.[5] Although Morton had long wanted to be interior secretary, the job was not formally offered until after Peterson announced her retirement. It's questionable whether she would have accepted the chairmanship if it had, in fact, been offered.

After the "troika" was announced, Massenburg wrote Peterson that Morton had told her he had wanted Peterson to be chairman, "but when he knew he could never get you, he settled on Pat Hitt and fought right up to the President on that; said only way we could make any points publicly would be having a woman."[6] To her sister, Peterson described Dole as "an ultra conservative yes man."[7]

Armstrong told Broder the assistant chairman's job had been retitled "to give women a lift." Morton said it was his idea to have two cochairmen "so that we wouldn't downgrade the ladies." But Peterson wasn't totally on the sidelines; Dole told her that a letter she had sent on Armstrong's behalf was "most persuasive." Armstrong later recalled that Peterson had been "fearless" in her support of women and had made her "much more knowledgeable about women's issues and far more caring about them."[8]

In Peterson's final month at the RNC, HEW secretary Robert Finch had sent a memo to the White House, urging it to act on the growing list of women's concerns. Finch said that "the best women" had been keeping a close eye on appointments.[9]

Nixon responded by appointing Barbara Franklin, an assistant vice president at Citibank, as "staff assistant to the president for executive *man*power," a title that stuck in the craw of the women reporters covering the announcement. The offending portion of her title was eventually changed.[10] In addition, Nixon directed agency heads to adopt plans for appointing and promoting women; Franklin was responsible for monitoring their progress.

In a later oral history, Franklin said she didn't start from scratch "because some ground work had already been done at the White House in terms of reviewing the status of women in the federal government." But because she arrived after Peterson had left, she said she did not know if Peterson's staff was responsible.[11]

At the time, Franklin observed, some women pioneers displayed what she called a "Queen Bee Syndrome"—women "who had fought so hard to get to wherever they were that when they got there, they were not about to help anybody else." But Peterson, she noted, "was certainly not a queen bee."[12]

Shank had warned Peterson that "you'll find the transition to complete nonentity a trifle hard at first. Everyone does."[13] Peterson had told her mentor she was thinking of writing a memoir, and in her first months of retirement she began working on a draft. JoAnn Hawkins, newly married and living in Georgia, offered feedback and editing suggestions in hopes they could get the manuscript published.[14]

The project seemed therapeutic for Peterson. Within a few months, the wannabe journalist pounded out 160 typewritten pages, capturing the story of her life in politics and the nitty-gritty lessons she had learned, as well as the frustrations she had endured.

In a June 9, 1971, letter, Hawkins observed to her former boss that "you seem to [b]oggle down in the 'meat' (the futility, the questioning sections) and that's probably because you *feel* more than you can express."[15]

Comparing this text with the memoirs she published later for her family suggests that Peterson's perspective changed as she got older. Fresh off her frustrating months at the RNC, Peterson's 1971 draft ended with an emotional conclusion, which she later dropped. She wrote:

> This has not been easy to write. It is, or would be, much easier to accept the fame of a sort that has been awarded me—and the friendships made throughout the country—and let the problems rest for somebody else. But that is partly what is wrong with the country today.
>
> Too many people don't want to recognize that their own personal disinterest has created some of the monumental problems of the day, not Viet Nam, nor the economy, but the problem of people living with people and people loving their neighbor.

She went on to express her disappointment that Nixon had failed "to build a strong, vital, exciting party" the way Romney had in Michigan. "This is what I failed to realize, that time is short and men are eager for power, their own power, not that of a party or a nebulous group of leaders—some effective, some ineffective, some with it, some way out of it. The job of President, itself, makes a politician a statesman and the con-

cerns of the party are left to advisors, who, in too many cases are not political." Her hero Romney, she concluded, "was an 'accident of fate.'"

Moderates, she added, "fail in this regard to build strong parties with
their philosophy for they are based too often on men of power, interested
largely in themselves while conservatives are based on an idea, a philosophy. They therefore are ready to accept a new leader if he offers them what
they want in the way of ideas—to heck with his personality or appearance.

"This then is the bitter pill I learned to swallow—that the ideas I have
dreamed and thought of for so many years, yes, and worked for, simply
will not come to pass."

She wrote that she realized "just how burned out I really was" when
shortly after her retirement she met with an old friend who was a former
Democratic state official. They had a conversation about their mutual
frustrations, and then the other woman left the table for a moment. Peterson recalled:

> [T]he moment of truth came to me during those quiet minutes. Al-
> ways before, in a conversation such as this, or in the frustrations I
> had encountered at the national level, excitement grew in me. The
> adrenalin started, the juices flowed, I was ready for another battle.
>
> In that quiet moment I found this to be true: There was no
> adrenalin, no juices flowing, no excitement, and no interest in fight-
> ing on through the maze of problems and prejudice. I was not disin-
> terested as a citizen, as a voter, but I found I simply and surely didn't
> care any more. I just thought, "Bag it. I've done what I can. I have
> done my share. Let someone else carry the water."

Her goal in capturing her thoughts, she wrote, was to try to get someone else to begin working to "make political parties meaningful and interesting to all ages." She added, "I thought if I could do this then I can afford
to lose a friend or even make an enemy."

She concluded:

> Politics has been so good to me, better than to most women. I like to
> think I have given more of myself than many women have been will-
> ing or able to give. I know that all the heartaches and the discour-
> agement, all the frustrations and the defeats, can be discounted for
> the friends and for the high excitements of those minutes, brief as

they may have been, when you feel, when you know, you have laid a brick in a great foundation.

I wish it could have been more.[16]

But over time, Peterson had second thoughts about how pointed her criticism should be. She wrote Hawkins, "I feel now the book should be reviewed carefully so it is not bitching in any way—I may get a little too tough on our Richard—I don't want it that way or whiney or any thing like that—so I would like your eagle eye on that." And, she suggested that perhaps she should solicit the recollections of others, such as Romney, Lindemer, and Shank, demonstrating her own tendency toward self-deprecation.[17]

Peterson did not mention Fisher by name in her 1971 manuscript. In recalling her salary cut, she left things vague.

Over and over again it was emphasized that I was the only person who could "lead them out of the wilderness"; this was a time when the organizational talents I had and the people I knew could be of the utmost value. Why, I could repair the damaged [sic] friendships, I could help raise the money to pay off the debts, indeed I was some "punkins." "But, after all, Elly, you are a woman and it would not be quite fitting to pay a woman the same salary as we paid a man." I thought about this for some time, about whether I should stand and fight, or just give in the way women did over and over again in Michigan politics.

My problem was two-fold. I was never in politics for the money. I had by now convinced myself that with the support indicated I could do a job putting the pieces back together again and flattery does get people someplace. It was sort of a kick in the head to try out the ideas I had. . . .

It is still a pain to be a woman and have this constant battle over equality of wages and representation.[18]

Hawkins speculated that Peterson still wanted to be able to play in Michigan politics and was not ready to burn those particular bridges behind her.[19]

Even in retirement, Peterson could still make headlines, as she did when she became identified with the fledgling "citizens' lobby," Common

Cause. The year before, John Gardner, Johnson's HEW secretary, had invited 225,000 Americans to join his new nonpartisan organization to reform government. By year's end, the mailing had attracted 6,334 members, and newspaper ads in four cities attracted 6,700 more.[20]

In a letter to Broder, apparently sent soon after his adulatory column, Peterson mentioned her interest in the group. On March 20, he wrote back.

> I wish you were back in Washington—for a lot of reasons, but mainly because there's no one with your sense or insights to talk to about what's going on. Personally, I am increasingly of the opinion that we're going to have another change of Presidents next year, but I fear very much that it will not be any more productive of the change and redirection and rebirth of energy and purpose—any of these things—than the last one was.
>
> You mention doing some work with Common Cause. I'd be interested in your views on that organization. The incredible response Gardner has had certainly seems to indicate a hunger—among a certain segment of the public, at least—for a credible guy who says, damn it, let's turn things around, not by violence, but by using the system intelligently to force some changes in the system. I've heard this same theme from people all over the political spectrum in the last few months, but I don't know whether it can become a *political* movement in the next election.[21]

In a June column, Saul Friedman observed that Peterson and Jane Hart, the senator's wife, both "charter members" of Common Cause, would be excellent choices to direct the Michigan chapter. Peterson, he said, had been recruited as a consultant to help reform the state's voter registration laws.

The Republican, he wrote, had "scoffed angrily" when the RNC had recently attacked Common Cause for its "leftism, liberalism and radicalism." She had responded, "Common Cause has my full support, and if it does its job it's going to offend somebody. If no one is offended, then it's doing nothing." Peterson said she had pledged to stay out of politics for at least a year, but that she "helps Common Cause when [she] can."

Friedman observed that "in her voice there was a hint of sadness that the enthusiasm she used to see in party work has now been transferred" to the new organization.[22]

Meanwhile, without Peterson's care and tending, the action centers were already dying, even in Detroit. In July 1971, she was sent a draft of the Ripon Society's research paper on the Detroit action center by a self-described Peterson "kid," whose "personal feelings" made her feel conflicted about her negative assessment. "I think we have to admit for starters the obvious," she wrote. "It [the center] didn't make it. I do not feel however that this represents only an indictment on a political party but the larger picture is that we still have a long way to go before black and white America understand, trust or can work with each other."

The letter writer added, "In the black-white situation any one of us who is white and sticks our neck out or our nose in, as the case may be, is eventually asking to be in the middle of a troubled situation. It should not negate what we try to do but it certainly leaves one with feelings of frustration and even anger. I would guess you have (or had) those feelings. . . . I just wanted you to know that I admire you for what you did with the Action Center and its ultimate failure is not yours. Its all of ours and damned if I know what's the answer."[23] Peterson, however, remained a believer, telling a student eight years later that if the RNC had continued the program, "I feel the party would have made significant gains in urban areas during the next four to five years."[24]

Peterson was also monitoring women's issues, particularly progress on the Equal Rights Amendment. In February, NFRW President O'Donnell asked if she would sign a letter to help drum up support for the amendment, noting, "We feel it would add much prestige to this appeal."[25]

Since January, Betty Friedan, cofounder of the National Organization for Women (NOW) and now a regular columnist for *McCall's*, had been talking to prominent women about organizing a bipartisan political caucus for women. But she butted heads with newly elected U.S. Rep. Bella Abzug, who wanted to build an organization of left-leaning women. A diverse group attended a June 9 planning meeting in New York, but no Republicans were present.[26]

As the plans went forward, Friedan approached Peterson about becoming involved. Peterson, Friedan recalled, "had been the most powerful woman in the Republican party—its traditionally powerless lady vice-chairman." She was among the "politically oriented women who hadn't been interested in women's rights before" who "were ready now to organize such a caucus."[27]

Peterson wrote Hawkins, "My latest is that Betty Friedan is after my warm body to join her movement to get more women elected to office. She has gone respectable you know with *McCall's* and has quite a list of women lined up who are meeting in Washington on July 10–11 to get this thing off the ground." Peterson noted that her friend Virginia Allan was involved, but so were Abzug and U.S. Representative Shirley Chisholm. She concluded, "I don't think I have the time."

In midletter, Peterson was interrupted by a phone call from O'Donnell. When she hung up, she continued, "She has checked out the Friedan thing and says it is definitely just the same women[']s lib people"—Abzug, Friedan, Gloria Steinem, and Chisholm—"with a few people who probably don't know." Peterson said O'Donnell had talked to Republican Representative Margaret Heckler, "who is avoiding it—so I called and said no dope."[28]

In her memoir, Peterson did not mention her decision to bypass the founding meeting of the National Women's Political Caucus (NWPC). For starters, its organizers were predominately Democratic, liberal, even radical women. The reaction of Democrat Liz Carpenter, a Peterson peer, is instructive: Carpenter recalled listening as Steinem told an organizing session: "Looking around this room, I see there is at least one thing we all have in common—a vagina." Carpenter said, "I jumped about two feet. I had never heard that word except in my gynecologist's office."[29]

But in the end, three hundred women *did* attend the founding meeting. At the time, there were only twelve female members of the House of Representatives, one woman senator, and not a single female governor or U.S. Supreme Court justice. That represented virtually no progress in the seven years since Peterson had run for the Senate. On top of that, women filled only 1.6 percent of top government jobs. That, Abzug declared, was "more like a pinprick than a breakthrough."[30]

By the end of the meeting, the women took steps to institutionalize the caucus's wide-ranging diversity, including a guarantee of representation for Republicans.[31] Its first twenty-one-member policy council included Republicans Allan, who was still chair of the president's women's task force, and Jo Ann Evans-Gardner, a candidate for the Pittsburgh City Council and a national board member of NOW.[32]

The caucus faced the same challenges as any new, diverse political coalition. Ronnie Feit, who organized the first meeting, observed a decade later that it had taken "conscious effort" and flexibility on the issues to keep the group together. Commitment to the caucus "by a few strong Republican women" and "the conviction of others that the Republicans must be included if the caucus was to have real power," she said, led organizers to take "several concrete steps" to overcome the organization's early domination by Democrats.[33]

The record suggests that after the founding meeting, Peterson began to play an important role in that. United Auto Workers executive Olga Madar returned from Washington eager to organize a Michigan caucus. On September 7, Allan informed Madar's staff that Peterson would serve as chairman of the Michigan Republican Women's Caucus and would attend the next National Policy Council meeting in New York. Allan also said she would not rush to call a meeting in the state because she believed in "planning and organization and from observation the National Caucus could be characterized as unstructured and disorganized." She advised Peterson that if Madar forged ahead on her own, it "would end the chance of the Women's Caucus in Michigan. It would turn into a Democratic Caucus."[34]

At the Policy Council's September meeting, Peterson asked that it begin "by fairly representing both major political parties," according to the minutes. She pointed out that in many states, the caucus was thought of "as a group of Democrats," and sought a policy decision to involve both parties and "all 11 Congresswomen and all powerful women in the country." She also said the caucus "needed numbers and needed to be able to get out a vote."[35]

The next day, the Council voted to add Peterson, Lorraine Beebe, and White House staff member Barbara "Bobbie" Kilberg as Republican members. Peterson was assigned to the Operating Committee and later to the Legislative Committee and an ad hoc committee on the Supreme Court.

Ten days later Peterson reported back to Armstrong and O'Donnell. She was warming to the caucus's leaders, even as she still cast her own participation in pragmatic political terms.

> Briefly, I believe the operation of [the caucus] is not so much Democratic per se as heading towards their own goals whether it be day care centers or helping Chicanos. They are totally disorganized since they had no real political people on the top committee. They were completely receptive when we talked organization—and I believe that if we have the fortitude to stick in there we can really help the Party—as well as the President in the coming election.

If we do not, then I think we are going to be wiping out a goodly number of working women and civic women—for it cannot be dismissed as simply "kooks" as we were at first inclined to do. Women like Martha Griffiths and Liz Carpenter, with nationally fine reputations, are now taking an interest—we cannot leave it to them, in my judgment.

Peterson also said the Republicans should form a national Women's Rights and Responsibilities Committee and suggested some possible names: "I would hope [these] women would encourage Republican women to take an active part—instead of sitting back and letting the entire thing be taken over by Democrats BECAUSE OF OUR OPTING OUT OF OUR RESPONSIBILITIES." She noted, "This might be a good spot to put people like me, on the shelf—but still known state wide—and able to make a few points."

Peterson observed that after the word got out that Allan, Beebe, and herself were involved, "we have all heard from women in various groups— farm, Republican, business, civic—that they are interested in joining it. There is a great response from younger activist women. If we are involved we can perhaps set them right on points about national and local candidates they otherwise will not know."[36]

A month later, she reported back to Armstrong on a two-day meeting of the National Policy Council in Detroit. "I would say that now the top committees are about equally divided between independents, Dems and Reps—the Dems are by no means together . . . the most unified group you might say were the New York Jewish crusaders except even here Bella Abzug and Betty Friedan do not see eye to eye." She reported that they were "all bitterly disappointed over the Supreme Court." After considering several women judges, Nixon had instead nominated William H. Rehnquist and Lewis F. Powell to the court.

Peterson also observed:

I really am most disappointed to find the Republican leadership in some states coming out against the Caucus rather than getting in and taking part—and having a say in things. It is another strike against us for ignoring masses of people and while I do not believe it will hurt the President in his bid for reelection necessarily it is surely going to hurt below that—and especially the membership in the Republican Party (and I feel this is especially so after seeing the poll that rates us at 24% of the population—how can we wipe off ANY-BODY with that rating?)[37]

About the same time, Peterson wrote two state Republican leaders, "Bella Abzug is funny as a crutch but so is Liz Carpenter so I hope sometime you two get to see them in action. I didn't find any died in the wool—hope to die Democrats—they are pretty much disgusted with the picture of their leadership and I think we can help adding to that by attending—and keeping on top of everything."[38]

Feit recalled that Abzug had initially been antagonistic to more moderate Democrats like Carpenter, whom she viewed as a Johnson apologist. But, she observed, "I watched Bella grow and see that even Republican women could be dealt with. You could see a gradual lowering of her distrust."[39]

Still, despite the developing relationships, the caucus's future was by no means secure. By mid-November, it had raised only thirteen thousand dollars to cover its operations; Peterson was one of only forty persons or organizations who had contributed twenty-five dollars or more.[40]

The caucus's immediate goal was to promote equal representation for women at the 1972 nominating conventions. In a November 2 letter to Dole, Peterson noted that the Republican Party had not yet agreed to implement a proposal calling for equal representation by the 1976 convention.

She also expressed concern that in calculating proportionate representation, the party might count alternate delegates and delegates together. This, she said, "would again derogate women to a second class, nonvoting status." She called on the party to publicize its delegate selection rules and to actively recruit women delegates. She also observed that because women represented 52.4 percent of the population, simple parity did not amount to "equal representation."[41]

Talking points for the caucus's meeting with Dole detailed what Republican women were up against. At the 1968 national convention, women accounted for only 17 percent of delegates, three delegations had had no women members, and twenty-two states did not have the four women necessary to a supply a female representative to all four of the convention's standing committees.[42]

Peterson was also actively involved in planning the first meeting of the

Michigan caucus, which took place on November 6 at Michigan State University, with Democratic activist Anne Wexler as keynoter.

With certain audiences, Peterson was already finding a sharper voice. In an early 1972 article for *Politéia,* the journal of the American Association of Political Consultants, she warned, "Many consultants will find that that great volunteer force of little old ladies in tennis shoes is just not there this time. . . . I'm a firm believer that for most male tongues it's biologically impossible to lick an envelope. It's an art they lost along with their gills which they weren't using either."

"The women's movement," she said, "is finally gaining momentum and the 70's will be to women what the 60's were to blacks. We'll get the attention and action we have wanted." She noted that since its founding, the NWPC "had become more moderate, more rational, more sensible. People like Bella Abzug and Gloria Steinem are still involved and are already veterans of this fight for women's rights. The Caucus has also drawn the attention of people like Liz Carpenter and myself, who are also veterans but have waged our wars quietly within the political parties."[43]

But when the Republican National Convention finally rolled into Miami Beach in August 1972, Peterson remained on the sidelines. Instead, friends and protégées pursued the fight for more representation and platform planks in support of the ERA, day care, and equal pay. Thirty percent of the delegates were women, and Armstrong became the first woman to keynote a national convention—eight years after Peterson made her own prime-time speech.

Still, old habits died hard. Three-fourths of the male delegates said "most men are better suited emotionally for politics" than women; about 43 percent of the female delegates agreed.[44] By the end of the tightly scripted event, Nixon was poised for a landslide victory in November. And the party seemed in little danger of growing "old and obsolete," as Peterson had warned the year before.

But she was not looking back. She had a new candidate.

In late July, Michigan's Probate and Juvenile Court Judges' Association began pushing their president, Calhoun County probate judge Mary Coleman, to run for the Michigan Supreme Court. Coleman knew she would need a substantial amount of money and better name recognition to win. On top of that, the state convention was only a month away; at the time, candidates had to be nominated by a party but ran on a nonpartisan basis.

Coleman left the judges' meeting without making a decision. But within days the state Supreme Court handed down a ruling on juvenile inmates that she thought was "one of their bigger abominations." She was "fussing and fussing" when her husband, Creighton, a state Circuit Court of Appeals judge and former state Senate majority leader, said, "Why don't you quit complaining and run for the Supreme Court?"

She said, "I'll do it," then promptly asked her spouse, "What do you do when you run for a statewide office?"

Call Elly Peterson, he replied.

Coleman knew Peterson had retired but phoned to ask if she would manage her campaign. Peterson first protested that she really had retired. But after a moment, she said, "A woman has never run for that Court before, and I know you, and yes, I'd like to do it. When shall we meet? Tomorrow morning?"

"That," Coleman concluded, "was Elly."

The convention was now just weeks away, and Coleman didn't have a hotel reservation or a list of the delegates. But that didn't faze her campaign manager. Coleman recalled:

> We had to get all kinds of agreements with the post office and the United Parcel Service. We had to get a place, a headquarters, equipment, etc. so we called together a few friends, community leaders and others. We met in our living room. Elly at one point said, "You should have a shower. You could have people bring anything they want including their own volunteer services.". . .
>
> We managed to obtain a headquarters right downtown, and that was really interesting. People would bring paper clips, paper, typewriters, and all kinds of things to start the business. It was quite exciting. In any event, Elly just took over.[45]

It had been two years since Peterson had attended a state party convention, but when she walked into the September gathering in Detroit, she was greeted by chants of "Mother, Mother's back."[46]

Recalled Molin, "She had been somewhat in the background. . . . Her presence was acknowledged, her leadership was respected, her word was listened to, but Elly had not really been the commander of the troops. And then all of a sudden she surfaced at the convention with Mary Coleman as the Supreme Court candidate. And you could just see her get reenergized."[47]

The Republicans could make two nominations to the court. The conventional wisdom was that Oakland County Circuit Court judge James S. Thorburn would capture the first spot and Coleman would have to battle two other male judges for the second. But, as one reporter recounted, "Enter Elly, whose touch in the convention backrooms and corridors has been awesome to Republicans."[48]

Thorburn's supporters tried to talk Coleman into conceding the first spot to him, arguing that all of the local chairmen would deliver their delegations. "They couldn't," Peterson recalled. "We went below them, to the delegates themselves, and WE could! After Coleman won the first position, Thorburn's backers asked Peterson to stay off the floor while they battled the other male judges for the second spot. She simply laughed and stayed out of the way."[49]

"Two of the toughest and most resourceful pros in state politics have teamed up to elect the first woman to the Michigan Supreme Court," wrote a reporter a few weeks later. "Mary, the legal pro, needed Elly, the political pro, and together, they could be tough on the rest of the field."[50]

From the outset, Peterson insisted that Coleman do things "her way," and that meant running the campaign on a shoestring. That suited Coleman, who didn't want to have to raise a lot of money. In the end, the campaign cost only about forty-six thousand dollars, roughly the job's annual salary.[51]

Peterson insisted on mailing a simple, inexpensive, black-and-white brochure. Coleman covered many of her own expenses, and Peterson and others worked on a volunteer basis, accepting only token financial gifts at the end of the campaign.

The campaign paid a small salary to another Peterson protégée, Cindy Sage, who served as press secretary. Peterson's marching orders were simple and drawn from experience: she wanted three stories every time Coleman made an appearance. "I want them to announce she's coming, I want them to get a picture while she's there, and I want a story at the end."

Peterson pushed Coleman to call on every editor in the state, including those working for African American and ethnic newspapers. "I tried not to miss anybody," Coleman recalled, "even in the Upper Peninsula in all those little areas, so that, in itself, took time."

Coleman turned out to be Peterson's "perfect candidate." She was "very popular," with "charm, beauty and brains," a woman who "belonged to everything." The only negative was Creighton Coleman, "a pain in the ass" who, Peterson said, "didn't comprehend" her meticulously detailed schedule and would line up competing speaking invitations.[52]

The ten-candidate field was the largest in the state's history for the court's two open seats. In the end, Coleman finished second, just behind Appeals Court judge Charles Levin. Levin spent more than four times what Coleman spent, and she spent less than half of what the third-place finisher did. Peterson wrote later, "I believe a great deal of the success was due to the fact that attention was paid to SMALL details and individual voters . . . too many men in the past few years feel that MONEY buys elections."[53] Among the lawyers Coleman bested were Thorburn and Ferency, now running under the banner of the Human Rights Party.

On Thanksgiving Day, Coleman wrote Peterson:

> I have started several letters to you—both on paper and in my mind—none have said what I really feel, and perhaps none can. It does seem appropriate, however, that I write to you today and try again to express the tremendous respect I have for you as a person, as a citizen and as a force in our state and nation. I have felt so very grateful and fortunate—and most humble—that you consented to lead my ("ours," really) campaign to its unusual success.
>
> As I have said many times, it could not have been done without you. I have enjoyed your personal prestige all over Michigan and have had many occasions to admire your capacity for leadership and your integrity. Personally, I could in no way be involved in a political campaign which was not honest and honorable and so it was of great importance to me that I could go where calendared and do what was expected of me with the greatest of confidence. . . .
>
> Some day, I hope we can return even a small portion of your great kindness, hard work and confidence. In the meanwhile, we love you, honor you and most deeply appreciate you.[54]

Peterson's "kids" would remember the Coleman race as her "statement campaign."

"I think she felt an awful lot of re-energizing and redemption in that," Molin recalled. "She'd been through her own Senate campaign, and through the Lenore Romney campaign. There'd been some tough times in there. . . . And then all of a sudden she had a candidate back in *her* state, that was embraced by *her* party, and they led a united run for a quality candidate for a critical post. They made a statement about women. They made a statement about public service."

And, for the first time in many years, he said, "they enjoyed a campaign."[55]

# CHAPTER TEN

---

# The Show

---

IN THE EARLY MONTHS OF 1973, the Watergate cover-up began to unravel. In October, Vice President Agnew resigned, pleading no contest to tax evasion and money laundering. In December, Gerald Ford was sworn in to replace him.

Peterson was among hundreds of Michigan Republicans who traveled to Washington to attend the swearing-in ceremony. She wrote afterward:

> [It] was more than a ceremony to me. I was viewing an old friend and co-worker being [sworn] into the No. 2 spot in the nation. I was looking at a man who had undergone more investigation, more examination, than any previous Vice President (or President for that matter)—and I was watching a man who had come through all these investigations as a symbol of integrity.
>
> As old friends greeted each other—there was a feeling of confidence and inspiration—Here was a man from Michigan—the first from our state ever to be in the Executive Office—but more important than the historic first, was the belief by all those there, that it was a beginning—for a return to confidence in government.[1]

At a party that night, she predicted that if Ford became president before the end of Nixon's term he would "make a great President." She added, "And there could be a chance that he will get to be President."[2]

In eight months, that prophecy was fulfilled.

As the Nixon administration's dirty tricks and cover-up were revealed, it would have been easy for Peterson to have smugly said, "I told you so." But there is little of that in her papers. Instead she observed in her memoir that the scandal had "a tremendously adverse effect on me. I had BELIEVED Richard Nixon and Spiro Agnew could do a fine job of governing the country. I was devastated by their actions."[3]

Still, throughout her life, Peterson always tried to separate the political from the personal, and to relate to people on a human level, even when it was difficult. Although she was never close to the Agnews, she apparently reached out to them after the vice president resigned. "Spiro and I appreciate your lovely note more than I am able to say," Judy Agnew wrote in response. "Thank you for your expression of friendship and for remembering us at this very, very difficult time."[4]

But, like other members of the Greatest Generation, Peterson was taught to bury her emotions and keep moving forward. Two weeks after Nixon resigned in August 1974, she wrote Griffin, outlining what the Republicans should do to reach out to women and other constituencies. She made no reference to Nixon, Agnew, or Watergate.

But she *was* concerned that *she* was still persona non grata in some circles. "On sober reflection," she cautioned, "I believe the idea should be sold to others without mention of my name. It is not a *personal* thing and should not be covered as such. I will simply funnel to you any info you might need to enlarge upon the subject."[5]

For a time, Peterson remained on the periphery of politics, staying in touch with old friends and offering advice when it was solicited. After Romney became chair of the National Center for Voluntary Action, she was retained in June 1974 as its director of organizational relations, a job she managed by commuting part time from Charlotte.

In November 1974, she led a "Delegation for Friendship among Women" on a trip to Egypt, where she met Jehan Sadat, the Egyptian president's wife, and then on to Lebanon, Iran, Iraq, Kuwait, and Syria. The trip helped cement friendships with women in other countries, as well as her American traveling companions.

Virginia Knauer tried to push her name for Ford's liaison to women, but the job went to U.S. Air Force general Jeanne Holm instead. Peterson asserted in her memoir that it would have been "impossible" for her to take the job because she lived in Hawaii for half the year.[6] But in 1975 she did win an appointment—probably with Knauer's help—to the White House Consumer Advisory Council. That same year, Eastern Michigan University recognized her with an honorary degree.

Nevertheless, some part of her still itched to be in politics. In August 1975, Griffin wrote the Ford campaign, expressing Peterson's interest in an assignment. But the senator received a noncommittal response from Chairman Howard "Bo" Callaway and no specific job offer for his friend.[7]

* * *

In other Washington offices, women's groups, including the National Federation of Business and Professional Women's Clubs (BPW) and the League of Women Voters, were becoming increasingly frustrated about the Equal Rights Amendment. Although thirty of the requisite thirty-eight state legislatures had voted to ratify the amendment in the first year after it cleared Congress in 1972, ratification had since bogged down—thanks largely to the opposition of Schlafly and her organization, Stop ERA. Supporting groups had formed an informal Ratification Council, but were struggling to work together. As Mariwyn Heath, who emerged as the BPW's point person, recalled, "You were starting to get the fight among organizations, that inability to agree on anything unless it is (1) talked to death and (2) that kind of turf problem that groups always have on 'how come we should do it just because it's your idea?'"[8]

The council enlisted the help of the National Commission on the Observance of International Women's Year (IWY), which Ford created by executive order in 1975. The commission, in turn, created an ERA Committee, cochaired by Heckler and actor Alan Alda, to take charge. In August, the committee brought together several political and public relations experts to make recommendations on how to reinvigorate the ratification drive.

Several pointed to the same problem. As consultant Richard Cohen put it, "We believe rather strongly that one of the great problems has been the lack of any kind of central organization, the lack of any kind of primary focal point. . . . I think one of the reasons the opposition is so easily identified and gets such good coverage is because they do have a single focal point. They have a lady. There is a place to go to."

What supporters needed were some standard-bearers, "people who cover a broad political spectrum, who have come together on this issue," in the words of consultant Barry Jagoda. Democratic representative Barbara Jordan and Republican Clare Boothe Luce were suggested.[9]

In October, Peterson took off on another overseas trip, this time to the

People's Republic of China as a member of the first women's delegation to be formally invited since the country reopened its doors to the West.[10] When she landed back in San Francisco in November, a telegram was waiting, signed by Jill Ruckelshaus, the head of the Republican Women's Political Caucus and the IWY Commission, and Virginia Allan, who was now deputy undersecretary of state. The time had come, they said, to launch a united effort to ratify the ERA, and they wanted Peterson and Democrat Liz Carpenter to lead it.

In a telegram, BPW president Maxine Hays urged Peterson to accept the job: "Women need your guiding hand as never before in the history of our struggle for equality."[11]

By January 5, 1976, Peterson and Carpenter were telling potential financial supporters that they had agreed to be "the bi-partisan, gray-haired, hopefully experienced co-chairs of ERAmerica."[12]

The organization was formally launched at a February 25 press conference. Peterson said she had been convinced "that the most effective way to ratify ERA was by waging a political campaign. . . . I believe that this is the single most important political campaign being launched this year. . . . After many years spent in the women's movement, I want to be a part of the inclusion of women in the Constitution."[13]

In April, she told the Indiana Women's Political Caucus, "We are doing this rather than work on a political campaign—and, as many of you know, I have spent many years in just that occupation."[14]

Peterson may have been sincere when she said she viewed the ERA as the year's most important political issue, but another political campaign was also beckoning.

The day before ERAmerica was launched, Ronald Reagan had nearly defeated Ford in the New Hampshire primary. Ford and his aides had not expected Reagan to challenge a sitting president. As a result, their campaign organization was in a state of chaos and riven by infighting among factions in the White House and the campaign.

Rogers Morton had been named counselor to the president and liaison to the campaign committee. In February, he wrote Peterson that he was "really concerned" and observed that "the system here is kind of like concrete."[15]

Peterson was also receiving alarming reports from friends in Michigan. On March 15, four days before the deadline, Republican national committeeman Peter Fletcher discovered that the Ford campaign had not yet filed the necessary petitions to get on the state's primary ballot. He wrote Peterson that when he alerted the campaign, "the big legal brains said I was wrong. Sent them back to their law books and they called back confessing I was right." Fletcher was asked to wait at Detroit Metropolitan Airport so he could hand deliver the papers. They never arrived. He concluded cynically, "Renews my confidence in the strong hands of leadership in which we have entrusted the future of our nation." Fletcher finally received the affidavits, and he delivered them with only two hours to spare.[16]

Later that spring Morton took charge of the President Ford Committee (PFC) after Callaway was forced to resign over allegations of financial improprieties. It was at PFC headquarters that Peterson finally caught up with her old colleague and was stunned by what she found. Morton had been diagnosed with cancer, and the "great big strapping man" was all "gray and bent over." Morton asked Peterson if she would come onboard to help build support among women voters.

"We loved each other," she recalled. "My heart almost broke because his cancer was so bad. . . . I wanted to do everything I could to help him."[17] In another version, she wrote, "There is no one I loved more, or enjoyed working with more, than Rog. . . . I wondered, after spending the evening with him, how he could hack it, but his spirit was strong, and he was determined to get the nomination through."[18]

Summertime was approaching, and that meant returning to Charlotte, with Pete on the golf course and nothing much for her to do. When her husband once again gave her the go-ahead, she accepted the offer.[19]

The fact that she was also serving as the public face of the ERA campaign was of little concern. She told a reporter that she would leave most of that work in the hands of Carpenter and the professional staff. "Much of the groundwork for ERA has been laid and there is only one state which will vote on it this year, Illinois, so there just isn't so much going on." She wrote her sister that she didn't think the Ford job "can be harder or more discouraging than dealing with state legislators on ERA." She had two ERA speaking commitments that summer, "but they can both be worked into this job, too. The President knows I am completely committed to it—and since he is for it, it is okay."

Peterson did meet with Ford for about half an hour "over what could be done and I said it was awfully late, etc." But, she reported to her sister, "He looks just fine—it seems a shame he has had such poor back up."[20]

For a woman who started as a secretary in a grungy state party office, a presidential campaign was certainly "the show." And even if she was juggling multiple jobs and a challenging travel schedule, it would have been hard for Peterson to turn down one of the highest jobs ever offered to a woman in a presidential campaign.

"I believe Ford and Morton thought I was to be an integral part of the campaign—both of them were used to me and my ways," she recalled. "We had all worked together over a long time. And I believe, too, that I was one of the few women politicians both Ford and Morton were comfortable working with and having around on a daily basis." She told a reporter she had no interest in a permanent administration post.[21]

Peterson acknowledged later that the two jobs turned out to be among the most frustrating—if not *the* worst—of her political lifetime. Still, even at sixty-two, she was still receiving calls for help. And in 1976, she still said "yes," not once, not twice, but ultimately three times—even against her better judgment.

* * *

Peterson arrived at the PFC as the primaries were ending but Ford's nomination still not secured. She wrote her family that she was "inundated with problems and people with problems and things to do. . . . I have been moving about 14 hours a day or more—and I think I am more an ombudsman now than anything else."[22] A reporter wrote that "one of the satisfying aspects of her campaign job is that she is being paid on the same scale as male members of the committee." The article quoted Peterson as saying, "They've taken me in on an equal basis. I have the authority to run my own program."[23]

But by the end of the first week she concluded it had been a mistake to take the job.

She had thought Morton was in charge, but that was not the case. The chairman lacked the energy and organizational skills that the campaign still desperately needed. He was putting in only half days because of his health, and his reputation had never recovered from the primary night when he had made what one reporter called "the most impolitic crack of the year."[24] In the wake of Ford losses in Indiana, Alabama, and Georgia, Morton had snapped, "I'm not going to rearrange the furniture on the deck of the Titanic." Possibly worse, he had been photographed, disheveled, in front of empty liquor bottles—most of which had actually been consumed by the press.

The first thing Peterson discovered was that Morton had apparently never told Stuart Spencer, the campaign's top political strategist, that she had been hired. Even under the best of circumstances, it was not an auspicious way to begin a professional relationship.

Spencer had come from California, where his consulting firm had been a pioneer in transforming campaigns "from an amateur back room business, managed for the most part by familiar 'old pol' types" into "a slick, high-powered profession that merchandised candidates as effectively as advertising agencies sold brands of soap, toothpaste, tobacco, and deodorant," in the words of reporter Haynes Johnson, who added, "They were political entrepreneurs; the products they sold were candidates. . . ."[25] The late Lyn Nofziger once observed that Spencer was "a hired gun" who had "no particular philosophy." Spencer "could have been a Democrat if things had worked like that, and it wouldn't have bothered him."[26]

James A. Baker III, the campaign's chief delegate counter, recalled in his own memoir that Spencer "was political, but he was not politic." Baker did not report to Spencer, and "initially," he conceded, "this was a source of tension."[27] In his early months, he recalled appealing to Morton to referee a battle with members of Spencer's staff.

Spencer could be blunt, gruff, and direct. In the final months of the campaign, he went so far as to tell the president, "You're no f——ing good as a campaigner." Reporter Jules Witcover observed that Spencer was quick to acknowledge that he was "no administrator" and, in fact, had turned down the chairman's job.[28]

Jack Stiles, a close aide to Ford, had detailed Spencer's liabilities a few months before Stiles died in an auto accident. "Stu Spencer is a 'doer,'" Stiles wrote the president. "He is great at making field decisions and fighting brush fires. He is not an overall planner. He puts out one fire at a time. As we get further into the heat of the campaign this will become a problem. He cannot rush to every fire and keep the station house operating at the same time. He likes to function as a 'loner' with his own tight-knit team. That's OK for fighting brush fires, but in the meantime the overall planning will not get done. When we come to the month of May with 16 Primaries in one month, it will be chaos."[29]

Spencer had no prior experience working directly with Peterson and probably no appreciation of her skills. She was thirteen years older, a veteran of a very different political world—and one that was rapidly disappearing.

Peterson later described her campaign experience as a "shocker" and an "eye opener." Except for her short stint with Lenore Romney in 1968, she had never actually worked in a presidential campaign. An accomplished organizer, she could be easily frustrated by chaos and incompetence. An extrovert whose personal style was inclusive, it would have been painful to be recruited for a top campaign job and then excluded from key meetings.

Her unhappiness colored her memories. As Ford himself moved farther to the right, she found herself working with persons who were much more conservative than she was. Peterson recalled that she was "dumbfounded" at the number of top Reagan aides that she found in the Ford campaign. The woman who had once preached the gospel of party unity increasingly was defining people by their prior political associations.

Still, there *were* differences between the candidates, particularly on issues important to Peterson. "While Ford supports the Equal Rights Amendment," *Time* said, "Reagan opposes it as encouraging 'sex and sexual differences [to be] treated as casually and amorally as dogs and other beasts treat them.' He also has highly exaggerated fears that the amendment would lead to sexually integrated rest rooms, the drafting of women into Army combat units and wholesale rewriting of the laws on divorce, child support and rape—to the detriment of women's rights."[30]

Peterson wrote her sister, "As time goes by I think I am closer to being retired!!! . . . It makes me sad for Jerry Ford but on the other hand he can read the papers and see the reports and you would think he would want to shake things up." She added that she was "happy I am not emotionally involved here. I could not take it!!"[31]

In Peterson's most cynical frame of mind, she believed that Reagan's conservative supporters had deliberately sabotaged the Ford campaign so that their candidate could run four years later. She faulted others for exploiting Morton's problems for their own purposes. Exhibit number 1 was the liquor bottle wirephoto. She blamed campaign aides for not protecting Morton—certainly not the way *she* would have watched out for him: "Normally, a good press agent would never permit a picture like this to be taken, much less to be printed. . . . Over and over again, tricks like this were played on Rog by the Spencer group. Rog wasn't himself, and they would tell the press (confidentially, of course!!!) that he was sick, he was ineffective, he was failing, etc."[32] She hewed to a professional code that placed personal loyalty ahead of political expediency. But in a struggling campaign organization, that was not necessarily appreciated.

In a later oral history, Nofziger acknowledged that there *were* many Reagan supporters working in the Ford campaign. They had expected Reagan to run in 1976, but their plans were thwarted when Nixon "screwed up." "So a lot of people who would have liked to have been with Reagan didn't think we would run. And being activists, they wanted to get involved. So they signed on with Gerald Ford."[33]

Peterson distrusted Spencer because he had worked in Reagan's 1966 and 1970 gubernatorial campaigns. But Spencer had also directed Rockefeller's 1964 presidential campaign in California and had worked on Riegle's 1966 congressional campaign, two liberal candidates she did not acknowledge. After the 1968 convention, Spencer had had a falling out with Reagan's palace guard, and in 1975, White House chief of staff Donald Rumsfeld recruited him for Ford's campaign.

"Here I am, a Reagan guy, and I'm in the Ford campaign," Spencer recalled twenty-five years later. "All these [Reagan] people were making damn sure I wasn't in the Reagan campaign. That didn't bother me. . . . I liked Gerald Ford. I've always had the philosophy that you don't run against a sitting incumbent in your own party. . . . It wasn't a matter of being vindictive. It was an opportunity professionally to go national with a sitting president in my own party, knowing full well I was never going to be invited into the primary process any other way." He added that even though Ford's people wouldn't admit it, he thought his Reagan experience was "a real plus," because "I was the only guy who understood him."[34]

The slights Peterson experienced could have been the result of miscommunications, power struggles, or simply the pressure-cooker atmosphere of a struggling campaign. Or they may have been rooted in differences of personality, politics, gender, and age. Stiles, who was three years younger than Peterson, expressed emotions similar to hers: "It is too bad, but I seem to be regarded as an old man who doesn't know much but is a friend of the President who must be kept on the payroll and tolerated. I naturally don't like playing this role. I have less responsibility in 1976 with the Ford campaign than I had in 1960 with the Nixon campaign. . . . I would have thought my performance record since 1948 would have justified a little more authority."[35]

Morton installed Peterson in a nearby office, and told her to get the public relations staff to issue a press release announcing her appointment. There was, after all, some positive publicity to be gained, particularly among moderate Republican women. But, although she marked up a draft with corrections, she said the press release was never distributed.[36]

But the news got out through her own press contacts. The *Washington Post* reported on May 28 that she would be in charge of "organizing special voter groups such as ethnic groups." The *Detroit News* version described her as one of four deputy campaign directors, on an equal footing with Spencer, Baker, and Royston F. Hughes, deputy director for administration. The assumption was that Ford would win the nomination because "she is joining the staff too late to have much impact on the remainder of the primary campaign."[37]

Morton took her to a meeting with Ford to discuss who would serve as the president's floor manager at the August convention. Texas senator John Tower had wanted the job but failed to get elected as a delegate. Peterson suggested Griffin, noting that he was close to Ford and had managed his campaign for House minority leader. Ford called Griffin and offered him the job.

When they told Spencer, he was, Peterson recalled, "really ticked off." It was obvious, she wrote, that "Bob Griffin, conservative though he might be, was no choice of his [Spencer's]. Perhaps he felt Bob couldn't be handled???" Peterson undoubtedly viewed the decision as Ford's to make, but Spencer likely resented the fact that *he* had not been consulted first.

While Morton and Baker "were meticulous about inviting me to every meeting," Peterson recalled, she believed that Spencer deliberately excluded her, particularly from White House meetings. "It was more than silly at times to have to figure out ways to keep informed in order to do the job for which I was hired." It felt, she recalled years later, "like a Stranger in a Strange Land."

Soon after the Griffin episode, her office was moved to another floor—"about as far as possible from the main operation." This was emotionally painful for "Mother," but in the closing days of a chaotic campaign, there was no one to whom she could appeal.[38]

But Peterson did not typically engage in political infighting on her own behalf. Rather, she reverted to her old role, trying to be useful and straightening up whatever needed fixing. She was first struck by the staff's poor morale. The campaign, Evans and Novak wrote, was "contaminated by recriminations, backstabbing and personal power plays," which had brought it "to the brink of anarchy." The secretaries, Peterson observed, were cleaning up their desks at 4:30 and leaving at 5:00, and she thought, "You cannot win a presidential campaign when your own staff isn't interested."[39]

She blamed Spencer for putting his own people in key roles and failing to integrate volunteers who were close to the Fords. But the party builder in her probably placed more importance on motivating and retaining volunteers than did a campaign tactician like Spencer.

She devised a project to build a "Women for Ford" list. Daily the staff tracked the number of names that had been added, a "ploy" she acknowledged, that was designed more to motivate the volunteers than to actually produce a long list.

The project was very successful but ultimately very frustrating. Within a matter of weeks, Peterson and her team identified 240,924 women willing to work for the president's election; she and Ford had initially agreed that if they got 50,000, they'd be doing very well. The names were keyboarded and a letter prepared that was supposed to go out as soon as Ford clinched the nomination.[40]

She worked with Richard Cheney, then Ford's chief of staff, to put together a meeting of prominent women who were interested in the Fords because of the couple's support for women's issues. But the meeting turned out to be "a fiasco." The Fords arrived from Camp David a few minutes before the start, and Betty was evidently in great pain, on sedatives and "completely spaced out." During the meeting, the press corps asked White House press secretary Ron Nessen for details. He checked with Spencer, who advised him that it was, as Peterson retold it, "purely a social meeting, no politics—and 'women of no importance.'" When a story on the event appeared, she said, most of the invited women responded to an invitation to become more involved with a "Thanks but no thanks."[41]

A few days later, she wrote "Rog and All the Powers that Be."

It is important to know the role expected of women in this campaign. If you want us to put together a public relations job to the extent we can sans time, money and staff, we will do so—

But it was our understanding in the beginning this Womens Division was to play a part in every way it could. . . .

We are picking up hundred of volunteers who have not been given a thing to do. . . .

The attitude by some of your leadership that no planning is necessary for the general campaign reveals, I think, one of the major weaknesses apparent—that of planning for the day thereof.[42]

In a memo she prepared for an August 11 event where Ford was scheduled to thank the volunteers, she stressed the importance of promoting his "Woman's Army." She observed that two announcements "have been blown" and the number of signatures "is unbelievably high and should be a positive effect on the delegates at Kansas City." She also hoped to make the most of the event among the women journalists she knew.[43]

Peterson still believed the case could be made that the Republican Party and the Ford administration welcomed women. She looked for ways to make them more visible, starting with her own appointment and publicizing the women she hired as her key assistants.

Spencer was not sympathetic. "It was the start of the feminist movement," he recalled in his oral history. "The women who worked for me were always having meetings and then coming and seeing me. I was not much help in some of these areas. One day they got me to agree that they weren't to be called secretaries. They were all going to be called somebody's assistant. I said, 'I don't give a damn, just do your job.'"[44]

When the last of the state conventions was held on July 16, both campaigns claimed they led in the delegate count.[45] With most of the staff now focused on nailing down the uncommitted delegates, Peterson suggested that she focus on keeping committed delegates happy. She set up a volunteer operation to phone the delegates, thank them for their support, and respond to any issues.

As the convention approached, she expressed concern that only two women were scheduled to speak, compared with the dozen women who had appeared at the Democratic convention in July.[46] She suggested five names to Ford for a potential running mate—William Ruckelshaus, Elliott Richardson, Gov. Robert Ray, Gov. Dan Evans, and Sen. Howard Baker—now that Vice President Rockefeller had removed himself from consideration under pressure from conservatives. She said she wanted to see "(1) a man of absolutely un-questionable honesty and integrity (2) a man with whom you and your people can work closely (3) a man who has given a lot of himself to building the Party and a record of achievement

(4) a man whose wife would be a credit and a help." Ironically, she did not suggest Anne Armstrong, now ambassador to the Court of Saint James, who—along with Ruckelshaus and Howard Baker—actually did make Ford's short list.[47] She later professed "amazement" at the support that delegates expressed for Armstrong in a preconvention survey, and was still skittish about the prospect of a female vice president. She told a reporter it "could be a very difficult move for the President. I'm not sure the country is ready for it."[48] Ultimately, Ford chose Dole instead.

In a July 29 memo to Morton and Spencer, and another undated memo to "Bill," presumably William J. Baroody Jr., assistant to the president for public liaison, Peterson also proposed creating an umbrella organization with a name such as "Ford Americans" to provide a new approach to organizing the campaign's special interest groups. She positioned this as an alternative to having "little bundles of people wrapped up as Polish-Americans for Ford, Farmers for Ford, etc."

"Most important now and immediately following the convention is ACTION," she wrote. She called for using surrogates to make speeches, a massive push to explain the president's programs, and more extensive use of Ford family members. She added, "It would be well to weave some of the 'strange faces' into our overall campaign organization, not just as field people. . . . I mean a black public relations person, a woman director of some group, etc."[49]

Peterson's skepticism about some targeted groups was based on experience. A month before, she wrote of the ethnic groups, "We have visited with quite a few of these individuals and those representing groups—and there is little to be done without money or staff—On the other hand if you had those the war would break out over that." The twenty-two persons she had spoken to "dislike each other, are jockeying for position and much more recruitment can be accomplished in other ways. . . . There is not enough time or money in the world to make a place for every unhappy ethnic. . . ." Later, she observed, "The old timers don't want to give up their prerogatives or their privileges. It was a fight to get Arabs included."[50]

In another memo to Morton in late July, she made the case that it was important to integrate the campaign's volunteer and political divisions. If the organizations were kept separate, "you take away the bodies needed for the actual political work." The memo indicates she knew her volunteer projects would only be effective if they reported through Spencer, suggesting she didn't care what the organizational chart looked like as long as it produced results. She also observed, "There would be field men who would have nothing to do with blacks—in some instances, ethnics—maybe in some instances, senior citizens, but each of them would surely want to have a stable of women and young people to call on for the work they needed to do."[51]

At the beginning of August, she also made a pitch for some of her staff members. She wrote Hughes, Spencer, and Morton, "It would be helpful if you decided on whether you are going to mount a PFC Committee attack—and if so, with what people. They need to be advised [on] what their mission will be—their budget, headquarters, etc. We are getting calls on this and they are getting antsy."[52]

When the convention came, she flew out on the staff plane and shared a room with Knauer on the floor "with the big boys." Bill McLaughlin had arranged for her to serve as an alternate delegate from Michigan so that she was assured of a good seat.[53]

She was among those who were concerned that the party might not adopt a plank in support of the ERA. Before the Platform Committee deliberations, she wrote New York Republican activist Tanya Melich, "I had drafted some material and wanted to try to be TUFF—I am so sick and tired of approaching [Phyllis Schlafly] and her troops with reason and have them counteract us with lies—emotion, etc. . . . I do hope we can keep ERA in—I think it would be the saddest mistake in the world to go backward and just what this beaten up party does not need."[54]

In a statement read on her behalf, Peterson questioned why her party would even consider reversing its long history of support for the amendment. In an apparent reference to Schlafly, she wrote, "We do, of course, understand that sometimes people who cannot be elected to party or government positions need a platform for their views. Too, we understand the political significance of the opposition. But we find it discouraging and disheartening that these people, labeling themselves Republicans, contribute to the malaise affecting this nation by stationing themselves" against the presidents, members of Congress and governors who supported the amendment. She also archly observed, "Since the strengthening and the building of the Republican Party has been almost a lifetime project for me," it was notable that only 18 percent of the electorate now identified themselves as Republicans, compared with 32 percent when she and the Platform Committee chair had been state party chairmen.[55]

In the end, the women preserved a plank that supported the ERA but only after Peterson telephoned Ford and persuaded him to intercede.[56] Overall, the convention proceedings were, in her memory, "gruesome." "The right wing was so unbending, so grim, and it was a reliving of the agony of 1964 as far as I was concerned."[57]

Peterson was one of thirty-two key aides from whom ideas for Ford's acceptance speech had been solicited.[58] In a memo to speechwriter Robert Hartmann, she suggested that a distinction be made between the Republicans and the Democrats' willingness "to wrap people into small packages carefully labeled—so no one is an American—but they are a little package of blacks, and a little package of other minorities and a little package of each ethnic group and a little package of senior citizens, etc. . . . Some are even hyphenated."

She called for a

> speech about the future—with a recognition of the problems of the cities and the unfortunate but bringing the thoughts of America back to the time when we worked together to solve problems, when we were compassionate towards each other, when we attempted to understand [whether] it was young towards old, black towards white, minority towards ethnic, rural towards city. We cannot omit any part without weakening the whole. . . . A campaign where we do not have Ethnics for Ford and Blacks for Ford and Women for Ford and physicians for Ford but one where we all work together—as people should in America—under one banner
> FORD AMERICANS.[59]

In the end, Ford won the nomination by a margin of 1,187 to 1,070 votes. And when he made his acceptance speech, he did, in fact, echo some of the themes that Peterson had suggested: "As I try in my imagination to look into the homes where families are watching the end of this great convention, I can't tell which faces are Republicans, which are Democrats, and which are Independents. I cannot see their color or their creed. I see only Americans."[60]

The speech, observed *Newsday,* "wasn't just the best speech of Ford's lackluster career before the microphone, it was the finest oratory heard by a party that had summoned all its best campaigners to Kansas City."[61]

Earlier in the summer, Peterson had told her sister that if Ford won the nomination, "then of course I am stuck until early November."[62] But by now she had had enough.

In a *Detroit News* analysis, Peterson said she had agreed to serve in the campaign "only on an interim basis" and denied that she was jumping ship. "Sure, there have been disagreements, but I never intended to stay after the convention, anyway. I'm getting too old to jet around the country for a fall campaign."[63] The *Free Press* reported she was quitting and was "unhappy with some of Ford's strategists because she believes they have ignored key social issues and the Republican left and because she was given no role in policymaking."[64]

Helen Milliken, the governor's wife, recalled that Peterson came home from the convention "just sick." She remembered Peterson predicting, "They're going to lose it, because those men at the top have written off the women's vote and the cities aren't even going to try because they don't think certain segments are available and won't try for them. They will not listen to me on the folly of this."[65]

Soon after the convention, the campaign's top strategists—"naturally, men only," Peterson observed—gathered in Vail, Colorado, to plan the fall campaign. By then Baker had replaced Morton. The new chairman phoned Peterson in Marion, Illinois, where she was visiting her brother Charles en route home. She recalled the conversation.

> Would I come back to work for the Ford campaign through the general election? No. Would I come back if the President called me personally? No. I explained to Jim Baker, as best I could, without using names, telling him of the primary activities. I said I was sure an ultra-conservative woman would do a better job than I possibly could for what they seemed to have in mind. . . .
>
> The calls continued. Jim Baker was to run the campaign, Rog had resigned . . . and the march was on by Reagan people to join. I finally agreed to come back for the two months.[66]

The *New York Times* reported that Peterson had told friends she had resigned "because of a belief that the Ford campaign had been inattentive to moderate voters and social issues." Ford "was reported to have telephoned her this morning and to have persuaded her to withdraw the resignation." The campaign's press aides maintained that Peterson had headed back to Michigan to take care of personal business and had not decided "whether she would have time to remain in her campaign post." But the reporter noted that the aides could not then explain why it had been necessary to reappoint Peterson.[67]

In later years Peterson said she often wondered why she was recruited for the job. She decided Ford had concluded it would "be easier with me because he knew me and he didn't know probably a lot of women in politics." She added that she had ultimately accepted the job out of respect for Betty Ford and the first lady's support of the ERA.[68]

By then, the election was only eight weeks away. As Witcover wrote, "It seemed, in fact, an intimidatingly short time to the masterminds of the Ford campaign, as they studied their polling data and their computer charts, their oftimes uninspired candidate, and their beleaguered minority party. They knew it would take a near-perfect campaign, and some missteps by the usually sure-footed [Democratic nominee Jimmy] Carter, to keep Gerald Ford in the White House."[69]

On the surface, at least, the Ford campaign playbook seemed tailor-made for a person with Peterson's skills. Michigan was a key swing state, money would be tight, the president needed independents and ticket splitters, and special efforts were necessary to reach out to Catholics, Jews, farmers, and other "constituency groups."[70]

Peterson was, in fact, placed in charge of outreach to women, minorities, and ethnic groups, under the umbrella of "People for Ford." As she explained her organizational vision in a memo:

> The point is that it would be a totally different approach to a campaign than ever attempted before if we worked to unite behind the Fords as people individually coming together to work for better government for all—rather than as parts of simplistic compartments which may or may not speak for their whole. We can get the jump on Carter and, with operating committees in every state, we would utilize leadership at the level at which it is most valuable—beginning with the precinct.[71]

Or, as she put it more succinctly to her family, "I tell people I have everyone but white men ages 24 to 60 and I get them if they are business or professional men."[72]

Things were also better now under Baker: "The office group generally is exceptional. Jim Baker has taken a real hold, is great fun to work with but you find yourself wanting to do your damnedest for him. The PR group are also effective."[73]

She began hiring her team. "One thing you learn quickly in politics," she wrote, is that "you assemble your own troops in order to accomplish your goals." This she did by tapping into her networks. In this way, she said, she knew exactly what was going on, even if Spencer wasn't telling her.[74] Of course, Spencer had naturally done the same thing, building up the campaign staff from among *his* political contacts.

Peterson's organizational chart showed five direct reports. Longtime aide Pam Curtis was in charge of the women's desk and five People for Ford regional coordinators. Jim DeFrancis from Griffin's staff was hired as deputy for advocacy/press coordination, and Tom Ruffin, an Arab American she had met when he was an Orthodox priest in Detroit, came on as deputy for administration. Robert Keyes, an African American who had worked for Lockheed, served as another deputy, with responsibility for special projects, as well as the black desk.

Her regional directors included former state party chair Lorraine Orr of Nebraska; former West Virginia State senator Louise Leonard; Pat Bailey, a thirty-nine year old who had just graduated from American University Law School; Angie Rietz, a twenty-four year old from California; and Judy Petty, who had chaired Arkansas Citizens for Reagan during the primary campaign. Rietz and Bailey had both been involved in the NWPC's Republican task force.

Despite her lofty vision, there were still separate "desks" for blacks, women, ethnics, farm groups, and the rest. Her staff also rode herd on celebrity volunteers, including jazz musician Lionel Hampton, actress Eva Gabor, and the Ford children.

By the standards of a modern-day campaign, some of Peterson's approaches—such as state-level "caravans" of politicians, Ford family members, and other celebrities—might be viewed as old-fashioned. But the 1976 campaign was different in at least one important respect. Thanks to the post-Watergate reforms, the campaigns were limited to roughly one-third of what Nixon had spent in 1972 against George McGovern.[75] Television, Baker observed, "could reach millions, so the challenge for both campaigns was to win as much airtime as possible for as few dollars as possible."[76] Creating "events" to attract free local media coverage thus made political—and financial—sense.

A September 20 game plan, prepared for the campaign's top leadership, called for building up President Ford Committees in every state through October 8, with volunteer members of People for Ford. Between October 8 and 23, state-level rallies and caravans would be held. After October 23, the focus would shift to getting out the vote through phone banks and other approaches.[77]

But Peterson continued to feel that her efforts were undermined at every turn, and she blamed the conservatives who had ascended in the campaign. In her memoir, she recalled that two weeks after putting her staff in place "we got the word Spencer was setting up 'his' districts, choosing men as his chairmen, and [it] seemed to be more a competition than a joint effort. The infighting was on.

"Our women were in the states first. They would have the rally, caravans, etc. all set up with the speakers they wanted. . . . Then Spencer's men would roll in and tell the local leaders the women had no authority. 'Don't listen to them. We will be telling you what to do later.' Then our phones would begin to ring."[78]

On September 21, in a memo to Baker and Spencer, she complained about members of Spencer's staff who knew nothing about People for Ford. Working in Iowa, she said, her staff "had everyone enthused and excited about the campaign" when Peter McPherson arrived "and told them we don't need two parallel organizations that the PFC is so good we don't need the PFF [People for Ford] program—he did not understand that PFF is the support organization for the PFC. . . . In the interests of not arguing in front of the Iowa people last night the matter was dropped."[79]

In her memoir, she complained:

Early on, we could see we would be taking one step forward and two back. The White House staff continued to be cooperative. Women's staff were encountering difficulties in the field but I told them that from now on NO independent decisions would be made or it would simply anger Spencer and go against Ford. Every step they took, every program they worked on, a written report was to go to Baker and Spencer.

At the first staff meeting in the White House the President asked Spencer if he had the campaign manuals ready and he said they were being worked on. We all returned to the office and one of his "gofers" came to me and asked me to write the part for ethnics, blacks and women. I just . . . put it together and returned it. A week later, at another White House meeting, Spencer handed the finished product to the President, and turning to me, gave me a copy with this remark: "I would appreciate your checking this to see if we left out anything on the groups in your charge." When I read it, it was word for word what I had turned in![80]

She was frustrated by many episodes in which plans would be put in place, arrangements made, print materials ordered, and then others would cancel the events after funds were committed. Phone banks were organized without a plan for who would actually make the calls. Her aides were expected to scramble at the last minute to staff them with women volunteers.

On September 17, 1976, she sent a sarcastic memo from "the ole girl" to Baker.

We must at all times keep our minds on the idea that our primary duty is not to elect the President—or build his credibility. . . .We must each one keep our own credibility with the press. We must, in fact, be sure to explain and re-explain what the President does wrong . . . and we must carefully point out everything that is considered a negative.

She also railed against aides who were expressing doubts Ford could win.

If the next time I go on television and find I am not defending the President, explaining his stands, working on his positive image—but trying to explain why his aides and ours are saying adverse things about his ability and the campaign—I shall return, stamp their bones into pulp, put them in a sack and deliver them at your door.[81]

The same day, the *New York Times* said she was among the strategists who said the campaign would "succeed or fail principally in the major industrial states stretching from the Northeast to the Middle West." The comments came as Ford was about to launch a trip through the Deep South to put Carter on the defensive there.[82]

Peterson likely feared that focusing on the South would only serve to push the party rightward. And her instincts turned out to be correct: In the end, the South—with the exception of Virginia—held for Carter. If Ford had captured Ohio and Wisconsin, both of which he lost by fewer than two percentage points, he would have won.

Despite her many years in politics, she still could get excited about the perks of being close to a president. In mid-September, she was invited to join the Fords when they traveled to the University of Michigan to kick off the fall campaign. She took the presidential helicopter to Andrews Air Force Base. "That was an experience," she wrote her family members, "but Air Force One even more so. . . . I kept thinking how lucky I was to be included." A few days later she recounted that "the most exciting part" of the flight was when she was invited into Ford's private cabin with members of Congress and White House aides. "We had drinks and a political talk all the way back to Wash Made me feel like I was ONE OF THE BOYS."[83]

And in the final days of the race, Vice President Rockefeller's office invited her to campaign with him in Michigan and Minnesota "for the last swing either of us would ever make." Later she observed to her sister, "We had a ball. . . . He will always be the greatest in my mind for being natural." When Rockefeller was vice president, she said she met weekly with him (presumably when she was in Washington). But this trip marked the last time she would see him.[84]

The week before the election, the campaign finally mailed the letter to women she had prepared before the convention. By then, Peterson rued, the letter was "useless" and made them "look a little weird!"[85]

As always, she shared her frankest observations with her sister. She expressed her frustration that time could not be found on Ford's schedule for him to pose with the leadership of the black Baptist ministers, ten thousand of whom were meeting in Philadelphia while the president was in town. "Once more I say it can't come too soon," she wrote, presumably referring to Election Day.[86]

Of a trip to rally volunteers in Pennsylvania, she wrote:

> I talked to my 300 women and men—there were quite a few blacks in the audience but I found out although the phone bank is not really properly manned the white women don't like black women coming in!! That was exceeded only by Connecticut Pres. Ford chairman deciding they didn't want to pass out the Jewish brochure (even though Conn. is loaded with Jews and a key state) because "it is too Jewish" and has a picture on the front of Ford with Rabin. If we win this we can be sure there is a plethora of bigoted intolerant white people in this country!![87]

Through it all, however, she kept her sense of humor. The transmittal letter for a final, October 30 report to Baker, Spencer, and Cheney aide Jim Field was sent from "Feminists for Ford" and noted, "In return we expect:"

Five cabinet poooosts

Four assistant secretaries

Three general counsels

Two heads of bureaus

AND ONE SUPREME COURT JUSTICE!![88]

The last weekend of the campaign, a tricky episode landed in her lap. On Sunday, October 31, Carter's church in Plains, Georgia, canceled its services when a black minister, Rev. Clennon King, turned up, seeking membership. In Witcover's words, King's appearance "had all the earmarks of a partisan effort to embarrass Carter, who eleven years earlier had opposed the policy of exclusion when it was originally approved by the deacons."[89] Carter aides scrambled to respond. "If nothing else," Peter Teeley, the PFC's deputy press spokesman, said, "it shows up some of the inconsistencies about Carter's beliefs on civil rights and religion."[90]

However, it was revealed that the PFC had sent telegrams to four hundred black ministers that asked, "If the former Georgia governor and lifelong member of the Plains Baptist Church cannot influence the decisions and opinions of his own church, can we expect him to influence the issues and opinions of the United States Congress?" According to wire service reports, the telegram was signed by Baker. When Carter campaign aides got hold of it, they noted that it had been distributed at virtually the same time the original story broke, suggesting the incident was a dirty trick orchestrated by the Ford campaign.

When asked to respond, PFC staff members engaged in ducking and weaving. Ron Weber, a committee spokesman, denied that Baker had authorized the letter, pointing instead to Martin Dinkins and others on People for Ford's "black desk." Weber said that on Sunday afternoon the desk had heard about the episode on Associated Press Radio "and sort of took it upon themselves to send [the telegram] out." He added that the letter should have been cleared with top campaign officials, who would not have authorized it.[91]

Dinkins told United Press International that the telegrams were sent in response "to a number of calls we got about why the church was closed. It was also in response to a number of ministers who were quite enraged and wanted to know if this was true."[92] Witcover characterized that excuse as "a transparent alibi." He added, "Baker said later that it was a mistake to have sent the telegrams, which he said were cleared" through Peterson and Spencer. But Baker asserted, that as far as he knew the committee had had nothing to do with Rev. King's application for membership.[93]

In her memoir, Peterson provided a different view.

> The whole campaign came to an unhappy conclusion the weekend before the election when the news came out about Carter and his church. . . . The Black Desk wished to send out wires to their black ministers to call this to their attention. Now most of the campaign leaders had gone to the game—a big baseball game being played in Washington, so I told the desk to call Spencer to get his permission. Baker could not be reached. Stu okayed it, the wire went out and it created quite a stir. It suddenly became "My black desk," "my problem," "my error." I never did know if Jim Baker realized what had happened: that, as always, it had been cleared through Stu Spencer. I suppose he did because he really didn't miss much.[94]

The story reflects the extent to which she *had* become demoralized by the end of the campaign, no longer seeming to care how the matter was ultimately resolved. Bob Keyes, her African American deputy, did not mention the episode in the memo he prepared at the end of the campaign. Instead he complained that the campaign had written off the black vote and that blacks "felt that the Black desk was a showpiece with absolutely no muscle, no ability to deliver the President or key administration people for appearances in the Black community or secure messages that would show concern for their interests."[95]

In the end, Ford did manage to climb back from a deficit of 33 percentage points before the convention to lose by the closest Electoral College margin in sixty years.[96] A mere eight thousand votes in Hawaii and Ohio deprived him of victory.[97]

Looking back on her dispiriting experience, Peterson wrote, "I guess I am one of the few who was bothered by it as it did not seem to faze Jerry Ford. . . ." That was how she came to grips with the defeat: "I decided if it didn't bother him, it shouldn't bother me!"[98]

Others on her staff were more emotional, once again expressing the kind of affection that Peterson attracted. "Pat," presumably regional director Patricia Bailey, was one of them. Shortly after Election Night she wrote:

> All I want to tell you is that I thought I managed everything pretty well Wednesday until I had to say goodbye to you. That was tough for me, dearie.
>
> The thing is—I got to thinking on my way home that I hadn't really known you so well for very long, but that you had managed somehow to have a fairly sizable impact on my life in that short period.

Bailey said she did not feel she had been a particularly effective political organizer. Still, she said, "What you did for me was give me a chance to really get my feet wet, to learn from you, and *now* I'll be ready if there is a next time." She asserted, "I'm not sorry I did it and most of all I will remember for all of my life how wonderful it was to work for you—to be around you, to watch you and to marvel at your enormous ability and courage—and your energy dear god you wore me out."

She closed by thanking Peterson—"for all that you have done for me. . . . My heart is so full of things I'd like to express to you, but I don't really know how to write them down."[99]

A "Betsey," presumably Betsey Bellows, a former aide to Sen. Jacob Javits who served as coordinator for People for Ford, struck a similar note.

> I'm sure I could never add to the accolades you've received over the years—and I'm equally sure that you feel I probably don't understand "the big fight."
>
> But better than you know I differentiate the realities of the public battles and their consequences, the battles you fight for all of us and those that touch you. And I just want you to know how much I love you not only for what you've done for all of us, but especially because I know there is a pricetag to you.[100]

Baker wrote her, "We came a long way in a short time, and I for one know that your efforts had a lot do with that—a heck of a lot! You brought a lot of class to the team and energized the campaign with that particular flair for the inventive that you possess. . . . As always, you lent a lot of spirit and a big heart to a meaningful cause."[101]

Ford's nearly successful campaign would seem to refute those, like Peterson, who suggested that conservatives deliberately tried to sabotage the campaign. Certainly important factors in Ford's defeat, starting with his pardon of Nixon and his Eastern Europe gaffe in the second presidential debate, were of his own making. Ford also ultimately bore responsibility for his hires and his choice of Dole as a running mate.[102]

But Peterson wasn't the only moderate who remained suspicious. Tanya Melich wrote later, "In some of his campaign appearances, Reagan lauded the GOP platform and never even mentioned the president. His followers did even less. Whether or not this was a calculated strategy, as Lyn Nofziger said later, 'I'm still not sure that things didn't work out for the best in the long run. The nation needed Jimmy Carter in order truly to appreciate a Ronald Reagan.'"[103]

Hartmann said that at the close of the convention, Rockefeller reminded Ford that in early 1975 he had warned him that "there were people around you who didn't want to see you succeed . . . who don't want to see you elected." Hartmann added that he, Rockefeller, and Morton used to debate "Rockefeller's theory that the White House contained a fifth column dedicated to Ford's failure as a President. Certainly a great many things happened to confirm that hypothesis. . . . I cannot accept Rocky's neat conspiracy theory, but neither can I entirely reject it." Hartmann was more inclined to target White House aides Rumsfeld, Cheney, and Nessen as culprits, concluding, "Now I am persuaded they were really shooting at the President, and it is hard to find any better reason than that they wanted Ford off the scene at the end of his caretaker term."[104]

Years later, Ford, too, acknowledged his own anger over Reagan's decision to challenge him in the primaries and his failure to campaign on his behalf. Biographer Douglas Brinkley wrote that "even though Ford insisted he didn't hold a grudge against Reagan, he clearly did." He then quoted Ford: "There was no question in my mind that if [Reagan] had campaigned for me in Mississippi, Wisconsin and Missouri, I could have beat Carter. . . . He just wasn't a party player that year. It was all about himself."[105]

Ford reiterated the same complaints in a 1995 interview with historian Michael Beschloss. This time, he listed Ohio, Louisiana, and Mississippi as the states he might have won, if only Reagan had helped.[106]

Spencer said later, "I have always maintained—and a lot of his right-wing friends think I am nuts—that Reagan was lucky he got beaten in the 1976 primaries. He would not have won that race: Jimmy Carter was going to carry the South, and without the South, Reagan could not have won in 1976."[107]

Since the start of Peterson's political career, the number one sin in her book had been failing to get behind your party's guy. Near the end of her memoir, she wrote, "When Ronald Reagan can attack a sitting conservative Republican President which results in the election of a Democrat as President—then surely my old belief that you MUST vote Republican, whether or not you respect the candidate, goes out of the window." [108]

Six years later, she showed that she meant it.

# CHAPTER ELEVEN

## A New Crusade

IN 1976, THE PRESIDENT FORD COMMITTEE couldn't figure out how to make the best use of a gray-haired matron with a national reputation for grassroots political organizing. Ironically, that was precisely what the mainstream women's movement decided it needed. Nevertheless, ERAmerica turned out to be nearly as frustrating for Peterson as the Ford campaign, an experience tempered only by her close friendship with Liz Carpenter, her "greatest happiness" of that difficult time.[1]

Carpenter and Peterson first met in 1971 through their work with the NWPC. Peterson was "instantly likeable and friendly," Carpenter recalled. "She was much more open-minded than some of the Republican women." When Carpenter, a vice president of the Hill and Knowlton public relations firm, was approached about cochairing ERAmerica, she said she had suggested Peterson as her Republican counterpart.[2]

"We felt we needed the kind of comfortable but identified old pols to lead this movement," recalled Mariwyn Heath. The women's groups, she said, "had sat for nine months," reviewing their bylaws, then negotiating an organization that "everyone could identify with. . . . And at that point, everyone bought into ERAmerica with those two co-chairs."[3]

"Well, we are on the way!" Carpenter wrote Peterson in mid-January 1976. "I want us to work out a 'soft shoe' routine in which our grey heads will knock them dead—some historical references, some humor and a real plea for passage. . . . So, Elly, get off that beach, grab your hat and that delightful brain of yours and let us know when you are coming and what your time-plans are." She wanted to start visiting anyone "we could get some help from on how to get those four states," the number still needed for ratification.[4]

Peterson plunged in enthusiastically, but was also impatient as she tried to plan her schedule from Hawaii. She wrote Carpenter, "I, too, am growing concerned about getting the show on the road." She planned to come back to the mainland by April, "but can come any time before then for anything important—just would like to have it well planned and moving."[5]

In early January, a letter went out over Peterson's and Carpenter's signatures, seeking commitments by the end of the month of at least $3,000 from forty organizations. "We must have at least $100,000 to begin," it read. "State legislatures will begin their 1976 sessions in a matter of days. To have its maximum effect, ERAmerica must be at work by January 31."[6]

In another solicitation, ERAmerica consultant Betsy Crone pointed to the recruitment of "two nationally prominent co-chairs" and donated office space as signs of progress. She said the organization was awaiting the initial "seed money" before making further hires.[7] The National Education Association (NEA) provided office space; the League of Women Voters and BPW each detailed staff members. Staff of the IWY Commission's ERA Committee transitioned to the new organization.

But it is unclear how much money ERAmerica actually had in hand as its first press conference was scheduled. There was also apparent confusion about the roles Peterson and Carpenter were expected to play. Mary Brooks, the league staffer serving as ERAmerica's field operations coordinator, said it was expected that the cochairs would work "fulltime in the near future." Although Peterson implied to a friend that she expected to work full time on the ERA when she was in Washington, there is no evidence that either of the cochairs ever anticipated working as full-time professionals. Years later Peterson told an interviewer that she could work "quite hard" for the five months of the year she was back on the mainland, "but it was very difficult for me to come back from Hawaii. That's an expensive trip and time consuming." At the time, Peterson and Carpenter were covering many of their own expenses.[8]

The deadline for ratification was now three years away. Carpenter told a reporter they hoped their work would be completed in two. Peterson said they didn't expect to capture the necessary states in 1976 but that ERAmerica planned to "put in motion the political strategy for effective 1977 action."[9]

In an apparent reference to Schlafly, Peterson told the launch press conference they regretted that the campaign "was not formed two years ago before the lies and misrepresentations of the opposition were allowed to be planted. It makes the job more difficult but it still will be [done]."[10]

From the start, the strategy of positioning Peterson and Carpenter as ERA spokeswomen seemed to work. The launch was well covered, and the two women were asked to counter Schlafly's arguments. Two weeks later they were the subject of a lengthy *New York Times* profile that was picked up by many papers.

> One is a Democrat, the other a Republican. That is their biggest difference, but from there on, Liz Carpenter and Elly Peterson have a lot in common: They are articulate, silver-haired and matronly-looking. They are feminists, but not the shrieking and shouting kind. And they are longtime party warhorses with a lot of outstanding political debts owed to them.
>
> This combination of nonmilitant feminism and political savvy was probably the main reason that the two old friends were chosen to head up ERAmerica. . . . Their major strategy, the two co-chairmen said here the other day, is a nationwide campaign, run along the lines of a political campaign, only this time the candidate isn't a human being. . . .

Said Carpenter, "Because of our many years in politics, we can get governors and lieutenant governors and speakers of the house on the telephone. That is what clout is all about, and that's why there are two of us." Added Peterson, "We both have our political debts, and now we'll cash them in."

But they rejected a suggestion that the coalition was snubbing other women's organizations. Carpenter asserted that they would be working with women's groups "because that's what gave us birth. We'll work with anyone who gives us assistance. We both consider ourselves strong feminists. We won't de-emphasize feminism to get the votes that we don't have."

Judy Klemesrud concluded her article:

> When all is said and done, then, do the two women think it is really possible for a Republican and a Democrat to work harmoniously to-

gether on a nationwide campaign of this sort? Both women nodded and smiled.

"We'll part ways on election day," Liz Carpenter said, "but then we'll get back together again."

"I don't mind that Liz is a Democrat," Elly Peterson added. "Frankly, I have more problems with her being a Texan and all those stories she tells."[11]

The two women had "a great working relationship," recalled Kathleen Currie, who joined the ERAmerica staff the following year. "The thing that was great about their politics is that . . . they were such political animals, they understood that 'you can influence this one more than I can,'" and each focused on the people she knew best.

But Currie recalled that the women were still "very different personalities." Carpenter, she said, was more intense than Peterson. "She was doing ten things at once." Elly would do her best, but she "had this ability to let go." She was "very zenlike in some ways. . . . And yet they got along extremely well. And I think part of that was because Elly really understood people, and she understood how valuable Liz was."[12]

Klemesrud reported that ERAmerica anticipated raising a million dollars in corporate and individual contributions. Plans were under way for a benefit concert by singer Helen Reddy at Constitution Hall later in March, followed by benefit performances of "Eleanor," Eileen Heckart's one-woman play, at Ford's Theater later that spring. Carpenter and Peterson began booking speeches and reaching out to potential supporters, including, in Peterson's case, Mamie Eisenhower and Pat Nixon and her daughters.[13]

But all the positive public relations also raised unrealistic expectations. And within a matter of weeks, Peterson and Carpenter realized that ERAmerica faced some major challenges that they had not anticipated before they signed on.

The management of any political coalition can be difficult, particularly when its members have different long-term agendas and organizational structures. But ERAmerica was expected to win battles all across the country while heading off amendment rescission drives in fifteen other states.

Although ERAmerica presented itself as a coalition of more than two hundred national organizations, fewer than thirty groups were directly involved. And only a few of those provided substantial, consistent financial support. The league was asked to contribute ten thousand dollars but initially provided only a thousand and Brooks's services for three months. Later in the year the National Organization for Women withdrew from the coalition to pursue its own strategy.[14]

It was not as if the founders hadn't been warned. At the hearing of the IWY Commission's ERA Committee, consultant Douglas Bailey, who had worked for BPW, noted that "at the state level there is insufficient money to go beyond what I would think accurately described is sort of the traditional women's volunteer charity kind of organization approach. . . . I don't know of a single state organization that has the capacity to raise the kind of funds necessary to produce the kind of fulltime staff at the state level, much less to help significantly with the fund-raising nationally."[15] Heath noted that Bailey's firm had advised BPW it would take eight million dollars to do the kind of national media campaign it felt would be necessary to ratify the amendment. And, Heath said, "this is the crowd that thought $250,000 was all the money in the world."[16]

"A coalition is a terrific thing when you are working on an idea," recalled Sheila Greenwald, a Peterson protégée who joined the staff later that year. "It is the least efficient way to run a campaign. . . ."

"The job of the national organizations was membership building and membership services," she added. "It's very difficult for them to go into a coalition for a campaign which essentially benefits, on a day-to-day basis, others than just their organization. There were constant jealousies, constant staff changes, very differing levels of participation." She paused, then added, "And also at that time there was no money."[17]

Peterson's memoir focused on her frustrations over the defeat of the ERA rather than her frustrations with ERAmerica. But her personal papers make clear that despite the positive attitude she and Carpenter projected in public, it was a different story behind the scenes.

Peterson was in Washington only sporadically until late May, when she joined the Ford campaign full time. As she looked for a place to live, she had sticker shock over the cost of hotel rooms in Washington during the Bicentennial summer. Carpenter came to her rescue, inviting her to stay in her home near American University, which still seemed too empty two years after her husband's death. The arrangement made the women even closer friends. "The joy for me was living with Liz," Peterson recalled.

"That was what got me through the summer. . . . Even if we were just home, we were always laughing."[18]

By early May, Peterson had observed enough problems that she wrote Jane Wells, ERAmerica's executive director, a diplomatic memo, detailing the steps she believed should be taken to save the organization.

Wells had represented twelve counties on the Texas State Board of Education when she was hired to direct ERAmerica. She was apparently the second choice of the ERA Committee staff members, who offered her the job after touching base with the cochairs. A newspaper clipping at the time described her as a "longtime advocate of women's rights" who would be commuting to Washington and traveling to various states. She, too, had stayed with Carpenter during her first days in town.[19]

Peterson had always disliked fund-raising, and now she wrote:

> During the meeting in the fall when IWY, the initiators and original promoters of ERAmerica called together the organizations and urged Liz and me to head this group we were advised that we were in effect asked because of our political backgrounds and that we would not be expected to raise money. I believe I can state for Liz that neither of us would have accepted had we understood this to be our jobs. I do not believe that either of us intended to be "honorary" or fund raisers.[20]

Despite her history with Max Fisher, she had previously been pragmatic enough to recommend to Wells that they reach out to his wife and several other wealthy Republican women for help. "Max [is] a fund raiser for the President so it is a way of getting him involved for us especially within the Jewish community," she wrote.[21] But Peterson also told Wells that she needed to stay in Washington and manage the organization. "Part of the morale problem is your heavy travel schedule—and this is serious, I do feel." Peterson expressed frustration that she had "no idea what we are operating on."[22]

Late in life, Peterson reflected that as she had moved up the party ladder she had been well prepared for each successive job. But ERAmerica, she acknowledged, "sort of threw me. . . . That was all new to me."[23]

Still, Peterson tried to make constructive suggestions. One problem was deciding how to spend ERAmerica's limited funds: "I look upon this much as we would do in a congressional district—if you can't find a good candidate and then good people to back a candidate, you surely are not going to raise any money to put on a campaign. Same thing." She complained that after four months educational materials still had not been produced and that field staff were not filing any reports: "Salesmen the world over write reports on their calls—and we should have hard and firm legislative counts in every file." She also said that "regular staff meetings should be held, complete with an agenda and every person in the office must feel they are part of the campaign."[24]

The fund-raising challenges were detailed in another memo found in Peterson's papers. Although undated and unsigned, it appears to have been written in early summer, probably by Norma Munn, who had been hired as director of finance. The memo observed that ERAmerica lacked "leadership" for fund-raising, "insofar as Liz and Elly do not wish to fund raise."[25]

What Peterson and Carpenter *had* been willing to do was to lend their names, their political connections, and their formidable speaking skills to the cause. At first, this was done in a haphazard way. In April they were keynote speakers at the Indiana Women's Political Caucus convention. Later that month, Peterson spoke to the League of Women Voters of Virginia. In early May, they both spoke at the annual conference of the Women's Equity Action League, raising three thousand dollars in the process. In late May, they spoke at a fund-raising dinner for the Florida Women's Political Caucus and met with other local supporters.

Following that trip, they received a handwritten note—decorated with hearts and flowers—from "the rejuvenated leadership of Florida N.O.W." It read, "We enjoyed you. We love you. We learned from you. We were re-energized. We promise hard work as proof that we are worthy of your attention."[26]

But Peterson had to fit these appearances around commitments back in Michigan, including two speeches about her China trip and the senior girls' annual tea in Charlotte.[27]

In early June, Peterson spoke with Alan Alda at the annual convention of the American Nurses Association. In mid-June, Peterson and Carpenter wrote the chairman of the North Carolina Republican Party, deploring the choice of Schlafly as the keynote speaker at its upcoming convention. Peterson also strategized with Michigan friends about new moves to rescind the ratification vote of that state's legislature.

But a consultant observed that publicity for their speeches was "done on a catch as catch can basis." While the women "are two of the campaign's most important resources," their time needed to be scheduled wisely "to take absolute advantage of their prestige and persuasiveness." The goal should be "scheduling only the most helpful events and smoothing out the wrinkles in the trip so that every minute of the co-chairs' time may be spent on promoting ERA."[28]

But the ERAmerica financial memo highlighted the overriding problem. The author complained that the organization "should not have opened its doors without a substantial sum of money in the bank.... Prior to becoming operational it was possible to seek funds for the concept of ERAmerica...; now we are expected to accomplish something, to function, which requires staffing, direction and management."

The memo observed, "Given the presidential elections, we can probably afford this lull now; we cannot afford it after Nov. 2." The author closed by writing:

> What cannot continue is no direction, no decisions and no campaign. That campaign can be fund raising and limited political work for a brief period, but unless we move very quickly we are going to lose this one last chance to give the ERA a national focus. We have to get away from pie in the sky and become realistic, and most of all, we must start being honest with the states about what we can offer them. I am now embarrassed to answer the phone when someone calls from a state. I know they have been promised things we cannot possibly deliver.[29]

Shortly after Peterson joined the Ford campaign, she celebrated her sixty-second birthday. Carpenter organized a backyard party to mark the occasion, inviting sixty feminist and media friends. She served champagne, peppermint and vanilla ice cream balls, and a large cake that spelled out ERA—"Elly's Remarkable Ability."[30]

But Carpenter also knew how to attract positive public relations, and the party provided another opportunity. "Some people might call them the Odd Couple," the *Washington Star* account began, again stressing their bipartisanship. The article noted that Peterson had recently joined the Ford campaign but that "she plans to continue her role in ERAmerica, even though she can give less time to it. 'After all, President Ford supports

ERA,' she said. Carpenter, hailing the decision, said: 'It's a mark of the President's commitment to the issue, and we think it will give Elly more clout in pursuing our cause.'"[31]

But the festive atmosphere masked what was happening downtown. The day the *Star* article appeared, Peterson wrote another tough memo, this time to Carpenter. She proposed terminating most of the staff but offering to help them find new jobs "if they go along." She then proposed, "We will then have the press in your backyard (?) and tell them it took us these three months to decide a course of action—that we tried various means, etc.—that we believe now we need a small, hard-hitting staff, etc."

She laid out plans for relying more on volunteers, finding the funds to cover their pared-down fixed expenses, and creating an advisory committee of key women's leaders who would meet every two weeks. She also said they should meet with Heckler, Ruckelshaus, and Allan—"since they got us into this"—and lay out several issues, including "the fact that we have had little support from individuals or groups as was originally expected" and "the fact that national organizations have *not* made this a priority— nor have most of them done anything below national convention level."[32]

One person whom Peterson hoped to retain, at least on a part-time basis, was Sheila Greenwald, who had worked for the Michigan Republican Party in the mid-1960s. Greenwald had been working as a part-time consultant, focusing on states where rescission drives were under way.[33]

On July 22, as her consulting job was ending, Greenwald wrote her mentor a frank memo.

> I no longer believe that the nationwide ratification effort is being helped by ERAmerica. All of the positives of the state coalition operations and the travels of Liz and Elly cannot overcome the dismal failure of this operation. Indeed, ERAmerica is now draining resources from the states that should be used for their statewide efforts.
>
> As the Board meets this week, you must face and respond to the problems of financial disaster, lack of staff and complete lack of management.
>
> It is my opinion that ERAmerica should be shut down. The public explanation should be that we have accomplished the goal of setting up state campaign operations and believe that the monies raised in the future should go directly to the states. Although the states have wanted a national entity, they have gotten little else. Any

monies raised from the direct mail should go to pay bills and if anything is left, it should be sent to the states. . . .

The national organizations will be meeting next week to review
the ERAmerica situation and their individual efforts for ratification.
Whatever your decision, you know that I am ready to be helpful to you.

As you also know, I have hung on longer than I have had hope
[*sic*] but I very much wanted this to work.[34]

That same day Wells tendered her resignation. The board of directors
scheduled a meeting in early August to review the organization's future.

The frustrations with ERAmerica echoed from Colorado, which faced
a November referendum on nullifying the state's own ERA. ERAmerica
staff members were sympathetic, but knew they had to marshal their limited resources for the national battle.

The Colorado women had hoped to organize a fund-raising concert
and sought help in finding a headliner. Later, they asked if they could have
a few thousand dollars to help underwrite the salary of a campaign director. They also expected to receive a newsletter from the organization.

Through their BPW connections, Peterson and Carpenter committed
to speak at the federation's national convention, which was to be held in
Denver in late July. But not everybody was satisfied. Two weeks before the
convention, Gail Booms Vila and Jan Caniglia of ERA Colorado sent a sarcastic memo to "the cleaning person for ERAmerica," writing, "We know
that it is not your job to dispatch memos. However, our influence with the
'top people' doesn't work. Perhaps you, or one of your friends could help
gain their attention long enough to give them the enclosed letter."

The letter read:

It would be an easy matter to say that there has been a lack of communication between us, but somehow we feel we have tried. It would
also be appropriate to say that "we are in this together" and that Colorado has had an ERA, that Colorado has actively supported you
from the beginning, that our plight in November directly influences
national ratification—but we don't feel that it is of any use either.

What we want to say is that we are EXTREMELY frustrated with
this situation.

The women pointed to the waste of resources at the Colorado Republican Convention, which the Fords had been expected to attend "because

you had told us that was what we could expect." When they didn't, "a phone call from you would have helped. To put it mildly, we feel shafted." On "talk of money and promises of help," they wrote, "we see the bottom line in this situation as zero." Regarding the BPW convention, they said:

> [S]omehow we felt a BPW convention in our home was something we could be part of. . . . Even if BPW feels that our state president doesn't express our situation well, it seems to us that you, ERAmerica, could have given us some guidance and support in this instance. . . .
>
> As one campaign to another, we expected more courtesy on basic levels and more effort between us than "tea, sympathy, spit curls and white gloves."[35]

Their caustic tone undoubtedly pained Peterson because it highlighted both the organization's problems and her problems connecting the Ford campaign and women's groups. Too, the letter reflected stylistic and strategic conflicts between newer, more militant organizations such as NOW and older, more moderate organizations such as BPW.

But Peterson and Carpenter were able to dissipate tensions like these through the force of their positive personalities. Peterson recalled that when women at the convention were "bemoaning the fact that they had no money," she and Carpenter began auctioning off their political buttons, raising more than three thousand dollars. The fund-raising coordinator for ERA Colorado wrote, "The positive, generous attitude of the women, engendered by you, gave a needed boost to our still-emerging fund-raising abilities."[36] Meanwhile, Jane Culbreth, BPW's national president, told the cochairs that their "performance" was "a masterpiece: You left the members enthused and determined that everything possible must be done to unite and focus our ERA campaign."[37] Vila and Caniglia, in turn, expressed their appreciation to Culbreth "for the support given us by the national convention." ERAmerica and its cochairs later sent congratulations to the two Colorado women when nullification was rejected in November.[38]

ERAmerica's links to mainstream women were reflected in press coverage of the convention: "For those who are preoccupied with image and appearance, Liz Carpenter and Elly Peterson don't look like firm-footed feminists. But, they are."

The "two matronly veterans of public life," spoke to several thousand women, "none of whom seem any more radical than the pastel polyester pantsuits so many are wearing." Peterson reminded her audience, "No one thinks of us as bra burners."[39]

Merging her Ford and ERAmerica assignments on the eve of her party's convention, Peterson said, "As a Republican, I will never vote for any candidate on any ticket who's not for the ERA." The story noted that Reagan was the only major candidate who fit that bill.[40]

As fall approached, a plan was developed to keep ERAmerica alive for at least three more months in hopes that it could eventually become viable. About this time, Carpenter apparently drafted a memo, "Re: The Future of ERA America [sic] and the Alternatives," for the two cochairs to send. They detailed their current projects and speaking invitations and asked how the proposed reorganization would manage them.

Carpenter complained that nothing had been budgeted to provide them with administrative support or cover their travel expenses.

> I simply am not going to continue to carry the entire load of schedule arranging from Texas; nor Elly from Hawaii when the major function ERAmerica has had in rallying new action among organizations is our joint appearance in unratified states.
>
> So, this will have to be included in the Steering Committee plan or you can find some other two people. Both of us are battered by extending ourselves while holding other jobs.

Of the sponsoring organizations, Carpenter complained, "Many have paid nothing; many paid far less than promised. There is no reason Elly and I should pay for the dubious honor of working to keep alive what we did not request but was requested of us. . . . Both Elly and I have given all our spare time (and this was often 3 days out of every week), imposed on our respective jobs to carry the ERA banner. We need additional relief after a year of it. ERAmerica deserves that. And when you add it up, both of us have given more time and money to the cause of ERAmerica than many of the organizations."[41]

However their concerns were eventually communicated, the coalition's leaders apparently got the message. On September 16, Rosalyn Baker of the NEA wrote them on behalf of the steering committee.

> In addition, we understand that, due to your heavy, demanding schedules, you are interested in resigning your corporate board positions

and continue in the capacity of "honorary" co-chairs of ERAmerica. In essence you would be [relieved] of the operational minutiae in the day-to-day workings of ERAmerica but continue as ERAmerica's and ERA's articulate proponents and advocates in the field.

We sincerely hope that you will indeed continue your relationship with ERAmerica and us by remaining as our co-chairs. Your activities on behalf of ERA since ERAmerica's inception have had a tremendously positive impact nationally. And while we have seemingly been caught up only with organizational details, we do appreciate all you've done!

As "an expression of our good faith and appreciation," Baker said the budget would include "some travel funds," and that the board would try to provide "appropriate staffing" to assist them.[42]

The immediate crisis was resolved; Peterson and Carpenter stayed on as cochairs but stepped down from the board. Greenwald took over as executive director, facing a debt of thirty-five thousand dollars. She later said that she took the job only because key coalition members said they would help out. "But that took a long time and in the meantime, this is October, November, December and January starts the new legislative sessions with the unratified states. And so you're paying off a debt, you have no money to run a campaign and yet you're supposedly the national coalition."[43]

In early October, Peterson and Carpenter sent a letter soliciting prominent persons to speak on the amendment's behalf.[44] A few weeks later, Peterson wrote the president of Ad Women in New York that "ERAmerica has been re-organized to handle the upcoming legislative ratification campaigns. I believe that we are on the right course to give the key unratified states the resources and direct help they need."[45]

Amid all of these stresses, of course, Peterson was also trying to help Ford win an election. But other than Carpenter's memo, there is little evidence that Peterson felt overwhelmed by doing the two jobs. It's possible that if the Ford offer had come first, she might have declined the chance to lead ERAmerica. But, despite the headaches, she tried to fulfill both responsibilities.

In late October, after eight months of effort and nothing to show for it, Peterson wrote a memo to Greenwald, the ERAmerica board, and the coalitions in unratified states.

The past few months have taught me an important lesson that I think can be applied to ERAmerica's campaign in the unratified states. One or two people coming into a state occasionally are not enough to carry the message and get it through to the people. We must hammer at the theme incessantly—secure every bit of media possible—cover as many people as we can—and sell sell sell sell. . . .

In other words—we ought to campaign just like we do to elect someone—and the enthusiasm would be bound to spill over. Plus I do not think the opponents have the capacity to deal with a really hard hitting day in and day out campaign like this.[46]

Two weeks after Election Day, a new fund-raising pitch went out, again over the signatures of Peterson and Carpenter. They noted that sixteen ERA opponents had just lost their races, but too many state legislators were still sitting on the fence. "The question is," it read, "'How much do you want the Amendment ratified?'"[47]

But Election Day marked another milestone—and again Peterson sought to turn over some duties to the next generation. She wrote the NWPC's executive director, saying it was time for her to step down from its board and let "some of our younger, BRIGHTER women" take her place. She suggested nine names, including several from the Ford campaign: "I think the addition of new faces would be helpful plus the idea that the Republican Party no longer has a HANDFUL of moderates but many committed to the Caucus."[48]

A difficult year came to an even sadder close as Phil Hart, her political adversary but longtime friend, was dying of cancer. On September 10, he had sent her a handwritten card that read, "Yours was a wonderfully kind and welcome note. Just what a fellow needs on days like this. Again, thanks and love. Phil." Hart died in Washington, surrounded by his family, the day after Christmas.[49]

The new year brought a new president and a chance for ERA supporters to regroup. Two days after the inauguration, ABC broadcast a special report, "ERA: The War between the Women."[50] Originally, the show's producers had planned to frame the debate around two women, Carpenter and Schlafly. But Carpenter objected, insisting that the broadcast must reflect the breadth of the amendment's support. Ultimately, the show did include interviews with more supporters, including Peterson, Alda, and

Ruth Bader Ginsburg, then an expert on discrimination law. For the opponents, the spotlight remained on Schlafly.

Asked to supply a "simple definition" of the ERA, Peterson told Howard K. Smith, "It is simply an amendment, a very simple amendment which will guarantee women equal protection under the law, basic rights. That's all it is. That's all it was intended to be. And the idea that people have added so many things to it is one of the problems we have."

Challenged on whether most of supporters' goals had already been achieved by new antidiscrimination laws, Peterson replied, "If the legislature gives it to you, the legislature can take it away. We want an amendment so that these things are not subject to the whims of the person who happens to be elected that year. And . . . in just about every state, there are laws on the books that are discriminatory."

The show included a clip of Peterson drawing applause from the Junior League of Atlanta when she said, "The ERA opponents have done an effective job in spreading myths and lies about the Equal Rights Amendment. And when you listen to them, you realize that Merrill Lynch isn't the only one who has bull for America."

At the end, Smith observed, "Arguments of backers are strong. . . . But the opponents of ERA are proving better publicists just by sowing profound doubts. . . . The mere fight over ERA has brought progress. . . . But if they're to win this advantage, they must overcome the most formidable foe there is—the unknown."[51]

Reaction to the show was mixed. Carpenter wrote Peterson, "Bad as I thought our ABC show was—the people here [North Carolina] liked it and felt it showed the anti-ERA's as 1-woman and the pro's as many. That is good. Your part was as clear and brilliant and candid as always."[52]

Early in the year the cochairs continued their road show. In a frank letter to her sister, Peterson described her exhaustion after a trip to Florida. Referring to a meeting with women legislators, she wrote, "It is also tough because their first attitude was we were a couple of Washington sharpies, they were doing okay, etc., so we had to sell sell sell not only the damned legislators but our own troops as well. Believe me bed never looked so good. Up for a 7:45 breakfast with [League of Women Voters] and [American Association of University Women]—all jockeying for their own positions, not understanding even basic politics and so the day went. . . ."[53]

Meanwhile, ERAmerica was still struggling for its life. At the March 10 board meeting, Greenwald reported that "ERAmerica had accomplished what it set out to do—clean up debts and function as a clearinghouse. However ERAmerica had no control over organizations, nationally and at state level, state coalitions or the White House."

In an undated letter, apparently written in early 1977, Greenwald vented to the cochairs. She reported that she had tried to get the national groups together to allocate the available dollars to the remaining states. But the meeting had broken down over tensions between NOW and some of the other organizations. The result, she said, was "No one will give a penny."

"I'm sick of the whole bunch," she complained. "I'm tired of playing social worker to a bunch of employees of national organizations. . . . Elly, it's like precinct politics [and] they'd rather fight over who will be chair than win the ERA fight."

Greenwald outlined steps for getting "thru these next few months with dignity," including providing state organizations "some planning help in running against the guys that screwed them." Her last goal was to "find another outlet for my enormous talent that does not depend on a bunch of loons."

She concluded, "I think my most sad feeling is that this thing could not be 'righter' for you two."[54]

In another letter, addressed to "Moms," Greenwald wrote:

This coalition business at the national level and at the state level is irrelevant to the campaigns. The coalition in Indiana was so bad, it had not one thing to do with the ratification. In Florida, we have two separate coalitions, which cannot get together and will be fighting about which is THE coalition until after the vote. . . .

The way we beat Phyllis in that Federation fight was with a well organized disciplined campaign, with one purpose in mind, this campaign is so damn fragmented from organization to organization, no one will give it top priority and unless we can raise significant money . . . and have our own campaign org. we will be at the mercy of these other groups from NOW to BPW and you can forget a cohesive campaign.[55]

Heath recalled: "Money became a serious problem. You can't mount a campaign and you can't go into states and suggest that they do one, two three, four and not provide the funds for them to do it. And a lot of these people now were nearly burned out. They'd been at this since 1972, and they wanted to be paid, too, and they were tired of the volunteer role."[56]

Currie observed:

> This was supposed to be a campaign, but this campaign went on and on and on and nerves start to fray and coalitions are really hard to keep together anyway. . . .
>
> It also had to do with state legislative politics. And it was different in every state. And it wasn't just like, "Okay, well, if we're just rational and we explain this, we're going to make our case." [The ERA] became a kind of political football, but the politics of Illinois was very different than the politics of North Carolina or the politics of Florida. And you've got all kinds of other political issues embroiled in it. And so it was a real can of worms.

Still, Currie admired what Greenwald did accomplish. She "had a really good understanding of what needed to be done, and I think it was a tribute to Sheila's political skills that she was able to manage all of that."[57]

The year 1977 provided a special challenge—and opportunity—for ERA supporters: the National Women's Conference. The November event in Houston was remembered by many as an emotional gathering of thousands of diverse women activists. Peterson experienced some of that, but she was more concerned about the conference's potential impact on the dimming prospects for ratification.

Peterson had been in England when the first International Women's Year gathering took place in Mexico in 1975. Afterward activists had successfully lobbied President Ford for an executive order creating a follow-up U.S. meeting and Congress for a five-million-dollar appropriation. Preparatory meetings were to be held in every state and territory to elect delegates and prepare resolutions.

Peterson helped recruit the forty members of Ford's International Women's Year Commission, which was chaired by Judge Betty Athanasakos of Florida. Thus, she was distressed when President Carter "bumped nearly every Republican from the committee" and installed the recently defeated Bella Abzug as chair. Peterson wrote Greenwald, "I am het up about the IWY too as I think turning that into a Democratic women's caucus with Bella at the head can just murder us."[58]

Then feminists watched with horror as Schlafly gained control of delegations in nearly a dozen states. But that, in Peterson's view, "was not the only problem. In two states, the left moved—New York and California—and a big push was made by the gay community."[59]

In May, Peterson wrote Audrey Rowe Colom, the outgoing NWPC president, "I am truly worried as a result of the press the IWY group is getting and I do hope some thought will be given to combatting this BEFORE the meetings start. Somehow it has got to be put across that Phyllis has trained her members in sabotage of a meeting, disruption, etc.—and, instead of coming to these meetings and taking part, they are coming for this purpose alon[e]."

She continued, "I can be sure of the fact knowing her for so long that she will be in as many states as possible . . . and, of course, unhappily Bella will be the worst possible person to face her especially in those right wing states we have not yet secured."[60]

Currie recalled, "There were feelings among many people that [the IWY meeting] was not a great thing to do, period. . . . And it really took a lot of time and effort to make sure that [the ratification drive] didn't fall apart."[61]

Peterson was confident Schlafly supporters would not prevail in Michigan "IF our people turn out—and that is the key."[62] On June 10–11, two thousand women gathered at the Lansing Civic Center. The session began with Bernice Zilly, the loser in the 1965 state federation fight, objecting to the rules for approving the state's delegates.

Ranny Riecker, then vice chair of the Michigan Republican Party, recalled that expansive eligibility rules had been put in place to thwart the conservatives. "Theoretically those meetings were open to anyone over 16 in the state," she recalled. All that was necessary to prove a Michigan residency was a Michigan fishing license, which she observed "was a little peculiar."

Participants were to elect forty-eight delegates. State representative Daisy Elliott, Helen Milliken, and Lorraine Beebe were the top vote getters, with close to 900 votes each. Peterson finished in the forth-eighth spot, with 594 votes. Zilly was elected first alternate with 491. Riecker, who was also elected, attributed Peterson's relatively low finish to the fact that her politics were well known and conservatives would not have supported her. Peterson had also lived in the state only part-time for more than seven years; when nominated, her home was misidentified as Charlevoix.[63]

ERAmerica looked to the national conference as a chance to raise money and reenergize supporters. It succeeded on both fronts. The BPW organized a day-long ERA seminar, which was attended by twelve hundred delegates and the national presidents of many coalition members. Peterson and Carpenter capped it off with a segment called "Political Lies," which poked fun at Schlafly. Peterson said she and Carpenter were going to start a newsletter called "the Lizelly Record" so that they, too, could make "a quarter of a million."

> Now we are not going to copy her on everything—just the money. We are not going to demand of you that you write letters, wear pink, bake pies or march. No, we simply say, "Send us your complete devotion—[and] your $100." . . .
>
> And, dear friends, we do not encourage you to bake pies and cakes and bread for the legislators. No. No—we say to you, "Get into the basics. Learn to make the dryest martini in town and the best hors [d'oeuvres."] I tell you from my heart that most of the legislators I have met will be a push over for this combination.[64]

Later that afternoon, ERAmerica held a reception at the Hyatt Regency that raised one hundred thousand dollars—double what its board had anticipated earlier in the year. Fire marshals ordered the doors closed after four thousand people filled the room.

Dozens of actors, politicians, and other celebrities had signed on as sponsors of the event. In the end, participants joined upraised hands, producing a triumphant wire photo of first ladies Rosalynn Carter and Betty Ford, the reception's honorary cochairs, along with Peterson, Carpenter, Friedan, Abzug, and Ruckelshaus, in front of an ERAmerica banner.

Supporters imposed tight discipline on the actual conference proceedings to ensure that the ERA resolution actually passed. They were frustrated, however, that Schlafly could still draw substantial media coverage for a "pro-family" rally of fifteen thousand across town—even though she was not a delegate. While more than 250 members of the press covered ERAmerica's fund-raiser, Currie noted that in several unratified states "positive ERA coverage was eclipsed by coverage of the votes on more sensational issues," such as a resolution in support of gay rights.[65]

Afterward Peterson wrote Lenore Romney, "It was my most exhilarating political experience since the first Romney campaign. I was just uplifted—as I saw those women begin to do what I have preached for lo these many years . . . come together—understand the essence of power in politics and finally one and for all believe that others are interested in their problems and are willing to help THEM if they but reach out their hand."

Of the gay rights resolution, she added, "One woman came to ask me how I could, as a Christian, set myself up to be better than the lesbians? Anyway, I thought to myself if I had had that group 10 years ago organization would be a dream. But I think it has taken these 10 years to season them and make them understand politics."[66]

After the meeting, Milliken wrote Peterson that the conference had been "truly one of life's great experiences, one of which was enjoying your incomparable company. No wonder you are 'mother' to and loved by so many."[67]

A college student wrote Peterson:

I know I've changed a lot because of that conference and I must add that you had a lot to do with it. I guess I used to be what you could call a closet feminist, but seeing you and Liz Carpenter at the ERAmerica fund raiser sure made me think! It's sad, but I guess that I had always thought (through books or T.V. or whatever) that most intelligent, working women, especially those in politics, strove for power, which is not bad in itself, but also tended to treat other women about the same way as the male chauvinist would. . . . But I was really wrong! You, and many other women in Houston, opened my eyes to the fact that women can be intelligent and capable and also compassionate. . . . And, consequently, I have come back and have been able to establish much better relationships with other women than I have ever thought possible.[68]

Greenwald wrote Peterson, "The best part of Houston was being able to spend that much time with you. If it was a treat for me and I know you as well as I do, you can imagine how thrilled the kids on the staff were. Everyone commented that your presence in our whole operation gave it the humor and quality that was important."

But the two women continued to share candid concerns. Greenwald was about to go to South Carolina

to try to iron out some of the problems that have occurred with our participation down there. The Democratic Party wants to be involved but everyone has a different idea of what that involvement should be. It is hard to iron out things by phone and I want to go in there with the folks from the League of Women Voters and get them to commit their money and have it all go the same direction. "Very complicated to run a campaign with all these egomaniacs[.]" Quote from our new lobbyist.[69]

Peterson continued to accept speaking invitations. Particularly meaningful was a speech to more than two hundred officers at the Army War College in Carlisle, Pennsylvania, the first time, she later said, that the "the women's movement" had been included in the curriculum. Her presentation, which lasted 3 1/2 hours, covered "where women in this country started—and where they are today—and where they will hope to be tomorrow." She also spoke at the Air Force War College at Maxwell Air Force Base in Alabama and the Army Chaplain Center and School at Fort Wadsworth on Staten Island.

At the Army War College, she expressed her pride that Pete had served "with honor" in the military and attended the school. "It has never appeared in a biography or in an introduction but I expect most of the people who come into contact with me will know it at once: I am a flag waver! . . . more than that, a flag-waving American. . . . I feel so strongly about the great privilege we have of being Americans—of having the right to vote (or not to vote)—of being able to accept the responsibilities of volunteerism—of helping build this country at every level, and most particularly, the community level."[70]

For a time, Peterson and Carpenter were threatened with a lawsuit, filed by the attorneys general of Idaho and Missouri (the latter future U.S. attorney general John Ashcroft), challenging a boycott that encouraged organizations not to hold gatherings in unratified states. (The lawsuit, based on the Sherman Antitrust Act, eventually was filed solely against NOW and was not successful.)

But despite the coalition's efforts—and twenty-five separate legislative votes after 1977—not a single additional state voted to ratify the amendment after that year, even after the ratification deadline was extended to June 30, 1982.

In November 1978, Peterson wrote Carpenter that she had decided to resign in midmonth, when she would return to Hawaii. It was vital that "the Republicans have someone who can travel and work diligently through months before March, 1979 in the hopes that they can get some action from Republicans. . . . Should we lose—perish the thought!—someone must then take to the road and give a good three years of hard work. This I cannot do."

"Facing age 65," she continued, "and increasing personal responsibilities with my family—I feel it is time to hang up the track shoes. . . . I hope I don't have to tell you that the joy of this crusade has been in getting to know you and to admire you and respect you—My prayer is that friendship continues."[71]

At the same time, she wrote Milliken, "As I approach the big 65 I feel I want to be like Martin Luther King—'free at last—free at last'—and I just want to smell the roses and lay aside the crusades. I have assured Liz and ERAmerica that I will do what I can within the framework of being the laziest woman in Michigan." She told Pat Goldman, chair of the Republican Women's Task Force, that "with my resignation, goes my intention to withdraw from any partisan political activity." She wrote Greenwald, "We want the very best efforts toward ratifications in the months ahead and I believe this can be handled much better by someone active and 'on tap' at all times."[72]

By the next board meeting, Peterson and Carpenter had both managed to extricate themselves, passing the torch to two women Greenwald had recommended, Milliken and Sharon Percy Rockefeller, wife of the then Democratic governor of West Virginia, John D. "Jay" Rockefeller IV. Greenwald proposed that Peterson and Carpenter remain "honorary" cochairs, "so that it doesn't look like you have changed your positions."[73]

After the transition, Milliken wrote Peterson, "Well, you have probably heard the news by now that Sharon and I have accepted the mantle which you and Liz are relinquishing. I am sure we can never wear it with the same flair or élan, but what an act to follow!"[74] Through these years, the friendship between Milliken and Peterson deepened through frequent letters. Later Milliken wrote, "Without you as a role model I'd be a quiet house frau sitting at home doing stitchery. And here I am out on the ERA stump getting picketed."[75]

Currie observed:

The thing about Elly, she was not one of these people who needed to be in the spotlight, needed to take all the credit, needed to be in charge. She was someone who really saw the value of mentoring and letting other people do the things that she felt they might be better at. And that was really an important lesson from her. She was so smart, and so savvy, but also understood, "I don't have to be on the podium for this to work." And "Why do you need me when we could have Betty Ford?" . . . She didn't have this enormous ego, which in politics is so rare. . . . She was in it because she really truly believed in what she was doing.[76]

Later that summer, at a strategic "ERA Get Together" in Washington, Peterson reflected on the ratification struggle. Gone were the jokes of the "Liz-and-Elly soft-shoe routine."

> We have worked at this so long we could have entitled the meeting, "How long, Oh Lord, how long?" . . . just think back. In 1972 we were so hopeful. The worst was behind us. It had been a battle but a worthwhile one. . . . The states were coming through—and everyone turned their attention to other problems.
>
> Then came the slow down and during this period ERAmerica was formed. Even then, the job ahead didn't seem too difficult. We just had to get all the groups working closely together, shepherd our money, not waste our efforts (I always play a little violin music here) but in 1976 no one seriously thought the end was not in sight.
>
> I believe, in retrospect, our problems began to mount in Houston. Most of us thought that it would be a plus for the women's movement and, of course, in many ways it was. But in terms of the ERA, it gave new impetus to the anti group. On the plus side we came out of the convention with many new groups pro-ERA and many many new faces. The women learned politics at long last. . . and they had also learned the sad lesson that they couldn't always trust their legislators.
>
> But out of it came trouble, too. The convention had been ordained and funded by Congress and was an official act. The agenda had been worked over in 50 state meetings and many seminars . . . and what happened? The press gave equal coverage to a jack leg religious rally which wouldn't have been covered with one inch of press any other time.

Peterson went on to detail a litany of complaints against Schlafly and her right-wing male supporters, and then concluded:

I dislike the necessity of recognizing that they exist, that they are powerful due to their money and fanaticism—but I dislike more being used as a Republican and a woman in what appears to be worst [sic] tactics than Joe McCarthy ever dreamed of. He was ONE MAN. Now it is a handful of men, to be sure, but backed by well financed organizations. It means the ERA is in real danger, I believe and that to pull it out of the fire before 1982 will take a massive effort of everyone working together.

The whole thing is repugnant to me—but I believe it is absolutely necessary that we wake up, become hard nosed politicians—and fight this thing TO WIN.

As Susan B. Anthony told us, "Failure is Impossible."[77]

* * *

Later that year, the ratification fight became more personal for Peterson. The Mormon church had emerged as one of the ERA's staunchest opponents and George Romney as one of its most formidable spokesmen.

In a letter written two years before, Lenore Romney had argued that the Mormon church's position on ERA was misunderstood and that it had, in fact, been supportive of women's rights. She asserted that church leaders had, in fact, encouraged her to run for the Senate. But now she, too, was parroting Schlafly's arguments, writing, "The homos and lesbians are the main reason for opposition for they believe the next step after ERA will be acceptance of family unions of homos with further deterioration of the sacred relationship of marriage as an institution."[78]

Now Governor Milliken had appointed his predecessor to the board of trustees of Wayne State University. And in public statements Romney was tying the amendment to abortion rights, homosexual marriages, and the disintegration of the American family. Romney said that at the IWY meeting "lesbians and the homosexuals and the moral perverts [cited] this amendment as a means of eliminating any basis of moral criticism of their conduct." He also said that the amendment "is basically the product of many individuals who had been making a concerted attack on the family and on morality as taught by the prophets through the ages."[79]

On December 21, the former governor sent a letter to "My dear Elly": "Terribly sorry we disagree on how to achieve equal rights for women.

Hopefully you don't doubt our dedication to the need for that." He signed the letter, "Your devoted friend and admirer."

Peterson turned to Helen Milliken for advice on how to respond. On December 26, she wrote the first lady, "And the clips still come. I think he is so much over his head now and won't admit it—just like the mess he got into, when governor, with the Michigan National Guard." It was a rare reference to the episode that had disrupted her Senate campaign. At the end of a long reply, Milliken wrote that "the sparks set off by this Romney ruckus will help the cause—if we can avoid being overcome by some of the smoke along the way."

Early in the new year, Peterson received another letter from Lenore.

> The press reports concerning ERA have been shattering and I am more distressed knowing that it must bring pain to you. . . .
>
> I never felt discriminated against in my church but had a taste of it during my campaign, especially through some members of the press, in union halls and in some areas of Michigan. I do know that women have been and are discriminated against in many circumstances and I abhor [sic] this as deeply as do you.
>
> Fortunately, good friends do not have to agree on every point nor to question one another's motives. . . .
>
> I would be devastated if I thought this publicity would effect [sic] my relationship and George's with you. Your friendship is one of our most precious possessions.

Peterson continued to wrestle over how to respond. Michigan ERA activist Laura Carter Callow wrote, "My heart has ached for you. I had always admired the Romneys from a distance. I still felt a personal sense of betrayal. For you, a close friend for years, it must be devastating."

Milliken wrote Peterson, "I do have a fairly good idea how traumatic this experience has been for you, because the element of your past friendship enters in. . . . However, it does occur to me that even your silence would be a strong message. But perhaps one good blast (BLAST) would be more cleansing, and even less destructive of a friendship."

She noted that in a televised interview Romney had been asked if he considered the two of them to be "moral perverts." She recounted, "I held my breath as he responded, 'Why, yes, I know them and regard them highly, and as a matter of fact Elly Peterson was one of the first state chairmen (he didn't say chairwomen) and I supported her, etc.' But frankly I thought he was more defensive than the praise fulsome."

The next day, Peterson finally did respond. In a letter addressed to both Romneys, she wrote that "the entire matter saddens me, especially in view of our past association." She tried, in measured words, to counter their arguments. But then all the frustrations of her political lifetime spilled over.

> George, I am in this battle because of the many inequities I have en-dured in my political career. For example, being asked to run for the Senate—assured if I would do this there would be no financial prob-lems, etc. When Gert Powers and I both had to BEG for money, it was degrading to us both.
>
> Another time was when I was told I was the ONLY one to run for State Chairmen [*sic*]; to bring the party out of its problems . . . then, when I was too far down the road to back out, told that I wasn't worth the money paid to other State Chairmen BECAUSE I WAS A WOMAN.
>
> There are so many women every day, in politics and business, who face these same inequities.
>
> Well, so be it . . .

She closed by extending "best wishes for the New Year" from herself, Mary, and Pete to them "and also to your family."

Romney replied about ten days later. He asserted that he and his wife had not taken their position "lightly or just because of the church." He ob-served, "I was burned once before (Vietnam) by taking a position I had to change because I hadn't studied the problem thoroughly first."

He said he saw "no point" in responding to her arguments "because I'm sure your position is one you believe is right." Then he added, "I am sorry about your experience as Senate candidate and State Chairman. If it was my fault, please forgive."

He noted that his wife had "suffered at disagreeing with you in partic-ular and was happy you haven't completely disowned her." In closing, he asked her to "give our love to Pete and Mary and reams full to you."[80]

Later that summer, the Republican Party gathered in Detroit for its national nominating convention. Helen Milliken and Pam Curtis were among those who tried, in various forums, to get the party to support ratification of the ERA. Peterson and others appealed to the Fords for help.

Peterson then joined some twelve thousand white-clad women and men at the front of a downtown march in support of the amendment. But when the speeches were over and Reagan nominated for president, the Republican Party left the city with a platform that did not endorse the ERA—for the first time in forty years.[81]

A few years later, Peterson observed, "The Republican Party, without a qualm, wrote off women by taking pro-choice and equality out of their platform, where the Party had traditionally been the leader in both human and civil rights." The party "broom[ed] away all its social advances of a century. . . . It took a lot of good women out of the Republican ranks."[82]

# CHAPTER TWELVE

# The Turning Point

Two years later, on June 30, 1982, the second ratification deadline for the Equal Rights Amendment expired.

"Proponents did everything they were told," Suone Cotner, ERAmerica's executive director, wrote in her final report:

> wear skirts; involve religious groups; involve traditional organizations; apply pressure from national figures; don't use national figures; rally; don't rally; use constituents to lobby; use professional lobbyists; poll the districts; work in and contribute to campaigns etc. . . After meeting all those criteria and changing no votes, the only logical conclusion is that legislators and political leaders were more interested in making proponents jump through hoops than really assessing constitutent [*sic*] support for the issue. Time and again, as soon as one excuse was defused, another rose in its place. And when those excuses ran out, legislative sleight-of-hand took over.

Of her organization, Cotner added, "The original concept of ERAmerica, a political/lobbying coalition headed by politically recognized professionals—Liz Carpenter and Elly Peterson was the correct image for the issue. However, initially the financial support was not forthcoming in sufficient measure to promote the kind of activity that would have made Carpenter and Peterson totally effective and recognized spokespersons for the issue."[1]

In the mid-1980s, Peterson wrote that the ERA failed "primarily in the last hours because of Ronald Reagan making it chic again to be anti-women. It also failed because it took the women so long to get organized and political."[2] In her final years, she acknowledged that the campaign had been challenging "because you had all these individual groups that had their own way of doing things." But she and other feminists believed that, ultimately, all the resources in the world would not have made a difference: "I don't think we could have won regardless. We couldn't have gotten those last three southern states. And I don't think you could get them today."[3]

Her relationship with the Romneys was still colored by their political differences. Lenore wrote her:

> I have let you down—you, my star supporter—and I am beset with sadness. First, I let you down in the Senate race, and now, I feel abject about the ERA situation. I want women to have EVERYTHING and you to realize your dearest dreams.
>
> I do not apologize for what I am—for that is my identity as a child of God, but I do apologize for offending you. . . .
>
> It is impossible to describe what your friendship has meant to me and how dearly I have cherished your good opinion and respect.[4]

For some activists, political scientist Jane J. Mansbridge observed, "The ERA became a public symbol of their own lives' meaning."[5] Peterson was clearly one of them.

* * *

Back in Michigan, Peterson's longtime friends and protégées had become more and more depressed as it became clear the amendment would fail. But they still weren't ready to give up. Margie Cooke, then director of the Michigan Women's Commission, organized a meeting of the Republican Women's Task Force. "We felt," she recalled, "that we needed to do something to let the world know that we weren't going away."[6]

Their answer: Women's Assembly III, a gathering of delegates from thirty women's organizations, ranging from the League of Women Voters to NOW, from the American Association of University Women to the YWCA, from BPW to the Women's Department of the United Auto Workers. The event would be scheduled for June 25–26, right before the ratification deadline.

Bernadine Denning, then chair of the Women's Commission and one of the assembly's three chairs, said the assembly "was to deliberate and agree upon a non-partisan, Michigan, feminist women's platform. The platform seemed necessary because women's rights are systematically being eroded at the federal level and a strong stand had to be taken in order to avoid even greater assaults in the future."[7] The assembly planned to use the platform as a basis for evaluating statewide candidates that fall.[8]

Helen Milliken was asked to approach Peterson about serving as keynoter. Milliken told her the organizers "would especially like to have you talk about the New Right, but whatever would be fine with us."[9] Peterson accepted.

She began her address to the three hundred attendees by acknowledging that the speech "is perhaps one of the most difficult assignments I have ever tried to fill in many years of speechmaking. It is a time of great disillusionment for hundreds of thousands of men and women: it is a time of discouragement as they see the dreams of many years shot down by a handful of bigoted, narrow-minded male legislators but perhaps saddest of all, for a Republican woman, is the fact that these bigots have been aided, abetted and encouraged by a sitting Republican President."

For most of her career, Peterson had been the picture of politeness. But she would no longer joke about Schlafly. Reviewing the ERA's "stumbling blocks," she said:

First, Phyllis Schafley [sic]—opportunist—a born loser until she could identify AGAINST her own sex. Unable to get elected to Congress, unable to get elected to head the Republican Women, unable to get on the advisory boards for the conservative Presidential candidates, unable to get a good Washington appointment—or any appointment for that matter—then came ERA. It gave her a chance to shine and the media helped make her the Grande Dame of Negativism. But an interesting sidelight, her little band of Women against Women never grows: It's Phyllis who appoints the regional and state leaders; it's Phyllis who does the national press things; it is Phyllis who collects the money, makes no accounting, runs the show.

In emotional terms, she challenged other right-wing leaders, then said:

I am here because I believe the women of *my* generation let *YOU* down. . . . I am here, too, to apologize to you because I LET YOU

DOWN. I have been far too complacent, believing that an occasional $100 check, letters to politicians or to friends to urge them to help, [and an] exchange of clippings, was a worthwhile contribution. And I learned how miserable I had been—what little effect I had REALLY had—in about two minutes.

The time it took for me to look into the faces of those seven fasting women in Illinois. MY GOD . . . these women are young, they were ready to give their lives to a cause to which they were dedicated . . . and I had had the temerity to think I had been doing something to help!

She closed by saying:

But to those who have decided that women's issues are their first priority—to those who have made the sometimes painful decision to be *feminists first,* I say

This can be *your* year to make your voices heard. This can be *your* year to take the first step to lead instead of accepting. This *can* be *your* year to feel the heady success of *real* power where it counts.[10]

The assembly represented diverse constituencies. At the meeting, Denning said, "emotions ran high, verbal interchange was lively, and women agreed to disagree. The climate was positive and constructive. Compromise wording was the order of the day." In the end, delegates approved a platform with dozens of positions on six key issues.[11]

Cooke recalled that it was "a very unusual thing to get all those groups to agree. I think they realized that with the ERA going down, that they had to do something. We had to make a statement."

When it came time to develop the assembly's candidate questionnaire, Cooke recalled, the group agreed to award fifteen points if a candidate supported the ERA, five points if he or she was pro-choice, and one point each for supporting a range of other issues. The Republican women, she explained, wanted to make sure that their party's likely gubernatorial nominee, Lt. Gov. James H. Brickley, would not be opposed by the assembly. Brickley was the most moderate of the four Republicans seeking to replace retiring Governor Milliken. Brickley was a Catholic and pro-life, but, in Cooke's words, "not aggressively so."

The assembly, she said, did not plan on endorsing a candidate. They knew the likely Democratic nominee, four-term U.S. representative James Blanchard, would get the highest score, but they wanted to keep Brickley close. So they proposed giving greater weight to support for the ERA, and the Democrats agreed.[12]

There was only one problem: Brickley didn't win. In the final weeks before the August 10 primary, insurance executive Richard Headlee came from behind with a thirty-two-city blitz and 150,000 phone calls from his supporters.

Headlee was a Romney protégée and, like the former governor, a Mormon and self-styled citizen activist. As founder of Citizens United for Tax Limitation, he had won a state constitutional amendment that required voter approval of new taxes and prohibited the legislature from approving new state services without providing the means to pay for them. Like Romney, Headlee was opposed to the ERA. But unlike the former governor, he was cast from a distinctly conservative mold.

Headlee won by about twenty-six thousand votes, capturing about a third of Republican primary voters in the four-man field. Observers blamed Brickley's loss on the economy—Michigan's unemployment rate had soared as high as 15.9 percent that year—and his ties to Milliken, who had supported a temporary increase in the state income tax.

Two days after Headlee's victory, Peterson wrote NOW president Eleanor Smeal from Hawaii.

> By now you know a Morman [sic] anti every woman's issue was chosen as the Republican gubernatorial candidate. . . . It is an unhappy state for the Republican feminists and I have not yet heard what they plan to do. It means, of course, a complete change in Republican politics from the Milliken era—and I expect no place for women who have fought for ERA, pro-choice, etc.[13]

"Enough had been said so women's issues were out there," Margie Cooke recalled. And so when Headlee was nominated, "the media started wondering what the women were going to do about it."[14]

It was then that the moderate Republican women convened their secret meeting at Peterson's home in Charlotte. Some of the participants were party activists. Some held jobs in the state government. Others were running for election that year.

Many of the latter said they would have to support their party's nominee. The women decided to take "a 'wait-and-see' approach," Cooke recalled, "to try to see if there was any wiggle room with Headlee in order to keep everyone in the room happy."

The first order of business for the gubernatorial candidates was to complete the rest of their slates for the statewide offices.

Headlee's campaign manager, future governor John Engler, approached several women about running for secretary of state, including Cooke and Virginia Nordby, then director of affirmative action for the University of Michigan. Cooke said Engler figured that "if they could get a good woman, that would take care of it, and put that issue to rest."

Cooke phoned Peterson for advice. "Well, dearie," her mentor replied, "that's an interesting idea." On the positive side, Peterson told her, "You'd get your name all over the state." But then she challenged Cooke to name the last five people who had sought the post.[15] Cooke turned down the offer, and Headlee eventually picked Elizabeth Andrus, president of Northern Michigan Railway. For his running mate, he tapped former state Supreme Court chief justice Thomas E. Brennan, who also opposed abortion rights.

Blanchard, meanwhile, was revising his campaign strategy. Having recently won a congressional bailout package for Chrysler Corporation, he knew he could count on several large voter blocs. As he described his position a quarter century later: "I've got all of labor lined up behind me, the African-American vote lined up behind me, the new Democratic kind of suburban [voter] . . . lined up behind me, so I had a very broad coalition. . . . So when they nominated Headlee instead of Brickley, it was a perfect opening for me to do well with moderate Republicans. So we were obviously targeting moderate Republicans from the get-go."[16]

Blanchard one-upped the Republicans by luring seventy-year-old Martha Griffiths out of retirement to be his running mate. "I didn't automatically assume I had to have a woman," he recalled. He wanted "someone of stature, like a former member of Congress or a CEO of a company." Approaching Griffiths, he acknowledged, was "a real longshot." But the ERA's congressional sponsor accepted the offer. "I think that helped solidify things with women," Blanchard recalled, "that I had a premier woman from their point of view."[17]

At the first meeting at Peterson's home, state representative Connie Binsfeld, who was running for the state Senate, agreed to set up a meeting with Headlee. It did not go well. Cooke tried to make the point that women's issues were economic issues, involving day care and children. Headlee replied, "I understand that. And that's why my goal is to make every household a one-income household where the mother can stay home with her children."[18]

As the campaigns swung into high gear after Labor Day, women's issues were moving to the forefront. The *Grand Rapids Press* noted, "While women's issues are not the most critical facing Michigan at the moment, they do manage to draw a sharp line between the Republican and Democratic teams."[19]

In a September interview, Helen Milliken warned that activist Republican women could desert their party in November. "There's a lot of soul-searching going on. . . . Those of us who worked very hard in Michigan for ERA are not going to suddenly walk away from those issues and vote against them. Women are going to vote their consciences."

In the same article, Peterson was quoted as saying she was "very deeply distressed" by Headlee's opposition to the ERA. She also took a swipe at the Republican Party's failure to support the ERA in its 1980 platform, saying, "Men treat the women's movement so lightly, as a social disease without even attempting to understand it."

She demonstrated anew how her perspective had evolved since her 1964 campaign. Ultraconservative Republicans, she noted, say the big issue of the year was economics. "But we do, too," she protested. "We're talking about the feminization of poverty. We want to see women have an equal place in the marketplace and in the home."[20]

A few days later the *Detroit Free Press* reported on a private meeting between Headlee and the Republican women. It said Headlee had opened the meeting by remarking, "Women are superior beings. They have more money because they live longer—so they inherit their husbands' money—and they're pretty." The remarks, the paper's Lansing bureau chief wrote, "fell flat with at least some of the audience," which included state legislators and legislative aides.[21]

Nevertheless, Binsfield and Ruth McNamee, another Republican legislator, released statements stating that Headlee, in Binsfield's words, "better understands our concerns [now] and we left with a much stronger understanding of his viewpoint." They noted that Headlee had a woman campaign manager and a day care center for his campaign staff and that his insurance company had two high-ranking women executives and provided "flex time" for employees.

The Republican women met again at Peterson's home, their ranks now a bit thinner. Cooke said Peterson's closest friends knew *she* had no intention of supporting Headlee. "But the question became, 'Did we do nothing? Did we just sit out the election?'"

Cooke said the tipping point came when Headlee "started off on" Helen Milliken, who had just been diagnosed with breast cancer and was about to undergo a mastectomy.[22]

A Headlee speech in Muskegon was typical. "There's no room for self-serving, single-issue militants to start threatening this party," he said, expressing concern that opposition from Republican women could diminish his chances. While he did not name the first lady, he complained, "You never saw my wife out organizing 'Republicans for Fitzgerald' four years ago," a reference to the 1978 Democratic gubernatorial nominee.[23]

Cooke said Headlee's attack on Milliken "really made us mad. . . . Prior to that, we were each going to do our own thing, and probably endorse Blanchard, but not make a big deal of it." But after Headlee criticized Milliken, she recalled, "at that point, it was no holds barred." The women decided to formally endorse Blanchard as a group. And Peterson, she said, "was pretty much the strategist of when that opportune time would come."[24]

But the pressure was on. Hugh McDiarmid, the *Free Press*'s political columnist, wrote a September 19 column headlined, "It's Time Feminists Spoke Out on Headlee."

"Helen Milliken and the other Republican feminists probably ought to quit playing games with Dick Headlee," he wrote. "If they can't stomach him, which seems obvious . . . well, they ought to look him in the eye and say so." McDiarmid noted that Peterson and Milliken had so far refused to take a position in the race, then concluded, "But a lot of this talk seems calculating, if not disingenuous. These women . . . have been living and breathing feminist issues for several years now. . . . It appears they have no intention of voting for Dick Headlee. If so, it's time they said so . . . or said nothing."[25]

But, Cooke recalled, "[T]hat was the last thing we were going to do because *we* wanted to be *the* issue." By counseling patience, Peterson instinctively knew that Headlee would continue to self-destruct.

A few days later the *Detroit News* reported on a Headlee appearance in Mount Clemens. The candidate, the item said, "was miffed over recent feminist criticism," and boasted from the podium, "Blanchard has one son; I have *nine* children. So who doesn't like women?" The column quoted "one GOP feminist" as saying, "Can you believe that Headlee equates his reproductive powers with women's rights? What an insult."[26]

Late in her life, Peterson said she could not recall many of the details of how the Republican women's endorsement of Blanchard was engineered. Her papers include a September 24 letter from Pamela Harwood, cochair of Women for Blanchard-Griffiths, who said she was forwarding some tickets at the request of Pat Short, cochair of the Republican Women's Task Force. An enclosed agenda, Harwood wrote, "reflects our substantive, as opposed to partisan, support of the candidates and is designed to highlight our issues as much as the candidates. Needless to say, your appearance will serve to strengthen our issue-oriented image."[27]

Blanchard recalled that his staff "started hearing from Republican women," which naturally excited them. There were meetings with campaign staff members and phone conversations with the candidate. "They knew I was good on the issues, but they wanted to know, if they broke ranks with the Republican Party, that they would have someone who would not be a hard partisan, who would not be a [party hack]," he recalled. Several of the women held jobs in the state government, and they were seeking assurances that if he won they "wouldn't be rooted out because they had been Republicans or because they had been Milliken people."

"I remember that Elly was worried about some of her protégées, and not being punished," Blanchard added. "They could get punished by the Republicans, but she didn't want them getting punished by *my* people." But, he added, from the vantage point of contemporary Washington, the partisan differences were "really pretty soft stuff. It's not like it was some big backroom deal. They were reasonable people and we worked together and we had common goals and we had a meeting of the minds."[28]

Meanwhile, the *Detroit News* tried to douse the growing bonfire. On September 26, it published an editorial, "Harassing Headlee," that noted that the state Republican Women's Federation, with a membership of two thousand, had endorsed Headlee and "is working overtime to get him elected." The Michigan Republican Women's Task Force, the paper said, is "a much smaller group," ranging in size from sixty-two to two hundred, but "sources who have attended meetings of the *ad hoc* organization claim the active membership is even smaller than that."

"Some members," the editorial continued, "have now dissociated themselves from the group on the Headlee question. Dare we suppose that all who remain are Helen Milliken and a few close friends?" The editorial added that the group "has no credibility as the voice of Republican women. Nor do we think political reporters are playing straight when they suggest that Republican women are about to defect *en masse* to the Democrats."[29]

Over the next week, Headlee continued to try to define his position on the ERA. "Women and men are different, equal but different," he told a small audience of women in Kalamazoo. "I've got four sons and five daughters, and I don't want any of my girls to serve in the infantry." The ERA, he contended, was "seriously flawed." In the same speech, he likened Milliken and GOP women who opposed him to "the Birch Society," because of their unwillingness to come up with a compromise on the ERA that would make allowances for gender differences. "I get criticized because I think women are pretty," he added. "Maybe it's a hormonal imbalance." He blasted State representative Mary Brown, a chair of Women's Assembly III, urging her to put a graph of the rising unemployment rate of minority city youths "on her mirror when she shaves every morning."[30]

On October 5, the "opportune" time had, at last, come. At a twenty-five-dollar-a-plate luncheon for Blanchard's women supporters, Peterson "came out" with her fellow Republicans and endorsed the Democratic nominee. The GOP women first met privately with Blanchard, his then wife, Paula, and Griffiths, and then entered the banquet room, where the more than five hundred attendees greeted them with cheers.

In a front-page story, the *Detroit News* reported that "three dozen prominent Republican feminists, led by the 'mother' of the modern-day Michigan GOP, repudiated their party's standard-bearer."

"None of these women are leaving the Republican Party," Peterson said. "They just do not feel Richard Headlee represents the party." Peterson was described as still "affectionately called 'mother' by some party regulars."[31]

"I gave my 15 years of my life . . . 24 hours a day to build a broad-based Republican Party," Peterson told the *Free Press*. "When I left in 1970, I felt completely convinced that Bill Milliken would carry on and build an even greater Republican Party. And to find now that we're reversing all that. . . . I guess you have to say I'm a Michigander and a woman before I'm a Republican." Peterson, the article noted, spent most of the year in Hawaii but maintained a home near Lansing.[32]

Connie O'Neal, a former Milliken aide then working for the state Department of Transportation, quoted Headlee as claiming he was opposed only by "Helen Milliken and her nine friends from the Women's Task Force." She added, "We want to tell him it's definitely more than nine and counting."[33]

Janet Good, described by the *News* as a neighbor of the Headlees in Farmington Hills, said the candidate's remarks "have been absolutely repugnant. . . . They [politicians] have to know there is a women's vote." Maxine Swanson, GOP chairman for the Tenth Congressional District, faulted Headlee for "polarizing" voters and said she was advising people to "vote their conscience."[34] The *Free Press* noted several more Republican women in attendance, some of whom said they remained undecided or would vote for a candidate "who shares [their] views."[35]

Nearly twenty-five years later, Cooke recalled, "We came down this flight of stairs together, the TV cameras were blaring, we were on every newscast in the state. At that point, we were quite giddy with our power."[36]

The next day, McDiarmid described the luncheon, "featuring," he wrote, "Elly Peterson, the retired-but-still-formidable GOP political matriarch, and a group of about 25 like-minded Republican women moderates.

"Oh," he continued, "they weren't *called* honored guests, and they didn't sit at the head table . . . but they were what it was all about." The Republican women, he reported, "were paraded in like show-biz celebrities on opening night." And while "the parade was certainly no surprise," McDiarmid acknowledged that "still, it was effective."

Headlee, he noted, had "kissed off the GOP defectors" as "pro-choice diehards who oppose him because he's anti-abortion." But Peterson, McDiarmid wrote, "begged to differ." She noted that the women supported Rep. Phil Ruppe, the Republicans' anti-abortion candidate for the U.S. Senate, and they had also supported Brickley. Headlee, she said, "just doesn't understand."

Peterson said a primary source of her disaffection was what she called "the polarization of Michigan." She accused Headlee of an "unconscionable" attempt to pit Detroit against outstate Michigan, a move she felt would dismantle much of the base of the Republican Party. Peterson, McDiarmid noted, was "no Johnny-come-lately to the GOP."[37]

In the same edition, the *Free Press* ran an editorial cartoon by Jack Ohman, showing Blanchard, covered with lipsticked kisses, taunting Headlee with "Elly Peterson Says Hello."

At the time, Peterson had no formal leadership role in either politics or the women's movement. Still, "Mother" was the best known of the dissident Republicans, and she rapidly emerged as their spokeswoman. A week later the *State Journal* said that the women "epitomize a growing split in Republican ranks" and that Peterson, "the mother of moderate Michigan Republicanism," was leading "the revolt." Headlee's "struggles to extricate himself from his problems with women voters," the article said, "often sidetrack him from the main thrust of his campaign."[38]

The paper cited a poll that showed Blanchard leading Headlee by 48 to 32 percent, a margin that widened to 52 to 29 percent among women voters. Headlee, the polling firm noted, was attracting only 62 percent of the GOP vote, compared with the 90 percent of Democrats who supported Blanchard.

Almost immediately, Peterson began hearing from angry Republicans. Former state representative Weldon O. Yeager, secretary of the state party, wrote, "It was with a great deal of astonishment and pain that I witnessed on television last night your embracing of Martha Griffiths and Jim Blanchard. I never thought I would live to see Elly Peterson becoming a liberal Democrat!" He went on:

> You know, over the years, there are many of us who supported you and the Millikens when we did not always agree with your position on some issues, but we swallowed that and went ahead and worked for you, contributed to you, and voted for you, knowing that the greater good would be served in the long term. I do not understand people like you and the Millikens who have such a poor philosophical base and such a poor memory. What happened to your often quoted statement "The Republican Party is broad enough to include everyone"?

Yeager concluded, "I am personally very disappointed that you, who are no longer a resident of Michigan, would come back here and get involved in this campaign."[39]

A few days later, Peterson fired off a reply. In response to the charge that she had become "a liberal Democrat," she wrote, "Voting for one Democrat would hardly classify me as such . . . and it is a great disservice to the many women and men who feel as I do (and the list grows daily as I hear from people). It is precisely what I am talking about: MY Republican party is open to all and it is not necessary that we think precisely alike, as we goose step along! These women (and men) not for Headlee are strong, activist Republicans—long time workers. For you (and Headlee) to write them out of the party is sad, indeed."

After discussing the issues, she wrote, "Your last statement about the fact I am no longer a resident of Michigan comes as quite a suurprise [*sic*] to both Pete and me. Our voting residence, our home, our property, our church affiliation and our community work is all here in Charlotte. We DO get away for the winter months as do thousands of other Michiganders so if you are going to declare all of them Democrats—as well as non-residents of Michigan—you have quite a job on your hands."[40]

State representative Charles L. Mueller also criticized her for being a carpetbagger: "Since you have not been active in local Michigan politics for the past several years, I would suggest it would be in the best interests of the Republican Party and all the candidates who are working so hard to become a majority in Michigan that you strongly consider returning to Hawaii and keeping your nose out of matters that no longer concern you."[41]

Peterson replied that she had asked her own legislator to let Mueller know she was a tax-paying resident of Charlotte. She also noted that Headlee had endorsed a Democratic candidate for the legislature because of the Democrat's opposition to abortion. "Of course," she noted tartly to Mueller, " you will want to speak to him [Headlee] about the majority."[42]

Excerpts from the letters were shared with the press.

About a week after the Blanchard luncheon, Peterson covered her bases by writing then vice president George Bush, who had been campaigning for Ruppe. Peterson contended that Headlee was "weakening the base we have spent 20 years in building in Detroit—totally destroying the black vote we were beginning to get in enough numbers to win and completely out of step on every woman's issue."

Peterson concluded, "There is no need for you to answer this. I just wanted you to know I did not take this step lightly, am very comfortable with it—and only hope somehow the party leadership will be separated from him, Peter Secchia [then the state's Republican national committeeman] and others of that ilk." The letter was copied to Jim Baker, her Ford campaign colleague who was now chief of the staff to Reagan.[43]

Continuing to manage press coverage adroitly, Peterson reported in another news item that only four of the nearly one hundred letters she had received were negative. The item said, "Included among those was one wishing her to be afflicted with a painful and—to-date—incurable vene-real disease; another contained a racial slur, and a third suggested that Pe-terson move back to Hawaii." Peterson commented, "I've had so much positive response."[44]

That provoked several more Republicans to write. Secchia's wife Joan said, "I would like to go on record as being one of many who disagree with what you've done. As a former head of our state party, your vision should be broader than your behavior demonstrates. Backing our opponent is unforgiveable."[45]

Ingham County Republican chairman David W. McKeague also wrote Peterson: "I would hate to have you think that silence by me or others . . . is any evidence that we condone or support your actions. . . . I have been a great admirer of your's [sic] over the years. . . . I am at a loss to explain, however, your actions as a former Party leader, to our many loyal volun-teers in the Lansing area that either knew you or knew of you when you were active with the Party."[46]

Peterson responded to McKeague with another passionate letter.

For the years I was active—15 in all—the party leadership believed strongly in broadening the base—Detroit, Upper Peninsula, out state, metropolitan counties—all were included. Black and white, men and women—all wanted. Now our candidate in a couple short months appears to wipe out the gains made over 20 years. . . .

In December, 1970, I resigned from the Republican National Committee and decided to spend the remaining years working in an area where I felt I had some expertise . . . and some hopes of success . . . the women's movement. . . .

My work with the womens [sic] movement has been satisfying, stimulating and educational . . . and led in part to my recent state-ments.

So, David, don't try to lay a guilt trip on me. In the first place, af-ter being out of Republican politics for 12 years, my contacts are minimal . . . and in the second place, please note that a number of Republican candidates are having rough sailing due to Headlee's statements . . . and his politics. . . .

Wake up, David. It is young men and women like you and oth-ers who should be leading this Party to be more than an elitist white male organization. . . .

> We must each march to his own tune ... and mine is certainly that
> I must be a loyal citizen AND woman, before I become partisan.[47]

Meanwhile, Louis K. Cramton, a former Republican legislator from Midland, sent a letter to the editor of five papers, referring to the women's defection: "It is hard to imagine the difficulty in making that decision and making it public, for women who have given so much of their lives to building the Republican party and supporting its candidates. It took overwhelming conviction [and] no other choice was left to them.

"It took great courage."[48]

The feminists, however, were not finished. On October 18, Women's Assembly III released its candidate rankings. Blanchard had received fifty-five points out of a possible sixty; Headlee drew only nine, placing him forty-third among the forty-eight candidates that were reviewed. At a press conference, Cooke and Brown noted that the assembly spoke on behalf of the hundred thousand members of its organizations but emphasized that the coalition was not endorsing a candidate. In response to media inquiries, Headlee retorted, "Who's this umbrella group? Never heard of it."

Cooke noted that, in fact, Headlee had attended part of the Women's Assembly III debate on the issues and had been given a copy of the coalition's platform in early September. "He said," she observed, "there were only 55 days of the campaign left, and 'I don't have time to read a book.'"[49]

The platform itself then became part of the story as Headlee scrambled to defend himself. Women's Assembly III had supported ratification of the ERA and opposed "all discrimination against lesbians and gay males" in such areas as licensing and adoptions.

In a October 21 interview with the Central Michigan University student radio station, Headlee responded to a softball question about his position on the ERA by saying, "It doesn't mention women anywhere in the ERA. It doesn't mention women's rights anywhere in it. It talks about sex. They are proponents of lesbian marriage, homosexual marriage, things of that nature, which I categorically resist and categorically reject as a basis for a sound society." He and his campaign contended that the assembly had "a hidden agenda" and knew that those policies might be enacted if courts were asked to interpret the ERA.[50]

Radio station staff members double-checked their tape, consulted their professor-adviser, and then called the Associated Press.[51] It resulted in another cycle of critical front-page responses from Republicans. National committeewoman Ranny Riecker termed Headlee's comments "shocking and disgusting." The women, she added, were "intelligent and responsible people—and they're people we [Republicans] need." Riecker acknowledged, however, that she was not yet prepared to support Blanchard.

Even Peter Secchia conceded that Headlee's "wording could have been better."[52]

In the same article, Romney contended that Headlee "was being utterly honest and frank" about the potential impact of the ERA, but he acknowledged, "It probably was not too smart politically."[53]

As the campaign wound to an end, Romney continued to campaign on behalf of Headlee, joining him in attacking the women's platform as "shocking and disgusting."[54] At the same time, both he and Lenore tried to cling to their old political friendships. On October 27, Lenore wrote Peterson, observing that Blanchard was ahead in the polls and expressing some astonishment that Peterson could vote for a candidate who enjoyed such strong support from the unions. But, she added, "This letter is to affirm my friendship and devotion to you and all we have stood for together."[55]

In a November 1 letter to Joyce Braithwaite, Romney wrote, "It distresses me that you and Elly feel as you do about me, because I value your friendship and always will." Romney attached a *Detroit News* editorial that had been critical of the Women's Assembly resolutions, then added in a postscript:

> I can't believe you and Elly, or Helen Milliken have read all the Assembly's resolutions and that you agree with them all.
>
> We are distressed at what we hope is a temporary rupture in relationships with you, Elly, and the Millikens. Even though we disagree on the means of achieving them, we believe as passionately as all of you do in equal rights for women, just as we all did and do believe in equal rights for blacks. Lenore and I have not enjoyed being classed with the Klu Klux Klan [*sic*] and others of that ilk on the women's issues by Helen Milliken because of our religious faith.
>
> We are actually taught and believe that not only are women equal to men, but superior and that they should have some superior rights and protections.[56]

But *Ann Arbor News* columnist Don Faber, for one, remembered when Peterson had put herself on the line for Romney. Noting that her "Republicanism" had been challenged, he wrote:

> I thought elephants had long memories. It wasn't so many years ago that Elly Peterson *loyally* ran for Senate against Phil Hart when it was conceded early on she or anyone else didn't have a chance. . . .
>
> Elly Peterson did her part to save the Michigan GOP from galloping Goldwaterism. Now *that's* loyalty.
>
> And methinks Elly was faithfully toiling in the party vineyards when some of her critics of today were still thumbsucking their way through "how a bill becomes a law."[57]

By that point in the campaign, there was not much left to do but count the votes. A week before Election Day, *Free Press* editor Joe H. Stroud wrote, "In the 14 years I have been in Michigan I have never seen such a mélange of bizarre social attitudes, self-righteousness, meanness and prejudice. Much of what [Headlee] says is so needless and so mean-spirited that it is, on its face, self-defeating. He represents an incredible aberration in the history of the Michigan Republican Party. . . . If he hasn't alienated a substantial part of the women's vote in this state, then it surely can't be alienated."[58]

Going down to the wire, all the polls projected that Blanchard would win by a comfortable margin. A quarter century later he recalled that his thirty-point lead in the polls narrowed considerably but that he never resorted to negative campaigning. " I remember," he said, "that Headlee's people bashed us for the whole last month, and in today's world we'd bash right back." But his campaign "had so much to give up" in terms of margin that it felt no need to respond in kind.[59]

On October 25, Peterson wrote Griffiths that she was leaving for Hawaii later that week ("after voting!") and "so am sending you early congratulations and best wishes." The Blanchard-Griffiths campaign, she said, "was a model of positive thinking, high spirit and hope and I am proud to have been a part."

She then encouraged the new administration to retain Cooke, either as head of the "Women's Division" or in some other job, "as she went out on a limb and some of the king makers will be after her." She encouraged Griffiths to create a Women's Advisory Council of her own. She also urged her to keep in touch with the Women's Assembly and to involve "those Republicans who came out for you."[60]

On Election Day, Blanchard won by a margin of 52 to 45 percent, and incumbent U.S. senator Donald Riegle (now a Democrat) defeated Ruppe. Although the state was operating under a new redistricting plan that was expected to favor Republicans, for the first time in forty-five years Democrats retained control of both the House and Senate and captured the governor's mansion, too. Two women—Democrat Lana Pollack and Republican Connie Binsfield—captured seats in the state Senate, returning women to that body for the first time in twelve years.[61]

The next day, the Republicans began a very public round of finger-pointing. Secchia cited the Republican women's endorsement and Milliken's criticism as signs of a lack of discipline on the part of the state GOP: "The Marine Corps taught me to shoot deserters. [Party leaders] didn't call those people into line. If you have no loyalty, no discipline, then you have no organization and no party. I don't think abortion and women's issues have anything to do with building a party. Those reflect a candidate's personal preferences, like whether you take a vacation in July or August. . . ."[62]

In the end, Blanchard captured every population segment but white males. But as political commentator Jack Casey wrote at the time, "Blanchard, not Headlee, will be top man (make that top *person*) in Lansing through 1986 because Michigan's women said so. They could have elected Blanchard with no additional help, since women went for the new governor by a landslide of almost sixty percent to forty percent."

The Republican women were clearly energized by the campaign. Coming off the battle for the ERA, it was satisfying to "win one" for a change. However, it is hard to quantify precisely what impact their endorsement had on the election's outcome. Casey's polling found that Blanchard held a twenty-point lead on October 2, three days before the endorsement. About 1 million voters remained undecided at that point. Over the next three weeks, Blanchard captured just over half of the 617,000 voters who made up their minds during that period. But Headlee actually captured a majority—53 percent of voters—who made up their minds in the final weekend of the campaign.[63]

In the weeks before Election Day, Peterson made several speeches, in some cases filling in for the still recuperating Milliken. Asked at Eastern Michigan University why she had endorsed Blanchard, she replied, "To wake up the Republican party, wake up the male leadership and make them understand that women are here, they're here to stay and they're a potent force."

Asked if it was "personally painful" to oppose her party, she responded, "Yes it was. That was the first time I had ever done that. We, those 200 Republican women, tried every way we could to wake them up, to make the party open up and understand what we were talking about. We were laughed at, we were given the crude remarks that Mr. Headlee made about how his reproductive abilities, the fact that he has nine children, meant that he could govern the state. That was very offensive to women."

In the same interview, she was also asked, "When you left partisan politics and decided to devote your energy to coalition-building within the women's movement, did you expect to see what you've seen in the last 12 years?"

Her response was characteristic Peterson, the view of a mother who was ready for her children to take over but was proud of what she—and her daughters—had accomplished.

"When I left partisan politics, I talked to Richard Nixon, I talked to the national chairman, I talked to the state chairman, and I said at my age I had just so much energy, just so much money and just so much time to devote. And I wanted to do this, and therefore I would step out. I also strongly believe that when you have been a leader and given your ideas, you should be willing to let somebody else have a shot. Nobody should hold a job forever. I felt in moving aside, I would help that. But I think it's been a dramatic 10 years, to see the way women have been on the move. . . . Women are just moving ahead in every field. I hope I live to see it."[64]

It was the last time Peterson would figure in a campaign. Politics was, of course, still a serious business. But it was also supposed to be fun. And when she and Cooke shared memories of the 1982 campaign a few years later, Cooke recalled that Peterson told her she "had never enjoyed anything more." It was, she said, "liberating."[65]

# Epilogue

A YEAR AND A HALF AFTER BLANCHARD'S VICTORY, Peterson's seventieth birthday provided an opportunity for old friends and political adversaries to gather for a "Tribute to Elly Peterson." The dinner was billed as a benefit for the Republican Women's Task Force; Blanchard's office, for one, bought $1,280 worth of tickets.

Reflecting again on the campaign, Hugh McDiarmid wrote, "Arguably, Elly Peterson and a handful of her feminist Republican pals did more to help elect Blanchard—and defeat Dick Headlee—in 1982 than any other small, single-issue group in the election."[1] That same year, 1984, she was installed in the Michigan Women's Hall of Fame in its second class of inductees.

Of the Blanchard campaign, Peterson wrote, "Being unable to get any of the party leaders in Michigan to realize the importance of the women's vote and to understand that certain issues made a difference with women, drastic steps were taken." Headlee, she asserted, was "overbearing and boorish, bragging about how much more 'productive' he was" since he had nine children and Blanchard had one. "And so the business of a number of Republican women coming out for Blanchard was not for him per se . . . it was a protest, a statement, a SCREAM to be heard and to be considered."

She contended that the Reagan White House *had* paid attention, appointing women to more offices, including an RNC job for Reagan's daughter Maureen. "So maybe," she concluded, "the effort was for the general good."[2]

In 1985, "Mrs. E.C. Peterson" received a direct-mail solicitation for the Fund for America's Future, directed to "Dear Ellie" over the signature of

Vice President Bush. She replied to him tartly, saying, "I cannot join this Fund, because I do not wish to support many of the oncoming [*sic*] Republican candidates." She said she had supported "certain Republicans" with three checks that year. "But we will not join PAC's—because we believe many candidates supported are not the kind of Republicans who should be running, or indeed acting as civil servants."[3]

To those who asked, she would say she was an independent. Although she still believed in fiscal conservatism, she declared in a 1995 interview for the Michigan Political History Society, "I don't believe that I would work in the Republican Party today."[4]

Peterson remained engaged, writing letters to her far-flung "children" and making an occasional speech. She continued to travel widely and to wait for Pete to come home from his golf games and hunting trips. "I have often said he goes into a duck blind in September and comes out in time for Christmas," she told one reporter.[5]

She stayed in touch with the Romneys, and visited them when she returned to Michigan. Lenore was not well, and so George would make lunch. "But it never was quite the same," she recalled, "because we couldn't talk about the Equal Rights Amendment or choice." So they talked about people. "And they were always happy to hear about the people out in the states."[6]

As the Petersons grew older, they decided to move closer to their nieces and nephews on the mainland. Mary was reluctant to leave Hawaii, even to be closer to her own son, but Elly and Pete insisted. They sold their farm in Charlotte and the condo in Hawaii and bought adjoining condos in a retirement community on a golf course outside of Winston-Salem, North Carolina. At eighty-one, Elly dusted off a speech one more time, this time for a local men's group. She and Pete were still the life of the community's parties, dressing up one year as Mr. and Mrs. Santa Claus.

Like any mother, she could take pride in her children's achievements. Christine Todd Whitman was elected governor of New Jersey, then served as administrator of the Environmental Protection Agency. Nancy Risque Rohrbach, another aide from her RNC days, went on to serve as cabinet secretary and as an assistant secretary of labor. John McClaughry served in the Vermont legislature. Pat Bailey served nine years on the Federal Trade Commission. Willie Lipscomb, who directed the Detroit Action Center, became chief judge of Michigan's Thirty-sixth District Court in Detroit.

John Marttila built a political consulting firm in Boston that advised Democratic campaigns, including the presidential quests of John Kerry and Joe Biden.

Forty years after he resigned from the RNC staff, Marttila's voice was full when he recalled working for Peterson: "She was an inspiration to me, period. . . . She just showed me that really wonderfully positive, powerful people *can* make things happen. . . . I always loved her."[7]

But Peterson also lived long enough to experience the acute pain of a parent who outlives a child. Pam Curtis died of cancer in 1990 at the age of forty-eight; Sheila Greenwald died nine years later at fifty-nine.

Pete became seriously ill while on a hunting trip with Jim Brickley. When he was confined to a nursing facility, she learned to sleep in a bedside chair so he wouldn't be lonely at night. He died in November 1994.

She learned yet another painful lesson about being a woman as she found herself ill-prepared to manage their personal finances. Once again, she put her emotions on paper, in an article she submitted to the American Association of Retired Persons: "I am 81 years old. Several months ago my husband of 59 years, died. And I found overnight I was in the midst of a different life: alone, facing a totally new life style and with one resource: myself."

She cataloged the practical financial lessons she had learned, then concluded, "Life will never be quite the same. But with . . . a pleasant demeanor, a thought for the happiness of others, and faith and determination, life will be good."[8]

In September 1995, the Michigan Women's Foundation and the Michigan Political History Society marked the seventy-fifth anniversary of women's suffrage with a dinner honoring Peterson and Democratic labor activist Mildred Jeffrey. More than three hundred people attended, raising twenty-seven thousand dollars. The women have shown, the *Detroit Free Press* said in an editorial, "that there is no conflict between combativeness and civility. They have been partisans—on occasion stubbornly combative partisans—but they also have been extraordinarily good citizens, people who see political service as a part of citizenship."[9]

Peterson was hailed as "a living legend" who "opened doors for women to get involved in politics as they rallied around her trailblazing activism." George Romney had just died, and the program noted that Peterson "remembers the patronizing attitude of even those men who were supportive of her efforts, particularly Romney's description of her as someone who 'thinks like a man, looks like a woman, and works like a dog.'"[10]

Back in North Carolina, she was again serving as a nurse and caregiver, as Mary entered the same nursing center where Pete had died. Elly's much beloved older sister passed away in 1999.

In 2004, Peterson celebrated another milestone birthday, this time her ninetieth, providing a smaller circle of family and friends the chance to surprise her with a party. Joyce Braithwaite-Brickley and Bill McLaughlin were among those who made the trip to Des Plaines, Illinois, where she had moved to be closer to one of Pete's nephews.

Those who couldn't make the trip sent messages. Dorothy Stuck, who met Peterson when they were trying to build the Arkansas Republican Party, wrote:

> What is it about this woman that elicits such admiration and awe? It's an abiding belief in the American dream and a dogged determination to keep it from becoming a nightmare for those denied access to its promise. It's knowing how to build a power structure by drawing on the strengths of others rather than playing on weaknesses. It's taking what she does and believes in more seriously than she takes herself. Above all, it is having a big heart with room for all in need of its interest and understanding.[11]

On another occasion, Helen Milliken wrote, "There are always individuals in our lives whose impact sometimes is so deep-rooted that awareness continues to grow. Elly Peterson is such an individual in my life. . . . She was a groundbreaker and a pioneer. Along the way she gathered beneath her wing scores of young women to mentor in the political process. She also gave us a belief in ourselves—one of many gifts given with love and irrepressible humor. No wonder so many young women called her 'Mother.'"[12]

In 2005, at the age of ninety-one, Peterson was back in the news as a *Boston Globe* columnist reviewed the shifting positions on abortion of another Romney, Massachusetts governor Mitt, as he was beginning a campaign for the presidency. Thirty-five years after Lenore Romney's Senate campaign, the columnist tracked down Peterson to check her recollections of Mitt's mother's stance on the issue.

Peterson was described as "dumbfounded" by Mitt's assertion that his mother had supported abortion rights. "If it happened, I'd remember it. It didn't, and I don't. The issue in 1970 was jobs, jobs, jobs and that is what we talked about: the Michigan economy."

"The idea that Lenore would defy her church is hard to believe," she added. "I can't rule it out, but I think I would remember it."[13] Romney subsequently produced a document from his mother's campaign that seemed to support both abortion rights and the rights of the unborn.[14]

Back in Michigan, the fruits of Peterson's long labors on behalf of women were continuing to pay off, even if it was mostly for the Democrats. In 1997, women judges achieved a majority of the seats on the Michigan Supreme Court. In 1998, Democratic prosecutor Jennifer Granholm was elected attorney general. In 2000, Democrat Debbie Stabenow was elected to the U.S. Senate, the office that had eluded both Peterson and Romney. Two years later, Granholm was elected governor. Peterson also lived long enough to see women elected as governor or senator from her adopted states of Hawaii and North Carolina.

Meanwhile, the disappointments of the ERA campaign gave birth to "a younger more successful daughter," in the words of Kathleen Currie.[15] In 1985, she and 24 other women gathered in the basement of activist Ellen Malcolm's home to combine Rolodexes and build a network of pro-choice Democratic women. By the next year, Emily's List (for "Early Money Is Like Yeast—it makes dough rise") had 1,155 members and had raised more than $350,000 for two Senate candidates. By its twenty-fifth anniversary, the organization had grown to more than 100,000 members and had raised a total of $78 million, becoming one of the country's largest political action committees.[16]

Peterson recalled of her years of traveling around Michigan, "I met a lot of different characters and made a lot of good friends. It made every day an adventure." In retrospect, she realized how naive she had been. But back then, she said, "I KNEW that ONE meeting, one more organization, would mean that Republicans would take over." Her enthusiasm was founded on the novitiate's view that her newfound God could do no wrong. "The Republicans, after all, were more capable, more honest, more everything on the side of justice, morality, love of Mother, God and country!" she wrote years later with tongue-in-cheek. "Let's face it, we all have to learn sometime!"

Later on Peterson came to believe that her emphasis on personal involvement and voluntarism had become "hopelessly outdated" in "the age of paid workers, electronics, millions collected, and millions spent." Reviewing the manuscript she wrote when she left the RNC, she observed, "I filled pages with our ideas of programming, organizing, building, but it does not seem worth the paper now."[17]

But others were not so quick to dismiss the enduring value of her approach. David Broder, for one, observed, "It's different now, but [that kind of organization] is still important." The Internet, he noted, is making that kind of organization work easier, and "so things are cycling back."

"She liked that kind of politics," he recalled of his days of watching Peterson in action. "It is much healthier." The voter thinks, "You are coming to me individually."[18]

The Michigan Political History Society also appreciated Peterson's skills. In a 2003 survey of its members, she was ranked as "the greatest" state political party chair of the previous fifty years.[19]

Peterson ended her last memoir on a different note than the one she had written in frustration when she left the RNC. She was still disappointed, but she had moved beyond bitterness to acceptance. She wrote:

> Politics was my great good fortune, bringing me strong friendships and extraordinary experiences. That it was instrumental in making me cynical is also significant.
>
> But the sum total of all these experiences is ME. I am sure I became a flag waver partly as a result of my experiences of 22 months overseas in World War II. And I became an ardent feminist as the result of my own experiences and those of others with whom I came into contact. And I became less of a straight-down-the-line Republican as I learned, to my sorrow, that Republican men are just normal men, subject to the crimes and sins and mischief of ordinary men. And I became convinced of the beauty and the necessity of volunteerism in all fields because I was there and saw it work.[20]

In early 2008, as her health was declining, she watched as a Democratic woman came tantalizingly close to winning her party's presidential nomination. Peterson contributed six hundred dollars and followed the campaign when she was well enough to track the closed captioning on the TV set in her nursing facility near a niece in Grand Junction, Colorado. She hoped Hillary Clinton would win. But she was also intrigued by the candidate who was challenging her: the junior senator from her native Illinois, born in her beloved Hawaii, and, incredibly, an African American. She was eager to find out more.

On June 7, 2008, Clinton formally ended her campaign. And two days later Elly Peterson died gently in the night, a few days after her ninety-fourth birthday.

In 1985, when Charlotte had honored its most famous resident on "Elly Peterson Day," she had noted that there were now women governors, senators, astronauts, and pilots. And she observed without regret, "I tell myself I was there when the door was opened. And maybe that is enough for anyone's life, to be able to say you were there when the door was opened for someone else."[21]

# Notes

PROLOGUE

1. Margaret Cooke, interview by author, November 1, 2005, and e-mail message to author, November 18, 2005.


CHAPTER 1

1. Janet Chusmir, "First Female Party Chief: 'Effort, Time and Energy,'" *Miami Herald*, August 5, 1968, C1.

2. Elly Peterson, "Just Me," unpublished childhood remembrance. Unless otherwise indicated, details of Peterson's childhood are from unpublished remembrances that were provided to the author.

3. Peterson letter to author, August 31, 2005.

4. Elly M. Peterson, *Elly! Confessions of a Woman Who Walked the Streets,* privately published, 1997, 69. Hereafter cited as EMP, *Elly!*

5. Estimate derived from U.S. Bureau of the Census, *Statistical Abstract of the United States, 1934,* comparing Chart 30: Age Distribution (39) and Chart 107: Universities, Colleges and Professional Schools (107), http://www2.census.gov/prod2/statcomp/documents/1934-01.pdf (accessed November 22, 2010); Elly Peterson, interview by author, Grand Junction, Colorado, February 5–7, 2006.

6. Peterson letter to author, August 31, 2005.

7. Peterson interview; Elly Peterson, interview by Karen Farnham Madden, Advance, North Carolina, August 29–31, 1996, 20 (transcript provided by Margaret Cooke).

8. Peterson interview.

9. Louise Timberlake Shearon, interview by author, March 29, 2006.

10. Peterson interview; Peterson to Nancy Randle, January 11, 1982, EMP Papers, Box 17 Correspondence, 1980–1985 Folder (3), Bentley Historical Library, University of Michigan. Randle was writing a story for *Savvy* magazine on famous women who had worked as secretaries.

11. James Brickley, remarks delivered at the memorial service of W. Merritt Peterson, April 29, 1995, citing the memories of his wife, Joyce Braithwaite-Brickley, transcript provided to author.

12. Peterson interview.

13. Madden interview (1996), 2.

14. EMP, *Elly!*, 69.

15. Madden interview (1996), 1.

16. "City Acclaims Landon Today," *Chicago Tribune,* October 9, 1936, 1.

17. EMP, *Elly!*, 69–70.

18. Cooke interview.

19. Peterson letter to author, April 2, 2006.

20. EMP, *Elly!*, introduction.

21. Peterson letter to author, October 21, 2005.

22. Jane Allen Edelheit, letter to author, April 22, 2006; Peterson letter to author, May 24, 2006.

23. Edelheit letter; Peterson letter to author, August 31, 2005.

24. Chicago Historical Society, *The Electronic Encyclopedia of Chicago,* 2005. Cited at www.encyclopedia.chicagohistory.org/pages/543.html and www.encyclopedia.chicagohistory.org/pages/478.html (accessed November 22, 2010).

25. Peterson letter to author, August 31, 2005; Peterson interview.

26. JoAnn DiBella Hawkins, e-mail message to author, June 4, 2007.

27. These persons included the author's mother, who became friends with the Petersons when they were all in their seventies.

28. Peterson letter to author, August 31, 2005.

29. EMP, *Elly!*, 1.

30. Peterson interview.

31. EMP, *Elly!*, 1.

32. In both of her self-published memoirs, Peterson credits Joyce Braithwaite for encouraging her to compile and publish excerpts from the letters.

33. Peterson interview.

34. EMP, *Elly!*, 2.

35. Peterson interview.

36. Peterson to Mary Richmond, February 13, 1944; Peterson to "guys," March 8, 1944, EMP Papers, Box 22, 1943–1945 American Red Cross WWII (original letters and bound and typed excerpts of correspondence). Much of Peterson's World War II correspondence is included in her memoir, but in some cases a letter was edited from the original, which can be found in the Bentley Historical Library. Perhaps not surprisingly, Peterson excluded many references to Bob Allen in the versions published in her memoirs.

37. EMP, *Elly!*, 4, 16.

38. Ibid., 6–7.

39. Ibid., 14–15.

40. Ibid., 8.

41. Ibid., 5, 10.

42. Peterson interview.

43. Peterson to mother, May 22, 1944, EMP Papers, Box 22, 1943–1945 American Red Cross WWII Correspondence.

44. Peterson to family, June 6, 1944, EMP Papers, Box 22, 1943–1945 American Red Cross WWII Correspondence.

45. EMP, *Elly!*, 19.

46. Ibid., 23.

47. Ibid., 25–27.

48. Ibid., 29.

49. Ibid., 30

50. Ibid., 30–31.

51. Ibid., 32.

52. Ibid., 33.

53. Ibid., 36–37.

54. Ibid., 39–40.

55. Ibid., 40.

56. Ibid., 43.

57. Ibid., 45–46.

58. Ibid., 45.

59. Ibid., 48.

60. Ibid., 49–50.

61. Ibid., 50. The V-2 was a long-range ballistic missile developed by the Germans and targeted at southeastern England and Belgium during World War II.

62. Ibid.

63. Ibid., 58.

64. Ibid. In a later interview, Peterson could not recall the meaning of the acronym E.B.I.

65. Ibid., 60.

66. Ibid., 59.

67. Gus to Maude McMillan, June 6, 1945, EMP Papers, Box 22, 1943–1945 American Red Cross WWII Correspondence.

68. EMP, *Elly!*, 62–63.

69. Ibid., 68.

70. Ibid.

71. Ibid., 69.

72. JoAnn DiBella Hawkins, e-mail message to author, June 3, 2007.

73. In 1954, the Petersons took a year off to travel around the world, and Elly and her sister made an annual overseas trip for many years after that. Elaine Jennings, "Elly Peterson Calls Politics Way of Life," *State Journal* (Lansing), February 17, 1963, B7.

74. EMP, *Elly!*, 13.

75. Peterson to mother, February 3, 1944, EMP Papers, Box 22, 1943–1945 American Red Cross, WWII Correspondence.

76. EMP, *Elly!*, 16. "You have never seen marching until you see them in action—they really swing out," she wrote in a March 19, 1944, letter. EMP Papers, Box 22, 1943–1945 American Red Cross WWII Correspondence.

77. Madden interview (1996), 7–8.
78. EMP, *Elly!*, 18.
79. Madden interview (1996), 7–8.
80. EMP, *Elly!*, 69.

CHAPTER 2

1. Peterson interview.
2. Undated obituary of Col. William M. Peterson, believed to be from the *Winston-Salem Journal* (North Carolina), circa November 15, 1994, provided to author; Peterson letter to author, October 21, 2005; Peterson interview; Peterson letter to author, August 31, 2005.
3. Elly McMillan, "To the Ladies," *National Bowlers Journal and Billiard Revue,* July 1946, 11, and February 1947, 31, EMP Papers, Box 20, Writings/Observations Folder. In a 2006 letter to the author, Peterson said she was unimpressed with Cuba and thus never mentioned it in subsequent recollections of her world travels.
4. Peterson interview.
5. Keith Molin, interview by author, February 21, 2006.
6. Cooke, e-mail message to author, March 1, 2006.
7. Peterson letter to author, August 31, 2005.
8. EMP, *Elly!*, 53.
9. Madden interview (1996), 13.
10. Elly Peterson, "Partying in Big C," unpublished remembrance provided to author.
11. Joyce Braithwaite-Brickley, letter to author, February 24, 2006.
12. Peterson letter to author, September 19, 2005.
13. Madden interview (1996), 4.
14. Ibid.
15. Jo Freeman, *A Room at a Time: How Women Entered Party Politics,* (Lanham, MD: Rowman and Littlefield Publishers, 2000), 199–200.
16. Madden interview (1996), 1.
17. EMP, *Elly!*, 70.
18. Ibid., 71.
19. Ibid.
20. Ibid.
21. In EMP, *Elly!*, Peterson names Max Murningham, the future mayor of Lansing, Lansing attorney Chuck MacLean, and Wendell and Ruth Hobbs of Ann Arbor as other leaders of the "revolt" (72).
22. Ibid.; Lawrence Lindemer, interview by author, March 24, 2006.
23. Madden interview (1996), 9.
24. Peterson interview.
25. EMP, *Elly!*, 72.
26. Ibid. Lindemer interview; Arnold Levin interview by author, March 24, 2006.

27. EMP, *Elly!*, 72.

28. Ibid., 73.

29. Levin interview.

30. Lindemer interview.

31. "Don't Be Taken In!," newspaper advertisement for Charlotte City Council candidates, EMP Papers, Box 1, 1958 Chronological Folder.

32. Peterson letter to author, August 31, 2005.

33. Elly Peterson, videotaped interview by William S. Ballenger, Governor James J. Blanchard Living Library of Oral Histories, Michigan Political History Society, May 1, 1995. Hereafter cited as Peterson MPHS oral history.

34. Lindemer interview.

35. Madden interview (1996), 2.

36. EMP, unpublished manuscript supplied by JoAnn DiBella Hawkins, "EMP Beginnings," 21–22.

37. Madden interview (1996), 2–3.

38. Lindemer interview.

39. Madden interview (1996), 5.

40. EMP, *Elly!*, 76.

41. Madden interview (1996), 6.

42. Lindemer interview.

43. EMP, *Elly!*, 76.

44. Freeman, among others, provides details of these conflicts (101–7).

45. Peterson to Catherine Gibson and Helen Dean, memorandum, April 27 (1958), EMP Papers, Box 1, 1958 Folder.

46. Peterson interview.

47. EMP, *Elly!*, 77.

48. Peterson form letter hand-addressed to "Mary," January 12, 1961, EMP Papers, Box 1, 1961 Folder.

49. EMP, *Elly!*, 78.

50. Ibid.

51. Elly Peterson, interview by Karen Farnham Madden, Advance, North Carolina, February 21, 2000, 4 (transcript provided by Margaret Cooke).

52. Lois V. Nair, flyer addressed to County Chairmen, Vice Chairmen, and Delegates to the Republican State Convention, EMP Papers, Box 22, Scrapbooks 1960–1961 Folder.

53. EMP, *Elly!*, 78–79. In her memoir, Peterson did not identify the other woman; in an October 5, 2009, interview with the author, Ranny Riecker, also from Midland, identified her as Jane Gerstenzang.

54. EMP, *Elly!*, 79.

55. Ibid., 80.

56. Ibid.

57. Ibid., 81. "Charlotte Woman Begins Duties as GOP Vice Chairman," an undated, unidentified Charlotte area newspaper clipping, reported that her margin of victory was even larger, 1,069 to 435 (EMP Papers, Box 22, 1960–1961 Scrapbook).

58. Richard I. Millman, "A Farewell to Elly," *Grand Ledge Independent*, December 23, 1970, 4, in EMP Papers, Box 22, Scrapbooks.

59. Ray Courage, "Van Peursem Heads GOP: Democrats Select Collins," *Detroit Free Press,* February 5, 1961, A1.

60. Peterson MPHS oral history.

61. "Local Woman to Head GOP Field Staff," undated, unidentified newspaper clipping, hand labeled "1961," EMP Papers, Box 23, 1961–64 Folder.

62. Romney's early political career is well covered in Clark Mollenhoff, *George Romney: Mormon in Politics* (New York: Meredith Press, 1968).

63. Madden interview (1996), 6.

64. Stephen Hess and David S. Broder, *The Republican Establishment: The Present and Future of the GOP* (New York: Harper and Row Publishers, 1967), 116, quoting a remark made to Alan L. Otten of the *Wall Street Journal.*

65. Mollenhoff, 5.

66. Hess and Broder, 117.

67. T George Harris, *Romney's Way* (Englewood Cliffs, NJ: Prentice-Hall, 1967), 217.

68. Mary Ann Richmond, e-mail message to author, October 15, 2006.

69. EMP, "Just Me."

70. Joyce Braithwaite-Brickley, letter to author, March 3, 2006.

71. Mary Ann Richmond, e-mail message to author, March 5, 2006.

72. Lindemer interview.

73. Molin interview.

74. EMP, *Elly!,* 82.

75. Peterson to State Vice Chairmen, undated memorandum regarding "Advisory Council," EMP Papers, Box 11, Undated Folder.

76. Ibid.

77. Keith Molin, remembrances provided to Margaret Cooke, April 21, 2004.

78. Molin interview.

79. Virginia Redfern, "Republican Women Sponsor Fashionable Benefit; Fashion Show, Hair Styles, Plus Luncheon," *State Journal* (Lansing), September 27, 1961, 33, EMP Papers, Box 22, Scrapbooks.

80. Virginia Redfern, "GOP Women Get Inside View of Con-Con," *State Journal* (Lansing), November 8, 1961, 36, EMP Papers, Box 23, Clippings, Republican Party Activities, 1961–64 Folder.

81. Corinne Smith, "Life of the Party; Politics Is TOO for Women," *Detroit News,* January 7, 1962, E1.

82. "Confidential Report on Counties in Michigan," EMP Papers, Box 1, 1962 Folder.

83. Madden interview (1996), 6.

84. EMP, *Elly!,* 84–85. At the time, Peterson noted, the only female reporter in Lansing was the society editor of the *State Journal.*

85. Ray Courage, "Mrs. Out to Win: Romney's Wife Enters Campaign," *Detroit Free Press,* June 6, 1962, A3.

86. Glenn Engle, "Mrs. Romney Hits Trail of Politics 'for Duration,'" *Detroit News,* June 6, 1962, A3.

87. EMP, *Elly!,* 85–86.

88. Harris, 236.

89. Madden interview (1996), 11.

90. Mollenhoff, 183.

91. Ibid.

92. Harris, 234.

93. Michigan Republican State Central Committee, *1962 Annual Report*, Republican Party (Mich.) State Central Committee, Box 1, "Annual Reports," 1962 and 1967 Folder, Bentley Historical Library.

94. EMP, *Elly!*, 87.

95. Ibid.

## CHAPTER 3

1. Elly M. Peterson, "Petticoats in Politics," *Michigan Challenge*, December 1962, 30–31; EMP Papers, Box 1, December 1–December 10, 1962 and Undated Folder.

2. EMP, *Elly!*, 111.

3. Ibid., 88.

4. Harris, 220.

5. Madden interview (1996), 8.

6. EMP, *Elly!*, 88.

7. Peterson, MPHS oral history.

8. Clare Shank to Peterson, October 23, EMP Papers, Box 15, Chronological 1971–1979 Folder.

9. Glenn Engle, "2nd GOP Leader Leaving: Elly Peterson to Lead Women's National Section," *Detroit News*, September 22, 1963, A1.

10. *Washington Post*, "GOP Names a Grass Roots Expert: Michigan Woman Gets High Post," September 24, 1963, A18.

11. Marion K. Sanders, "Issues Girls, Club Ladies, Camp Followers," *New York Times Magazine*, December 1, 1963, 38. This figure was nearly twice what the party leadership had claimed a few months before.

12. Paul A. Miltich, "Elly Is Charmer for Republicans: Mrs. Peterson Has Flair for Soft Sell," *Flint Journal*, EMP Papers, Box 23, 1961–64 Clippings Folder.

13. Ruth Hobbs to Peterson, October 2 [1963], EMP Papers, Box 1, Correspondence, Undated Folder.

14. Freeman, 106, quoting a postscript to Clare B. Williams, *The History of the Founding and Development of the National Federation of Republican Women* (Washington, DC: Republican National Committee, 1962), 37.

15. Ibid., ix.

16. EMP, *Elly!*, 88.

17. Michigan National Guard press release, November 18, 1963, supplied by Peterson.

18. Miltich.

19. EMP, *Elly!*, 90–91.

20. Ibid., 89.

21. Ibid., 89–90.

22. Ibid., 89; Madden interview (1996), 10–11.

23. Sample Mabel Cards, EMP Papers, Box 3, March 7–9, 1964 Folder.

24. Mrs. John W. Lewis to Peterson, March 14, 1964, EMP Papers, Box 3, March 13–14, 1964 Folder.

25. Joseph A. Loftus, "G.O.P Will Dine to Fill Its Purse: 21 Fetes Jan. 29 to Hear 8 Party Personalities," *New York Times,* January 16, 1964, 21.

26. EMP, *Elly!*, 91.

27. Peterson to Mary Richmond, hand-labeled February 28, 1964, EMP Papers, Box 3, February 28–29, 1964 Folder. In the letter, Peterson called the organization "Delta Sigma Chi"; she reported that one member said of Higgins, "Well, there is some question as to whether she IS a woman."

28. EMP, *Elly!*, 90.

29. Walter DeVries, interview by author, November 8, 2006.

30. Ibid. In Elly M. Peterson, *Elly! Memoirs of a Republican Lady!,* unpublished, Bentley Historical Library, University of Michigan (hereafter cited as EMP, *Republican Lady*). Peterson went to great lengths to extol the virtues of O'Neil and Meany (70).

31. DeVries interview; EMP, *Elly!*, 95–96; Peterson to Richmond, February 28, 1964.

32. EMP, *Republican Lady,* 71.

33. EMP, *Elly!*, 95–96.

34. Peterson to Richmond, February 28, 1964.

35. Tom Shawver, "Elly Peterson Eyes Senate Race: GOP Aide to Run?" *Detroit Free Press,* February 28, 1964, A1.

36. Glenn Engle, "Mrs. Peterson Primped for Race against Hart," *Detroit News,* February 28, 1964, A3.

37. Maxine Cheshire, "'Housewife's Friend' Faced with 'Joan of Arc,'" *Washington Post,* March 23, 1964, B3.

38. J. F. Ter Horst, "Top GOP Woman Eyes Hart Seat: Mrs. Peterson Drafted," *Detroit News,* March 20, 1964, A1.

39. Engle. The article noted that in 1940 Matilda R. Wilson served for forty days as an appointed lieutenant governor.

40. Edward A. Meany Jr. to Peterson, March 1, 1964, EMP Papers, Box 3, March 1–2, 1964 Folder.

41. Peterson to Edward A. Meany Jr., March 4, 1964, EMP Papers, Box 3, March 3–4, 1964 Folder.

42. Louise Hutchinson, "It's Busy Day for Woman in Senate Race: Gives New Look to Politics in Michigan," *Chicago Tribune,* October 9, 1964, A4.

43. Levin interview.

44. Peterson to Richmond, February 28, 1964.

45. Glenn Engle, "Mrs. Peterson Boomed for Senate by Women," *Detroit News,* March 14, 1964.

46. Audrey Seay to Peterson, EMP Papers, Box 3, March 3–4, 1964 Folder.

47. Katherine Willis to Peterson, March 9, 1964, EMP Papers, Box 3, March 7–9, 1964 Folder.

48. Lillian Wright to Peterson, March 2, 1964, EMP Papers, Box 3, March 1–2, 1964 Folder.

49. Mrs. Robert D. (Shirley) McFee to Peterson, March 20, 1964, EMP Papers, Box 3, March 20–23, 1964 Folder.

50. Peterson to John T. (Jack) Dempsey, March 2, 1964, EMP Papers, Box 3, March 3–4, 1964 Folder.

51. Peterson to Dean Dody, Nan Smith, and Colonel W. Merritt Peterson, schedule, March 11, 1964, EMP Papers, Box 3, March 10–11, 1964 Folder.

52. *Detroit Free Press,* "Elly Appears Ready to Run," March 25, 1964, A9.

53. Peterson to Mary Richmond, Saturday (hand-labeled March 1964), EMP Papers, Box 3, March, 1964 (Undated) Folder.

54. Ella Koeze to The WACS, March 13, 1964, EMP Papers, Box 3, March 13–14, 1964 Folder.

55. *New York Times,* "Michigan Woman in Senate Race," March 27, 1964, 11.

56. William Baird, "Elly's Chapeau in Senate Race," *State Journal* (Lansing), March 26, 1964, A1.

57. United Press International, "Woman Candidate for Senator Reveals Her Views on Politics," *Battle Creek Enquirer and News,* March 26, 1964, 23.

58. *Detroit Free Press,* "Millinery in State's Ring," March 30, 1964, A6.

59. Glenn Engle, "Mrs. Peterson Gets into Senate Race," *Detroit News,* March 26, 1964, A1.

60. James S. Brooks, "Woman Runs for Senate," *Christian Science Monitor,* EMP Papers, Box 3, March 27–28, 1964 Folder.

61. *Battle Creek Enquirer and News,* "There's Trouble on Horizon for Sen. Hart This Year," March 28, 1964, EMP Papers, Box 3, March 24–26 Folder.

62. Bob Vosges, Associated Press, "Gallant Pair: GOP Hopefuls 'Welcome' Elly," *State Journal* (Lansing), March 27, 1964, A7.

63. Marilyn Gardner, "Candidate Ready to 'Unmess' Politics: Active Campaigning for Senate Seat to Begin after GOP Conference," *Milwaukee Journal,* April 8, 1964, EMP Papers, Box 4, April 24, 1964 Folder.

64. Ter Horst.

65. Isabelle Shelton, "Administration Confused, G.O.P. Speaker Declares," *Evening Star* (Washington, DC), April 7, 1964, A11; Robert S. Boyd, "Elly Urges Unity of GOP Women: Calls Johnson 'Huckster,'" *Detroit Free Press,* undated clipping, EMP Papers, Box 4, April 22, 1964 Folder.

66. Amelia Young, "Romney, Scranton Roundly Applauded," *Evening Star* (Washington, DC), April 12, 1964, D9.

67. EMP, *Elly!,* 92; *National Observer,* "GOP Ladies Have 'Win Workshops,' but Some Face Up to Pessimism," April 13, 1964, 2.

68. EMP, *Elly!,* 97.

69. Peterson to Mrs. S. Carl (Clare) Shank, March 26, 1964, EMP Papers, Box 3, March 24–26 Folder.

70. EMP, *Elly!,* 97.

71. *Detroit Free Press,* "It's Official: Mrs. Peterson's Hat Is in the Ring—I'll Beat Senator Hart, She Vows," March 27, 1964, A3; EMP, *Elly!,* 97.

72. The challenges faced by women reporters in Washington at this time are detailed in Nan Robertson, *The Girls in the Balcony: Women, Men, and the New York Times* (New York: Fawcett Columbine, 1992).

73. John McClaughry, interview by author, October 17, 2006.

74. Gardner.

75. James Robinson, "Elly's Campaign Weapon—Lots of Talk about Her," *Detroit Free Press,* April 14, 1964, C8.

76. Elly M. Peterson and Margaret Price, "Two Open Letters to Teen-Age Girls," *Seventeen,* September 1964, 233. Peterson may not have known whether she would still be a candidate by the time the article was published. She was identified by an RNC job that she no longer held.

77. Jo Ann Hardee, "Senate Drive Begun by Mrs. Peterson," *Detroit News,* April 16, 1964, C11.

78. Virginia Redfern, "Elly's Home Reflects Her Taste," *State Journal* (Lansing), undated clipping, EMP Papers, Box 3, March 1964 (Undated) Folder.

79. Peterson to Richmond, Saturday (hand-labeled March 1964), EMP Papers, Box 3, March 1964 (Undated) Folder.

80. Redfern; Robinson; Hardee.

81. Madden interview (1996), 13; EMP, *Elly!,* 98.

82. Allen L. Otten, "Difficulty in Enlisting Top-Flight Candidates Dims Republican Hopes," *Wall Street Journal,* April 20, 1964, 1.

83. Walter DeVries Papers, Box 5, Senate Race 1964 Folder, Bentley Historical Library.

84. Richard W. Oudersluys, "O'Neil Sweeps Poll of GOP's Senate Choice: Many Undecided," *Detroit News,* July 7, 1964, A1.

85. Eric Sevareid, CBS News, "Campaign '64: Republican National Convention," July 12, 1964, accessed at The Paley Center for Media, New York City.

86. Frances Lewine, "Women Playing Prominent Roles at GOP Convention," *Charleston Gazette* (West Virginia), July 13, 1964, 7.

87. *Oakland Tribune* (California), "Women Enjoying Conclave," July 14, 1964.

88. Helen Thomas, United Press International, "Will TV Commercials Blackout Elly's Talk: Women Speakers 'Poison,'" *State Journal* (Lansing), July 12, 1964, D13.

89. Marie Smith, "In GOP Camp, Men Still Big-Heap Chiefs: Only One Squaw Rates Time on Squawk Box," *Washington Post,* June 28, 1964, F5. Smith's role was described in an in-house advertisement in the *Post* (July 11, 1964, E19).

90. Marie Smith, "They're Backstage and in the Spotlight," *Washington Post,* July 12, 1964, F1.

91. Smith, June 28, 1964.

92. Ranny Riecker, interview by author, Midland, MI, October 5, 2009.

93. EMP, *Elly!,* 92; Elly M. Peterson, Address, Second Session of Republican National Convention, July 13, 1964, EMP Papers, Box 25, Speeches, National Republican Committee, 1964 Folder.

94. *Washington Post,* "Drastic Change Is Termed Folly: By Elly Peterson," July 14, 1964, B6.

95. Peterson interview.

96. *Holland Evening Sentinel* (Michigan), "Elly Peterson Blasts Great Society Plea," July 14, 1964, 11.

97. Frances Lewine, Associated Press, "Candidates' Wives Find Convention

Lively, Wearying," *State Journal* (Lansing), July 14, 1964, B6. Bobby Baker, a long-time aide to Lyndon B. Johnson, was forced to resign his post as secretary to the Senate Democrats in October 1963 amid allegations of political corruption.

98. *State Journal* (Lansing), "Elly Blasts Dems at Convention: GOP Aide Basks in Spotlight; Accuses LBJ Regime of Trying to Scrap U.S. Traditions," July 14, 1964, A7.

99. Bulletin to Elly Peterson Campaign Committee, EMP Papers, Box 4, July 9–10, 1964 Folder; Newspaper advertisements, EMP Papers, Box 23, Clippings 1964 Senatorial Campaign Folder.

100. Christine Todd Whitman, interview by author, July 17, 2007.

101. Anita Stauffer letter to Peterson, July 14, 1964; Deborah C. Paul letter to Peterson, July 14, 1964, EMP Papers, Box 4, July 14–15 Folder. Peterson's notations indicate she responded to both a week later.

102. EMP, *Elly!*, 92.

103. Ibid., 93.

104. Ibid. The actual tally for Goldwater was 883 votes.

## CHAPTER 4

1. EMP, *Elly!*, 97–99.

2. Braithwaite-Brickley, February 24, 2006.

3. ". . . And Now We Come to a Top Woman Candidate's Husband," undated newspaper clipping hand-labeled "the *Redford Observer*, the *Livonia Observer*, the *Plymouth Observer*, the *Farmington Observer*," EMP Papers, Box 22, 1964 Senate Campaign Scrapbook.

4. Gene Schroeder, "Early Rush Hints Peak in Primary," *State Journal* (Lansing), September 1, 1964, A1.

5. United Press International, "Elly Wins GOP Race for U.S. Senate, Defeats O'Neil, Meany: Charlotte Woman Faces 'Underdog' Role Again against Hart," *State Journal* (Lansing), September 2, 1964, 1.

6. United Press International, "Peterson Primary Cost Was $23,157, Elly Reports," undated clipping, EMP Papers, Box 22, 1964 Senate Campaign Scrapbook.

7. Associated Press, "Volunteers' Work Did It, Elly Claims," *State Journal* (Lansing), September 2, 1964, A2.

8. *Washington Post*, "Romney Magic Being Tested: Conservative Gaining in Michigan Primary," August 2, 1970, A1.

9. William McLaughlin, "Politician: Remembrances of 20 Years at the Political Grass Roots," 95, undated manuscript provided to author.

10. *State Journal* (Lansing), "Primary Pleases Romney," September 3, 1964, A2.

11. *Detroit Daily Press*, "Vote, Victors Prepare for Final Fight," September 3, 1964, 1.

12. EMP, *Elly!*, 99–100.

13. "Elly Peterson: Your Choice for U.S. Senate" brochure, EMP Papers, Box 20, Later Correspondence and Memorabilia Folder.

14. EMP, *Elly!*, 96.

15. Peterson interview.

16. Jon Lowell, interview by author, October 27, 2005.

17. DeVries interview.

18. McClaughry interview.

19. EMP, *Elly!*, 98–100.

20. Jon Lowell, "Elly Rips Hart over Sleeping Bear: Calls It 'Bargain Basement Steal,'" *Grand Rapids Press*, October 7, 1964, 28; *Muskegon Chronicle*, "Voters Here to Get Woman's Touch," October 2, 1964, 13; Jon Lowell, "Elly Carries Ike's Endorsement in U.P. Tour," *Grand Rapids Press*, October 15, 1964, 6. While these stories were the work of a single reporter, they appeared in multiple papers. Ranny Riecker also recalled Peterson taking off her gloves for dramatic effect in some speeches.

21. *Muskegon Chronicle.*

22. Madden interview (1996), 13.

23. Lowell interview.

24. EMP, *Elly!*, 100.

25. Ibid., 100–101.

26. John Marttila, interview by author, June 5, 2010.

27. Lowell interview.

28. Hutchinson.

29. EMP, *Elly!*, 101–2.

30. Hutchinson.

31. Jon Lowell, "100,000 Join 'Elly's Army,'" *Grand Rapids Press*, October 3, 1964, 7.

32. Peterson, MPHS oral history.

33. Jon Lowell, "Elly Pinpoints Effectiveness as Basic Issue in Campaign," *Grand Rapids Press*, October 2, 1964, 3.

34. Lowell, *Grand Rapids Press*, October 7, 1964.

35. Jon Lowell, "End Draft, Bids Mrs. Peterson," *Grand Rapids Press*, October 9, 1964, 9.

36. Jon Lowell, "Elly Asks Fight on Delinquency," *Grand Rapids Press*, October 6, 1964, 9.

37. EMP, *Elly!*, 99.

38. McClaughry interview.

39. Levin interview.

40. McClaughry interview.

41. Peterson interview.

42. Michael O'Brien, *Philip Hart: The Conscience of the Senate* (East Lansing: Michigan State University Press, 1995), 99.

43. United Press International, "Hart 'No Shows' Shake Up Staff," *Grand Rapids Press*, October 3, 1964, 12.

44. United Press International, "Hart-Peterson Meeting Hardly a Big Debate," *State Journal* (Lansing), October 9, 1964, A10.

45. EMP, "Elly," 101.

46. Lowell interview.

47. McClaughry interview.

48. EMP, *Elly!*, 102–3.

49. Bill Burke, "Political Figures, Military Officers Got 'Bargain' Lots," *State Journal* (Lansing), October 9, 1964, A1; William Baird, "Romney Shuffles Military," *State Journal* (Lansing), October 9, 1964, A1.

50. United Press International, "Romney Decries Charge by Ferency: Guard Scandal Takes Political Turn," *Grand Rapids Press*, October 11, 1964, 1.

51. McClaughry interview.

52. *Grand Rapids Press*, "Elly Defends Husband in Guard Land Scandal," October 12, 1964, 1.

53. *State Journal* (Lansing), "Lot Purchase Not an Issue—Hart," October 12, 1964, B2.

54. Robert Lewis, "Hart Denies Elly's Charge He Questioned Her Integrity," *Grand Rapids Press*, October 13, 1964, 9.

55. *State Journal* (Lansing), "What Others Think: Ferency Tactics Are 'Disgusting,'" October 16, 1964, A10, quoting *Jackson Citizen Patriot* editorial.

56. United Press International, October 11, 1964.

57. *State Journal* (Lansing), October 16, 1964.

58. EMP, *Elly!*, 103. Peterson said National Guard adjutant general Ronald McDonald, a family friend, "was completely vindicated." It took McDonald more than three years, and a legal battle he pursued to the State Supreme Court, to clear his name. In January 1968, the court agreed that Romney had removed him illegally and ordered him reinstated—at least temporarily—and back pay restored. McDonald's legal battle was supported by a bipartisan group of citizens. See United Press International, "McDonald Plans to Pursue Court Battle over Ouster," *Holland Evening Sentinel* (Michigan), July 27, 1966, 20; and United Press International, "McDonald Placed on Retired List," *Holland Evening Sentinel* (Michigan), February 9, 1968, 1.

59. Jon Lowell, "Elly Mends Political Fences in U.P.," *Grand Rapids Press*, October 14, 1964, 4.

60. EMP, *Elly!*, 102.

61. James S. Brooks, United Press International, "Candidates Grumbling after Tour: Members of 'Team' Given Minor Roles in St. Clair Blitz," *State Journal* (Lansing), October 19, 1964, A11.

62. James Brooks, United Press International, "Romney Responds to Campaign Criticism: Calls Report on GOP Team Tour Inaccurate," *State Journal* (Lansing), October 20, 1964, A7.

63. EMP, *Elly!*, 102; Peterson letter to author, September 25, 2006.

64. EMP, *Elly!*, 99.

65. *State Journal* (Lansing), "State Polls Draw over 3 Million: Mild Weather Slated to Boost Turnout above Prediction," November 3, 1964, 1.

66. EMP, *Elly!*, 103.

67. Harris, 241.

68. Associated Press, "Hart Beats Elly by 2-to-1 Margin: Dem Incumbent Returned to Senate," *State Journal* (Lansing), November 4, 1964, A3.

69. Associated Press, "Dems Gain in Both Houses of Congress," *Michigan Daily* (Ann Arbor), November 4, 1964, 1.

70. Lowell interview.
71. Molin interview.
72. DeVries interview.
73. EMP, *Elly!*, 103.
74. Ibid., 100.
75. Peterson interview.
76. Molin interview.
77. McClaughry interview.
78. EMP, *Elly!*, 104.
79. Associated Press, "Hart Beats Elly by 2-to-1 Margin," November 4, 1964.

## CHAPTER 5

1. Madden interview (1996), 8
2. EMP, *Elly!*, 104; Peterson, MPHS oral history.
3. D. Duane Angel, *Romney: A Political Biography* (New York: Exposition Press, 1967), 152.
4. EMP, *Elly!*, 104–5. Peterson's memoir said the meeting occurred on January 23, but news coverage at the time places it during the previous weekend.
5. Dick Barnes, Associated Press, "GOP Hierarchy Hoping Elly Can Rekindle Fire in Party," *State Journal* (Lansing), January 18, 1965, A7; United Press International, "Romney Hires Elly Peterson," *Holland Evening Sentinel* (Michigan), January 16, 1965, 6.
6. EMP, *Elly!*, 105.
7. *State Journal* (Lansing), "Pair Proposes Elly for GOP Chairman," January 16, 1965, A1.
8. Braithwaite-Brickley letter, February 24, 2006.
9. Madden interview (1996), 12.
10. EMP, *Elly!*, 87.
11. Ibid., 105.
12. Ibid., 106.
13. Angel, 151–52.
14. *State Journal* (Lansing), January 16, 1965.
15. EMP, *Elly!*, 106; James S. Brooks, United Press International, "Mrs. Peterson Slated for Elliott's GOP Post," *State Journal* (Lansing), January 17, 1965, A1.
16. EMP, *Elly!*, 106.
17. Freeman, 118. As of late 2010, the Web site of the National Federation of Republican Women (http://www.nfrw.org/republicans/women/2.htm) still asserted that Peterson was the first woman of either party to chair a state party organization (accessed November 27, 2010).
18. Dick Barnes, Associated Press, "A Serious Party-Planner," *Los Angeles Herald Examiner*, February 24, 1965. The same story also appeared in the *St. Petersburg Times*, March 1, 1965, and *Florence Morning News* (South Carolina), February 23, 1965, among other papers.
19. Barnes, January 18, 1965.

20. Dick Barnes, Associated Press, "Elly Apparently Will Become First Female State Chairman," *State Journal* (Lansing), January 24, 1965, clipping provided by Margaret Cooke.

21. Elizabeth A. Conway, "Elly Energetic, Eager, Effective," undated newspaper clipping, circa early 1965, provided by Margaret Cooke.

22. Melda Lynn, "Elly Peterson—Michigan's Mrs. Republican," *Blade Sunday Magazine* (Toledo), April 18, 1965, 4.

23. Richard Dougherty, HTNS, "It's Becoming a Pretty Good Spring for the Country's Romney-Watchers," *Chronicle-Telegram* (Elyria, Ohio), April 24, 1965, 3.

24. *State Journal* (Lansing), "Ferency Praises Elliott: 'Dumped Wrong Guy,'" January 18, 1965, A7.

25. DeVries interview.

26. Arnold Levin to Peterson, EMP Papers, Box 20, "A Tribute to Elly Peterson," 1984 Folder.

27. Levin interview.

28. The term was popularized by Jane O'Reilly's cover story, "Click: The Housewife's Moment of Truth," in the inaugural issue of *Ms.* magazine (spring 1972).

29. EMP, *Elly!*, 106.

30. Peterson, letter to author, October 21, 2005.

31. Madden interview (1996), 13–14.

32. Peterson, letter to author, October 21, 2005.

33. Cooke, e-mail message to author, October 7, 2006.

34. Elly M. Peterson videotaped interview, 2003, Kathy Banfield Shaw, executive producer, Michigan Women's Hall of Fame, Michigan Women's Studies Association, 2006.

35. United Press International, "'Elly' Is New GOP Chairman," *Holland Evening Sentinel* (Michigan), February, 22, 1965, 9.

36. Madden interview (1996), 14.

37. EMP, *Elly!*, 107.

38. McLaughlin, 31.

39. Lindemer interview; Riecker interview.

40. Braithwaite-Brickley letter, February 24, 2006. In her interview for the Michigan Women's Hall of Fame, Peterson said she gave herself a raise the following year.

41. *Detroit News*, "D. Ahrens, M. Fisher Named Republican Committee Chairmen," March 4, 1965, clipping provided by Margaret Cooke.

42. Barnes, February 24, 1965.

43. EMP, *Elly!*, 107; Peterson, MPHS oral history. These versions of the story differ on whether the committee meeting started at the club or in Fisher's office.

44. EMP, *Elly !*, 107.

45. DeVries interview.

46. Sara M. Evans, *Tidal Wave: How Women Changed America at Century's End* (New York: Free Press, 2003), 1.

47. Peterson, MPHS oral history; EMP, *Elly!*, 107–8. In interviews and memoirs, Peterson provided slightly different versions of her response to Bliss. In

one, she said she told him she had learned the expletives during her own wartime service.

48. EMP, *Elly!*, 108; John J. Green, "First, Let's Check with Mother," *Detroit News,* March 12, 1967, newspaper clipping, EMP Papers, Box 23, Republican Party Activities, 1965–1970 Folder; *New York Times,* "Nebraska GOP Elects," January 30, 1967, 12. The midwestern governors apparently drafted Peterson as secretary of their regional group (EMP Papers, Box 9, Undated [4] Folder).

49. Braithwaite-Brickley letter, March 3, 2006.

50. Braithwaite-Brickley letter, February 24, 2006.

51. Lynn, 6.

52. Braithwaite-Brickley letters, March 3, 2006, and February 24, 2006.

53. McLaughlin, 31–33. In his memoir, McLaughlin calculated his commute at 250 miles a day.

54. Molin interview.

55. Cooke interview.

56. EMP, *Elly!*, 108–9.

57. Ibid., 109.

58. DeVries interview.

59. EMP, *Elly!*, 109. Reagan continued this practice until the mid-1970s, when aides advised him that this was not the way to build political loyalty. Lyn Nofziger oral history, Miller Center, University of Virginia, Ronald Reagan Presidential Oral History Project, March 6, 2003, 24, http://millercenter.org/scripps/archive/oralhistories/detail/3229 (accessed November 29, 2010).

60. EMP, *Elly!*, 109–10.

61. Braithwaite-Brickley letter, March 3, 2006.

62. United Press International, "Claims LBJ Is Dictator," *Holland Evening Sentinel* (Michigan), January 25, 1966, 5.

63. EMP, *Elly!*, 109–11. The subtitle of Peterson's memoir *Elly!* is *Confessions of a Woman Who Walked the Streets.* The author of the poem is unknown.

64. Molin interview.

65. Cooke interview.

66. *Grand Rapids Press,* "Moderate-Conservative GOP Women Prepare for Showdown," May 1, 1966, 16.

67. Tom Shawver, "GOP Women Fight for Command," *Detroit Free Press,* undated clipping circa September 1965, supplied by Margaret Cooke.

68. Elly Peterson to Dorothy McHugh and others, memorandum, EMP Papers, Box 14, Republican Women's Federation Folder.

69. Virginia Redfern, "Harmony Engulfs GOP: R.W.F.M. Session Ends," *State Journal* (Lansing), September 23, 1965, F1.

70. Peterson to McHugh.

71. Peterson to Ella Koeze, memorandum, September 30, 1965, EMP Papers, Box 7, Correspondence, September 16–30, 1965 Folder.

72. "Carolyn" to Peterson, October 5, 1965, EMP Papers, Box 14, Republican Women's Federation Folder.

73. Art Elliott to Peterson, telegram, September 23, 1965, EMP Papers, Box 14, Republican Women's Federation Folder.

74. Jim Hayes to Peterson, September 23, 1965, EMP Papers, Box 14, Republican Women's Federation Folder.

75. Ruth Hobbs to Peterson, October 3, 1965, EMP Papers, Box 14, Republican Women's Federation Folder.

76. EMP, *Elly!*, 118.

77. McLaughlin, 44–45.

78. Ibid., 53.

79. Hess and Broder, 130.

80. Ibid., 129–30.

81. Ibid., 122.

82. Angel, 145.

83. Hess and Broder, 123.

84. McLaughlin, 55.

85. Hess and Broder, 123.

86. Ironically, one Republican candidate who was *not* successful that year was Lindemer, who lost to the incumbent, Attorney General Frank Kelley.

87. Colleen O'Brien, "'Other Woman' Behind George," *Detroit Free Press,* November 10, 1966, C1.

88. Braithwaite-Brickley letter, March 3, 2006.

89. United Press International, "Romney, Griffin Ride GOP Crest: Win Boosts Governor's Prestige," *Holland Evening Sentinel* (Michigan), November 9, 1966, 1.

90. Walter Rugaber, "Romney Edges toward Race for '68 Nomination," *New York Times,* November 10, 1966.


CHAPTER 6

1. Angel, 235, citing a September 1966 *Newsweek* survey; Mollenhoff, 251; EMP, *Republican Lady,* 87.

2. EMP, *Elly!*, 113.

3. Ibid., 113–14.

4. Marttila interview.

5. EMP, *Elly!*, 114.

6. Ibid., 115.

7. Harris, 244.

8. John Marttila to Peterson, "Report on the Metropolitan Action Committee for the Year 1967," November 30, 1967, EMP Papers, Box 8, Correspondence November 16–30, 1968 Folder.

9. EMP, *Elly!*, 115.

10. Ibid., 116; Harris, 246.

11. "This Was 1967," Annual Report, Republican State Central Committee of Michigan, supplied by Margaret Cooke.

12. EMP, *Elly!*, 115.

13. Ibid., 116–17.

14. Harris, 245; EMP, *Elly!*, 117; "This Was 1967."

15. EMP, *Elly!*, 116–17.

16. Freeman, 106.

17. *New York Times*, "2 Bandy Charges in Race to Head G.O.P. Women," May 3, 1967.

18. Catherine E. Rymph, *Republican Women: Feminism and Conservatism from Suffrage through the Rise of the New Right* (Chapel Hill: University of North Carolina Press, 2006), 180. The battle is also described in detail in Donald T. Critchlow, *Phyllis Schlafly and Grassroots Conservatism: A Woman's Crusade* (Princeton: Princeton University Press, 2005), 137–62.

19. EMP, *Elly!*, 123.

20. Madden interview (2000), 3.

21. Carol Felsenthal, *The Sweetheart of the Silent Majority* (Garden City, NY: Doubleday, 1981), xviii. Felsenthal acknowledged that she had set out to investigate Schlafly but "came away with nothing" and in the end found much to admire in her.

22. Phyllis Schlafly, *Safe—Not Sorry* (Alton, IL: Pere Marquette Press, 1967), 168–69.

23. Gladys O'Donnell to Peterson, August 21, 1965; Peterson to O'Donnell, August 27, 1965, EMP Papers, Box 7, Correspondence, September 1–15, 1965 Folder.

24. Katherine K. Neuberger to Peterson, May 9, 1966, EMP Papers, Box 7, Correspondence, May 21–30, 1966 Folder.

25. Mrs. Neal (Janet) Tourtellotte to Peterson, March 13, 1966, EMP Papers, Box 7, Correspondence, March 11–20, 1966 Folder.

26. Peterson to Dorothy McHugh, June 13, 1966, EMP Papers, Box 7, June 13, 1966, Correspondence, June 1966 Folder.

27. Peterson to George Anna Theobold, December 11, 1966, EMP Papers, Box 7, Correspondence, December 1966 Folder.

28. Ibid.

29. Ibid.

30. Peterson to Honorable Hiram Fong, April 10, 1967, EMP Papers, Box 8, Correspondence, April 1967 Folder.

31. Peterson to Mrs. George (Bobbie) Mills, April 13, 1967, EMP Papers, Box 8, Correspondence, April 1967 Folder.

32. Elly Peterson, speech to Interchange, Madison, Wisconsin, November 3, 1979, EMP Papers, Box 25, Speeches 1979 Folder.

33. "A Few Good Women" Oral History Collection, 1938–2000, MGN 984, Penn State University Archives, Special Collections Library, University Libraries, Pennsylvania State University, Patricia Reilly Hitt oral history, September 23, 1997, 56.

34. Schlafly, 164–65.

35. Ibid., 153–54.

36. Peterson to Mrs. George (Bobbee) Mills, May 15, 1967, EMP Papers, Box 8, Correspondence, May 1–20 Folder. Based on earlier correspondence, the author assumes a typographical error was made in Mills's first name.

37. Elly Peterson, Report of NFRW's Convention, May 8, 1967, EMP Papers, Box 14, Republican Women's Federation Folder.

38. Redfern, September 23, 1965.

39. Felsenthal, 194.

40. Sheila Tobias, *Faces of Feminism: An Activist's Reflections on the Women's Movement* (Boulder: Westview Press, 1997), 141.

41. Felsenthal, 186.

42. EMP, *Elly!*, 123. In "Revolution from the Right" (*Smithsonian*, August 2008, 50), Rick Perlstein wrote that some delegates to the 1964 GOP convention reported receiving as many as sixty copies of Schlafly's book *A Choice Not an Echo.*

43. Two years later, O'Donnell received a "bootlegged tape" of a 1968 meeting at which Michigan conservative Dick Durant was captured instructing Schlafly supporters "in the gentle art of 'taking over' meetings, disrupting them and 'bleeding all over the floor.'" Forewarned by the tape, O'Donnell succeeded in beating back another attempt to take over the federation in 1969. See Vera Glaser and Malvina Stephenson, "Detroiter in the Middle as GOP Gals Feud," *Detroit Free Press*, November 4, 1969, D12.

44. Warren Weaver Jr., "G.O.P. Women Split as Parley Opens," *New York Times*, May 6, 1967, 13.

45. EMP, *Elly!*, 118–19.

46. There is one tantalizing reference in a letter sent to Peterson, apparently on May 30, 1967, from a Wisconsin Republican woman. She wrote, "I'll be anxious to hear how you make out at your June 5 meeting with Len Hall and Company." "Chris" to Peterson, "Tuesday the 30th," EMP Papers, Box 1, Undated Correspondence Folder.

47. In Hitt's oral history, she said Richard M. Nixon approached her in 1967 about becoming cochairman of his presidential campaign but she declined for personal reasons. Hitt later served as the volunteer head of Women for Nixon in 1968. In 1972, Jean Westwood served as an adviser to the McGovern campaign from her position as chair of the Democratic National Committee. In 1976, Peterson was hired as a deputy chairman of President Ford's campaign.

48. Mollenhoff, 253–54, 290.

49. Details of the Gordon interview are provided in ibid., 290–313. A later perspective can be found in Neil Swidey, "The Lessons of the Father," *Boston Globe Magazine*, August 13, 2006, 24. Their transcripts of the interview differ slightly.

50. EMP, *Elly!*, 121–22.

51. Peterson to "Chris," October 9, 1967, EMP Papers, Box 8, Correspondence, October 1967 Folder.

52. "This Was 1967." The annual report noted that the State Central Committee's public relations arm was responsible for transmitting Romney's announcement by telephone to more than sixty large radio stations, including twenty in New Hampshire, the first primary state. The committee also distributed more than forty thousand copies of a brochure entitled "The Romney Way to GOP Victories" after Republican David Serotkin won a special election for a state House seat in May 1967.

53. EMP, *Elly!*, 119–21.

54. Ibid., 119.

55. Ibid.

56. Robert B. Semple Jr., "Romney Decision Urged by His Aides," *New York Times,* March 1, 1968, 17.

57. EMP, *Elly!,* 122. On March 1, 1968, the *New York Times* reported that when the decision was made Fisher was in Acapulco, Mexico, "for a brief rest."

58. "The Story of Wednesday, February 28, 1968," EMP Papers, Box 18, ERA Miscellaneous, 1968–1980 Folder.

59. *New York Times,* "Decision Shocks G.O.P. in Michigan: Leaders and Staff Told Only Three Hours before Public," February 29, 1968, 23.

60. EMP, *Elly!,* 122.

61. Ibid., 122–23.

62. Associated Press, "Romney Declares His Party Is United," *New York Times,* August 10, 1968, 12.

63. EMP, *Elly!,* 127.

64. Jerry M. Flint, "Nixon Is Believed in Michigan Lead," *New York Times,* September 8, 1968, 81.

65. David S. Broder, "Four Days on Trail of Two Candidates," *Washington Post,* October 27, 1968, B1.

66. McLaughlin, 76; Theodore H. White, *The Making of the President, 1968* (New York: Atheneum, 1969), 391.

67. Peterson to McDill "Huck" Boyd, November 6, 1968, EMP Papers, Box 8, Correspondence, November 1–15, 1968 Folder.

68. EMP, *Elly!,* 126. In this account, Peterson did not name Lockwood, but in her MPHS oral history she said he accompanied her to the California meeting. Mitchell, she said, was "perhaps the worst chauvinist" she ever encountered (127).

CHAPTER 7

1. EMP, *Elly!,* 127.

2. C. Calvert Knudsen to Peterson, December 30, 1968, EMP Papers, Box 8, Correspondence, February 1968 Folder.

3. Peterson to Ilmar Heinaru, February 7, 1969, EMP Papers, Box 9, Correspondence, February 1969 Folder.

4. Peterson to William H. G. Fitzgerald, January 6, 1969, EMP Papers, Box 9, Correspondence, January 1–17, 1969 Folder.

5. Peterson to William Broomfield, January 28, 1969, EMP Papers, Box 9, Correspondence, January 16–30 Folder.

6. Sen. Robert P. Griffin, "The Remarkable Elly Peterson," *Congressional Record,* February 7, 1969, Extensions of Remarks, E925.

7. Rep. Garry Brown, contribution to "Michigan's 'Mrs. Republican'—Elly Peterson," *Congressional Record,* February 6, 1969, Extensions of Remarks, E874.

8. David S. Broder, "Tribute to Elly Peterson," *Washington Post,* December 15, 1970, A21.

9. McLaughlin, 92.

10. Lindemer interview; transcript of Margaret Cooke interview with Jerry Roe, February 27, 2004, provided by Cooke; *Republican Party of Michigan State Fi-*

*nance Committee Bulletin,* February 17, 1969, EMP Papers, Box, 9, Correspondence, February 1969 Folder.

11. *Chicago Tribune,* "Eyed by HUD," March 18, 1969, A8.

12. EMP, *Elly!,* 124.

13. William Kulsea, "Romney, Elly, and Max Fisher Pleased by Creation of Action Bureau," *Grand Rapids Press,* May 13, 1969, F9.

14. Don Oberdorfer, "Nixon Seeks Social-Aid Volunteers," *Washington Post,* January 26, 1969, 1.

15. Kulsea.

16. Peter Golden, *Quiet Diplomat: A Biography of Max M. Fisher* (New York: Cornwall Books, 1992), 143–44, 178–79, 181, 184.

17. EMP, *Elly!,* 124.

18. Associated Press, "Elly Gets Post She Wanted," undated, unidentified newspaper clipping, EMP Papers, Box 22, Scrapbook 1969–1970 Folder.

19. EMP, *Elly!,* 125.

20. Ibid.

21. Kulsea.

22. "Elly Peterson to Address Child Study Association Saturday," undated, unidentified newspaper clipping, EMP Papers, Box 22, Scrapbook 1969–1970 Folder.

23. *Washington Post,* "Old Job Beckons," April 2, 1969, B4.

24. Donnie Radcliffe, "For Your Information," *Sunday Star* (Washington, DC), March 30, 1969, E16.

25. Ibid.

26. Tom Ochiltree, "Elly Peterson's Job: Ensure Nixon's Re-Election," *State Journal* (Lansing), April 15, 1969, A12.

27. Tom Ochiltree, "Elly's Task: Change Image of Republicans," *State Journal* (Lansing), May 18, 1969, A12.

28. Robert Longstaff, "GOP Gives Elly New Prominence," *Grand Rapids Press,* April 8, 1969, D5.

29. Esther Van Wagoner Tufty, "No. 1 GOP Woman: Elly Peterson," *Macomb Daily* (Michigan), September 5, 1969, EMP Papers, Box 22, Scrapbook.

30. "Tuesday," EMP Papers, Box 15, Chronological, 1971–1979, Undated Folder. The context of the document places it in the spring of 1969.

31. EMP, *Elly!,* 149. When Ferency was thanked by party organizers for participating, Peterson said he wrote back that she would have done the same thing for him "except that the Democrats weren't smart enough to put on a party like that!"

32. Marguerite Davis, United Press International, "Elly Peterson: 'Best Woman Pro in Politics,'" *Deseret News* (Salt Lake City), August 12, 1969, A15. This wire story appeared in many other papers.

33. EMP, *Elly!,* 125.

34. Ibid.

35. Davis.

36. "Speaking Engagements," EMP Papers, Box 14, Schedule Folder.

37. Rogers Morton to Peterson, memorandum, May 22, 1969, EMP Papers, Box 9, Chronological Files, 1969 Folder.

38. Alice McKee, "GOP Keeps Her Moving; Washington-Michigan Commuter," *Fort Lauderdale News and Sun-Sentinel,* June 7, 1970, EMP Papers, Box 23, Scrapbook.

39. "'Elly' Is Off Again for GOP Candidates," undated clipping, EMP Papers, Box 23, Scrapbook.

40. McKee.

41. EMP, *Elly!,* 125–26.

42. *Women Power,* Republican National Committee Women's Division, undated booklet, circa 1969, provided by Margaret Cooke.

43. Christine Todd Whitman, *It's My Party, Too: The Battle for the Heart of the GOP and the Future of America* (New York: Penguin Press, 2005), 65.

44. Whitman interview.

45. Hawkins, e-mail message to author, June 3, 2007.

46. Ibid.

47. Whitman interview.

48. EMP, *Elly!,* 125.

49. Ibid., 126.

50. Ibid., 128.

51. Willard Clopton Jr. and Mike Causey, "The Federal Diary: Patronage Hunters Find Pickings Slim," *Washington Post,* April 8, 1969, B13.

52. Davis.

53. Elly Peterson to National Committeewomen, memorandum, May 16, 1969, EMP Papers, Box 9, 1969 Folder.

54. John Osborne, *The Nixon Watch* (New York: Liveright Publishing, 1970), 74, from the column "The Rise of Harry Dent."

55. Rowland Evans and Robert Novak, "Backstage Struggle over Patronage Angers GOP National Committee," *Washington Post,* August 1, 1969, A19.

56. EMP, *Elly!,* 128.

57. Evans and Novak, August 1, 1969.

58. Ibid.

59. EMP, *Elly!,* 128.

60. EMP, *Elly!,* 129.

61. Ibid.

62. Elly Peterson, Unidentified remembrance beginning "As the newspapers faithfully reported," EMP Papers, Box 15, Chronological 1971–1979, Undated Folder.

63. EMP, *Elly!,* 127.

64. Dean J. Kotlowski, *Nixon's Civil Rights: Politics, Principle, and Policy* (Cambridge: Harvard University Press, 2001), 226, 258.

65. EMP, *Elly!,* 136.

66. Marie Smith, "Nixon Woos Women, Vows a Bigger Role," *Washington Post,* October 17, 1968, K1.

67. "A Few Good Women," Vera Glaser oral history, August 19, 1997, 3–5. *Washington Post,* "Nixon: Purpose Must Supplant Fear in Support of NATO," transcript of White House Press Conference, February 7, 1969, A10.

68. Cited by Kotlowski, 228, Rogers C.B. Morton Papers, Box 205, Peterson to Morton, May 28, 1969, Department of Special Collections, Margaret I. King Library, University of Kentucky, Lexington.

69. EMP, *Elly!*, 133.

70. Ibid., 133–34. Peterson named Jack Crawford at HUD, Alan May at the Department of Health, Education, and Welfare, and a State Department official as men who tried to be gracious and helpful.

71. Ibid., 134.

72. Rep. (Florence) Dwyer to The President (Richard M. Nixon), memorandum, July 8, 1969, EMP Papers, Box 14, Nixon and Women Folder.

73. Davis; Louise Hutchinson, "Nixon Pledges to Seek Jobs for Women," *Chicago Tribune*, July 9, 1969, 4.

74. Elly M. Peterson, "Women in Public Service," *Republican Women's Federation of Michigan Bulletin* 10, no. 9 (September 1970): 6, EMP Papers, Box 23, Scrapbook; "Top Women Appointments in the Nixon Administration," EMP Papers, Box 14, Nixon and Women Folder; EMP, *Elly!*, 135.

75. "A Few Good Women," Virginia Allan oral history, August 30–September 1, 1998, 8.

76. Kotlowski, 231.

77. EMP, *Elly!*, 136.

78. Esther Van Wagoner Tufty, "Elly Plans to Round Up a Passle of Volunteers," *Flint Journal*, May 13, 1969, EMP Papers, Box 22, Scrapbooks. Fisher resigned as chairman of the National Center for Volunteer Action in March 1970. Although Fisher said he believed the job should be rotated each year, the press speculated that he was unhappy with the Nixon administration's Mideast policy (Golden, 209–10).

79. Elly M. Peterson, "Take a Little Time for America," in *Action Now: Guidelines for Establishing a Republican Community Action Program*, booklet provided by Margaret Cooke.

80. Vera Glaser, "GOP Plans 10 Urban 'Action Centers': To Give Aid, Garner Votes," *Miami Herald*, September 8, 1969, D2; Marttila interview.

81. Carl P. Leubsdorf, Associated Press, "Young Look Ushered in at GOP Headquarters," *Evening Star* (Washington, DC), August 20, 1969, newspaper clipping, EMP Papers, Box 23, Republican Party Activities, 1965–1970 Folder; David S. Broder, "GOP Drive Is Aimed to Break Democrats' Grip on Ghettos," *Washington Post*, April 29, 1969, A17.

82. Glaser, September 8, 1969.

83. Clark Hoyt, "GOP Action Center in 13th Is a Model," *Detroit Free Press*, June 24, 1969, C11.

84. Broder, April 29, 1969.

85. Paul Hope, "Elly Peterson Builds Urban GOP," *Evening Star* (Washington, DC), September 15, 1969, A10.

86. Ibid.

87. Virginia Knauer, text of speech to the National Federation of Republican Women, September 27, 1969, EMP Papers, Box 22, Scrapbook.

88. EMP, *Elly!*, 131–32. Peterson made no comment on Nixon's observation about Jews.

89. "Monday, Jan. 12, 1970," Republican National Committee newsletter supplied to author by Margaret Cooke.

90. Kotlowski, 20.

91. Barbara Richardson, "Action Now Her Baby," *Dallas Times Herald,* March 20, 1970, E1, EMP Papers, Box 23, Scrapbook.

92. Nancy Hartnagel, "GOP Women Hear Call to Action," *Knickerbocker News* (Albany), November 22, 1969, EMP Papers, Box 22, Scrapbook.

93. Marie MacDonald, "Thursday Meeting to Inaugurate Wichita's Action Now Program," *Wichita Eagle and Beacon,* February 14, 1970, EMP Papers, Box 22, Scrapbook.

94. David Watson, "GOP Here Hears the Word—Be 'Solvers,'" *Tampa Tribune,* August 27, 1969, B1.

95. Jay Hensley, "GOP Official Praises Volunteers," *Asheville Citizen-Times,* undated clipping, circa December 1969, A1, EMP Papers, Box 22, Scrapbook.

96. George H. W. Bush, Inaugural Address, January 20, 1989, George Bush Presidential Library and Museum, http://bushlibrary.tamu.edu/research/pub lic_papers.php?year=1989 (accessed December 1, 2010).

97. "The Chairman's Report," EMP Papers, Box 22, Scrapbook 1969–70.

98. EMP, *Elly!,* 130.

99. Marttila interview.

100. EMP, *Elly!,* 148.


CHAPTER 8

1. EMP, *Elly!,* 127. The order of worship is found in EMP Papers, Box 23, January 1970–March 1970 Scrapbook.

2. Margaret Crimmins, "Peale Officiates at White House," *Washington Post,* January 12, 1970, B2.

3. Whitman interview. The Senate ultimately rejected the Carswell nomination, 51–45, on April 8, 1970.

4. Ibid.

5. "A Night to Forget," *Republican Battle Line,* January 1970, 7, EMP Papers, Box 23, January 1970–March 1970 Scrapbook.

6. Clark Hoyt, "Detroiter Recruiting Negroes Bolts GOP; Hits 'Racist' Policies," *Detroit Free Press,* March 22, 1970, A3.

7. John Marttila to Peterson, undated letter, EMP Papers, Box 9, Correspondence, Undated 1969–70 Folder.

8. EMP, *Elly!,* 132.

9. Marttila interview.

10. EMP, *Elly!,* 124. Peterson wrote that her other major regret was her failure to clarify RNC–White House relations before returning to Washington.

11. Research Group of the Detroit–Ann Arbor Ripon Chapter, "The Detroit Experience with the Republican Action Center Program," EMP Papers, Box 20, Republican Action Center Program, Ripon Meeting, 1973 Folder. The paper was discussed at a November 30, 1973, meeting of the Ripon Society.

12. William G. Milliken to Peterson, December 14, 1997, EMP Papers, Box 20, 1985–2000: Letters from Public Figures Folder. In telling the story, Milliken said Marttila's meeting was held in Detroit, but Marttila told the author it was in Boston with youthful staff members of his consulting firm.

13. EMP, *Elly!*, 138.

14. Ibid., 138–40.

15. Ibid., 139. In McLaughlin's memoir (114), he said Peterson wrote him in early January "of her concern that we were giving the impression that no one could beat Hart."

16. Robert A. Popa, "Huber Charges Partiality: Mrs. Peterson Blamed," *Detroit News*, undated clipping labeled "August," EMP Papers, Box 23, Scrapbook.

17. Tim Skubick, *Off the Record* (Ann Arbor: University of Michigan Press, 2003), 116.

18. Robert Pisor, "Mrs. Romney Seen Set for Senate Race," *Washington Post*, February 20, 1970, A1.

19. EMP, *Elly!*, 140.

20. Skubick, 116.

21. EMP, *Elly!*, 141.

22. McLaughlin, 117.

23. EMP, *Elly!*, 142. McLaughlin and contemporary news accounts identified the Milliken aides as John Stahlin and Emmett Tracey.

24. Peterson to Mary Richmond, "on the plane enroute from Marquette to Okla City–Sun nite," EMP Papers, Box 15, Chronological 1971–1979 Undated Folder.

25. EMP, *Elly!*, 143.

26. Skubick, 117.

27. EMP, *Elly!*, 143.

28. Robert L. Pisor, "Romney Power Play Keeps Lenore in Race," *Detroit News*, February 24, 1970, A1.

29. EMP, *Elly!*, 143.

30. Ibid., 143–44.

31. Vera Glaser, "Elly Peterson Raps GOP Senator, Aide," *Miami Herald*, March 20, 1970, F2.

32. EMP, *Elly!*, 137.

33. Ibid., 137–38; Dorothy McCardle, "Surprise Guest: The President," *Washington Post*, April 18, 1970.

34. EMP, *Elly!*, 137.

35. Hawkins, e-mail message to author, June 3, 2007.

36. Whitman interview; Hawkins, e-mail message to author, June 4, 2007.

37. Republican Women's Leadership Council program, April 15, 1970, EMP Papers, Box 23, Scrapbook.

38. Hawkins, e-mail message to author, June 4, 2007.

39. EMP, *Elly!*, 135.

40. *Washington Post*, "President Is Criticized by Women," June 14, 1970, 25.

41. Glaser, March 20, 1970.

42. Mary McGarey, "GOP Party Leader Challenges Ohio Women to Effective

Action: Elly Peterson Speaks in Columbus," *Columbus Dispatch,* August 27, 1970, EMP Papers, Box 23, Scrapbook. Later, after she had left the RNC, Peterson wrote of Mrs. Mitchell, "She gave me the impression some one had wound her up with a key tight as she would go—she flittered from male to male—kissing, hugging, ruffles and sling straps flashing—[an] up to date version of the southern belle" (EMP, Unidentified remembrance beginning "As the newspapers faithfully reported").

43. Undated Republican National Committee press release, RNC-87, EMP Papers, Box 14, Press Releases Folder.

44. Glaser, March 20, 1970.

45. Peterson to National Committeewomen and State Vice Chairmen, memorandum, EMP Papers, Box 14, Women in Politics Questionnaires Folder.

46. "Statement of Elly Peterson and Geri Joseph," May 4, 1970, EMP Papers, Box 23, Scrapbook.

47. EMP, *Elly!,* 134.

48. "Women's Tea," undated Republican National Committee press release, RNC-82, EMP Papers, Box 14, Women Miscellaneous Folder. Peterson was appointed to the Defense Advisory Committee on Women in the Services (DACOWITS) a few weeks before the event.

49. "Elly" to Republican Women Leaders, memorandum, August 17, 1970, EMP Papers, Box 9, Distributed Papers, 1970 Folder.

50. "Elly" to Republican Women Leaders, memorandum, September 9, 1970, EMP Papers, Box 9, Distributed Papers, 1970 Folder.

51. Kent Ward, "Maine Political Whirl: Elly Peterson Gets Praise as 'Best Speaker,'" unidentified newspaper clipping, hand-labeled May 2, 1970, EMP Papers, Box 23, April 1970 to June 1970 Scrapbook.

52. Hazel Lovett, "Effect on Second Term Unknown Says GOP Aide," page 1 clipping from unidentified newspaper, EMP Papers, Box 23, Scrapbook.

53. "What Kind of a Republican Are You?," prepared speech text supplied by JoAnn DiBella Hawkins.

54. Ward.

55. Untitled text of speech delivered at William Woods College, supplied by JoAnn DiBella Hawkins.

56. Peterson to Dr. R. B. Cutlip, April 28, 1970, EMP Papers, Box 9, Chronological File, 1970 Folder.

57. EMP, *Elly!,* 131.

58. Elly M. Peterson, "Remarks at the National Association of Colored Women's Clubs Convention," EMP Papers, Box 14, Speeches 2 Folder.

59. *Congressional Record,* Extensions of Remarks, August 24, 1970, E7895; "A Coat of Many Colors," brochure, EMP Papers, Box 23, Republican Party Activities 1965–1970 Folder.

60. "Elly" to Republican Women Leaders, memorandum, July 9, 1970, EMP Papers, Box 9, Distributed Papers, 1970 Folder.

61. Edith K. Roosevelt, "GOP Urged to Use Woman Power: By Offering Meaningful Roles in Politics," *Manchester Union Leader* (New Hampshire), July 28, 1970, EMP Papers, Box 23, Scrapbook.

62. McKee, June 7, 1970.

63. Hawkins, e-mail message to author, June 3, 2007.

64. Peterson to William Kulsea, November 23, 1970, EMP Papers, Box 9, Chronological File, 1970 Folder.

65. EMP, *Elly!*, 144.

66. Ibid., 145.

67. Molin interview.

68. Vera Glaser, "Elly Peterson Is Bowing Out as High GOP Aide," *Detroit Free Press,* October 17, 1970, A9.

69. Peterson to Republican Leadership, memorandum, October 29, 1970, EMP Papers, Box 13, RNC Files, Mass Mailings Folder.

70. Peterson to Rogers C. B. Morton, November 1, 1970, EMP Papers, Box 9, Chronological File, 1970 Folder.

71. Clare Shank to Peterson, October 23, EMP Papers, Box 15, Chronological 1971–1979, Undated Folder. The context of the letter suggests it was written in late 1970.

72. Richard Dudman, "Woman GOP Leader Shows Disenchantment," *St. Louis Post-Dispatch,* November 5, 1970, EMP Papers, Box 23, Scrapbook.

73. McLaughlin, 139–40.

74. Hawkins, e-mail message to author, June 3, 2007.

75. EMP, *Elly!*, 145. The following year, May won a nomination to the U.S. Tariff Commission (later known as the U.S. International Trade Commission).

76. David S. Broder, "Republicans Lose Governorship Edge," *Washington Post,* November 4, 1970, A1.

77. Peterson to Rogers C. B. Morton, "Final Report," November 9, 1970, EMP Papers, Box 9, Chronological Files, 1970 Folder.

78. Dudman, November 5, 1970.

79. Lenore Romney to Peterson, undated letter, EMP Papers, Box 9, Chronological Files, 1970 Folder.

80. Peterson, remarks to the Illinois Federation of Republican Women, Chicago, Illinois, November 19, 1970, EMP Papers, Box 23, Scrapbook

81. *Chicago Tribune,* "Blasts GOP," November 20, 1970, 2.

82. Elly Peterson, "Report on Action Now," December 3, 1970, EMP Papers, Box 23, Scrapbook.

83. Vera Glaser and Malvina Stephenson, "Offbeat Washington: High Level Exodus," *Sunday Star* (Washington, DC), November 29, 1970, G9.

84. Ben A. Franklin, "GOP Facing Its 2d Criminal Citation for Violation of Campaign Fund Law," *New York Times,* April 26, 1973, 34; John Anthony Maltese, *Spin Control: The White House Office of Communications and the Management of Presidential News* (Chapel Hill: University of North Carolina Press, 1994), 73; Jeb Stuart Magruder, *An American Life: One Man's Road to Watergate* (New York: Atheneum, 1974), 133–38.

85. "Elly," *The Republican,* December 1970, 13, EMP Papers, Box 23, Clippings from Retirement from RNC, 1970 Folder.

86. Peterson to Mary Richmond, undated ("Wednesday"), EMP Papers, Box 9, Correspondence, undated, 1969–1970 Folder.

87. David S. Broder, "Tribute to Elly Peterson," *Washington Post*, December 15, 1970, A21.

88. David Broder to Peterson, December 24, 1970, EMP Papers, Box 20, Letters from Public Figures, 1970–1974 Folder.

89. Peterson to Mary Richmond, "Wednesday."

90. Saul Friedman, "Elly Peterson a Real Loss to GOP," *Detroit Free Press*, December 21, 1970, A9.

91. Helen Thomas, "President Snubs Elly," United Press International, undated clipping, EMP Papers, Box 23, Clippings, Retirement from Republican National Committee Folder; Richard M. Nixon (RN) to Peterson, December 5, 1970, EMP Papers, Box 9, Chronological Files, 1970 Folder.

92. Rowland Evans and Robert Novak, "Mutiny among Republicans," *Washington Post*, December 31, 1970, A11.

93. Bill Kulsea et al. to Peterson, telegram, December 15, 1970, EMP Papers, Box 9, Chronological, 1970 Folder.

94. EMP, *Elly!*, 150.

95. Rogers Morton to Peterson, "Friday," EMP Papers, Box 20, Letters from Public Figures, Undated Folder.

96. Braithwaite-Brickley, letter to author, March 3, 2006.

97. Dudman, November 5, 1970.


CHAPTER 9

1. Saul Friedman, "Jane, Elly Find a Common Cause," *Detroit Free Press*, June 10, 1971, A7.

2. McKee, June 7, 1970.

3. "'Elly' Is Off Again for GOP Candidates," undated, unidentified newspaper clipping, EMP Papers, Box 23, April 1970–June 1970 Scrapbook.

4. Peterson interview; Peterson letter to author, August 31, 2005.

5. David S. Broder, "2 GOP 'Co-Chairmen' Named to Ease Criticism over Dole," *Washington Post*, January 15, 1971, A2.

6. Katherine Black Massenburg to Peterson, labeled "Tuesday," EMP Papers, Box 9, Correspondence, undated 1969–70 Folder.

7. Peterson to Mary Richmond, undated, "Thurs. nite," EMP Papers, Box 9, Correspondence, Undated 1969–70 Folder. The context of the letter indicates it was written shortly after Peterson retired.

8. Broder, January 15, 1971; Sally Quinn, "Co-chairmen for the Chairman," *Washington Post*, January 15, 1971, B1; Robert Dole to Peterson, January 26, 1971, EMP Papers, Box 15, Chronological Files, 1971 Folder; "A Few Good Women," Anne Armstrong oral history, March 24, 1998, 5, 21. In *Elly!*, Peterson praised Armstrong for what she was able to accomplish, noting tartly that she had not been "branded a Michigan liberal" (137).

9. "A Few Good Women," Barbara Franklin oral history, 11.

10. In her memoirs, Peterson described the circumstances surrounding Franklin's appointment but did not name her.

11. Barbara Franklin, e-mail message to author, May 31, 2010.

12. Franklin oral history, 88. Franklin, e-mail message.

13. Shank to Peterson, October 23.

14. JoAnn DiBella Hawkins, interview by author, September 14, 2007.

15. Hawkins letter to Peterson, June 9, 1971, provided to author by Hawkins.

16. Unpublished manuscript provided to author by JoAnn DiBella Hawkins, chapter entitled "Conclusion." This text reflects Hawkins's copy-editing.

17. Peterson to JoAnn DiBella Hawkins, undated but written before September 1971, provided to author by Hawkins.

18. Unpublished manuscript provided by Hawkins, "State Chairman," 69–70.

19. Hawkins interview.

20. Haynes Johnson, "'Common Cause' Catching On: Gardner Pushes Reforms," *Washington Post,* December 13, 1970, A1.

21. "Dave" to Peterson, March 20, 1971, EMP Papers, Box 15, Chronological 1971 Folder.

22. Friedman, June 10, 1971.

23. "Thiema" to Peterson, July 23, 1971, EMP Papers, Box 15, Chronological 1971 Folder.

24. Steve Lilienthal, "The Republican Party and the Black Electorate," research paper provided to author, quoting phone interview with Peterson, October 16, 1979.

25. Gladys O'Donnell to Peterson, February 4, 1971, EMP Papers, Box 15, Chronological 1971 Folder.

26. Sydney Ladensohn Stern, *Gloria Steinem: Her Passions, Politics, and Mystique* (New York: Birch Lane Press, 1997), 236–37.

27. Betty Friedan, *It Changed My Life: Writings on the Women's Movement* (New York: Random House, 1976), 168.

28. Peterson to JoAnn DiBella Hawkins, undated letter provided by Hawkins.

29. Liz Carpenter, *Getting Better All the Time* (New York: Simon and Schuster, 1987), 125.

30. Stern, 236.

31. Evans, 73–74.

32. *New York Times,* "Goals Set by Women's Political Caucus," July 13, 1971.

33. Rona F. Feit, "Organizing for Political Power: The National Women's Political Caucus," in *Women Organizing: An Anthology,* ed. Bernice Cummings and Victoria Schuck (Metuchen, NJ, and London: Scarecrow Press, 1979), 194.

34. Virginia R. Allan to Peterson, memorandum, September 7, 1971, EMP Papers, Box 20, NWPC Folder.

35. Virginia Allan Papers, "Minutes of NWPC National Policy Council meeting," September 10–11, 1971, Box 4, NWPC (2) Folder, Bentley Historical Library, University of Michigan.

36. Peterson to Anne Armstrong and Gladys O'Donnell, memorandum, September 17, 1971, EMP Papers, Box 20, NWPC Folder.

37. Peterson to Anne Armstrong, memorandum, October 25, 1971, EMP Papers, Box 20, NWPC Folder.

38. Peterson to Ranny Riecker and Lavon Bliesener, EMP Papers, Box 20, NWPC Folder.

39. Stern, 238.

40. "NWPC Financial Report," November 15, 1971, Virginia Allan Papers, Box 4, NWPC (2) Folder.

41. Peterson to Robert Dole, November 2, 1971, Virginia Allan Papers, Box 4, NWPC (2) Folder, Bentley Library, University of Michigan.

42. Phyllis N. Segal to Members of the National Womens [sic] Political Caucus Delegation to Republican National Committee Chairman Robert Dole, memorandum, Virginia Allan Papers, Box 4, NWPC (2) Folder, Bentley Library, University of Michigan.

43. Elly Peterson, "Run, Lady, Run!" *Politéia* 1, no. 3 (winter 1972): 41–44.

44. M. Kent Jennings, "Women in Party Politics," in *Women, Politics, and Change,* ed. Louise A. Tilly and Patricia Gurin (New York: Russell Sage Foundation, 1990), 240–43.

45. Mary S. Coleman, interview by Roger F. Lane, January 21–23, 1991, Michigan Supreme Court Historical Society, January, http://archive.lib.msu.edu/AFS/dmc/court/public/all/Coleman/ASO.html (accessed December 6, 2010).

46. Peterson interview.

47. Molin interview.

48. Don Hoenshell, "Elly Helps Mary in Try for High Court Seat," *Oakland Press,* September 21, 1972, B8, newspaper clipping, EMP Papers, Box 23, Scrapbook.

49. EMP, *Elly!,* 152. In her memoir, Peterson did not name Thorburn but referred to him as "a judge from Oakland County."

50. Hoenshell, September 21, 1972.

51. Elly Peterson, undated speech, EMP Papers, Box 25, Speeches, Undated, Miscellaneous Folder.

52. Peterson interview.

53. "Biography—Elly M. Peterson," June 15, 1973, EMP Papers, Box 16, EMP Personal Folder.

54. Mary Coleman to Peterson, "Thanksgiving," EMP Papers, Box 15, Chronological, 1971–79, Undated Folder.

55. Molin interview.

CHAPTER 10

1. Remembrances of the Swearing-in of Vice President Gerald R. Ford, EMP Papers, Box 20, Writings-Observations, 1972–88 Folder.

2. Dorothy McCardle and Donnie Radcliffe, "A Grand (Rapids) Celebration," *Washington Post,* December 7, 1973, B1.

3. EMP, *Elly!,* 167.

4. Judy Agnew to Peterson, October 30, 1973, EMP Papers, Box 15, August–September 1975 Folder.

5. Peterson to Robert Griffin, memorandum, August 22, 1974, EMP Papers, Box 16, Republican National Committee Folder.

6. EMP, *Elly!,* 156.

7. Bo Callaway to Robert Griffin, August 13, 1975, EMP Papers, Box 16, Memoes (6) Folder; James U. DeFrancis to Peterson, September 8, 1975, EMP Papers, Box 16, Memoes (6) Folder.

8. "The Fight for ERA: Leaders, Strategies, and Directions," Mariwyn Heath oral history, April 1 1983, conducted by Jennifer Jackman and Tamar Raphael, Women's Rights Collection, 1789–1999, Sophia Smith Collection, Smith College, Northampton, Massachusetts.

9. National Commission on the Observance of International Women's Year, ERA Committee meeting, September 15, 1975, transcript, EMP Papers, Box 20, International Women's Year Commission, ERA Committee Meeting, 1975 Folder. John Marttila was among the consultants who participated.

10. Willah Weddon, "China Trip a Rewarding Experience for Women," *Circadia,* December 1975, EMP Papers, Box 19, Women for International Understanding China Trip—"An Elly's Eye View of China," 1975 Folder.

11. Maxine Hays to Peterson, telegram, EMP Papers, Box 18, Undated Correspondence, ERAmerica Folder.

12. Elly Peterson and Liz Carpenter form letter, January 5, 1976, ERAmerica Records (1974–1982), Container 16, Good Ideas/Kreps Letter Folder, Library of Congress.

13. Text from Peterson's personal scrapbook provided to author and undated handwritten remarks for press conference, EMP Papers, Box 25, Speeches Folder.

14. Elly Peterson, Keynote speech to Indiana Women's Political Caucus, Indianapolis, Indiana, April 10, 1976, EMP Papers, Box 25, Speeches Folder.

15. Rogers Morton to Peterson, February 19, 1976, Elly M. Peterson Folder, Box 2486, White House Central Files Name Files. Gerald R. Ford Presidential Library.

16. Peter Fletcher ("El Pedro") to Peterson (Ms. E.R. America Peterson), May 17, 1976, EMP Papers, Box 15, Chronological, January–April 1976 Folder. Fletcher recounted the same story in the oral history he provided to the Michigan Political History Society on October 15, 2008.

17. Peterson interview.

18. EMP, *Elly!,* 156–57.

19. Peterson interview; ibid.

20. Mary Tuthill, "Elly Peterson at Work for the President," *Kalamazoo Gazette,* June 17, 1976, clipping, EMP Papers, Box 23, Clippings, President Ford Committee Folder; Peterson to Mary Richmond, undated letter, EMP Papers, Box 15, Chronological, 1971–79, Undated Folder.

21. EMP, *Elly!,* 157; Tuthill, June 17, 1976.

22. Peterson to family, undated letter, EMP Papers, Box 20, Loose Items from Scrapbook Folder.

23. Tuthill, June 17, 1976.

24. Jules Witcover, *Marathon* (New York: Viking Press, 1977), 420.

25. Haynes Johnson, *Sleepwalking through History: America in the Reagan Years* (New York: W. W. Norton, 1991), 80.

26. Nofziger oral history, 24.

27. James A. Baker III with Steve Fiffer, *Work Hard, Study . . . and Keep Out of*

*Politics! Adventures and Lessons from an Unexpected Public Life* (New York: G. P. Putnam's Sons, 2006), 39.

28. Witcover, 413.

29. Jack Stiles, "Report by Jack Stiles, 2/24/76," folder, "Presidential Campaign—Campaign Report by Jack Stiles," Box 1, Dorothy E. Downton Files, Gerald R. Ford Presidential Library.

30. *Time*, "The Star Shakes up the Party," November 24, 1975, http://www.time.com/time/magazine/article/0,9171,913715,00.html (accessed December 7, 2010).

31. Peterson to Mary Richmond, "Monday morning," EMP Papers, Box 15, Chronological, November 1976 Folder.

32. EMP, *Elly!*, 161–62.

33. Lyn Nofziger oral history, 13–14.

34. Stuart Spencer oral history, Miller Center, University of Virginia, Ronald Reagan Presidential Oral History Project, November 15–16, 2001, 35–36.

35. Stiles report.

36. President Ford Committee press release, May 27, 1976, EMP Papers, Box 16, EMP Personal Folder; EMP, *Elly!*, 158.

37. *Washington Post*, "Rockefeller Worried by Ford's Move to the Right," May 28, 1976, A3; *Detroit News*, "Elly Peterson to Join Ford Campaign Staff: GOP Leader in Michigan," undated clipping, EMP Papers, Box 16, EMP Personal Folder.

38. EMP, *Elly!*, 158–59; Peterson interview.

39. Rowland Evans and Robert Novak, "Chaos and Bitterness Inside the Ford Camp," *Washington Post*, July 10, 1976, A15; Peterson interview.

40. EMP, *Elly!* 160; Gerald R. Ford, "Remarks at President Ford Committee Headquarters in Washington, D.C., August 11, 1976, from John T. Woolley and Gerhard Peters, The American Presidency Project [online], Santa Barbara, CA, http://www.presidency.ucsb.edu/ws/?pid=6269 (accessed December 7, 2010).

41. EMP, *Elly!*, 159. Immediately after the event, there was no coverage in the *New York Times, Washington Post,* or *Washington Star*. Peterson undoubtedly was frustrated by what she viewed as lack of support from Spencer and Nessen, but the media may have also decided that other political events were more newsworthy. On June 14, the *New York Times* ran a short wire story announcing the launch of Jimmy Carter's "Committee of 51.3 Percent," the Democratic presidential campaign's organization for women supporters.

42. Peterson to Rogers Morton "and All the Powers That Be," memorandum, June 16, 1976, EMP Papers, Box 16, Memoes (6) Folder.

43. "Briefing Paper on visit Wed. to PFC Hdqs. by the President," EMP Papers, Box 16, Memoes (4) Folder.

44. Spencer oral history, 90.

45. Baker, 41.

46. *Grand Rapids Press,* "GOP Women Ask Big Spot in Convention," undated clipping, C16, EMP Papers, Box 16, EMP Personal Folder.

47. Peterson to Gerald R. Ford, memorandum, August 5 [1976], EMP Papers, Box 15, Chronological August–September 1976 Folder.

48. Susan Fleming, "Limelight Eludes GOP Women," *Detroit News*, August 17, 1976, A16.

49. Peterson to Rogers Morton and Stuart Spencer, memorandum, July 29, 1976, EMP Papers, Box 16, President Ford Committee, Undated Folder.

50. Peterson to Rogers Morton, memorandum, June 22, 1976, EMP Papers, Box 16, Memoes (5) Folder; EMP, *Elly!*, 163. After the election, Tom Ruffin, deputy director of People for Ford, complained to Peterson that the White House did not include the director of the Ethnic Desk in meetings to discuss the fallout over Ford's remarks about Eastern Europe in the second presidential debate. Tom Ruffin, "Analysis of People for Ford Operation," EMP Papers, Box 16, EMP Personal Folder.

51. Peterson to Rogers Morton, memorandum, August 6 [1976], EMP Papers, Box 16, Memoes (6) Folder.

52. Peterson to Roy, Stu, and Rog [Royston Hughes, Stuart Spencer and Rogers Morton], August 3 [1976], EMP Papers, Box 16, Memoes (2) Folder.

53. EMP, *Elly!*, 160.

54. Elly Peterson to Tanya, August 5 [1976], EMP Papers, Box 18, Correspondence July–December 1976. The author presumes that "PS" is a reference to Schlafly and that Tanya Melich was the recipient of this letter because of its context.

55. Statement of Elly M. Peterson before Republican Platform Committee, August 9, 1976, EMP Papers, Box 25, Speeches Folder.

56. Saul Friedman and Remer Tyson, "Ford Election Team in Tatters: Michigan Pros Worried," *Detroit Free Press*, August 20, 1976, A1.

57. EMP, *Elly!*, 161.

58. Robert T. Hartmann, *Palace Politics: An Inside Account of the Ford Years* (New York: McGraw-Hill, 1980), 401.

59. Elly Peterson to Bob Hartman[n], memorandum, undated, EMP Papers, Box 15, Chronological, August–September 1976 Folder.

60. Gerald R. Ford, Speech on his acceptance of the Republican presidential nomination, August 19, 1976, Gerald R. Ford Presidential Library, http://www.fordlibrarymuseum.gov/library/speeches/760733.htm (accessed June 17, 2010).

61. Hartmann, 402.

62. Peterson to Mary Richmond, "Monday morning," undated letter, EMP Papers, Box 15, November 1976 Folder.

63. Clark Hallas, "Ford Campaign Shaky? State GOP Frets at Strategy," *Detroit News*, August 23, 1976, D8.

64. Saul Friedman, "Ford Picks New Team to Manage Campaign," *Detroit Free Press*, August 26, 1976, A1. Friedman reported Peterson had turned down Baker's appeals to return to the campaign.

65. Karen Farnham Madden, "Ready to Work: Women in Vermont and Michigan from Suffrage to Republican Party Politics," PhD diss., Michigan State University, 2002, UMI Dissertation Services, 180–81.

66. EMP, *Elly!*, 162.

67. James M. Naughton, "Ford and 3 'Guests' Dining with Strategy as a Topic," *New York Times*, August 27, 1976, 20. Peterson's salary was set at thirty-eight thousand dollars according to a review of the campaigns by the National Organization for Women.

68. Peterson interview.

69. Witcover, 542.

70. Ibid., 536.

71. Peterson to "Bill," undated memo, EMP Papers, Box 16, Memoes (6) Folder. The recipient is presumed to have been presidential assistant William Baroody.

72. Peterson to Mary [Richmond], Adey and Cha[rle]s [McMillan] and all, "Friday," Box 17, Correspondence, 1972–1979 Folder.

73. Ibid.

74. EMP, *Elly!*, 159.

75. Witcover, cited in Baker, 55.

76. Baker, 55–56.

77. Peterson to James Baker et al., memorandum, September 20, 1976, EMP Papers, Box 16, PFF Staff Reports Folder.

78. EMP, *Elly!*, 162–63.

79. Peterson to James Baker and Stuart Spencer, memorandum, September 21, 1976, President Ford Committee Campaign Records, Box C27 People for Ford—Peterson (Elly) Memoranda, Gerald R. Ford Presidential Library.

80. EMP, *Elly!*, 163.

81. Peterson to Chairman [James] Baker, memorandum, September 17 [1976], EMP Papers, Box 16, Memoes (2) Folder.

82. James M. Naughton, "Ford to Campaign in Deep South in a Direct Challenge to Carter," *New York Times*, September 17, 1976, 16.

83. Peterson to Mary Richmond and other family members, "Friday," and Peterson to family, "Sunday night," EMP Papers, Box 17, 1972–1979 Folder.

84. EMP, *Elly!*, 165–66; Peterson to Mary Richmond, "Thursday afternoon," EMP Papers, Box 15, November 1976 Folder. After Rockefeller died on January 23, 1979, Peterson served on a committee that helped plan a political institute at Dartmouth College that was named for him.

85. EMP, *Elly!*, 162.

86. Peterson to Mary Richmond, "Wednesday afternoon," EMP Papers, Box 15, November 1976 Folder.

87. Peterson to Mary Richmond, "Sunday," EMP Papers, Box 15, November 1976 Folder.

88. "Feminists for Ford" to James Baker III, Stu Spencer I, and Jim Field I, final report, October 30 [1976], EMP Papers, Box 16, People for Ford Staff Reports Folder.

89. Witcover, 632.

90. James R. Dickenson, "Carter Won't Quit Church over Racial Bar," *Washington Star*, November 1, 1976, A6.

91. Associated Press, "Ford Vote Aide Disavows Wire to Black Ministers; Calls It 'Terrible Taste,'" *New York Times*, November 3, 1976, 21.

92. United Press International, "Ford Unit Seeks to Exploit Incident at Carter Church," *Washington Post*, November 2, 1976, A4.

93. Witcover, 635.

94. EMP, *Elly!*, 165. This excerpt demonstrates Peterson's readily professed lack

of interest in sports; the "big game" in Washington that day was actually a football game between the Washington Redskins and Dallas Cowboys.

95.  Robert J. Keyes to Elly Peterson, November 10, 1976, EMP Papers, Box 15, November 1976 Folder.

96.  Witcover, 541; Baker, 71.

97.  John Robert Greene, *The Presidency of Gerald R. Ford* (Lawrence: University Press of Kansas, 1975), 187.

98.  EMP, *Elly!*, 152.

99.  Pat, presumably Patricia Bailey, to Elly Peterson, November 11, 1976, EMP Papers, Box 15, November 1976 Folder.

100.  Betsey, presumably Betsey Bellows, to Elly Peterson, undated, EMP Papers, Box 15, November 1976 Folder.

101.  James A. Baker III to Elly Peterson, November 11, 1976, EMP Papers, Box 15, November 1976 Folder.

102.  Political observers at the time believed that Ford irreparably damaged his election prospects by his September 8, 1974, decision to pardon Nixon for any crimes he might have committed as president. The campaign suffered another major setback on October 7, 1976, when Ford asserted, in the second presidential debate, that "there is no Soviet domination of Eastern Europe" at a time when the Iron Curtain was still in place. Given a chance to correct his answer, Ford asserted that citizens in those countries did not believe they were "dominated by the Soviet Union." After the debate, Ford fueled the controversy by his reluctance to acknowledge that his remarks needed correction or clarification.

103.  Tanya Melich, *The Republican War against Women: An Insider's Report from Behind the Lines,* updated ed. (New York: Bantam Books, 1998), 81.

104.  Hartmann, 406–10.

105.  Douglas Brinkley, *Gerald R. Ford* (New York: Times Books, Henry Holt, 2007), 139–40.

106.  Michael Beschloss, "From Watergate to Iraq, Gerald Ford's Influence," *Newsweek,* January 8, 2007.

107.  Deborah Hart Strober and Gerald S. Strober, *The Reagan Presidency: An Oral History of the Era* (Washington, DC: Brassey's, 2003), 14.

108.  EMP, *Elly!*, 167.


CHAPTER 11

1.  EMP, *Elly!*, 164.

2.  Liz Carpenter, interview by author, November 15, 2005.

3.  Heath oral history.

4.  Liz Carpenter to Peterson, January 17, 1976, EMP Papers, Box 18, Correspondence January–June 1976 Folder.

5.  Peterson to Liz Carpenter, January 20, 1976, ERAmerica Records, Container 136, Elly Peterson Correspondence Folder, Library of Congress.

6.  Peterson and Carpenter, form letter, January 5, 1976.

7. Betsy Crone to ERA supporters, memorandum, January 5, 1976, ERAmerica Records, Container 16, "Good Ideas/Kreps Letter" Folder, Library of Congress.

8. Mary Brooks to Virginia Webb, memorandum, February 20, 1976, EMP Papers, Box 18, January–June 1976 Correspondence Folder; Peterson to "Pat," presumably Pat Goldman, January 22, 1976, EMP Papers, Box 15, Chronological January–April 1976 Folder; Madden interview (1996), 17.

9. "ERAmerica Launches National ERA Campaign," press release, EMP Papers, Box 18, News Releases, 1976–1980 Folder.

10. EMP Papers, Box 25, Speeches Folder.

11. Judy Klemesrud, "New Team to Unify E.R.A. Campaign," *New York Times,* March 8, 1976, 20.

12. Kathleen Currie, interview by author, December 10, 2009.

13. Peterson to Julie Eisenhower, April 19, 1976, EMP Papers, Box 15, January–April 1976 Folder. Betty Ford, Rosalynn Carter, and Lady Bird Johnson were the only first ladies identified as supporters of the ratification drive.

14. Janet K. Boles, "ERAmerica," in *U.S. Women's Interest Groups: Institutional Profiles,* ed. Sarah Slavin (Westport, CT: Greenwood Press, 1995), 179–82.

15. Equal Rights Committee hearing, 81–82.

16. Heath oral history.

17. "The Fight for ERA: Leaders, Strategies, and Directions," Sheila Greenwald oral history, March 1983.

18. Peterson interview.

19. "Austinite Heads ERA Campaign," undated unidentified newspaper clipping, ERAmerica Records, Container 148, Jane Wells Clippings Folder, Library of Congress; "Former SBOE Member Passes Away," *Texas Education Today,* January–February 2002, http://ritter.tea.state.tx.us/press/tet/febteto2.pdf (accessed December 9, 2010); Mariwynn Heath and Ellen Boddie to Peterson, January 7, 1976, EMP Papers, Box 15, Chronological January–April 1976 Folder. Carpenter to Peterson, January 17, 1976.

20. Peterson to Jane Wells, memorandum, May 3 [1976], EMP Papers, Box 18, Undated Correspondence Folder.

21. Peterson to Jane Wells, February 13, 1976, ERAmerica Records, Container 136, Elly Peterson Correspondence Folder, Library of Congress.

22. Peterson to Wells, May 3.

23. Peterson interview.

24. Peterson to Wells, May 3.

25. Memorandum, undated, unsigned, EMP Papers, Box 18, Correspondence July–December 1976 Folder. Norma Munn is believed to be the author because of the author's reference to her work on a separate report on fund-raising, which is found in this file under Munn's name.

26. Margaret Barowich et al. to Liz Carpenter and Elly Peterson, memorandum, May 26, 1976, EMP Papers, Box 18, Correspondence January–June 1976 Folder.

27. "Schedule for Em. Peterson, April, May 1976," EMP Papers, Box 15, Chronological January–April 1976 Folder.

28. Rothstein/Buckley to Jane Wells, memorandum, May 19, 1976, ERAmerica Records, Library of Congress, Container 145, Rothstein/Buckley Folder.

29. Undated ERAmerica Financial Memorandum.

30. Peterson to family ("The Clan Chief will get the 1st copy"), undated letter, EMP Papers, Box 16, Miscellaneous Folder.

31. Isabelle Shelton, "Politics Make Strange Parties, *Washington Star*, June 7, 1976, C2.

32. Peterson to Liz Carpenter, memorandum, June 7, 1976, EMP Papers, Box 18, Correspondence, January–June 1976 Folder.

33. Greenwald oral history.

34. Sheila Greenwald to Peterson, memorandum, July 22, 1976, EMP Papers, Box 18, Correspondence July–December 1976.

35. Gail Booms Vila and Jan Caniglia, ERA Colorado, to "The Cleaning Person for ERAmerica," memorandum, July 15, 1976, and Gail Booms Vila and Jan Caniglia, ERA Colorado, to Liz Carpenter, Ellie Peterson and Jane Wells, July 15, 1976, EMP Papers, Box 18, Correspondence, July–December, 1976.

36. Madden interview (1996), 18. Jill Miller to Liz Carpenter and Elly Peterson, August 5, 1976, EMP Papers, Box 18, Undated Correspondence Folder.

37. Jane Culbreth to Elizabeth Carpenter and Elly Peterson, August 5, 1976, EMP Papers, Box 18, Correspondence July–December 1976 Folder.

38. Gail Vila and Janet M. Caniglia to Jane Culbreth, August 5, 1976, ERAmerica records, Container 93, Colorado Folder, Library of Congress.

39. Joan McCoy, "Differences Set Aside in Campaign for ERA," *Rocky Mountain News*, July 28, 1976, 38, newspaper clipping, ERAmerica Records, Container 93, Colorado Folder, Library of Congress.

40. Bob Ewegen, "ERA—and Its Supporters—'Alive, Well,'" *Denver Post*, July 28, 1976, C21, ERAmerica Records, Container 93, Colorado Folder, Library of Congress.

41. Elly Peterson and Liz Carpenter, undated memorandum, EMP Papers, Box 18, Undated Correspondence Folder.

42. Rosalyn Baker to Liz Carpenter and Elly Peterson, memorandum, September 16, 1976, EMP Papers, Box 18, Correspondence July–December 1976 Folder.

43. Greenwald oral history.

44. Marjorie to Betsey, October 6, 1976, EMP Papers, Box 18, Correspondence July–December 1976 Folder.

45. Peterson to Marcia Allen, October 28, 1976, EMP Papers, Box 18, Correspondence July–December 1976 Folder.

46. Peterson to "Sheila [Greenwald], the Board and the unratified state coalitions," memorandum, October 24 [1976], Box 18, Correspondence July–December 1976 Folder.

47. Liz Carpenter and Elly Peterson to "ERA supporter," November 18, 1976, EMP Papers, Box 18, ERAmerica Corporate Board, 1976 Folder.

48. Peterson to Jane P. McMichael, November 23, 1976, EMP Papers, Box 15, Chronological November 1976 Folder.

49. Phil Hart to Peterson, September 10, 1976, EMP Papers, Box 15, August–September 1976 Folder.

50. "Activities Summary through July 30, 1976," EMP Papers, Box 18, July–December 1976 Correspondence Folder; Peterson and Carpenter undated memo.

51. ABC News Close-Up, "ERA: The War between the Women," broadcast January 22, 1977, accessed at The Paley Center for Media, New York.

52. Liz Carpenter to Peterson, undated letter, EMP Papers, Box 18, Correspondence 1977 Folder.

53. Peterson to Mary Richmond, undated letter, hand-labeled "1977," EMP Papers, Box 15, Chronological 1971–1979 Undated Folder.

54. Sheila Greenwald to Liz Carpenter and Elly Peterson, undated ("Sat. AM"), EMP Papers, Box 18, Undated Correspondence Folder.

55. Sheila Greenwald to Peterson ("Moms"), undated (received March 21, 1977), EMP Papers, Box 15, Chronological 1977, Undated Folder.

56. Heath oral history.

57. Currie interview.

58. Peterson to Sheila Greenwald, March 27, 1977, EMP Papers, Box 18, Correspondence 1977 Folder.

59. Elly Peterson, undated, unidentified speech, apparently delivered in Charlotte, Michigan, EMP Papers, Box 19, Speeches Folder.

60. Peterson to Audrey Rowe Colom, May 23, 1977, EMP Papers, Box 15, Chronological April–December 1977 Folder.

61. Currie interview.

62. Peterson to Colom.

63. International Women's Year Conference [Michigan] Meeting Minutes, June 10–11, 1977, EMP Papers, Box 20, International Women's Year Conference Folder; Riecker interview.

64. Elly Peterson, Remarks for Houston BPW seminar, November 18, 1977, EMP Papers, Box 20, IWY 1977–1978 Folder. Slightly different versions of this speech are found in Peterson's papers.

65. Kathleen Currie to ERAmerica Corporate Board, Steering Committee and Co-chairs, memorandum, December 15, 1977, EMP Papers, Box 18, Correspondence 1979 Folder.

66. Peterson to Lenore Romney, undated, EMP Papers, Box 15, Chronological 1971–1979 Folder.

67. Helen Milliken to Peterson, March 15, 1978, EMP Papers, Box 15, Chronological 1978–1979 Folder.

68. "Laura" to Peterson, February 5, 1978, EMP Papers, Box 17, Correspondence, 1972–1979 Folder. This is probably Laura Beckett, a student member of the Michigan delegation from Grand Rapids.

69. Sheila Greenwald to Peterson, undated, EMP Papers, Box 18, Undated Correspondence Folder.

70. Elly Peterson, Speech to the Army War College, August 23, 1978, EMP Papers, Box 25, Speeches Folder.

71. Peterson to Liz Carpenter, November 2, 1978, EMP Papers, Box 18, Correspondence 1978 Folder.

72. Peterson to Helen Milliken, and Peterson to Patricia Goldman, November 2, 1978, EMP Papers, Box 18, Correspondence 1978 Folder; Peterson to Sheila Greenwald, January 7, 1979, ERAmerica Records, Container 136, Personnel—Elly Peterson Folder, Library of Congress.

73. Sheila Greenwald to Peterson, undated, EMP Papers, Box 17, Republican Party Correspondence, 1972–1979 Folder.

74. Helen Milliken to Peterson, March 13, 1979, EMP Papers, Box 17, Correspondence 1979 Folder.

75. Helen Milliken to Peterson, April 30, 1980, EMP Papers, Box 17, Correspondence, 1980–1985 Folder (1).

76. Currie interview.

77. Elly Peterson, Remarks for the ERA Get Together, Washington, DC, August 18, 1979, EMP Papers, Box 25, Speeches 1979 Folder.

78. Lenore Romney to Peterson, Dec. 5, EMP Papers, Box 15, Chronological, 1971–1979 Folder. The letter was subsequently labeled "1975," but the context indicates it was written in December 1977, after the IWY meeting in Houston.

79. George Bullard, "ERA Backers Assail Romney, Mormon Church," *Detroit News,* December 18, 1979, and George Bullard and Joy Haenlein, "32 Angry Legislators Want Romney to Quit," *Detroit News,* December 19, 1979, clippings in the January 1980 edition of Michigan ERAmerica's "Coalition Update," Box 18, Coalition Update, EMP Papers, 1980–1982 Folder.

80. George Romney to Peterson, December 21, 1979; Peterson to Helen Milliken, December 26, [1979]; Helen Milliken to Peterson, January 4, 1980; Lenore Romney to Peterson, January 6, 1980; Laura Carter Callow to Peterson, January 6, [1980]; Helen Milliken to Peterson, January 8, 1980; Peterson to George and Lenore Romney, January 9, 1980; George Romney to Peterson, January 18, 1980; EMP Papers, Box 19, Romney Positions Folder. Because of the distance between Hawaii and Michigan, it is possible a particular letter was not received before the next one was sent.

81. At the time of the convention, it was widely reported that the party had failed to endorse the amendment for the first time in forty years. Jo Freeman notes, however, that despite widespread support, a plank supporting the ERA did not appear in the 1964 platform, nor in the 1968 platform, a development noted by the National Women's Party (209–12).

82. EMP, *Elly!,* 154, 166.

CHAPTER 12

1. Suone Cotner to ERAmerica Board of Directors, memorandum, July 12, 1982, EMP Papers, Box 18, Mailings to Board, 1980–1982 Folder.

2. EMP, *Elly!,* 155.

3. Peterson interview.

4. Lenore Romney to Peterson, September 14, EMP Papers, Box 20, Letters from Public Figures, Undated Folder.

5. J. Mansbridge, "Organizing for the ERA: Cracks in the Façade of Unity," in Tilly and Gurin, 329.

6. Cooke interview.

7. Bernadine Denning, "And They Said It Couldn't Be Done!," *Michigan Women* 6, no. 3 (fall 1982), publication of the Michigan Women's Commission, EMP Papers, Box 17, 1982 Michigan Gubernatorial Campaign Folder.

8. Cooke interview.

9. Helen Milliken to Peterson, April 29, 1982, EMP Papers, Box 17, Correspondence, 1980–1985 Folder (1).

10. Elly Peterson, "Are We Feminists First?," speech, Women's Assembly III Convention," EMP Papers, Box 25, Speeches 1980 Folder.

11. Denning.

12. Cooke interview.

13. Peterson to Ellie Smeal, August 12, 1982, EMP Papers, Box 17, 1982 Michigan Gubernatorial Campaign Folder.

14. Cooke interview.

15. Ibid.

16. James Blanchard, interview by author, July 12, 2006.

17. Ibid.

18. Cooke interview.

19. "Sex Fires Up State Politics," *Grand Rapids Press,* September 5, 1982, clipping provided by Margaret Cooke.

20. Sharon McGrayne, "State GOP Women in Bind," *State Journal* (Lansing), September 12, 1982, D1, clipping provided by Margaret Cooke.

21. James N. Crutchfield, "Headlee's Pitch to Women Misses Some," *Detroit Free Press,* September 15, 1982, clipping provided by Margaret Cooke.

22. Cooke interview. During this time, Peterson advised a friend that she was trying to "pick up" Milliken's schedule while she was hospitalized, "as well as my own." Peterson to Shirley McFee, October 17, 1982, EMP Papers, Box 17, 1982 Michigan Gubernatorial Campaign Folder.

23. Susan R. Pollack, "'You're Right,' Headlee Tells Foes of Abortion," *Detroit News,* September 26, 1982, A10, clipping provided by Margaret Cooke.

24. Cooke interview.

25. Hugh McDiarmid, "It's Time Feminists Spoke Out on Headlee," *Detroit Free Press,* September 19, 1982, clipping provided by Margaret Cooke.

26. Matt Beer and Kay Richards, "Yours Truly," *Detroit News,* September 23, 1982, clipping provided by Margaret Cooke.

27. Pamela Harwood to Peterson, September 24, 1976, EMP Papers, Box 17, 1982 Michigan Gubernatorial Campaign Folder.

28. Blanchard interview.

29. "Harassing Headlee," *Detroit News,* September 26, 1982, clipping provided by Margaret Cooke.

30. Barbara Walters, "Headlee Lashes out at Brown during Campaign Stop Here," *Kalamazoo Gazette,* September 27, 1982, clipping provided by Margaret Cooke.

31. Joanna Firestone and Susan R. Pollack, "'Mother' of New GOP Endorses Blanchard," *Detroit News,* October 6, 1982, A1, clipping provided by Margaret Cooke.

32. James N. Crutchfield, "GOP Women at Blanchard Lunch," *Detroit Free Press,* October 6, 1982, clipping provided by Margaret Cooke.

33. Ibid.

34. Firestone and Pollack.

35. Crutchfield.

36. Cooke interview.

37. Hugh McDiarmid, "See Elly Back Jim—See Dick Go Nuts," *Detroit Free Press,* October 7, 1982, clipping provided by Margaret Cooke.

38. Jerry Moskal, "Factional Dissent Hurting Headlee," *State Journal* (Lansing), October 18, 1982, B6.

39. Weldon O. Yeager to Peterson, October 6, 1982, EMP Papers, Box 17, 1982 Michigan Gubernatorial Campaign Folder.

40. Peterson to Weldon Yeager, October 11, 1982, EMP Papers, Box 17, 1982 Michigan Gubernatorial Campaign Folder.

41. Charles L. Mueller to Peterson, October 6, 1982, EMP Papers, Box 17, 1982 Michigan Gubernatorial Campaign Folder.

42. Peterson to Charles Mueller, October 11, 1982, EMP Papers, Box 17, 1982 Michigan Gubernatorial Campaign.

43. Peterson to George Bush, October 13, 1982, EMP Papers, Box 17, 1982 Michigan Gubernatorial Campaign Folder.

44. "Politics: Hate Comes in Amazingly Small Doses," undated newspaper clipping, EMP Papers, Box 17, 1982 Michigan Gubernatorial Campaign Folder. If Peterson received a hundred letters, she retained only a few for her personal papers.

45. Joan Secchia to Peterson, October 16, 1982, EMP Papers, Box 17, 1982 Michigan Gubernatorial Campaign Folder.

46. David W. McKeague to Peterson, October 15, 1982, EMP Papers, Box 17, 1982 Michigan Gubernatorial Campaign Folder.

47. Peterson to David W. McKeague, October 17, 1982, EMP Papers, Box 17, 1982 Michigan Gubernatorial Campaign Folder.

48. Louis K. Cramton, letter to the editor of the *Midland Daily News*, EMP Papers, Box 17, 1982 Michigan Gubernatorial Campaign Folder.

49. Sharon McGrayne, "Headlee 'Never Heard of Them,'" *State Journal* (Lansing), October 20, 1982, clipping provided by Margaret Cooke.

50. James N. Crutchfield, "Headlee: Pro-ERA Means Pro-Gay," *Detroit Free Press*, October 22, 1982, clipping provided by Margaret Cooke.

51. Hugh McDiarmid, "Headlee Stumbles over a 'Non-Issue,'" *Detroit Free Press*, October 24, 1982, clipping provided by Margaret Cooke

52. James N. Crutchfield, "Headlee Assailed for ERA Remark: 'Appalling,' 'Shocking,'" *Detroit Free Press*, October 23, 1982, A1.

53. Ibid.

54. Hugh McDiarmid, "What Issues? This Campaign Became a Morality Play," *Detroit Free Press*, October 31, 1982, clipping provided by Margaret Cooke.

55. Lenore Romney to Peterson, October 27, 1982, EMP Papers, Box 17, Letters from Public Figures, 1980–84 Folder.

56. George Romney to Joyce Braithwaite, November 1, 1982, EMP Papers, Box 17, 1982 Michigan Gubernatorial Campaign Folder. Two years later Braithwaite married Brickley.

57. Don Faber, "Thoughts from a Mind Benumbed of Politics," *Ann Arbor News*, October 24, 1982, EMP Papers, Box 17, 1982 Michigan Gubernatorial Campaign Folder.

58. Joe H. Stroud, "Headlee Takes Governor's Race to New Low," *Detroit Free Press*, October 24, 1982, clipping provided by Margaret Cooke.

59. Blanchard interview.

60. Peterson to Martha Griffiths, October 25, 1982, EMP Papers, Box 17, 1982 Michigan Gubernatorial Campaign Folder.

61. David Kushma, "Democrats in Driver's Seat in Lansing," *Detroit Free Press*, November 4, 1982, B9.

62. David Kushma, "Republicans Start Sifting the Wreckage," *Detroit Free Press*, November 4, 1982, A1.

63. Jack Casey, "Women: Michigan's New Political Powerhouse," *Monthly Detroit*, January 1983, 49–51, 98.

64. Bonnie DeSimone, "Trying to Wake Up the Republican Men," *Ann Arbor News,* October 22, 1982, A7, EMP Papers, Box 17, 1982 Michigan Gubernatorial Campaign Folder.

65. Cooke interview.

EPILOGUE

1. Hugh McDiarmid, "Bipartisan Tribute to a Ticket Splitter," *Detroit Free Press* clipping, EMP Papers, Box 20, Tribute to Elly Peterson Folder.

2. EMP, *Elly!,* 154. Although the memoir was published later, it appears these words were written between the elections of 1982 and 1984.

3. George Bush to Mrs. E. C. Peterson, August 21, 1985, and Peterson to Bush, September 4, 1985, EMP Papers, Box 20, Letters from Public Figures, 1985–2000 Folder. Bush responded with a personal note.

4. Peterson, MPHS oral history. Peterson reiterated that she considered herself to be an independent in a 1996 speech to the Bermuda Village Men's Breakfast Club in North Carolina (transcript provided to author).

5. Marion S. Grattan, "Elly Returns to Arena," *Jackson Citizen-Patriot* (Michigan), November 25, 1973, clipping, EMP Papers, Box 23, Clippings, ERAmerica Folder.

6. EMP interview.

7. Marttila interview.

8. Elly Peterson, "I am 81 years old. . . ," freelance article, EMP Papers, Box 20, Later Correspondence Folder, identified in interview by author.

9. "Millie and Elly: Two Women of Conviction," *Detroit Free Press,* September 12, 1995, A8.

10. "Millie and Elly" program for a benefit cohosted by the Michigan Women's Foundation and the Michigan Political History Society, September 19, 1995, provided to author.

11. Dorothy Stuck to Peterson, 90th Birthday Scrapbook, reviewed by author.

12. Helen Milliken, "Feminism Is Simple, but Never Easy," undated, unidentified clipping provided by Margaret Cooke.

13. Eileen McNamara, "Evolving History," *Boston Globe,* June 26, 2005, B1.

14. Stephanie Ebbert, "Romney Releases Mother's Statement on Abortion Issue," *Boston Globe,* June 28, 2005, B1.

15. Currie interview.

16. Reported at the twenty-fifth anniversary luncheon of Emily's List, Washington, DC, April 29, 2010.

17. EMP, *Elly!,* 74.

18. David S. Broder, interview by author, November 22, 2005.

19. "Michigan Political History Society Picks 'Greats' of Past Half-Century," *Inside Michigan Politics,* June 2, 2003, 4.

20. EMP, *Elly!,* 167.

21. Elly Peterson, Remarks as part of "The People Versus Peterson" skit, Elly Peterson Day, Charlotte, Michigan, June 30, 1985, EMP Papers, Box 21, Scrapbook.

# Index